China's Economy
into the
New Century

China's Economy into the New Century

Structural Issues and Problems

John WONG
LU Ding

East Asian Institute
National University of Singapore

SINGAPORE UNIVERSITY PRESS
NATIONAL UNIVERSITY OF SINGAPORE

World Scientific
New Jersey • London • Singapore • Hong Kong

Published by

Singapore University Press
Yusof Ishak House, National University of Singapore
31 Lower Kent Ridge Road, Singapore 119078

and

World Scientific Publishing Co. Pte. Ltd.
P O Box 128, Farrer Road, Singapore 912805
USA office: Suite 1B, 1060 Main Street, River Edge, NJ 07661
UK office: 57 Shelton Street, Covent Garden, London WC2H 9HE

British Library Cataloguing-in-Publication Data
A catalogue record for this book is available from the British Library.

CHINA'S ECONOMY INTO THE NEW CENTURY
Structural Issues and Problems

Copyright © 2002 by Singapore University Press and World Scientific Publishing Co. Pte. Ltd.

All rights reserved. This book, or parts thereof, may not be reproduced in any form or by any means, electronic or mechanical, including photocopying, recording or any information storage and retrieval system now known or to be invented, without written permission from the Publisher.

For photocopying of material in this volume, please pay a copying fee through the Copyright Clearance Center, Inc., 222 Rosewood Drive, Danvers, MA 01923, USA. In this case permission to photocopy is not required from the publisher.

ISBN 981-02-4788-5

Printed in Singapore by Mainland Press

Contents

Introduction ix

Part I: Growth and Structural Adjustments

1. China's Economy: Confronting Restructuring and Stability
   Woo Wing Thye ... 3

2. The Nature and Sources of Economic Growth in China:
   Is There TFP Growth?
   Liu Zhiqiang ... 43

3. Understanding China's Statistical System
   Part One: "Lies, Damn Lies, and Statistics"
   — The Problems with Chinese Statistics
   John Wong ... 63

   Part Two: China's National Bureau of Statistics:
   Its Functions and Structure
   Ren Caifang ... 75

4. China's Industrial Policy and Long-term Structural Planning
   Lu Ding ... 81

Part II: Fiscal Federalism and Reforms

5. Tax Reforms and Government Revenues
   Lin Shuanglin ... 113

6. Fiscal Decentralisation and Economic Growth
   Justin LIN *Yifu and* LIU *Zhiqiang* — 147

7. Too Many Fees and Too Many Charges: China Streamlines Fiscal System
   LIN *Shuanglin* — 175

8. From the Helping Hand to the Grabbing Hand: Fiscal Federalism and Corruption in China
   CHEN *Kang, Arye L.* HILLMAN *and* GU *Qingyang* — 193

Part III: Inter-regional Policy

9. China's Inter-Provincial Disparities: 1952–1995
   TIAN *Xiaowen and Ron* DUNCAN — 219

10. China's Drive to Develop Its Western Region (I): Why Turn to This Region Now?
    TIAN *Xiaowen* — 237

    China's Drive to Develop Its Western Region (II): Priorities in Development
    TIAN *Xiaowen* — 257

11. Economic Openness and Implications for Chongqing's Development
    John WONG — 273

Part IV: Infrastructure – Hard and Soft

12. China's Infrastructure Development
    LIN *Shuanglin* — 291

13. Building Up China's Telecommunications Infrastructure
    LU *Ding* — 325

14. Education and Development: Experiences from East Asia
    John WONG and LIU Zhiqiang   373

15. China's Drive to Attract the Return of Its Expatriate
    Talents
    YU Wing Yin   387

Part V: Regional Impact

16. Implications of China's Reform and Development
    on the Asia Pacific
    John WONG   405

17. Has The Asian Financial Crisis Eroded China's Export
    Competitiveness?
    Friedrich WU   425

Index   445

Introduction

The last quarter of the 20th century witnessed a phenomenal rise of the dynamic East Asian economic region comprising China, the four NIEs (newly industrialized economies) of South Korea, Taiwan, Hong Kong and Singapore (dubbed Asia's four "small dragons") and the ASEAN (Association of Southeast Asian Nations) economies of Indonesia, Malaysia, the Philippines and Thailand (dubbed Asia's "tiger economies"). All these economies had sustained strong economic growth at average rates of 6-8% for several decades until 1997 when they were hit, in varying degrees, by the regional financial crisis. The World Bank in one of its well-known development studies referred to the impressive economic success of these economies as the "East Asian Miracle".

Among these high-performance East Asian economies, China stood out with even more impressive economic growth track records. Thanks to its success in market-oriented economic reform, the Chinese economy has chalked up an annual rate of 9.7% real growth during 1979–2000. In absolute terms, China's total GDP sextupled between 1980 and 2000; and its per capita GDP quintupled. By 2000, China's total nominal GNP exceeded US$1 trillion, making it the world's seventh largest economy. In terms of PPP (purchasing power parity), the Chinese economy is now the world's second largest after the USA — although the PPP measures tend to overstate China's real GNP just as the conventional approach has seriously underestimated it.

On account of its successful open-door policy, China's economy has also achieved greater integration with the global economy. Over the past two decades, China's exports have increased at a hefty annual rate of 17%, from US$13.7 billion in 1979 to US$250 billion in 2000. China has now become the world's seventh largest exporting economy. China's efforts to attract foreign direct investment (FDI) have been even more successful. From 1988 to 2000, actual or utilized FDI in China increased at an annual rate of 23% to reach a cumulative total of US$339 billion. No other country in the world, besides the United States, receives more FDI. As a result of its success in exports and FDI, China's total foreign exchange reserves in mid-2001 reached US$180 billion, the second largest in the world next to Japan.

China's economic success is also reflected in several important physical indicators. China not only tops the world in grain production (necessarily so because of its large population) but also in coal, steel and cement. Before Deng Xiaoping introduced economic reform in 1978, home electronics manufacturing was trivial in China. Today, one in four of the world's colour TVs and one in five of the world's fridges are now produced in China. At the start of the economic reform, the whole of China counted only 2 million fixed-line telephone subscribers. By early 2001, China had 160 million fixed-line telephone subscribers, in addition to 111 million mobile phones and 45 million pagers. By the end of 2001, China expects to have 40 million people online as Internet users, just slightly behind Japan. Not just in the "old economy", China is also making rapid progress in "New Economy" areas.

It is not just that the Chinese economy has achieved spectacular growth performance over the past two decades. But it is also sufficiently clear that China's economy is carrying over its high growth momentum into this century, at least for the first two decades. Unlike the other smaller East Asian economies, which can easily exhaust their growth potential, China is a large and diverse continental-sized economy. It has sufficient internal dynamics to sustain growth for a much longer period. This is already evident in 2001 when economic growth in most parts of East Asia has plunged due to the slow-down of the US economy. Only China's economy is still able to keep to its original target of over 7% largely because of its reliance on domestic demand.

However, for China's economy to sustain continuing high growth in the next lap, China will have to come to grips with several structural and institutional constraints, including the unfinished business of economic reform. The two-decade long rapid growth has effectively strengthened China's economic power and raised its people's standard of living. It has also transformed China from a centrally planned economy to a "socialist market economy", one that operates increasingly in line with capitalist norms. Many structural problems, however, remain. Weaknesses in the half-reformed fiscal system breeds widespread rent seeking activities at the local levels and cause tensions in state budget. The flawed financial institutions and the biased ownership structure continue to distort resource allocation, leading to huge efficiency losses. Inter-provincial and inter-regional disparity is reaching a level that threatens national unity and social stability. Some of these structural issues will get more acute once China is exposed to greater global competition after its accession to the WTO. What needs to be done in the remaining areas of reform and restructuring will present enormous challenges to the Chinese leadership in the next lap of growth.

This volume is a collection of papers written by researchers and visiting scholars in the East Asian Institute to address the salient problems and issues currently facing the Chinese economy. It consists of five parts and 16 chapters. The first part (three chapters) provides a basis for understanding the long-term structural constraints on China's economic growth at the turn of the century. The second part (four chapters) discusses fiscal issues, ranging from central-local fiscal relationships and taxation/levy structure to their impact on efficiency of local governance. In a vast economy with 1.2 billion people, these fiscal issues are pivotal in shaping the pattern of development in future. The third part (three chapters) deals with the issue of inter-regional development disparity. This explains why Beijing recently vowed to step up efforts in "Western development" as its new frontiers of economic growth. Infrastructure, in the form of physical and human capital, has been and continues to be a major constraint on the nation's economic development. Hence the fourth part (four chapters) is devoted to the crucial issue of infrastructure development. As the Chinese economy becomes more integrated into the world economy, the impact of China's economic growth will be felt beyond its national borders. The volume thus ends with its last part (two chapters) to analyze the regional impact of China's growth and structural changes.

Many of the papers selected for this volume had been presented at the Institute's weekly seminars attended actively by academics, government officials, and business executives and consultants in Singapore and the region. Many chapters contained in this volume should be of topical interest to a wide range of readership.

PART I

Chapter 1, "China's Economy: Confronting Restructuring and Stability" by WOO Wing Thye, looks into the restructuring imperatives of the Chinese economy. Based on a discussion of the macroeconomic situation by the end of the 1990s, the author questions the rationale of the expansionary fiscal policy adopted by the Chinese government and warns of the long-term negative effects of the fiscal pump-priming measures on financial restructuring. WOO urges China's policy makers to implement fundamental changes in the capital market by bringing the nation's financial institutions closer to the operational norms of modern market economies. This, according to the author, will offer China the only chance to achieve sustained growth.

In **Chapter 2**, "The Nature and Sources of Economic Growth in China: Is There TFP Growth", LIU Zhiqiang reviews the literature on sources of China's economic growth and emphasizes the importance of productivity growth to the nation's long-term growth sustainability. The author identifies four contributing factors to productivity growth, namely, the efficiency gains at the micro level, the efficiency improvement in cross-sector resource allocation, the diffusion of technology through foreign direct investment, and the improved infrastructure. Acknowledging the progress of restructuring the state-owned sector restructure and the emergence of the entrepreneurial class, the author expresses optimism towards continuing productivity gains that China's economy can enjoy in the future.

Chapter 3 by John WONG and REN Caifang deals with a central issue of studying the Chinese economy: "Understanding China's Statistical System." Based on their rich experience in this field, the authors provide an objective evaluation of the quality of abundant statistical data published at surprising promptness by the Chinese authorities. This chapter offers a much-needed guideline for avoiding statistical pitfalls in China studies.

In its process of economic restructuring since the early 1990s, China's industrial policy regime has played an active and pivotal role. **Chapter 4**, "China's Industrial Policy and Long-term Structural Planning" by LU Ding describes the regime's features and discusses its impact on the economy's industrial structure and cross-sector resource allocation. The author argues that some strong interventionist features of the regime have to be phased out or modified once China is in the WTO.

Part II

The four chapters in this part investigate fiscal federalism and reforms. An indispensable part of China's two-decade economic reform is a series of fiscal restructuring efforts. From 1978 to 1993, the main thrust of fiscal reform was decentralization and revenue sharing between the central and local governments based on a contractual relationship. Since 1994, a systematic re-centralization of revenues has been phased in through reforms guided by fiscal federalism. These events are reviewed by LIN Shuanglin in **Chapter 5**, "Tax Reforms and Government Revenues in China". LIN notes the decline of government revenue as a proportion of GDP and discusses the factors that contributed to these trends. To tackle the revenue loss, LIN suggests unifying revenue sources, broadening the tax base, equalizing tax burdens, and reinforcing tax laws.

In **Chapter 6**, "Fiscal Decentralization and Economic Growth in China", LIU Zhiqiang and Justin LIN Yifu offer empirical evidence to show that fiscal decentralization from 1970 to 1993 made a positive contribution to the growth process. The duo also finds that, along with the fiscal reform, the rural reform, the non-state sector, and capital accumulation were the key driving forces for growth.

With fiscal decentralization, a notorious problem in China's fiscal system arising, that is, the irregularity of local governments' wanton levies on residents and businesses. In **Chapter 7**, "Too Many Fees and Too Many Charges: China Streamlines Fiscal System", LIN Shuanglin scrutinizes the sources of this problem in the context of "extra-budget" revenue system and the Central Government's "fee reform" since 1999. LIN observes that the "fee reform" is a process of legalization of revenue collection mechanism and its success therefore hinges on the improvement of the entire legal environment in China.

Changes in the fiscal system inevitably have significant implications for local officials' governing behaviour. CHEN Kang, Arye L. HILLMAN and GU Qingyang discuss impact of fiscal reform on the strategic interaction between the central and local governments in **Chapter 8**, "From the Helping Hand to the Grabbing Hand: Fiscal Federalism and Corruption in China". The trio produces empirical results to argue that the revenue re-centralization process after 1994 had a tendency to change local officials' "helping hand" to "grabbing hand" towards business. This observation offers a novel but controversial interpretation of the deteriorating bureaucratic corruption in China in recent years.

Part III

China's two-decade long economic growth was mainly driven by booms in its coastal (Eastern) region, thanks to the East-West sequencing of opening to external trade and investment. Such sequencing has left behind a legacy of a deteriorated inter-provincial livelihood disparity. This legacy and its relationship with unbalanced inter-region output growth are examined by TIAN Xiaowen and Ron DUNCAN in **Chapter 9**, "China's Inter-Provincial Disparities: 1952–1995". The duo attributes the widening inter-provincial livelihood disparities to the weakened state intervention in inter-region income distribution and the rise of provincial autonomy.

To tackle this problem, the Chinese government announced a shift in its national economic strategy at the dawn of the new century to develop its Western region over next 15 years. The motivation of this policy shift and its impact on the prospects of the Western region development are discussed in detail in **Chapter 10**, "China's Drive to Develop Its Western Region: Rationale and Priorities", by TIAN Xiaowen. The author identifies the government's four priorities in developing the Western region, namely, infrastructure construction, ecological protection, industrial structure adjustment, and the development of science, technology and education. TIAN points out that these priorities, although in line with the needs of the region, are financially and technically demanding. Their successful implementation hinges on the ability of the central and local governments to mobilize resources in an increasingly market-oriented economy.

As part of the policy shift, Chongqing, a metropolitan area formerly part of Sichuan province, was upgraded into a statutory province by the central government in 1999. In **Chapter 11**, "Economic Openness and Implications for Chongqing's Development", John WONG, after showing how physical isolation and "policy isolation" (i.e. lack of economic openness) can hinder economic development, assesses the opportunities for this newly designated province. WONG points out that Chongqing holds great promise for the region's development in the coming years.

PART IV

Infrastructure development requires private-sector participation as well as government guidance, co-ordination and public investment. The three chapters in this part look at how China is tackling this critical issue.

In **Chapter 12**, "China's Infrastructure Development", LIN Shuanglin reviews the physical infrastructure development in the economy over the past twenty years and concludes that infrastructure construction and maintenance have lagged behind the hyper economic growth. LIN recommends several policy adjustments to promote infrastructure financing and construction. According to the author, fiscal decentralization and better law enforcement are pivotal in improving inner city infrastructure and rural infrastructure in the future.

One area where China has successfully overcome its physical infrastructure bottleneck during the last two decades is the development of its telecommunications industry. **Chapter 13**, "Building Up China's Telecommunications Infrastructure" by LU Ding, delineates state policies that have supported the speedy expansion of the nation's telecommunication network. The author examines the impact of such success in policy making on the industry's development and discusses the challenges to the industry in the coming years.

Alongside the development of infrastructure hardware such as roads and ports are the equally crucial "software" components of development such as education, human capital, and legal framework, which are in fact becoming increasingly important for modern economic growth. In **Chapter 14**, "Education and Development: Experiences from East Asia", John WONG and LIU Zhiqiang evaluate China's human capital formation in light of the East Asian experience. The duo suggests that, while the government should continue to take the lead in education development, market forces should be allowed to play a bigger role in mobilizing financial and human resources in this sector.

Chapter 15, "China's Drive to Attract the Return of Its Expatriate Talents" by YU Wing Yin, looks into the measures Beijing has taken recently to facilitate a "reverse brain drain" by attracting overseas Chinese professionals back to China to participate in its economic modernization. The author notes that the policy towards Chinese going overseas to study has become remarkably liberal over the years and the enormous opportunities for entrepreneurship in China has been a magnet to draw back Chinese overseas talents.

Part V

China's dynamic economic growth has brought about significant geo-economic implications for the region to China's south. In **Chapter 16** "Implications of China's Reform and Development on the Asia Pacific," John WONG assesses the challenges and opportunities brought in by the rise of the Chinese economy to the Asia Pacific economies, in particular, the Southeast Asian economies. **Chapter 17**, "Has the Asian Financial Crisis Eroded China's Export Competitiveness?" by Friedrich WU, uses a shift-share analysis to show that the competitiveness of China's manufactured exports has clearly improved vis-à-vis that of the ASEAN-4 (Indonesia, Malaysia, Philippines, and Thailand) since 1994. The author hence dismisses the need for China to use the devaluation of the Chinese *Renminbi* to maintain its export competitiveness during the Asian financial crisis 1997–98.

Part I

Growth and Structural Adjustments

1

China's Economy: Confronting Restructuring and Stability[†]

WOO WING THYE[*]

1. INTRODUCTION

China has been the world's star performer in economic growth for the last two decades. China registered an average annual growth rate of 9.7 percent in the 1978–99 period. However, the growth rates for 1996–99 are not only below the average of the period, they have also declined monotonically from 9.6 percent in 1996 to 7.1 percent in 1999. Naturally, many questions and concerns have arisen about this four-year deviation from the average. How much of the deviation has been due to trend slowdown, how much to the internal economic cycle, and how much to the external shock from the Asian financial crisis? Furthermore, what could be done to offset the decline, and what are the long-term implications of these counter-measures?

[†]Reprinted with permission from *The Asian Financial Crisis: Lessons for a Resilient Asia*, edited by Wing Thye Woo, Jeffrey D. Sachs, and Klaus Schwab, The MIT Press, 2000, ©World Economic Forum.

[*]WOO Wing Thye is Professor at the Economics Department of the University of California, Davis. This paper was presented at an EAI Seminar on 21 March 2000.

In the public pronouncements of Chinese officials, the usual explanation for the slowdown was a drop in consumption and the stagnation of exports caused by the Asian financial crisis. Large-scale infrastructure investment programs were started in 1998 and 1999, and a third round of infrastructure spending is planned for 2000. The rationale is straightforward: infrastructure investment lifts aggregate demand to maintain full capacity usage and alleviates production bottlenecks to ease inflationary pressures.

The above diagnosis and cure have been rejected by a number of economists. In the opinion of Thomas Rawski (1999):

> This diagnosis is mistaken and the policy misconstrued. Weakness in the economy, which pre-dates the Asian crisis of 1997/98 runs much deeper than China's leaders appear to believe. The difficulties are structural rather than cyclical. Short-term pump-priming exacerbates structural problems and undercuts long-term reform objectives.

Nicholas Lardy (1998), while not offering an explanation for the slowdown, also deemed China's reflation program to be a mistake:

> China's leadership has made its short-term growth objective its highest priority. Longer-term structural reform of state-owned banks and enterprises is being postponed. Ironically, even if the program increases the rate of growth, ultimately, the costs of postponed reforms will be even greater, meaning it likely will fail to alleviate social unrest.

We agree with some elements in each of the above analyses but we differ in emphasis, and, sometimes also, in conclusions. In this paper, we argue that:

(a) the structural flaws in China's economy in 1995, if left uncorrected, would likely cause growth to slow down in the future, say within a decade, but these structural flaws were not responsible for the significant slowdown in 1996–99;

(b) the slowdown in 1996–97 was largely the result of the austerity program that Zhu Rongji had implemented since mid-1993 to simultaneously wring inflationary pressures out of the economy and to restructure the economy;
(c) the further slowdown in 1998–99 reflected the export decline caused by the Asian financial crisis; and
(d) the reflation program of 1998–99 did not represent a wavering of commitment to restructuring; its emphasis on infrastructure investment (as opposed to a generalised increase in investment) was a sensible response to a temporary external shock.

Thomas Rawski and Nicholas Lardy are correct that radical restructuring of the state enterprise sector and the state banks system is absolutely crucial to avoiding a drastic drop in the trend growth rate in the future. The maintenance of the 1996 status of the state enterprises and state banks is not a viable option in the long run because the economy will simply not be able to support the growing burden from these two sectors.

The Chinese view that under-consumption (high saving) has made macroeconomic management more difficult is correct, a point that we will develop later, but we do not see larger state spending, even if it is in infrastructure, to be the optimum policy response. The correct response is restructuring not stabilisation; there should be financial restructuring to create financial institutions that would quickly channel the additional saving to investments with the highest rates of return.

Our general view is that the short-run costs of economic restructuring may have been overstated. Restructuring state-owned enterprises (SOEs) could worsen short-term growth while improving long-term growth prospects; but restructuring state-owned banks could improve both short-term and long-term growth. Financial restructuring is a win-win reform activity because it will eliminate the liquidity trap that now exists in credit creation, and neutralise the short-run deflationary effects of higher saving. Finally, the macroeconomic record suggests the interesting possibility that a clear commitment to a restructuring strategy based on promoting the convergence of China's economic institutions to the norms of modern market economies improves the short-term tradeoff between growth and inflation.

This paper is organised as follows. Part 2 presents the case for economic restructuring. Part 3 analyses the macroeconomic record. Part 4 evaluates the post-1997 reflation package. Part 5 takes up the question of the susceptibility of China to the type of financial crisis that had hit Asia in 1997–98. Parts 6 examines the issue of under-consumption and the need for financial restructuring, especially in the rural sector, if China's high growth is to be prolonged. Part 7 discusses the issue of enterprise restructuring. Part 8 contains brief concluding remarks.

2. THE RESTRUCTURING IMPERATIVE

The successful completion of the bilateral US-China negotiations in November 1999 over the conditions of China's entry into the World Trade Organisation (WTO) marks a watershed on many fronts for China. First and foremost, China's admission into WTO marks an important improvement in the economic security of China. Trade and foreign investment have constituted an important engine of growth since 1978. The requirement for annual renewal by the U.S. Congress of China's normal trading relationship with the United States made China's economic growth vulnerable to the vagaries of American domestic politics. Through WTO membership, this engine of growth could no longer be unilaterally shut off by the United States without the action being a major violation of international law.

WTO membership also marks a watershed in China's public recognition about the primary source of its impressive growth in the last two decades. The WTO is an international economic organisation that specifies and enforces broadly similar economic policy regimes on its membership. China's willingness to join such an institution reflects more than a desire to protect itself from potential blackmail by the United States, it also reflects China's realisation that the active ingredient in Deng Xiaoping's recipe for conjuring up growth was the convergence of China's economic institutions to the economic institutions of modern capitalist economies, particularly of East Asian capitalist economies.

At the early stages of China's reform when most of the intelligentsia did not know the full extent of the economic achievements of their capitalist neighbours, and when most of the top leaders were ideologically committed to Stalinist-style communism, it was important for the survival of the reformist faction of that time that the changes to China's economic institutions were comfortingly gradual, conveniently located in areas far from Beijing, and cloaked in the chauvinistic rhetoric of experimentation to discover new institutional forms that are optimal for China's socialist system and particular economic circumstances. After twenty years of evolution in economic institutions, of rotation in political leadership, and of tectonic change in the political fortune of the communist parties in Eastern Europe and the former Soviet Union, the only organised opposition today to the continued convergence of China's economic institutions to international forms comes form a small group of sentimental Stalinists like Deng Liqun.[1] The social and political landscape in China has changed so much that the political leadership now incurs only minimal ideological liability when they introduce more capitalist incentives (e.g. differentiated pay, leveraged buy-out, stock options for managers) and capitalist tools (e.g. joint-stock company, bankruptcy law, unemployment insurance). The leadership is hence confident that its explicit embrace of capitalist institutions under WTO auspices would be seen by the general Chinese public (and the Chinese elite) as a step forward in the reform process rather than as surrender of China's sovereignty in economic experimentation.[2]

It must be underscored that WTO membership will involve considerable costs to China. China has agreed to reduce its industrial

---

[1] For recent warnings from this faction against perceived suicide by the Communist WParty, see "Elder warns on economic change," *South China Morning Post*, January 13, 2000, and "Leftists make late bid to slow reforms," *South China Morning Post*, February 10, 2000.

[2] This de facto public recognition by the government that the *deus ex machina* of China's impressive growth since 1978 is the convergence of its economic institutions to those of market economies will unfortunately not end the academic debate on this issue. Many China specialists have waxed eloquently about how China's experimentation has created economic institutions that are optimally suited for transition economies in general; see Sachs and Woo (forthcoming) for a survey of this debate.

tariffs from an average of 24.6 percent to 9.4 percent by 2005, and its agricultural tariffs from an average of 31.5 percent to 14.5 percent by 2004. China has also agreed to liberalise trade in many services, including telecommunications, insurance and banking. Compliance with WTO rules will create substantial dislocation in China, albeit for the sake of a better future. China is a natural food-importer and a natural factory-oriented society given its low land-man ratio. The agricultural sector employs over 320 million people, which is over two-third of the rural labour force. The bulk of China's state-owned sector, which employs over 40 percent of the urban labour force, survives only because of various forms of subsidies and import barriers, both of which contravene WTO regulations. The agricultural sector and the state sector together employed 47 percent of the total labour force in 1998. Conservatively, a fifth of China's workers may have to change jobs, and this could be a politically destabilising process if not handled adeptly, and if external shocks were to slow down economic growth.

The tradeoff between stability and restructuring that is so starkly brought to the forefront by China's admission into WTO is not a new tradeoff. China's WTO membership has really accentuated an existing dilemma and not introduced a new one. The government has always realised that the soft budget constraint of the inefficient state-owned enterprise (SOE) sector is a constant threat to price stability, and the diversion of resources to keep this sector afloat is a drag on economic growth. But serious restructuring of SOEs means much more than facing higher urban unemployment, it also means confronting the politically powerful industrial-military complex and the industrial-bureaucratic complex. Economic rents now pose a bigger obstacle to restructuring than ideological sentimentality, and, unlike the latter, it is not something that the mere passing of time will resolve.

Luckily for China, the job of restructuring had been made easier because China's economic structure in the early years of the reform could allow growth to occur without much restructuring. This is because China in 1978 was still an undeveloped economy dominated by self-subsistence peasant agriculture, unlike the urbanised Central European and Russian economies in 1989 which had an overabundance of heavy industries. This meant that the introduction of market forces caused economic development in China but economic restructuring in Poland and Russia, which translated, respectively, into output growth and output decline.[3]

The movement of Chinese labour from low-productivity agriculture to higher-productivity industry, and from the poor inland provinces to the richer coastal provinces produced an average annual growth rate of 10 percent in the 1978–95 period. The Chinese state sector certainly did not wither away in this period; it employed 18.6 percent of the workforce in 1978 and 18.0 percent in 1995, and therewere 38 million more state workers in 1995 than in 1978.[4] There was reallocation of labour from agriculture to industry but not reallocation of labour from state to non-state enterprises. China in 1978 was thence very different from Russia in 1991; extensive growth was still possible in China whereas it had run its course in Russia.[5]

Since China was in the fortunate situation of being able to postpone most of the pain of restructuring, it was quite understandable that China did so. The result is that after two decades of "reform and opening," the job of economic restructuring is far from done. Among the many daunting tasks left are:

- a government sector that is still too large (despite a recent cut in the size of the central bureaucracy), too intrusive, and susceptible to corruption;

---

[3] This argument is developed in Sachs and Woo (1994).

[4] The 18.0 percent for 1995 is calculated from the *China Statistical Yearbook 1996* because the total workforce data from 1990 onward was revised upward in the *China Statistical Yearbook* of the succeeding years by increasing the size of the rural workforce. The revised data is inconsistent across time, the growth in labour force between 1989 and 1990 is now 15.5 percent (!), while the old data shows an increase of 2.5 percent. Using the revised data, the SOEs employed 17 percent of total labour force in 1995.

[5] Easterley and Fischer (1994) showed that extensive growth came to a quicker end in Russia than would be in capitalist market economies because the elasticity of substitution between capital and labour in Russia was much lower.

- a state-owned enterprise (SOE) system that has proved itself resistant to numerous efforts to increase its efficiency and profitability;
- a state-dominated financial system where the banks lack the ability to assess the economic merits of proposed projects, and, worse, have shied away from lending to non-state enterprises, the most dynamic component of the economy; and
- inadequate institutional infrastructure to allow smooth running of a market economy; for example, an efficient commercial court system, speedy bankruptcy procedures, independent mechanisms to mediate labour conflict, uniform accounting standards, and social safety nets are really not yet in place.

It was only after the ascent of Zhu Rongji to the prime ministership in early 1998 that a decisive program of restructuring was implemented. The size of the central government was cut by a third, and the process of privatising many small and medium enterprises was speeded up. Twenty million workers left the payroll of state-owned units in 1998, compared to two million in 1997. This represented an 18 percent reduction in state employment in one year![6]

Now that China is entering WTO, it can no longer postpone the required restructuring of the inefficient components of its economy. However, the restructuring job was made more difficult in the last two and a half years because of negative external shocks. The Asian financial crisis caused Chinese exports to East and Southeast Asia to decline tremendously, and Chinese exports to North America and Western Europe to face increased competition from the Asia countries whose currencies had fallen in value against the Renminbi (RMB). Foreign direct investments amounted to $40 billion in 1999, down from $45 million in 1998. The result was a GDP growth rate of 7.8 percent in 1998 and 7.1 percent in 1999, despite the government's vigorous attempts to reflate the economy since mid-1998.

---

[6] This is such a large shift that it raises the discomforting thought that some of the shift may be a mere change in employment classification without change in work conditions; an issue that we cannot go into here.

3. The Macroeconomic Situation

Figure 1 summarises the growth and inflation record since 1978 when China embarked on the first steps toward a market economy. There have been two episodes of high inflation, 1988-89 and 1993–95, where the inflation rate exceeded both 10 percent. It is interesting that the output cost of wringing out inflation were very different in both episodes. The drop in inflation from 18.8 percent in 1988 to 3.1 percent in 1990 was accompanied by a 7 percentage point drop in the growth rate; whereas the drop in inflation from 24.1 percent in 1994 to 2.8 percent in 1997 saw less than a 4 percentage point drop in the growth rate.

What accounted for the drastically more favourable tradeoff between growth and inflation in the second episode? In statistical analysis not reported here, we found that the differences in the inflation and growth performance across the two episodes could not be systemically linked to differences in the credit polices that started and then ended the two high inflations. My hypothesis for the different tradeoffs in these two episodes is that consumers' confidence and investors' confidence about China's future were very different in the two stabilisation programs. The 1989–90 stabilisation occurred amid widespread doubt about whether the convergence toward a market economy would continue, if not reversed. Following the unfortunate Tiananmen tragedy in June 1989, economic policymaking returned to the hands of the central planners, and numerous announcements were made about reining in capitalist tendencies. The implementation of the 1994–97 stabilisation, in contrast, occurred after the 14th Party Congress in 1992 had pledged to build "a socialist market economy with Chinese characteristics." This denial of a universal norm for socialism was correctly read as renewed commitment by the Communist Party toward convergence to a market economy.

Our hypothesis is that this difference in anticipation about the future direction of China's economic policy had very different effects on the behaviour of consumers and investors. The heightened confidence in a prosperous future was largely why fixed capital formation contributed over 2 percentage points to GDP growth in 1996–97 compared to the negative 1.7 percentage points in 1989–90; and why consumption

12 China's Economy into the New Century

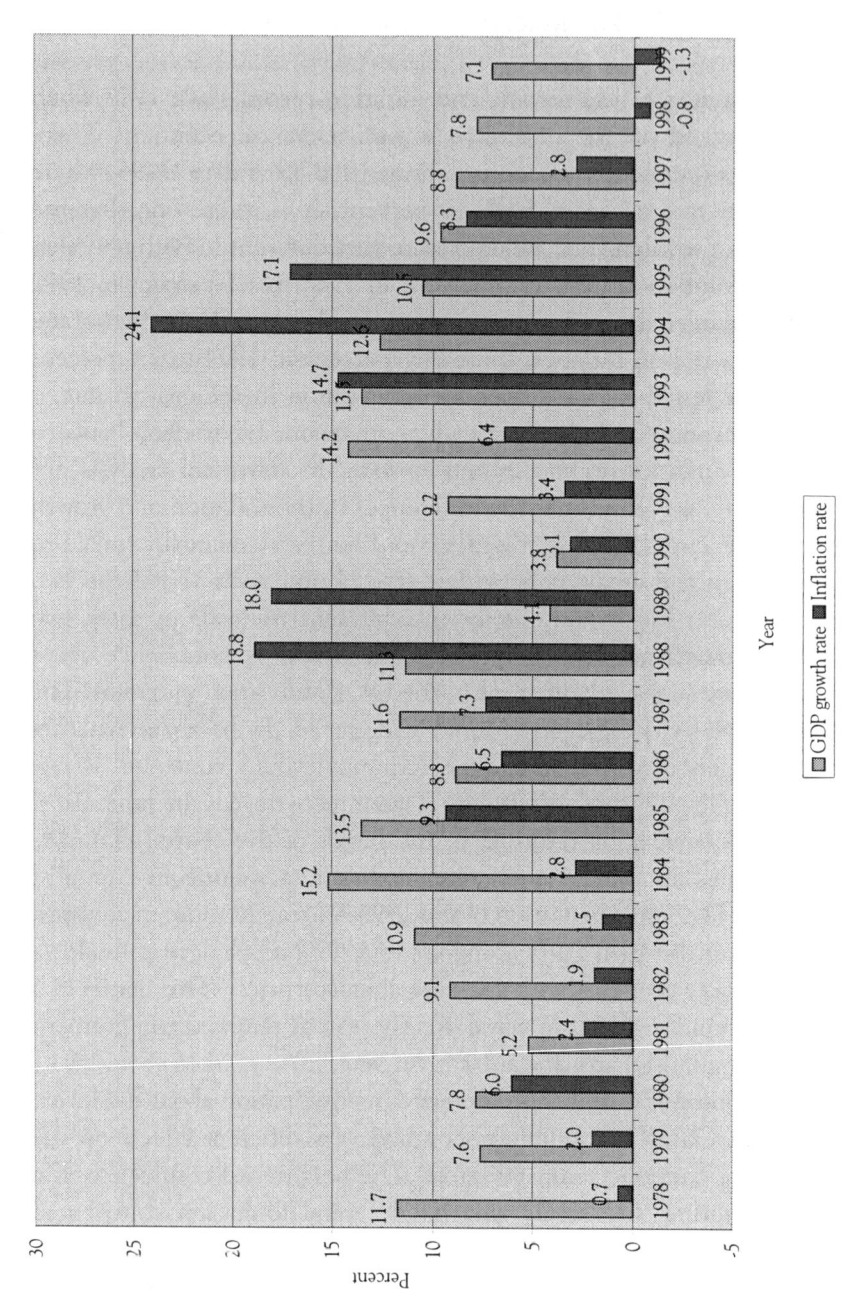

Figure 1. Growth and Inflation in China, 1978–1999

spending contributed an average 4.5 percentage points to growth in 1996–97 versus 1 percentage point in 1989–90 (see Table 1).

Since inflation in 1996 was down to 8.3 percent from 24.2 percent in 1994, and the 1996 growth rate of 9.5 percent almost equalled the average 10 percent growth rate of the 1978–95 period, one could say that the Chinese stabilisation program that started in mid-1993 had achieved soft-landing in 1996. Some observers have used this reasoning to describe the continuation of tight macroeconomic policies until early 1998 to be a case of "macroeconomic policy overkill." While the precipitous plunge in money (M1) growth from an inflationary 43 percent in 1993 to 20 percent in 1996 was desirable, the further drop to 10 percent in 1998:2Q was an overkill, as evidenced by the fall in the level of retail prices since October 1997.[7]

We do not dispute the macroeconomic consequences of the tight monetary policies and the tight controls over investment spending before mid-1998, but we note that these restrictive policies had succeeded in forcing considerable restructuring in the inefficient state-owned enterprise (SOE) sector. Because most loss-making SOEs did not receive their accustomed allotments of credit to continue production (a large portion of which went straight into inventory), the default outcome was that many were taken over by new owners[8] who reorganised the firms and changed the output mix. Our point is that a temporary slowdown in growth is many times necessary in order to force resources to move to a new growth path that would lead to a more competitive economy in the future. We have to recognise in the so-called "macroeconomic policy overkill" the audacity of the top Chinese leadership to choose to dislocate reforms to produce sustained dynamic growth in the future over Brezhnev-style maintenance of the comfortable status quo which would have led to a dismal future.

The "macroeconomic policy overkill" from 1997:1Q to 1998:2Q, in short, reflected a deliberate decision to accept growth rates that were

---

[7] Except in August and September 1998 when the heavy flooding disrupted supplies in several heavily-populated parts of the country.

[8] In many cases, the new owners were employees of the firms.

Table 1. Sources of Aggregate Demand in China in Reform Period, 1978–1998

	Annual GDP growth rate	Rural household consumption	Urban household consumption	Government consumption	Fixed capital formation	Change in inventory	Net exports	Total household consumption
Part A: Percentage Point Contribution to GDP Growth Rate by Each Expenditure Category
1979–98	9.8	2.4	2.3	1.2	3.3	0.3	0.2	4.7
1988	11.3	3.1	4.1	0.4	3.2	1.7	-1.2	7.2
1989	4.1	0.7	1.3	1.1	-4.0	5.2	-0.1	2.0
1990	3.8	-0.8	0.7	0.4	0.5	-1.0	4.0	-0.1
1991	9.2	0.9	2.2	2.2	4.7	-1.3	0.4	3.2
1992	14.2	2.5	4.0	2.1	8.8	-1.6	-1.7	6.5
1993	13.5	0.5	2.9	1.3	10.5	1.5	-3.3	3.4
1994	12.6	2.1	2.7	1.4	3.0	-0.1	3.5	4.7
1995	10.5	2.9	3.4	-0.2	2.2	1.6	0.5	6.3
1996	9.6	3.7	1.9	1.2	2.7	-0.4	0.6	5.5
1997	8.8	1.3	2.2	1.2	2.4	-0.4	2.0	3.6
1998	7.8	0.6	2.7	1.2	4.5	-1.4	0.3	3.3

lower than the 10 percent average growth rate of the 1978–95 period in order to ensure an acceptable rate of economic restructuring and to moderate the boom-bust cycles of the last two decades. The implicit growth range that policymakers appear to think is compatible with achieving the restructuring and stabilisation objectives seems to be about 7.0 percent to 8.0 percent. When the Asian financial crisis hit in 1998, causing China's exports to fall, and hence rendering growth lower than intended, it was only natural that the government undertook stimulation of domestic demand to reflate the economy.

4. Responding to the Post-1997 Deflation

The government responded to the onset of price deflation in 1997:4Q by cutting the average lending rate from 10.1 percent to 8.6 percent. However, the anticipated surge in credit expansion did not occur. This is largely because of the newfound reluctance of the state commercial banks to extend more credits to its traditional clients, the SOEs — especially the loss-making SOEs — creating a "liquidity trap" phenomenon that we will discuss later.

By early 1998, in the wake of the collapse of several important Pacific Asian economies, Chinese policymakers recognised that stronger reflation was required to offset the coming collapse in external demand. Furthermore, the SOE reform program announced at the 15th Party Congress in September 1997 was beginning to take bite and firms would soon begin to shed excess workers. So, stronger reflation was also desirable in order to induce the establishment of new urban enterprises to soak up the newly released SOE workers.

The reflation program sought to boost aggregate demand by trying to:

(a) increase investment by approving faster the backlog of investment applications;
(b) increase government spending;
(c) loosen monetary policy; and
(d) stimulate private spending through housing reform.

Faster Approval of Investment Applications

The State Planning Commission was literally put on an over-time schedule in early 1998 to speed up the approval of investment projects. "Increased economic openness" was a fortuitous byproduct of this measure. Approval was given to a number of large foreign projects that had been held up for several years because of concerns either about the possible domination of these particular lines of business by foreign firms or about the possible competition that they might provide to domestic firms of national strategic importance.

One unexpected check on approval acceleration as a reflation tool was that many local governments had not bothered to turn in local investment plans for 1998 because of the across-the-border rejection of local investment plans since the earnest implementation of the stabilisation program in 1994. The greatest obstacle to the effectiveness of investment approval as an economic stimulus is that approval does not necessarily translate into realisation. The translation of approval of investment into realisation of investment is usually low in times of declining aggregate demand. Hence, not surprisingly, many foreign and domestic firms postponed the actual investment until sustained economic recovery seems imminent. Partly, because of the low aggregate demand in China and abroad, but mostly because of the panic in international credit markets, actual FDI was US$40 billion in 1999, 10 percent down from US$45 billion in 1998 despite the "increased economic openness" noted above.[9]

Expansionary Fiscal Policy

In July 1998, the government announced the issuance of RMB 100 billion in bonds to finance <u>new</u> infrastructure investment by the central and local governments. (It seems that these bonds had been purchased mainly by state banks.) This announcement was quickly followed by new spending plans on telecommunications, railways, and roads. As the economy continued to slow steadily throughout 1999, a new fiscal stimulus

---

[9] "Foreign capital off the rails," *South China Morning Post*, February 16, 2000.

package of RMB 60 billion was implemented in August 1999. In March 2000, the government announced that it would soon issue RMB 100 billion of bonds to finance additional infrastructure investment, especially in the interior provinces.[10]

A natural question raised by the recent expansionary fiscal policy is whether the level of public debt in China is still at a level that would not be too heavy a burden in the future. The issue is what should be counted as "public debt" when so much of the economy is still state owned. If public debt is defined to be the stock of government bonds that has been issued to finance budget deficits, (and held by both domestic and foreign agents), then the public debt-GDP ratio was 7.3 percent of GDP in 1996 and 8.1 percent in 1997.

It has been argued, however, that since the government is the guarantor of the state banks, the nonperforming loans of the state banks ought to be counted as public debt. Estimates of the extent of nonperforming loans range from 20 percent to 50 percent of total bank loans.[11] If we take the NPL ratio to be 33 percent, then the broader definition of public debt would put the "broader public debt"-GDP ratio at 37.0 percent of GDP in 1996 and 41.1 percent in 1997.

What about the debt of SOEs and other state institutions (for example, the regional trusts and investment companies, TICs)? The government could be construed as being responsible for these bad debts just as they were construed to be responsible for the bad debts held by the banks. Since the bulk of the <u>domestic</u> borrowing of SOEs and state institutions is from the state banks, the inclusion of nonperforming loans of the state banks in the broader definition of public debt has already taken into account the bad debts of SOEs and state institutions that are owed to domestic agents.

---

[10] "Zhu pledges to keep cash flowing," *South China Morning Post*, March 6, 2000.

[11] This range reflects our selection of credible estimates (e.g. a missed interest payment does not necessarily mean that the loan is bad), so this range does not encompass all estimates that have been reported in the press. For example, Bloomburg News has reported that some analysts believed bad loans to be 70 percent of bad loans, *New York Times*, "China Hopes to Sell Bad Loans at Discount," January 5, 1999.

Foreign debts of SOEs and other state institutions may deserve different treatment from their domestic debts because of the government's great concern about China's continued access to international financial markets at favourable interest rates. In order to arrive at the "broadest" definition of public debt, we take into account all the bad debts that SOEs and other state institutions could potentially owe to foreigners. We constructed the "maximum" public debt as the sum of the broader public debt plus the entire foreign debt of SOEs and public institutions. The "maximum public debt"-GDP ratio was 50.1 percent of GDP in 1996 and 55.1 percent in 1997.[12]

Is a debt-GDP ratio of 55.1 percent too low or too high? Compared with the Italian, Swedish and U.S. situations where central government debt (after deducting intra-governmental debt) to GDP ratios were, respectively, 117.6 percent in 1995, 70.8 percent in 1995, and 50.5 percent in 1996, it might appear that there is still substantial room for the Chinese government to increase its borrowing to finance its expansionary fiscal policy without causing serious debt problems in the future. However, such conclusion would be overly optimistic. This is because China raises much less state revenue (as a share of GDP) than these other countries, and hence has a much lower capacity to service its public debt. The revenue-GDP ratio was 11 percent for China in 1995, 30 percent for Italy in 1995, 38 percent for Sweden in 1995, and 21 percent for the U.S. in 1996. The point is that until China increases its tax collection, there is a real tradeoff between restructuring the state financial sector and increasing infrastructure investment to stimulate the economy. And it is important to note that increasing tax collection is as much a political challenge as it is an administrative challenge.

Easier Monetary Policy

The People's Bank of China has cut interest rates several times since price deflation became obvious. For example, the bank lending rate was

---

[12] The terms "broader public debt" and "maximum public debt" are from Fan (1998), he differs from my calculations in that he assumes a NPL ratio of 25 percent.

reduced steadily from 10.1 percent in September 1997 to 5.9 percent in September 1999. Furthermore, the bank reserve ratio was lowered twice; from 13 percent to 8 percent in March 1998 and then to 6 percent in November 1999. However, the money (M1) growth rate continued its downward course from 25 percent in 1997:3Q and 1997:3Q to 13 percent in 1998:1Q, and then to 10 percent in 1998:2Q, prompting some Chinese economists, like their Japanese colleagues, in postulating the existence of liquidity traps.

This reluctance by banks to extend credit has its origin in the determined efforts of Zhu Rongji to improve the balance sheets of the state banks and to promote restructuring in the SOE sector since he took over as economic czar in mid-1993. By the end of 1997, the twin facts that Zhu Rongji would be promoted to become the Prime Minister in 1998 and that he had peremptorily dismissed bank managers when the proportion of NPLs in their banks had gone up had instilled a new sense of prudent lending in the entire state bank system. Until the typical bank manager faced personally severe consequences from an increase in the ratio of NPLs, he never had to respond to the knowledge that the demand for credit by bankrupt SOEs was always high because they really do not expect to repay any of their debts. The loss-making SOEs were engaging in a gamble of the desperate; new loans offered the only chance of a lucky investment that would pull them out of their seemingly hopeless financial straits. This new behaviour by bank managers is the reason why despite additional reductions in interest rates and required reserve ratios by the central bank, money growth continued to drop in line with the decline in GDP growth.

This slowdown in loans to the SOEs has unfortunately not been replaced by an increase in loans to non-state enterprises, the primary engine of growth in China's economy. The state banks are reluctant to lend to the non-state enterprises, partly because the latter's non-standard accounting makes risk assessments difficult. More importantly, a banker knows that while a NPL to an SOE is financially undesirable, a NPL to a private enterprise is more than that, it is also politically undesirable. The banker feared that the NPL to a private firm could result in him being accused afterward of working with capitalists to embezzle the state.

Thus, we have the present situation where the loans that state banks are most willing to make are infrastructure loans guaranteed by the central government.

It was only after the central bank implicitly assured the banks in mid-1998 that new NPLs incurred in support of SOEs that were producing saleable goods would be overlooked that money growth increased to 14 percent in 1998:3Q. But then caution reasserted itself as bank managers were rightly sceptical about the credibility of the government that the new NPLs would not count against them in the future. The result was that money growth, after the 14 percent spurt in 1998:3Q, declined steadily to 11.3 percent in 1999:3Q.

Hence, the practical short-run solution to this "liquidity trap" is for the government to undertake <u>new</u> infrastructure spending financed by the state backs (and ultimately by new reserves from the central bank). However, a larger sustained increase in credit is possible only if the state commercial banks would use the new deposits (new reserves) to extend new loans, i.e. only if banks act according to the standard "money multiplier" process. As the banks' willingness to lend depends now on finding truly economically viable projects, the government has sought to create new safe lending opportunities to the banks by announcing housing reforms, including privatisation of the housing stock. The hope is that the banks would then expand mortgage lending on the basis that the household debt would be fully (and, presumably, also safely) backed by a marketable asset, and hence boost aggregate demand.

Housing Reform as a Short-Run Stimulus

The majority of the urban population has, until very recently, lived in virtually free housing supplied by their employers.[13] In early 1998, the government announced that SOEs and other state institutions would stop providing free housing after July 1 and that the housing stock would

---

[13] Of course, housing and other subsidies are in fact largely paid for by the employees themselves; this is why their take-home pay is so low.

be privatised.[14] To compensate for the loss of free housing, and to encourage their workers to buy the houses that they are presently staying in, many local governments are giving subsidised mortgages to civil servants. By the end of 2000, government workers had purchased 60 percent of the public housing stock.[15] The marketization of housing is now in full swing, marking another significant milestone on the way to a market economy. The marketization of housing will enhance labour mobility and free the SOEs to focus on production and distribution of goods.

The *China Macroeconomic Analysis* (1998:3Q issue) estimated that, with a functioning mortgage system in place, the marketization of housing would increase the annual demand for housing by 20 to 30 percent. Since housing investment is presently about 4.3 percent of GDP, the housing reform would increase GDP growth by 1 percentage point.[16]

However, in our assessment, the short-run result of the housing reform was a decrease in aggregate demand even though the new steady-state level of housing demand under the market regime is higher than the old steady-state level of housing demand under the entitlement regime. First, the demand for new residential construction by SOEs stopped abruptly on July 1, 1998, and because it takes time for private agencies to appear to intermediate between the builders and the millions of disparate buyers, the immediate impact was more likely to have been a drop in housing demand than an increase.

---

[14] The practical method of privatising the housing stock is to offer the houses to the existing tenants at prices which approximate the present discounted value of the stream of low rent payments. By giving the existing tenants the right of first refusal, this method makes explicit whatever existing inequality there is in housing allocation. This method does not create new inequalities.

[15] "Civil Servants own 60% of public housing," *The Straits Times*, February 24, 2000.

[16] The Minister of Construction has claimed that the housing reform contributed 1.5 to 2 percentage points to the 1999 growth rate; see "Civil Servants own 60% of public housing," *The Straits Times*, February 24, 2000. The construction of housing might have contributed this amount, but the relevant question is whether the housing reform had actually increased the amount of construction without housing. We doubt this claim for the reasons given in the paragraphs below.

Second, the mortgage system was not yet in place. The banks need time to build up its expertise in mortgage lending, and the certification/registration system of house ownership is usually not standardised province-wide. More importantly, at the moment, only the richest 5 to 10 percent of the urban population can qualify for mortgage loans; and these well-to-do folks are likely to have already acquired most of the housing that they want.

Results of the Reflation Package

The reflation package has worked much better than expected by most observers. When the negative effects of the Asian financial crisis started hitting in early 1998, and slowing China's GDP growth, most observers steadily revised their forecasts of 1998 growth downward. For example, the Economist Intelligence Unit's (EIU) *Country Report on China* predicted a 1998 growth rate of 7.3 percent in the 1998:1Q issue, 6.7 percent in the 1998:2Q issue, and then 6.1 percent in the 1998:3Q issue. The credit spurt and investment splurge in the last half of 1998 disappointed all these forecasts by lifting GDP growth to 7.6 percent in 1998:3Q and 9.6 percent in 1998:4Q to produce an annual growth rate of 7.8 percent for 1998. The decomposition of aggregate demand in Table 1 shows that fixed capital formation added 4.5 percent points to the 1998 growth rate.

However, given the widespread expectation that the Asian financial crisis was going to be a long-drawn crisis, and doubts that China would be able to undertake sustained fiscal stimulus, the EIU continued to predict low growth rates for 1999 despite the falsification of its gloomy forecasts for 1998. The 1999:3Q issue predicted a 1999 growth rate of 6.7 percent. The actual 1999 growth rate turned out to be 7.1 percent, partly due to the additional fiscal and monetary stimulus in the last quarter, and partly to the rapid recovery of exports in response to the end of the Asian financial crisis.

It must be mentioned that a number of observers believe that the official growth numbers are wrong and that actual growth in 1998 was between 3 to 5 percent. The basis of this scepticism is the low usage of electricity, the low volume of goods being transported, and the continued fall in the level of retail prices. A well-known Chinese economist, Mao Yushi, was quoted as saying that: "The GDP figure is still dubious... There must be some local government trying to please the central government by reporting inflated statistics."[17] There is credibility in Mao Yushi's statements because Premier Zhu had criticised provincial leaders in early December for each reporting a provincial growth rate greater than 10 percent in the first half of 1998 when the national growth rate was only 7.2 percent.[18]

The 1999 growth rate of 7.1 percent, low as it is, also deserves scepticism for the same reasons. First, only two provinces, Shanxi and Sichuan, have reported growth rates below 7.1 percent. Second, the sum of all individually reported provincial GDP exceeded the official national GDP by 7 percent.[19]

In Woo (1998), we had found that the annual GDP growth rate in the 1985–93 period could have been overstated, on the average, by as much as 2 percentage points; and, after taking various factors into account, Woo suggested a downward correction of about 1 percentage point. The overstatement is less serious however, when the inflation rate is low. In light of our work, the negative inflation, and the scepticism expressed in the two preceding paragraphs, we think that the actual GDP growth rate could plausibly be about 7 percent in 1998 and around 6.5 percent in 1999.

Table 2 compares exports in each quarter to its level in the same quarter of the previous year. It shows that the negative effects from the Asian financial crisis reached their peak in the 1998:3Q to 1999:2Q. With the recovery of the Asian crisis economies in 1999, China's exports leaped to $54 billion in 1999:3Q. Since the Asian crisis countries are expected to continue their economic expansion in 2000, China now has more room to undertake continued restructuring.

---

[17] "China just misses 8 percent growth rate," *South China Morning Post*, December 30, 1998, updated at 2:43 p.m.
[18] "China admits to cooking the books: editorial," *Agence France Presse*, December 23, 1998, 4:31 p.m.
[19] "Beijing has $546b chasm in key data," *South China Morning Post*, February 29, 2000.

Table 2. Export Earnings (fob, in US$ million)

	Q1	Q2	Q3	Q4	Year Total
1996	28,249	35,803	39,979	47,166	151,197
1997	35,585	45,360	48,173	53,759	182,877
1998	40,072	46,488	47,190	49,839	183,589
1999	37,290	45,727	54,201	na	na

5. Susceptibility of China to a Financial Crisis

The Asian financial crisis was typified by (a) a collapse of the exchange rate because of heavy capital outflow, and (b) a collapse of the domestic financial system causing a shortage of working capital that, in turn, caused output to collapse. So how vulnerable is China to a meltdown scenario of this type?

A dramatic speculative attack on the RMB can be ruled out simply because the RMB is not convertible for capital account transactions in financial assets. It is difficult for a person to borrow RMB from a Chinese bank to buy US dollars to speculate against the exchange rate because the purchase of US dollars requires documentation to prove that the transaction is trade-related.

Capital outflow by foreign private agents has not occurred because most of *the foreign private investments* in China are foreign direct investments, and there is very little short-term foreign debt. At the end of 1999, short-term foreign debt was less than 20 percent of the total foreign debt of US$168 billion. The fact that China also had US$155 billion in foreign exchange reserves made defense of the exchange rate feasible even if all short-term foreign debts had been recalled.

Furthermore, foreign participation in the Chinese stock markets is limited to transaction in B-shares. Only foreigners can own B-shares, and B-shares are denominated in US dollars and transacted using US dollars. In short, an abrupt withdrawal by foreigners from the Chinese stock markets can affect the value of the yuan-dominated A-shares (that only Chinese can own) only if their withdrawal would cause Chinese speculators to revise their expectations of future Chinese growth downward.

Of course, capital flight can occur through channels like over-invoicing of imports and under-invoicing of exports. A successful speculative attack on the RMB via large and pervasive mis-invoicing is theoretically possible, but difficult to prove because the paper trial would point to trade imbalance rather than portfolio adjustment being the cause of the exchange rate collapse. An exchange rate collapse from mis-invoicing of trade requires that the government be rigidly committed to current account convertibility, but this is not credible. Any government like China that has in place a comprehensive administrative system that processes every import application to buy foreign exchange (in order to prevent capital movements) can be easily tempted to defend the exchange rate by delaying approvals of import applications. So imports could be compressed to a significant degree whenever a trade deficit threatens to materialise.

We turn now to the issue of whether China's banking system would collapse spectacularly as in the countries experiencing the Asian financial crisis. To a first approximation, when the won, baht, and rupiah went into free fall, many Korean, Thai and Indonesian banks were rendered insolvent through a combination of the following channels: the sudden increase in the value (measured in domestic currency) of their foreign liabilties; the default on bank loans by domestic corporation bankrupted by the soaring of their external debts; and the default on bank loans by exporters who could not get short-term credit from their foreign suppliers of inputs. Many of the Korean, Thai and Indonesian banks were already financially fragile before their collapse because of undercapitalisation, and because of considerable NPLs that had been hidden by accounting gimmicks. And the exchange rate shock pushed these fragile banks over.

Much alarm has been raised in recent months about the amount of NPLs in China's banking system, with estimate for NPLs ranging from 20 to 50 percent of total bank loans. It has even been raised as a serious possibility several times, that a run by depositors is almost inevitable, causing a banking collapse that would trigger a general output decline.

We find the likelihood of either a bank run or a collapse of the banking system to be minimal. Admittedly, there have been bank runs in China since 1978, e.g. in 1988. But these bank runs were motivated by anticipations of high inflation caused by imminent lifting of price controls, and not by anticipations of bank failures. Whenever the government began indexing interest payments to the inflation rate, the bank runs reversed themselves. In the present time of falling prices, inflation-induced bank runs will not occur.

It is true that there is no depositor insurance in China but this in itself is unlikely to cause a bank run induced by fear over the large amount of NPLs. This is because all but one of the banks are state-owned and the government has repeatedly pledged to honour all deposits in the state banks. This pledge is credible because the government is in a position to make good its promise. As pointed out earlier, the government can easily borrow to cover the NPLs; and assuming an NPL ratio of 33 percent, the borrowing would raise the public debt-GDP ratio to just 40 percent. Alternatively, the government could always raise taxes to cover the NPLs.

Even if a bank run does occur, there need not be a collapse in bank credit because the central bank could just issue currency to the state banks to meet the withdrawals. This expansion of high power money cannot be easily translated into a loss of foreign reserves because capital controls are in place. This expansion of high power money will also not have much impact on inflation because this is mainly a shift out of bank deposits into cash, and not a shift into goods.

Simply put, even if the state banks are truly insolvent as has been alleged, and even if the insolvency does induce bank runs, a collapse in bank credit does not have to follow. It is well within the technical ability of the government to accommodate the bank runs, and it is also well within the financial ability of the government to recapitalise the state banks. Furthermore, these two government actions would not cause much damage (if any) to the economy, like lower growth and higher inflation.

While China can prevent the NPLs of the state banks from maiming the payments system and crippling production, we recognise that the

NPLs have imposed real costs on the economy. With NPLs accounting for a third of total bank loans (our estimate), bank loans accounting for about a fifth of fixed investments since 1985, and fixed investments at about 35 percent of GDP, this means that about 2.3 percent of GDP has been wasted annually in the last decade. Moreover, since most of the bank loans are extended to SOEs with little going to the more efficient non-state sector, the performing loans are not in investments with the highest rates of return. In short, the productive capacity of the economy could be higher than what it is.

Of course, we also recognise that the NPL problem might be even worse at the non-bank financial institutions (NBFIs) like the regional trust and investment companies (TICs).[20] However, because NBFIs constitute only a small part of the national credit system, their failure is not capable of bringing down the payments system. The biggest dangers from the collapse of NBFIs are social instability (especially when the base of NBFIs is small depositors), and reduction in foreign credit.

In the 1998 closure of the financial arm of the Guangdong International Trust and Investment Company (GITIC), the central government assumed responsibility for all properly-registered foreign debt. Since trade-related credit with maturity of less than three months and foreign debts of GITIC's branch in Hong Kong did not require official registration, it is likely that a very substantial amount of GITIC's foreign debt will not be assumed by the Chinese government. In October 1999, GITIC's liquidation committee reported that, after rejecting illegal contingent guarantees issued by GITIC, the total liabilities had been reduced from US$4.7 billion to the range of US$1.7 billion to US$2.7 billion. The value of recoverable assets was put at US$0.9 billion.[21]

As discussed earlier, this assumption of all the properly-registered debt of state institutions and SOEs would raise the public debt-GDP

---

[20] According to the *Far Eastern Economic Review* ("TIC Fever: China's shaky trust and investment houses start to fall," October 22, 1998), "most of the country's 243 TICs are on the rocks." Lardy (1998b) reported the claim that 50 percent of the assets of the non-bank financial sector was not performing.

[21] "Illegal GITIC deals delay payout," *South China Morning Post*, October 23, 1999.

ratio to 55 percent — still a very low level when compared with the public debt-GDP ratios of most Western European countries. As a general principle, the government's decision to let NBFIs fail is important to reducing the moral hazard problem inherent in supervision of the financial sector. Both domestic depositors and foreign creditors have to be encouraged to assess and manage risks better.

As things stand at the beginning of 2000, it looks unlikely that China will soon succumb to a financial crisis marked by bank runs, capital flight, a severe shortage of working capital, and a deep recession.

6. The Importance of Financial Intermediation for Stabilisation and Growth

Part A of Table 3 shows that total household consumption has declined steadily as a proportion of GDP. It dropped from an average of 52 percent in 1979–1983 to 46 percent in 1994–98. However, this fall in consumption is not seen in all sectors. While rural consumption fell from 33 percent of GDP in 1979–83 to 23 percent in 1994–98, urban consumption rose from 19 percent to 23 percent. But since the share of population living in urban areas has gone up from 20 percent in 1979–83 to 30 percent in 1994–98, it is not surprising that urban consumption has risen relative to GDP, while rural consumption has fallen. The important analytical issue is whether urban consumption did increase relative to GDP, once the demographic shift has been controlled for.

Part B of Table 3 presents a decomposition of the change in rural and urban consumption behaviour after taking the rural-urban movements into account. The decomposition follows from:

Equation (1): $(C_i/GDP) = [L_i/L] * [(C_i/L_i)/(GDP/L)]$
where C_i = consumption in sector I
 L_i = population in sector i
 L = total population

The decomposition in Equation (1) can be described as:
(consumption in sector i as share of GDP)

= (share of population living in sector i) * (normalised per capita consumption in sector i)

Taking differences, Equation (1) becomes:

Equation (2): $D(C_i/GDP) = [(C_i/L_i / (GDP/L)]*D [L_i/L]$
$+ [L_i/L]*D[(C_i/L_i)/(GDP/L)]$
$+ [D (L_i/L)]*[D\{(C_i/L_i)/(GDP/L)\}]$

The decomposition in Equation (2) can be described as:

Percentage point change in (consumption in sector i as share of GDP)
 = Percentage point contribution from the shift in the share of population in sector i
 + Percentage point contribution from the shift in normalised consumption in sector i
 + Percentage point contribution from interaction of the two shifts

We note that the normalised per capita consumption in sector i can in turn be decomposed into:

$[(C_i/L_i)/(GDP/L)] = (C_i/Y_i) * [(Y_i/L_i)/(GDP/L)]$
(C_i/Y_i) = average propensity to consume in sector i
$[(Y_i/L_i)/(GDP/L)]$ = [(per capita income in sector i)/(per capita GDP)]
 = normalised per capita income in sector i

We now have a natural definition of chronic under-consumption, it means a secularly declining average propensity to consume.

Since per capita income in China's urban sector has risen faster than per capita GDP over the entire reform period, normalised consumption in urban sector would increase if average propensity to consume in urban sector has remained unchanged. A drop in normalised consumption in the urban sector could only mean that the average propensity to consume among urban residents has gone down, i.e. that there is chronic under-consumption in the urban sector.

A drop in normalised consumption in the rural sector is more ambiguous, it would be consistent with a drop or a rise in the average propensity to consume of rural dwellers because growth in per capita income in rural areas has lagged behind growth in per capita GDP.

Table 3. Consumption Shifts in China in Reform Period, 1978–1998

	Rural household consumption	Urban household consumption	Government consumption	Fixed capital formation	Change in inventory	Net exports	Total household consumption	Rural share of population
Part A: Expenditure Category as Proportion of GDP, 1978–1998								
1978	30.3	18.5	13.3	29.8	8.4	-0.3	48.8	82.1
1988	30.4	21.5	11.7	31.4	5.9	-1.0	51.9	74.2
1998	22.1	24.1	11.9	35.3	2.8	3.8	46.2	69.6
Period 1 1979–83	32.6	19.0	14.4	27.6	6.1	0.4	51.6	79.7
Period 2 1984–88	31.9	19.5	13.1	30.7	6.3	-1.5	51.4	75.5
Period 3 1989–93	26.5	22.2	12.9	30.0	7.7	0.7	48.7	73.0
Period 4 1994–98	22.8	23.3	11.9	34.8	4.7	2.6	46.1	70.5

Part B: Decomposing the Change in Consumption-GDP Ratio

	Change in Consumption-GDP Ratio	Percentage Point Change in Consumption-GDP Ratio Due to:		
		(a) Rural-Urban Shift	(b) Consumption Shift	(c) Interaction Effects
For the Rural Sector				
Change between 1978 and 1998	-8.2	-4.6	-4.2	0.6
Change between Period 1 and 4	-9.7	-3.8	-6.7	0.8
For the Urban Sector				
Change between 1978 and 1998	5.6	12.9	-4.3	-3.0
Change between Period 1 and 4	4.2	8.7	-3.0	-1.4

Part B of Table 3 shows that there is unambiguous chronic underconsumption in urban China, and that this is also likely to be the case in rural China. There has been a downward shift of 3 percentage points in the normalised consumption of urban residents between Period 1 (1979–83) to Period 4 (1994–98), and a downward shift of 6.7 percent points in the normalised consumption of rural residents. This much bigger downward shift in rural normalised consumption suggests that the rural average propensity to consume has also fallen.

Keynes pointed out in his paradox of thrift that a rise in the saving rate could, in the short run, depress aggregate demand, and cause the economy to produce below capacity. Only if financial markets were informationally perfect would the increased saving be translated instantaneously into investments, and the level of aggregate demand be maintained. The paradox of thrift is based on coordination failure between savers and investors, and the minimisation of its occurrence requires highly sophisticated financial intermediation. In a centrally planned economy, the paradox of thrift would not exist because the planner controls both the amount of saving and the amount of investment; but then, for well-known reasons, a large portion of the saving would be wasted on value-subtracting projects.

China's marginally reformed financial system contains the worst aspects of the preceding two financial systems: the coordination failure of the market financial system, and the allocation irrationality of the command financial system. China's high saving rate is actually also partly a reflection of this serious problem in financial intermediation. The steady liberalisation of the economy has steadily increased the number and range of profitable investment opportunities. But because of the refusal of the state banks to lend to private entrepreneurs to enable them to reap these high rates of return, the private entrepreneurs have to engage in self-financing, and this requires high saving to accumulate the required threshold amount of capital.[22] In short, the convergence of financial intermediation in China to the level of financial sophistication in the United States would lower China's saving rate as well as ensure

---

[22] A formal model and testing of this argument is in Liu and Woo (1994).

the full employment of saving and allocate it to the most profitable projects.

Most of the attention on China's financial sector has focused on its urban banks. This neglect of rural financial intermediation is most unfortunate because rural enterprises (popularly known as township and village enterprises, TVEs) have constituted the main engine of China's economic growth since 1984.[23] It has been clear since the 15th Party Congress in September 1997 that China has decided to sharply reduce the importance of state-owned enterprises (SOEs) by accelerating the diversity of ownership forms. The amendment of the constitution in March 1999 to accord private ownership the same legal status as state ownership is a logical development from the 1997 policy decision. Implicitly, TVEs are expected to become an even more important engine of growth in the future.

Woo (1999) argued that this expectation of continued high TVE growth may be unrealistic however, given recent investment trends. TVE investment in the 1990s has declined relative to both GDP and total fixed investment, in a period in which total investment went from 30 percent of GDP in 1987 to 33 percent in 1997 (Table 4).

Table 4. Investment and Output by Ownership Forms

	Fixed Investment as % of GDP		Share of Fixed Investment, %		Share of Industrial Output, %	
	1987	1997	1987	1997	1987	1997
All Ownership Forms	30.4	33.4	100.0	100.0	100.0	100.0
SOEs	19.2	17.5	63.1	52.5	59.7	25.5
TVEs	8.9	7.7	29.1	23.0	32.5	47.6

---

[23] The industrial output alone from rural enterprises accounted for about 31 percent of the increase in GDP between 1984 and 1993; calculated from Woo (1998).

So far, the TVEs have increased their output share not only without getting any of the investment share released by the shrinking SOE sector but doing so with a decreased investment share, from 29 percent in 1987 to 23 percent in 1997. This is unlikely to be a sustainable situation. It is hard to see how the TVEs could move up the value-added chain in production without significant capital investments in the near future. So, if China's market capitals continue not to allocate sufficient investment funds to the most dynamic sector of the economy, China's high growth rate is probably not going to continue in the medium run.

The Agricultural Bank of China (ABC) was established in 1955 to provide financial services to the rural sector, and to channel funds for the grain procurement purchases. Small-scale collectively-owned rural credit cooperatives (RCCs, *Nongcun Xindai Hezuoshe*) were started in the early 1950s, under the supervision of ABC, to be the primary financial institutions serving the rural areas. RCCs operate an extensive network of branches, savings deposit offices, and credit stations in market towns and remote areas. The number of RCC units rose from 389,726 in 1981 to 421,582 in 1984, and then fell steadily to 365,492 in 1995.[24] We want to highlight this decline in the number of RCC units after 1984 because this decline means a decrease in the effort to mobilise rural saving, and a decrease in the access of the rural community to investment financing.

In our opinion, the primary reason for the drop in TVE investment (as a share of GDP and as a share of total domestic investments) is that TVEs suffer from two big disadvantages in investment financing. The first disadvantage suffered by TVEs is that the still heavily-regulated financial system is directing too much of the investment funds to the SOE sector, thus starving the TVEs sector of investment funds. The second major disadvantage of the TVEs in raising capital is that, because of political discrimination against private ownership, many TVEs generally have vague, collective forms of property rights that cannot attract market-driven investment funds.

---

[24] The number of RCC units is the number of RCCs plus the number of branches, saving deposit offices and credit stations.

The deregulation of financial intermediation will allow the appearance of new small-scale local financial institutions that will mobilise local savings to finance local TVE investments. Our expectation is based on the impressive growth of folk finance (*minjian rongzhi*) since 1978 despite the absence of legal recognition and legal protection. According to Liu (1992), folk finance was the source of the development of TVEs in Wenzhou city in Zhejiang Province:

> Ninety-five per cent of the total capital needed by the local private sector has been supplied by "underground" private financial organisations, such as money clubs, specialised financial households and money shops ... .[25]

It cannot be over-emphasised that financial deregulation has to be accompanied by the introduction of adequate banking supervision and of prudential standards that comply with international norms. The rash of banking crises in Eastern Europe in the early 1990s and in East and Southeast Asia recently should serve as warnings of financial deregulation without adequate improvement in the government's ability to monitor the activities of the financial institutions. Besides deregulating rural financial intermediation, it is also important that the property rights of rural enterprises are clearly defined, protected legally, and freely tradable like the property rights of shareholding firms. The present trend of restructuring TVEs into shareholding cooperatives by dividing their assets among the workers (sometimes, among the original inhabitants of the community) is a natural convergence to an enterprise form which,

---

[25] The competition from the new rural financial institutions is likely to force the ABC-RCC system to improve its operations. This expectation is again based on Wenzhou's experience: "In order to compete with [the new folk finance institutions]... , as early as 1980, a local collective credit union, without informing the superior authority, abandoned for the first time the fixed interest rate and adopted a floating interest rate which fluctuated in accordance with market demand but remained within the upper limit set by the state. Despite the dubious legality of the floating interest rate, the local state bank branches and all the credit unions in Wenzhou had already adopted it before the central state officially ratified it in 1984" [Liu (1992)].

international experiences have shown, assures investors that managers would have the incentives to maximise profits in a prudent manner.

7. THE MANY DISAPPOINTMENTS OF STATE ENTERPRISE REFORM

When China started its SOE reform two decades ago, it followed the principles of market socialism to motivate the SOE manager to maximise profits. The state entered into a profit-sharing arrangement with the firm, and gave increasing operational autonomy to the manager. The official conclusion is that the decentralisation of decision-making to the firms has failed to improve their performance.

> The current problems of SOEs are: excessive investments in fixed assets with very low return rates, resulting in the sinking of large amounts of capital; and a low sales-to-production ratio, giving rise to mounting inventories. The end result is that the state has to inject an increasing amount of working capital through the banking sector into the state enterprises. (Vice-Premier Zhu Rongji, 1996)[26]
>
> The situation as regards the economic efficiency of [state] enterprises has remained very grim ... And the prominent feature is the great increase in the volume and size of losses. (Vice-Premier Wu Bangguo, 1996)[27]

There has been a steady increase in SOE losses since additional decision-making powers were given to SOE managers in 1985.[28] The

---

[26] "Guo you qiye sheng hua gaige ke burong huan," (No time shall be lost in further reforming state-owned enterprises), speech at the 4th meeting of the 8th People's Congress, *People's Daily, Overseas Edition*, March 11, 1996.
[27] "Losses of State-Owned Industries Pose Problems for China's Leaders," *The Washington Post*, November 3, 1996.
[28] Recent evidence suggest that past reports on SOE losses (e.g. two-third of SOEs make zero or negative profits) may be understated. A national audit of 100 SOEs in 1999 found that 81 falsified their books, and 69 reported profits that did not exist; and an

three most commonly cited reasons for this development are: the emergence of competition from the non-state enterprises, the failure of the SOEs to improve their efficiency, and embezzlement by SOE personnel.

The competition explanation is perhaps the weakest explanation because the profit rates of SOEs in the sectors of industry that experienced little entry by non-SOEs showed the same dramatic drop as the profit rates of SOEs in sectors with heavy penetration by non-SOEs. Fan and Woo (1996) compared the SOE profit rate and the proportion of output sold by SOEs in different sectors of industry in 1989 and 1992. In four of the five cases where the degree of SOE domination was unchanged, the profit rates were lower in 1992, e.g. the profit rate of the tobacco industry dropped 82 percentage points, and that of petroleum refining dropped 13 percentage points. The 1992 profit rates were lower in six of the seven cases where the degree of SOE domination had declined by less than five percentage points.

The failure-to-improve explanation has generated a heated debate in the academic literature. There is a wide range of total factor productivity (TFP) estimates, going from large negative to large positive, and they could be due to a whole array of factors like the possibility of Potemkin data sets, the functional form, the estimation method, and the choice of price deflators.[29] Our reading of the evidence is that any improvements in TFP was minor, and, most likely, temporary.

The attribution of China's SOE losses to embezzlement of profits and asset-stripping by employees (managers and workers) is reminiscent of the relentless escalation of SOE losses during the decentralising reforms in pre-1990 Eastern Europe. With the end of the central plan and the devolution of financial decision-making power to the SOEs, the key

---

audit of the Industrial and Commercial Bank of China and the China Construction Bank found that accounting abuses involving RMB 400 billion, of which RMB 200 billion was overstatement of assets. ("China: Finance ministry reveals widespread accounting fraud," *Financial Times*, December 24, 1999.) In January 2000, auditors in Hebei caught 67 SOEs covering up losses of RMB 600 million ("Beijing moving to improve quality of statistics," *South China Morning Post*, February 29, 2000).

[29] For a review of the empirical findings, see Huang, Woo and Duncan (1999).

source of information to the industrial bureaus regarding the SOEs were reports submitted by the SOEs themselves. This reduction in the monitoring ability of the state in a situation of continued soft-budget constraint meant that there was little incentive for state-enterprise managers to resist wage demands because their future promotion to larger SOEs was determined in part by the increases in workers' welfare during their tenure. The reduction in the state's monitoring ability combined with the steady reduction in discrimination against the private sector also made it easier for the managers to transfer state assets to themselves.[30]

Besides creating a fiscal crisis for the state, the "disappearing profits" at the SOEs have also contributed to social instability. The increasing public outrage over the inequity of the informal privatisation of the SOE sector is well captured in a recent book by He Qinglian who wrote that the SOE reform has amounted to:

> ... a process in which power-holders and their hangers-on plundered public wealth. The primary target of their plunder was state property that had been accumulated from forty years of the people's sweat, and their primary mean of plunder was political power.[31]

There can be little doubt that the Chinese leadership recognises the increasingly serious economic and political problems created by the agency problem innate in the decentralising reforms of market socialism. This is why the debate between the conservative reformers and the liberal reformers has progressed from whether privatisation is necessary to the question of the optimal form and amount of privatisation. The emerging consensus is that all but the thousand largest SOEs and the defense-related SOEs are to be corporatized, with part of their shares sold to employees and the general public. The preferred privatisation method for small and medium-sized SOEs has been employee (insider)

---

[30] It is hence not surprising that of the 327 cases of embezzlement, bribery and misuse of public funds that were tried in Beijing in 1999, "76 percent took place in SOEs" ("Judicial Attention to SOEs Pledged," *China Daily*, February 19, 2000).

[31] The translated quote is from Liu and Link (1998), p. 19.

privatisation. Even for the larger SOEs that are to be corporatized, the state need not be the biggest shareholder.

The thousand largest SOEs will be given preferential financing to develop into business groups (like the Japanese *zaibatsus* and the Korean *chaebols*) that allegedly will enjoy enormous economies of scale. The truth is more prosaic. Given the co-existence of conservative and liberal reformers, any SOE reform package needs to contain a component that appeases each group. The upshot is dual-track SOE reform: state-sponsored conglomerates for the conservative reformers, and publicly-traded joint-stock companies for the liberal reformers. However, in light of the 1997–98 external debt crisis in South Korea caused by imprudent borrowing by the *chaebols*, one should question the wisdom of creating such large state business groups.

We must emphasise that the key to SOE reform is not privatisation *per se*, but a transparent, legal privatisation process that society at large can accept, at the minimum, as tolerably equitable. Because an adequate privatisation program must compensate the retired and layoff workers, permit takeover by core investors, and respect the rights of minority shareholders, it is important that legal reforms be carried out simultaneously. Without a transparent, equitable privatisation process (overseen by an adequate legal framework), China is likely to repeat the mistakes of the Russian privatisation program implemented by Premier Chernomyrdin. Just as the creation of the new *kleptoklatura* in Russia has robbed the Yeltsin government of its political legitimacy, its occurrence in urban China could be socially explosive.

8. Concluding Remarks

We want to highlight one possible negative long-run result from the present reflation package. There is strong evidence that the larger credit growth in the third and fourth quarters of 1998 was achieved only after implicit assurances were given to bank managers that they would not be held responsible if the NPL ratio were to increase. A temporary deviation from the firm policy of cleaning up the balance sheets of the state banks may be defensible in the midst of the Asian financial crisis, but a prolonged deviation would underline the credibility of the commitment to reforming the state banks and mean a return to the traditional socialist boom-bust cycle.

The long-term answer to the NPL problem goes beyond punishing bank managers who experienced increases in the NPL ratio; the long-term answer lies in changing both the supply-side and the demand-side of the credit market. Many changes are required on both sides of the credit market, and the most fundamental changes include the transformation of the state banks and the SOEs into shareholding corporations to make profit-maximisation their primary objective, the establishment of a modern legal framework to promote transparency and reduce transaction costs, and the creation of a prudential regulatory body to reduce excessive risk-taking by banks.

The above complex institutional changes that are necessary in order to address the NPL problem adequately illustrate that most of China's economic problems cannot be individually addressed, success depends on systemic reform. This brings us to the basic point that while President Jiang and Premier Zhu deserve much credit for their competent handling of the current macroeconomic problems so far, their position in Chinese history will depend more on their success in addressing the many and varied long-term development challenges facing China. These challenges include the slowdown in agricultural productivity growth, the decline in job creation in the rural enterprise sector, the acceleration of losses by state-owned enterprises (SOEs), the relentless growth in nonperforming loans (NPLs) at the state banks, the inability of the legal system to meet the demands of an increasingly sophisticated economy, and the inadequacy of social safety nets to cope with the temporary dislocations that are characteristic of a fast-growing economy. The ability of China to maintain its international competitiveness after the Asian financial crisis is over is conditional upon the resolution of the above problems.

China's forthcoming accession into WTO reveals recognition by the top leaders that convergence of China's economic institutions to the institutional norms of modern market economies offers China the only chance to achieve sustained high growth, and, more importantly, it reveals the commitment of the top leaders to make sure that convergence will occur.

References

Easterley, William and Stanley Fischer, "The Soviet Economic Decline: Historical and Republican Data," Working Paper No. 4735, National Bureau of Economic Research, May 1994.

Fan, Gang, "Fiscal Stimulus and Debt-Financing: Potential and Constraints," manuscript, September 1998.

Fan, Gang and Wing Thye Woo, "State Enterprise Reform as a Source of Macroeconomic Instability," *Asian Economic Journal*, November 1996, pp. 207–224.

Huang, Yiping, Wing Thye Woo and Ron Duncan, "Understanding the Decline of the State Sector in China," *MOCT-MOST: Economic Policy in Transitional Economies*, Vol. 9 No. 1, 1999.

Lardy, Nicholas, "China Chooses Growth Today, Reckoning Tomorrow," *Asian Wall Street Journal*, September 30, 1998.

Lardy, Nicholas, "Financial reform: Fast track or back track," *Global Emerging Markets*, Credit Lyonnais Securities Asia, November 1998.

Liu, Binyan and Perry Link, "China: The Great Backward?" *The New York Review of Books*, October 8, 1998.

Liu, Liang-Yn and Wing Thye Woo, "Saving Behavior under Imperfect Financial Markets and the Current Account Consequences," *Economic Journal*, May 1994, pp. 512–527.

Liu, Yia-Ling, "Reform From Below: The Private Economy and Local Politics in the Rural Industrialization of Wenzhou," *China Quarterly*, No. 130, June 1992, pp. 293–316.

Rawski, Thomas, "China's Move to Market: How Far? What Next," manuscript, October 25, 1999.

Sachs, Jeffrey and Wing Thye Woo, "Structural Factors in the Economic Reforms of China, Eastern Europe, and the Former Soviet Union," *Economic Policy: A European Forum*, Vol. 9 No. 18, April 1994, pp. 101–45.

Sachs, Jeffrey and Wing Thye Woo, "Understanding China's Economic Performance," *Journal of Policy Reform*, Vol. 4 No. 1, 2000, pp. 1–50.

Woo, Wing Thye, "Zhongguo Quan Yaosu Shengchan Lu: Laizi Nongye Bumen Laodongli Zai Pei Zhi de Shouyao Zuoyong (Total Factor Productivity Growth in China: The Primacy of Reallocation of Labor from Agriculture)" in *Jingji Yanjiu*, Vol. 3, 1998b, pp. 31–39.

Woo, Wing Thye, "Some Observations on the Ownership and Regional Aspects in Financing the Growth of China's Rural Enterprises," translated into French as "La croissance des entreprises rurales selon les regions et la propriete", in *Revue d'Economie du Developpement*, Juin 1999.

2

The Nature and Sources of Economic Growth in China: Is There TFP Growth?[†]

LIU ZHIQIANG*

1. ASIAN PRODUCTIVITY DEBATE

An economy can grow by: (1) deploying more inputs, labour and capital, to production or by (2) becoming more efficient, i.e., producing more output per unit of input. The former is factor accumulation while the latter is productivity improvement. Input-driven growth is not sustainable because of the law of diminishing returns to capital. This leaves productivity the sole viable engine of long-term economic growth.

Alwyn Young (1992), an economics professor from Boston University, made an attempt to compute the contributions of input factors and productivity to the economic growth in Singapore and Hong Kong from 1966 to 1990 and reached an astonishing conclusion. The economic

---

[†] Reprinted with permission from *Post-Communist Economies*, Vol. 12, No. 2, 2000, pp. 201–214. ©Taylor and Francis Ltd., http://www.tandf.co.uk/journals.

*Dr. Liu Zhiqiang was Senior Research Fellow at East Asian Institute, National University of Singapore, 1999 to 2000. The author would like to thank Professor John Wong for his very constructive comments and suggestions and Mr. Gu Qingyang for his valuable help in reviewing the relevant literature. Thanks also go to Professor William T. Liu and Miss Nah Seok Ling for their useful suggestions.

growth of Singapore can be explained entirely by the growth in labour force and accumulation of capital, and there has been no productivity improvement. In the case of Hong Kong, productivity gains did contribute to the growth process, but still, increases in input factors were responsible for most of the growth. Jong-Il Kim and Lawrence Lau (1994) of Stanford University extended Young's work to include other Asian NICs in their analysis and reached essentially the same conclusion: that rapid economic growth of the Asian NICs has been primarily input-driven and there has been little, if any, productivity gain in these economies. A heated debate erupted within the academic circles [Goh and Low (1996), Felip (1999)].

It was Paul Krugman (1994) who popularized the debate on productivity and economic growth. Based on Young, and Kim and Lau, Krugman provided a controversial interpretation of the Asian miracle. According to Krugman, there was no miracle behind Asia's growth but only simple capital accumulation, and these countries would not be able to sustain their economic growth. Instead, it might end up like the former Soviet Union, which also experienced rapid, but input-driven economic growth some 50 years ago.

The Chinese economy has grown at record rates since the start of the market-oriented reform in 1978. What is the nature of that growth? Is the growth sustainable? Put differently, are there productivity gains in China's economic growth? What have been the sources of its productivity growth? What are the potential sources of productivity gains in future? These are important questions that we will try to address in this article.[1]

2. Total Factor Productivity and Its Measurement

Productivity is an indicator of efficiency with which inputs in a production process are used to produce output. There are several productivity measures. The first, and most widely used, is labour productivity. It is the ratio of output to labour input. The latter is measured in terms of

---

[1] For a recent discussion of the growth performance of the Chinese economy, see Wong (1999).

number of workers or man-hours. Governments around the world use labour productivity to gauge how well their economies are performing. The main attraction of this index is that it is intuitive and easy to compute. But it can be a very misleading indicator of overall performance. Labour productivity can grow because workers have truly become more efficient or because workers just have more capital to work with. If an increase in capital is the underlying reason for a rise in labour productivity, an overall productivity gain is not guaranteed. In economics jargons, labour productivity is a partial factor productivity index that ignores the fact that factors are substitutable among themselves. The same can be said about the partial productivity of capital.

To overcome this deficiency of partial factor productivity measures, economists turn to the concept of total factor productivity, or TFP for short. Intuitively, TFP is a measure of the quantities of output per unit of "aggregate" input. The latter is calculated as a weighted average of all inputs. The weights are either the factor shares in output or the estimated output elasticities of corresponding input factors.[2] Indeed, this is the first method adopted by economists to construct TFP as an index. Further details on the construction of TFP index are contained in Appendix 1.

A second way to estimate TFP is through the estimation of a production function, which shows how output is related to a combination of inputs. Since TFP measures the efficiency at which inputs are utilized, any change in TFP then is represented by a shift of production function; that is an increase in output without an increase in any input factor.

The third way to estimate TFP involves the estimation of a production frontier that represents the best practice among firms or economies in a particular sample. The distance between the frontier and a sample observation is the measure of technical inefficiency. The narrowing of

---

[2] Factor shares in output refer to the portions of the total output that are received, as compensation, by input factors. In the US economy, for example, labor compensation accounts for about 70% of its total national income. The other 30% goes to capital. In this case, the labor and capital shares in output are 0.70 and 0.30, respectively. Output elasticity is a technical term, measuring the percentage increase (or decrease) in output as a result of 1% increase (or decrease) in an input factor, say, labor, holding other inputs constant.

the gap represents gains in TFP. Furthermore, the frontier itself is not static, but it can shift out as a result of technological progress. This shift means that more output can be produced with the same amount of inputs and hence a gain in productivity. Therefore, by this approach TFP growth comes from two sources: improved technical efficiency and technological progress.[3]

The role of productivity gains in economic growth can best be described in the context of growth accounting equation.[4] The growth rate of output can be decomposed into factor accumulation and productivity gains. Usually, the rate of growth attributable to productivity is calculated as the difference between the growth rate of output and a weighted average of the growth rates of inputs (labour and capital).

This way of decomposing the growth rate leads to a powerful conclusion as to what type of growth is sustainable and what type of growth is not. Suppose that there is neither productivity improvement nor population growth in an economy. The only way then for the economy to produce more output and hence to grow is to invest more in physical capital, which means to save more. However, because of the diminishing returns to capital, each additional unit of capital will lead to a smaller increment in output as more capital investments are made. Therefore, in order to maintain a constant growth rate for a prolonged period, an economy has to devote an increasing share of its current output to capital accumulation. Put differently, a constant rate of growth in this case requires an ever-rising savings rate. Since savings rate in any economy cannot exceed 100%, this capital-driven growth is obviously not sustainable. The same can be said about labour-driven growth. Therefore, long-term and sustainable economic growth must rely on productivity growth, i.e., more output per unit of input.

---

[3] This separation of two sources has important policy implications for developing countries. TFP growth does not equal technological progress. Policies that put a greater emphasis on technological progress as a means of raising productivity may prove to be inappropriate in these countries, where technical efficiency improvement seems to be the more relevant part of the change in TFP.

[4] See Equation (5) in Appendix 1.

3. TFP IN CHINA'S ECONOMIC GROWTH PROCESS

There are numerous studies on China's economic growth and many focus on TFP growth. Some make use of national or provincial level data; others analyze data by sector; and still others rely on firm level samples. Although studies provide quantitatively different productivity estimates, most conclude that TFP has been an important driving force behind China's economic growth in the past twenty years or so. Appendix 2 contains a list of selected studies.

Studies at the aggregate level use either national or provincial data. Most of these studies estimate the contribution of TFP to economic growth by estimating an aggregate production function. The study by the World Bank (1997) is the most comprehensive and therefore deserves special mention. This study uses national level data and decomposes the rate of economic growth over the period 1978–1995 into four components — that attributable to capital accumulation, increase in labour employment, increase in human capital, and TFP growth. The last component is calculated as a residual. The decomposition suggestes that 46%, or 4.3 percentage points, of the 9.4% annual GDP growth during 1978–1995 can be attributed to TFP growth. The remaining 54% is accounted for by changes in capital (37%), labour (8%), and human capital (9%). It is worth noting that the contribution of TFP to economic growth has been substantially larger in China than in other countries such as Japan and South Korea over the period 1960–1993.

Sectoral studies generally confirm the findings from economy-wide studies. In agriculture, there was a surge in TFP growth in the period of rural reform in the early 1980s. Two factors are mainly responsible for the increase in productivity. The first is the introduction of the household responsibility system that made the household the unit of production. Farmers are required to remit a fixed amount of their outputs to the state and allowed to sell remaining outputs in the market. Essentially, the reform allows farmers to claim the right on any output increase beyond the state quota. The second contributing factor is the upward price adjustment for some agricultural products.[5]

Studies on industrial sectors are more numerous. The general conclusion is that there was little, if any, TFP growth until 1985. This is not surprising. Industrial reform did not really start until 1984. Similar to the rural reform, the industrial reform also provides individual firms, managers, and workers with greater incentives to improve efficiency. A variety of reform measures were implemented, such as substituting profit remission by corporate tax (*li gai shui*), contract responsibility system (*Qi Ye Cheng Bao Zhi*), enterprise leasing scheme (*Qi Ye Zhu Lin Zhi*), and shareholding (*Gu Fei Zhi*). Labour contract system was gradually introduced to replace the permanent employment mode of the central planning era. All these reform measures rewarded more productive firms and individuals while penalizing the less productive ones.

Another conclusion to be drawn from these studies suggests that non-state owned enterprises (urban collective enterprises (COEs) and township and village enterprises (TVEs)) have achieved higher TFP growth rates than state owned enterprises (SOEs) have. This is consistent with the popular belief that the non-state sector, especially TVEs, has become the most dynamic force behind the rapid economic growth in China in recent years.

It should be stressed that the validity of these estimates depends critically on how accurate outputs and inputs are measured. For instance, if capital, for some reason, is underestimated, the contribution of TFP to growth will likely be exaggerated. Indeed, this measurement issue has always been at the center of contention in the literature on TFP estimations. Unfortunately the problem is especially acute in the context of China because of the poor quality of its statistical data as well as the lack of market-determined prices.

There is also an additional methodological issue. Some of the empirical studies in the literature assume that competitive equilibrium

---

[5] According to McMillan, Whally, Zhu (1989), between 1978 and 1984 the average productivity growth rate in Chinese agriculture is 5.9%, of which 78% can be attributed to the household responsibility system and 22% to higher prices. Other studies also found significant TFP growth in the agriculture sector. However, the TFP growth rates in more recent years are generally lower albeit positive.

prevails in the Chinese economy. This assumption clearly did not hold in the 1980s, during which state planning still played an important role. Since 1990, however, prices have been largely determined by market forces. Therefore, recent studies, which showed positive TFP growth in China, are more reliable.[6]

4. THE SOURCES OF TFP GROWTH IN CHINA

According to the World Bank study as cited above, productivity and input accumulation each contributed about 50% to the 9.4% annual GDP growth rate over the period 1978–1995. Thus, China's economic growth has been both productivity-driven and input-driven. The increases in input factors are easy to understand. Rapid capital accumulation was supported by high savings rates; increases in the labour force came from a growing population and a rising labour force participation rate; and an upsurge in human capital was a result of increased investment in education. But what have been the sources of productivity growth?

We can identify four main factors. The first is efficiency gains at the micro level. As pointed out earlier, various reform measures were implemented at individual household, firm, and market levels. The rural reform started in 1978 with rapid de-collectivization of farm production.

---

[6] There are other reasons for us to have faith in these estimates. First, the main disagreement concerning the measurement issue is about deflators used to construct real output and capital stock. There was indeed a heated discussion in the literature on economic growth in China about what these deflators should be. See for example the arguments presented in Woo et al. (1994) and the responses and revisions made by Jefferson et al. (1996). But over time, the measurement problem becomes less serious as the quality of statistics improves and as market-driven prices become available. A second reason is that alternative estimation methods have led to essentially the same results. Some methods are more sensitive than others to the existence of measurement problems or particular types of measurement problems. If the same results, at least qualitatively, are obtained regardless of method used, we should accept these results with a great deal of confidence. There is a third reason. These results are quite robust in a sense that they are not sensitive to alternative data sets used. The positive TFP growth rates at the macro level receive confirmation at the micro level.

In four years' time the share of agriculture households that were subjected to the household responsibility system increased to 98.6% from zero in 1978. The share reached 100% in 1986. This, together with the price adjustment for agriculture products, provided farmers with strong incentives to increase output and improve efficiency. In the industrial sector, various reform programs were tried out by step. All aimed at boosting productivity by providing individual firms, managers, and workers with material incentives. Take the contract responsibility system introduced in 1984. Under this system, firm managers or sometimes the firm's entire work force agree to fulfill specific obligations, such as delivery of certain amount of profit to the state, in return for extensive control over enterprise operations, including the disposal of retained profits.[7]

The second source of TFP growth is improved efficiency in resource allocation: more resources have been allocated to more productive functions or reallocated from low-productivity to high-productivity sectors. Over the past two decades, there has been a significant shift of labour from the primary sector (low productivity) to the secondary and tertiary sectors (high productivity). This is a common phenomenon of development. But the economic reform in China, particularly the rural reform, has accelerated the pace of this industrialization process. At the start of the economic reform in 1978, 70.5% of the labour force was employed in the primary sector. This share reduced to 49.8% twenty years later in 1998. While the flow of labour from primary to secondary and tertiary sectors is a universal and necessary process of development, the migration of workers from the state to non-state sector in urban areas is a unique feature of China's transition from a command to market-oriented economy. As several comparative studies[8] have shown that, in terms of TFP growth, non-state-owned enterprises, especially the dynamic TVEs, have outperformed SOEs by a big margin. A reallocation of labour from the low-productivity state sector to high-productivity non-state sector would lead to a rise in the overall productivity of the industrial

---

[7] In 1985, 37% of SOEs signed up for the contract responsibility system. The share went up to about 45% by 1993.
[8] See, for example, Jefferson, Rawski and Zheng (1996).

sector. In 1978, SOEs employed nearly 80% of the total urban labour force. By 1998, however, less than 45% of urban workers were employed by SOEs. Furthermore, in 1996, non-SOEs outgrew SOEs for the first time ever since 1952 as a more important source of urban employment. More significant is the downward trend of employment in SOEs that begun in 1996 (see Table 1).

Table 1. Urban Employment (SOEs vs Non-SOEs)

Year	Total	Number of persons (in million) SOEs	Non-SOEs	Share in percent SOEs	Non-SOEs
1978	95.14	74.51	20.63	78.32	21.68
1985	128.08	89.90	38.18	70.19	29.81
1990	166.16	103.46	62.70	62.27	37.73
1998	206.78	90.58	116.20	43.81	56.19

Note: Non-SOEs include urban collective enterprises, joint-owned operations, shareholding companies, foreign-invested companies, companies funded by entrepreneurs from Hong Kong, Macao and Taiwan, private enterprises, individual-owned businesses, and other types of enterprises.
Source: *Statistical Survey of China*, China Statistical Publishing House, 1999.

Capital moved in a similar fashion. Although there were exceptions due to macroeconomic policies, the non-state sector received a growing share of the total investment in fixed assets in the past twenty years. Table 2 shows the total capital investment and its composition. SOEs accounted for over 80% of the total investment in fixed assets in 1980. The share declined steadily over the next twenty years or so, reducing to 55% by 1998.[9]

---

[9] By contrast, non-SOEs received a growing share of the total investment. The share went up from less than 20% in 1980 to 45% in 1998. The increases in capital investment in non-state- and non-collective-enterprises were particularly impressive. Between 1980 and 1998, the capital investment in these enterprises increased by more than 76 times, accounting for about one third of the total investment in fixed assets by 1998. Much of the increases were registered in foreign-invested enterprises.

Table 2. Total Investment in Fixed Assets by Ownership

Year	Total	In billion yuan SOEs	COEs	Others*	Share in percent SOEs	COEs	Others*
1980	91.09	74.59	4.60	11.90	81.9	5.0	13.1
1985	254.32	168.05	32.75	53.52	66.1	12.9	21.0
1990	451.70	298.63	52.95	100.12	66.1	11.7	22.2
1995	2,001.93	1,089.82	328.94	583.17	54.4	16.4	29.2
1998	2,845.75	1,566.20	371.73	907.81	55.0	13.1	31.9

See note to table 1.
Source: *Statistical Survey of China*, China Statistical Publishing House, 1999.

The flow of resources to more productive, non-state sector has generated remarkable results. In 1978, SOEs produced roughly 78% of the total industrial output. But this share fell steadily in the reform era, reaching an all-time low of 26% in 1997. The output shares lost by SOEs are shares gained by the non-SOEs. In 1993, non-SOEs' share grew to 53 percent, ending the dominant position of SOEs in the industrial sector. And the trend continued unabated in the following years. The reversal of positions between SOEs and non-SOEs in terms of output has been more remarkable given that non-SOEs employed less than 50% of the urban labour force and received less than 50% of the capital investment in 1993 (and up to 1997). In 1997, for example, non-SOEs produced 74.5% of the total industry output with 45% of the urban labour force and 47.5% of the total investment in fixed assets.

A similar, but by no means less dramatic, resource movement occurred in the rural sector: more people were employed in the high-productivity, non-farming segment. As Table 3 indicates that the employment share of the farming sector declined quite dramatically in the past two decades. Over 90% of the rural labour force engaged in farming activities in 1978, the first year of the rural reform. Since then this share has been in decline, dropping to 64.6% in 1996 (albeit gained marginally the following year). By contrast, the employment in the non-farming sector was more than quadrupled from 1978 to 1998, accounting for about 35%

and 25% of the total rural employment in 1996 and 1998, respectively.[10]

Table 3. Rural Employment

Year	Total	In million Farming	TVEs	Others*	Share Farming	TVEs	Others*
1978	30.638	27.811	2.827	0	90.8	9.2	0
1985	37.065	30.086	6.979	0	81.2	18.8	0
1990	47.293	36.424	9.265	1.604	77.0	19.6	3.4
1995	48.854	32.468	12.862	3.524	66.5	26.3	7.2
1997	49.393	36.113	9.158	4.122	73.1	18.5	8.4
1998	49.279	37.24	7.449	4.592	75.6	15.1	9.3

*Others private enterprises and individual-owned businesses.
Source: *Statistical Survey of China*, China Statistical Publishing House, 1999.

The diffusion of technology through foreign direct investment has been the third driving force of TFP growth. The annual foreign direct investment (actual realized) increased every year since 1979. From 1979 to 1997, the foreign direct investment totaled US$220 billion, amounting to 13% of the total domestic investment over the same period.

Foreign direct investment has played a dual role. One is that it provided China with much needed capital, which in turn helped alleviate unemployment pressure. The other and more important role of foreign direct investment is to serve as a means of technology transfer. Foreign direct investment in China covers a wide spectrum of industries, ranging from labour-intensive clothing and toy making to technology-intensive pharmaceutical and electronics manufacture. They brought to China not only advanced machines and equipment but also better managerial know-how, such as production and human resource management, new products, and marketing techniques. Domestic partners could directly

---

[10] The number of people in the farming sector is derived by subtracting from the total rural employment the number of people in TVEs and others. This tends to exaggerate the size of the rural work force engaging in farming activities, because it fails to take into account those who are classified as farmers but actually work in cities.

benefit and learn from their foreign partners. Other domestic firms could also benefit from foreign direct investment due to the latter's spillover effects.

The fourth impetus to TFP growth is the improved infrastructure. Infrastructure, such as road, power, and communications, has the characteristics of public goods. As a social capital, infrastructure exerts a positive external effect on all other forms of capital. For example, a well-built and -maintained road system would reduce the costs of delivering goods or services to customers of business firms. The past twenty years saw great progress being made in transport and communication networks in China as shown in Table 4. Between 1978 and 1997, the length of transportation routes rose by 18% for railways, 38% for highways, and 957% for civil aviation.[11]

Table 4. Length of Transportation Routes

Year	Rail-ways	Double Track	% DT	Auto blocking	% AB	High-ways	Paved	% paved	Civil Aviation	Int'l
1978	48618	7630	15.7	5981	12.3	890536	651068	73.1	148.9	55.3
1985	52119	9989	19.2	6921	14.0	942395	750331	79.6	277.2	106.0
1990	53378	13024	24.4	10370	19.4	1028348	883464	85.9	506.8	166.4
1995	54616	16909	31.0	12910	23.6	1157009	1043390	90.2	1129.0	348.2
1997	57566	19046	33.1	17344	29.2	1226405	997496	81.3	1425.0	504.4

The length of railways and highways is measured in km; the length of civil aviation is in 1,000 km.
Source: *China Statistical Yearbook* 1998, China Statistical Publishing House.

Table 5 shows China's telecommunication capacity for selected years. The number of long-distance telephone circuits increased from 18,800

[11] The 18% rise in the railway routes seems too little when compared with the 9.7% annual growth in GDP over the same period. But the improvement in the quality of railways has been considerable. In 1978, only 15.7% of railways were double tracking and 12.3% with automatic blocking design. By 1997, the shares for these two types of railways rose to 33.1% and 29.2%, respectively. The quality of highways also improved: 81.3% of the highways were paved in 1997, 8 percentage points higher than 1978's 73.1%.

in 1978 to 1,146,000 in 1997, a six-fold rise or an average 24% annual growth over a period of 19 years. Telephone capacity in terms of phone lines also recorded explosive growth over the same period with a robust 19% annual increase. Another indicator of telecommunication infrastructure development is the number of telephone sets per 100 persons. The number was 0.6 in 1980 and rose to 8.1 by 1997.[12]

Table 5. Growth of Telecommunication Capacity

Year	Long-distance Telephone circuits (1,000)	Capacity of telephone exchanges (1,000)
1978	18.8	4,058.5
1985	37.6	6,134.5
1990	112.4	12,318.2
1995	735.5	72,035.9
1997	1,146.1	112,691.7

Source: *China Statistical Yearbook* 1998, China Statistical Publishing House.

5. THE POTENTIAL SOURCES OF FUTURE TFP GROWTH

The four driving forces discussed above will continue to exert positive impacts on TFP growth in the future. Reforms at the micro level will intensify; labour force will continue to move from the primary sector to the secondary and tertiary sectors and from the state to non-state sector; foreign direct investment will continue to flow into China, perhaps, at a slower pace but with higher-technology content; and infrastructure investment will remain a top priority on the government's spending list. There are also other potential sources of TFP growth. Three factors

---

[12] As with many things, telecommunication system has been much better developed in urban than in rural areas. There were more than 65 million telephone subscribers in urban China in 1997, of which over 13 million were mobile phone users. That comes to one telephone line for every 7 city dwellers, not counting the 29 million-plus subscribers of paging service.

stand out prominently as the motive forces of the medium- to long-term TFP growth in China. They are: the on-going SOE and banking reforms, emerging entrepreneurs, and more R&D spending.

China's economic reform has not been completed. A large number of SOEs remain inefficient, loss-making, and debt-ridden. With rapid growth of the non-state sector and the establishment of unemployment insurance and social security system, it is time for SOEs to shed some of their burdens. Indeed, the process of laying off redundant workers has been going on quite successfully for 5 years now. Since 1993, millions of SOE workers have been laid off without causing any major social unrest, which the government feared the most. So far, redundancy lay-off appears to be a productivity-enhancing measure. Furthermore, the government seems to stick to its early reform strategy to "hold on to large-scale enterprises and let go smaller ones". Thus, the fate of SOEs is clearer: improve or perish.[13]

China's banking sector is notoriously inefficient. In the past, banks were essentially government's cashiers, operating on political rather than commercial principles. They provided the life supports for SOEs, funneling funds to inefficient loss-making SOEs, and as a result, deprived the more productive, non-state sector of a chance to grow. Banking sector reform is exactly designed to change such practice by making banks independent and profit-driven business units. As such, the banks will be able to channel scarce financial resources to the most productive uses, and thus contribute to the overall productivity growth.

Entrepreneurs will become an important force behind future TFP growth. Joseph Schumpeter links innovation to the entrepreneur, arguing that the source of private profits is successful innovation and that innovation brings about economic growth. The current economic condition in China is conducive to entrepreneurship development. First, the dominance of giant corporations in industries is not widespread. True, there are SOE monopolies in some industries. But they are

---

[13] Either way the reform will contribute to productivity growth, at least in the short to medium term. But for the reform to become a driving force for the long-run productivity growth, SOEs, irrespective of size, must be privatized.

inefficient and, therefore, are takeover targets for would-be entrepreneurs. Entrepreneurs can build their businesses either from scratch by being innovative or by means of expanding an existing firm. Second, the incentive for innovation is especially strong given the huge potential market for consumer products in China. Indeed, a class of entrepreneurs has already emerged in China. The Liu brothers of Geli Central Air-conditioners Manufacture Company and Liu Yong of the Hope Corporation in feedstock business are among the more successful entrepreneurs in China today.

Research and development will be the ultimate source of long-run TFP growth in China. There are some indications that China will break away from its laggard past in this area. The first is that China has consolidated its base for R&D undertakings. Table 6 shows the basic statistics on national research capacity. In 1990, there were 18,722 research institutions that engaged in R&D activities. Between 1990 and 1997, additional 3,809 research institutions were established, most affiliated with universities. Expenditure on R&D showed a four-fold increase in nominal terms over the same period. But in real terms the increase in research and development expenditure was smaller than the

Table 6. National Research Capacity

Items	Unit	1990	1997
Science and technology research institutions	Number	18,722	22,531
Research institutes	Number	8,990	7,558
Enterprises	Number	8,116	11,142
Universities	Number	1,666	3,343
Expenditures on research and development	Million yuan	12,500	48,200
Research and development expenditure as a share of GNP	%	0.7	0.6
Transaction value in technology Market	Million yuan	7,500	35,100
Number of patent applications	Number	41,469	114,208
University enrolment	1,000	2,063	3,174
Post-graduates	1,000	93	176

Source: *China Statistical Yearbook* 1998, China Statistical Publishing House.

increase in GNP. R&D expenditure as a share of GNP actually fell from 0.7% in 1990 to 0.6 & by 1997. By international standard, China's spending on R&D has been paltry. However, this is going to change in the near future.

The Chinese government has gradually realized the importance of R&D to long-term productivity growth and economic growth. The government has begun to commit more efforts to technological innovation and the development of advanced technologies. A favourable climate has been created for high-tech development as governments grant preferential policies to encourage technological innovation. Since 1988, 53 State-level technology zones have been established, which are home to 16,097 high-tech firms. In Shenzhen, a special economic zone, high-tech industrial value accounted for more than 35% of the city's total industrial output in 1998.[14] Commenting on a four-day national conference on technological innovation held in Beijing in August this year, Premier Zhu Rongji called for more support to enterprises, especially to private-owned small or medium-sized high-tech enterprises, which have scored marked success in recent years with a market-oriented perspective and the fast commercialization of cutting-edge technologies. In fact, nurturing high-tech industries and boosting agricultural production through advanced technology are the key elements of China's scientific development for the 10th Five-Year Plan (2001–2005).

[14] *China Daily*, 6 Oct. 1999.

Appendix 1

1. THE CONCEPT OF TFP

A convenient way to conceptualize the notion of TFP is to start with a production function. Let us express the relationship between the quantity of output and the quantities of inputs by the following equation,

$$Q = F(L, K, A), \tag{1}$$

where Q denotes output, L labour, K capital and A technology or production efficiency. Further, assume that technological change is disembodied and factor-neutral so that the technology indicator, A, can be separated from input factors as

$$Q = A\, F(L, K). \tag{2}$$

The total factor productivity is then defined as

$$TFP = A = Q/F(L, K). \tag{3}$$

Differentiating equation (2) with respect to time and dividing the resulting equation by Q, we obtain,

$$1/Q * dQ/dt = 1/A * dA/dt + \alpha * 1/L * dL/dt + \beta * 1/K * dK/dt, \tag{4}$$

where $\alpha = L/Y * \partial Y/\partial L$ and $\beta = K/Y * \partial Y/\partial K$ are output elasticities of labour and capital, respectively. Equation (4) is the famous growth accounting equation, which shows that the growth rate of output is equal to the growth rate of productivity plus a weighted average of the growth rates of labour and capital inputs. Rearranging equation (4), the growth rate of TFP can be expressed as,

$$1/TFP * dTFP/dt = 1/A * dA/dt = 1/Q * dQ/dt - \alpha * 1/L * dL/dt - \beta * 1/K * dK/dt. \tag{5}$$

Equation (5) shows that productivity growth is the part of output growth that is not accounted for by the growth of inputs.

2. THE ESTIMATION OF TFP

Equation (3) provides a basis for estimating TFP as an index. Suppose the production function is of Cobb-Douglas type, i.e., $Q = AL^{\alpha}K^{\beta}$, then $TFP = Q/L^{\alpha}K^{\beta}$. There are two ways to estimate the elasticities, α and β. The first is to assume perfect competition and profit maximization so that elasticities are equal to corresponding factor shares in output. However, in many cases, especially in applying the method to Chinese data, perfection competition and profit maximization cannot be assumed. To get around this problem, economists resort to the second approach, which obtains estimates of output elasticities of labour and capital by fitting a production function with data.

As an alternative to index method, one can also estimate the rate of productivity growth through empirical estimation of production functions. Suppose, again, the production function takes the Cobb-Douglas form,

$$Q = AL^{\alpha}K^{\beta}. \qquad (6)$$

Then we can estimate A by fitting the following regression model to actual data:

$$\text{Ln}Q = a + \gamma T + \alpha \ln L + \beta \ln K + u, \qquad (7)$$

where ln is the natural logarithm, a, γ, α, and β are parameters to be estimated, and u is a statistical random error. Since A, the productivity indicator, is approximated by a time trend, T, the estimate of γ shows the percentage of output growth that is attributable to TFP growth. To see this more clearly, differentiate equation (7) with respect to T (holding L and K constant). We obtain,

$$\gamma = \partial \ln Q/\partial T = 1/Q * \partial Q/\partial T. \qquad (8)$$

There is a third method to measure TFP. It involves the estimation of the so-called production frontier. The frontier represents the best practice. In this context, TFP can grow from two sources. The first is efficiency gain, often dubbed technical efficiency improvement, which is due to the narrowing of the gap between the current production position (i.e., the way inputs are utilized) and the frontier (the most efficient way of using the same amount of inputs), i.e., TE. The second component of TFP is the outward shift of the frontier itself, i.e., TC, which is due to technological improvement over time. Thus, by this interpretation and calculation, TFP = TE+TC.

REFERENCES

Chen, Jian and Fleisher, Belton M., "Regional Income Inequality and Economic Growth in China," *Journal of Comparative Economics* 22, 1996, 141–64.

Chen, Kuan; Jefferson, Gary H.; Rawski, Thomas G.; Wang, Hongchang and Zheng, Yuxin, "Productivity Change in Chinese Industry, 1953–1985," *Journal of Comparative Economics* 12, 1988, 570–591.

Chow, Gregory, "Capital Formation and Economic Growth in China," *Quarterly Journal of Economics*, 1993, 809–42.

See for example, Goh, Keng Swee and Low, Linda, "Beyond 'Miracles' and Total Factor Productivity," *ASEAN Economic Bulletin*, Vol. 13, 1996; Jesus Felipe, "Total Factor Productivity Growth in East Asia: A Critical Survey," *Journal of Development Studies*, Vol. 35, 1999.

Jefferson, Gary; Rawski, Thomas and Zhen, Yuxin, "Growth, Efficiency, and Convergence in China's State and Collective Industry," *Economic Development and Cultural Change* 40, 1992, 239–66.

Jefferson, Gary; Rawski, Thomas and Zhen, Yuxin, "Chinese Industrial Productivity: Trends, Measurement Issues, and Recent Developments," *Journal of Comparative Economics* 23, 1996, 146–80.

Kim, Jong-Il and Lau, Lawrence, "The Sources of Growth of the East Asian Newly Industrialized Countries," *Journal of the Japanese and International Economies*, 1994.

Krugman, Paul, "The Myth of Asia's Miracle," *Foreign Affairs*, Nov/Dec 1994.

Lin, Justin Yifu, "Rural Reforms and Agricultural Growth in China," *American Economic Review* 82, 1992, 34–51.

Lin, Justin Yifu and Liu, Zhiqiang, "Fiscal Decentralization and Economic Growth in China," manuscript, 1999.

McMillan, John; Whally, John and Zhu, Lijing, "The Impact of China's Economic Reforms on Agricultural Productivity Growth," *Journal of Political Economy* 97, 1989, 781–807.

Rawski, Thomas, "Productivity Change in Chinese Industry: Problems of Measurement," manuscript, 1986.

Svejnar, Jan, "Productivity Efficiency and Employment," in Byrd and Lin (eds), *China's Rural Industry: Structure, Development and Reform*, Oxford University Press, 1990.

Tian, Xiaowen, "Foreign Direct Investment and Economic Growth in China: Implications for Less Developed Countries," manuscript, 1999.

Tidrick, Gene, "Productivity Growth and Technological Change in Chinese Industry," *World Bank Working Papers No.761*, the World Bank, Washington, D.C. 1986.

Wen, Guanzhong James, "Total Factor Productivity Changes in China's Farming Sector: 1952–1989," *Economic Development and Cultural Change* 42, 1993, 1–41.

Wong, John, "China's Dynamic Economic Growth in the Context of East Asia," East Asian Institute, Singapore, 1999.

Woo, Wing Thye; Hai, Wen; Jin, Yibiao and Fan, Gang, "How Successful Has Chinese Enterprise Reform Been" Pitfalls in Opposite Biases and Focus," *Journal of Comparative Economics* 18, 1994, 410–37.

World Bank, *China 2020: Development Challenges in the New Century*, The World Bank, Washington D.C., 1997.

World Bank, *China's Long Term Development Issues and Options*, Johns Hopkins University Press, Baltimore, 1985.

Wu, Yanrui, "Productivity Growth, Technological Progress and Technical Efficiency Change in China: A Three-sector Analysis," *Journal of Comparative Economics* 21, 1995, 207–29.

Young, Alwyn, "A Tale of Two Cities: Factor Accumulation and Technical Change in Hong Kong and Singapore," *NBER Macroeconomics Annual* 1992, MIT Press.

3

Understanding China's Statistical System

Part One: "Lies, Damn Lies, and Statistics" — The Problems with Chinese Statistics

JOHN WONG*

SOMETHING REMARKABLE ABOUT CHINESE STATISTICS

Modern business decisions and government policy making critically depend on reliable statistical information. One central concern of foreign businessmen and investors operating in China is what to make of Chinese statistics. Particularly for those who are not familiar with China, their natural reaction is: How accurate and reliable are those numbers and figures coming from the official sources in Beijing?

China is actually a country that is marked by a proliferation of official statistics. Thanks to its central planning legacies, China has inherited a number of extensive and fairly sophisticated statistical reporting networks throughout China, from county to city, to province and then all the way up to the State Statistical Bureau (SSB) at the centre, which is now re-named the National Bureau of Statistics (NBS). The NBS system today employs more than 60,000 full-time statistical workers whose job is to collect and compile various kinds of economic and social statistics.

---

*Professor John Wong is Research Director of East Asian Institute, National University of Singapore.

Accordingly, the *China Statistical Yearbook 2000*, published by NBS, is a huge and comprehensive volume of 888 full pages. It presents a highly impressive array of China's economic and social statistics up to 1999. Divided into 23 sections, the volume covers all the usual statistical items from national accounts (complete with an input-output table for 1997) to population, employment, investment, consumption, production, prices, public finance, trade, tourism, education, science, sports, public health, and social welfare. Its last section contains major social and economic indicators of Macau, Hong Kong, and Taiwan. All headings, subtitles and descriptions are in English. Above all, most notions and terms used in this Yearbook have, with few exceptions, largely followed mainstream international practices.

Below the national level, individual provinces, individual cities and special economic zones, publish their own statistical yearbooks. Take the more developed Guangdong province as an example. The *Guangdong Statistical Yearbook 2000* dons 681 pages of economic and social statistics (with English subtitles and descriptions), while its provincial capital city Guangzhou puts out the 574-page *Guangzhou Statistical Yearbook 2000*. At the same time, its Special Economic Zones of Shenzhen and Zhuhai have separately put out the *Shenzhen Statistics and Information Yearbook 2000* (404 pages) and the *Zhuhai Statistical Yearbook 2000* (419 pages). Even the smaller county towns (those recently converted into cities) have also published their own statistical yearbooks, e.g., the *Statistical Yearbook of Dongguan* and the *Statistical Yearbook of Huizhou*.

In addition to the above general statistical compendiums, there is a third source. Many ministries and state commissions/agencies also regularly put out their specialized statistical yearbooks, whose data come from their own ministerial statistical network independent of the NBS system. The important ones include the *China Customs Statistical Yearbook*, *Rural Statistical Yearbook of China*, *China Population Statistics Yearbook*, *China Labour Statistical Yearbook*, and *China Statistical Yearbook of Science and Technology*. Major industries and trades also publish their own statistical yearbooks: e.g., the iron and steel industry, automobile industry, chemicals industry, machine-making industry, nonferous metals industry, and electronics industry. No other developing countries can match China in such extensive statistical detail and coverage. (See Table 1.)

There is, of course, a great deal of overlapping in coverage among all these statistical volumes. The statistical yearbook at the county/city level is inevitably summarized to appear in the provincial yearbook, which is, in turn, appropriately summarized to appear in the national yearbook. The local statistical bureaus, which publish local statistical yearbooks, are parts of the NBS's reporting system. Apart from the data generated from its own network, NBS also depends on various ministries and commissions/agencies for submitting specialized statistics: e.g., the General Customs Administration to supply foreign trade statistics, the Ministry of Education to supply education statistics, the People's Bank of China to supply banking and finance statistics, and so on.

The astonishing feature of China's statistical system is not just about its comprehensive coverage, but also its speed in the publication of national statistics. The national yearbook of the last-year data, for instance, is normally published in the third quarter of this year. Even more remarkable, such key economic performance indicators as industrial output, imports and exports, and CPI (consumer price index) of the current month, are normally released in the middle of the following month. Such quick release of important economic statistics is truly unusual, considering the size and diversity of China's economy. The NBS's huge manpower resources no doubt facilitate the prompt processing and publication of these numbers. But the main reason is because NBS has been authorized by the State Council (China's Cabinet) to release those key indicators directly by its spokesman without prior political clearance.[1]

The abundance of Chinese statistics and the speed of their publication have, ironically, created skepticism about their authenticity and reliability. There is a common feeling outside China that for a large and backward country like China, which is run by a Communist government, its statistics cannot be reliable. On many occasions, Beijing has in fact openly accused local officials of fudging statistics (adding *shuifen* or "water

---

[1] The release of the adjusted figures for the whole year is, however, delayed until April of the following year, because the whole set has to be formally presented at the National People's Congress, which usually meets in April. After the adoption by the NPC, the statistical figures will come out as the NBS's annual "Statistical Communique".

Table 1. Newly-Published Statistical Yearbooks by China Statistics Press

China Urban Statistical Yearbook-2000
China Foreign Economic Statistical Yearbook-2000
China Development Report-2000
China Industrial Statistical Yearbook-2000
China Fixed Assets Statistical Yearbook-2000
China Basic Statistical Units Yearbook-1999
China Construction Statistical Yearbook-2000
China Labour Statistical Yearbook-2000
China Civil Affairs's Statistical Yearbook-2000
China Energy Statistical Yearbook-2000
China Rural Poor Monitor Report-2000
China Rural Statistical Yearbook-2000
China Statistical Yearbook on Country and Town-2000
China Rural Household Statistical Yearbook-2000
China Population Statistical Yearbook-2000
China Social Statistical Yearbook-2000
China Food Industrial Statistical Yearbook-2000
China Market Statistical Yearbook-2000
China Statistical Yearbook-2000
China Statistical Abstract-2000
China Statistical Yearbook of Price and Urban Household Survey-2000
Western China Rural Statistics-2000
China County (City) Statistical Summary
Anhui Statistical Yearbook-2000
Bayinguoleng Statistical Yearbook-2000
Baoshan Statistical Yearbook-2000
Beijing Statistical Yearbook-2000
Changzhou Statistical Yearbook-2000
Chengdu Statistical Yearbook-2000
Dezhou Statistical Yearbook-2000
Dongguan Statistical Yearbook-2000
Fujian Rural Statistical Yearbook-2000
Fujian Statistical Yearbook-2000
Statistical Yearbook of Fuzhou Economic & Technical Development District-2000
Fuzhou Yearbook-2000
Gansu Yearbook-2000
Guang'an Statistical Yearbook-2000
Guangdong Rural Statistical Yearbook-2000
Guangdong Statistical Yearbook-2000
Guangxi Statistical Yearbook-2000
Guangzhou Statistical Yearbook-2000
Guiyang Statistical Yearbook-2000
Guizhou Statistical Yearbook-2000
Guilin Economic Social Statistical Yearbook-2000
International Statistical Yearbook-2000
Harbin Statistical Yearbook-2000
Haikou Statistical Yearbook-2000
Hainan Statistical Yearbook-2000
Handan Statistical Yearbook-2000
Hangzhou Statistical Yearbook-2000
Hebei Economic Statistical Yearbook-2000
Hebei Rural Statistical Yearbook-2000
Henan Rural Statistical Yearbook-2000
Henan Statistical Yearbook-2000
Heilongjiang Assarting District Statistical Yearbook-2000
Helongjiang Statistical Yearbook-2000
Hengshui Statistical Yearbook-2000
Hohhot Economic Statistical Yearbook-2000
Hubei Industrial Statistical Yearbook-2000
Hubei Rural Statistical Yearbook-2000
Hubei Statistical Yearbook-2000
Hunan Statistical Yearbook-2000
Huizhou Statistical Yearbook-2000
Jilin City Social Economic Statistical Yearbook-2000
Jilin Statistical Yearbook-2000
Jinan Statistical Yearbook-2000
Jiaxin Statistical Yearbook-2000
Jiangsu Statistical Yearbook-2000
Jiangxi Statistical Yearbook-2000

Continue Table 1

Jinhua Statistical Yearoook-2000
Jiujiang Statistical Yearbook-2000
Kaifeng Statistical Yearbook-2000
Lanzhou Yearbook-2000
Langfang Statistical Yearbook-2000
Liaoning Statistical Yearbook-2000
Linfeng Yearbook-2000
Liuzhou Prefecture Statistical Yearbook-2000
Liuzhou Economic Statistical Yearbook-2000
Luoyang Statistical Yearbook-2000
Mudaujiang Social Economic Statistical Yearbook-2000
Inner Mongolia Statistical Yearbook-2000
Nanchang Statistical Yearbook-2000
Nanning Prefectural Statistical Yearbook-2000
Nanning Statistical Yearbook-2000
Nanton Statistical Yearbook-2000
Nanyang Statistical Yearbook-2000
Ningbo Statistical Yearbook-2000
Ningxia Statistical Yearbook-2000
Pangzhihua Statistical Yearbook-2000
Pingdingshan Statistical Yearbook-2000
Qiqihrer Economic Statistical Yeatbook-2000
Qingdao Statistical Yearbook-2000
Qinghai Statistical Yearbook-2000
Rizhao Statistical Yearbook-2000
How to Use Statistical Yearbook
Sanmenxia Statistical Yearbook-2000
Shandong Urban Statistical Yearbook-2000
Shandong Statistical Yearbook-2000
Shanxi Statistical Yearbook-2000
Shaanxi Statistical Yearbook-2000
Statistical Yearbook of Shanghai Pudong New Area-2000
Shanghai Statistical Yearbook-2000
Shaoxing Statistical Yearbook-2000
Shenzhen Statistical and Information Yearbook-2000

Shenyang Statistical Yearbook-2000
Shihezi Statistical Yearbook-2000
Shijiazhuang Statistical Yearbook-2000
ShuanRyashan Statistical Yearbook-2000
Sichuan Statistical Yearbook-2000
Siping Statistical Yearbook-2000
Suzhou Statistical Yearbook-2000
Taizhou Statistical Yearbook-2000
Tai'an Statistical Yearbook-2000
Tangshan Statistical Yearbook-2000
Tianjin Statistical Yearbook-2000
Tolufan Statistical Yearbook-2000
Weifang Statistical Yearbook-2000
Wenzhou Statistical Yearbook-2000
Urumqi Statistical Yearbook-2000
Wuxi Statistical Yearbook-2000
Wuhan Statistical Yearbook-2000
Xi'an Statistical Yearbook-2000
Tibet Statistical Yearbook-2000
Xining Statistical Yearbook-2000
Xiamen Statistical Yearbook-2000
Xinjiang Production & Construction Group Statistical Yearbook-2000
Xinjiang Statistical Yearbook-2000
Xingtai Statistical Yearbook-2000
Xuzhou Statistical Yearbook-2000
Yanji Statistical Yearbook-2000
Yili Statistical Yearbook-2000
Yichang Statistical Yearbook-2000
Yichuan Statistical Yearbook-2000
Yunnan Statistical Yearbook-2000
Zhangjiakou Statistical Yearbook-2000
Zhejiang Statistical Yearbook-2000
Zhengzhou Statistical Yearbook-2000
Chongqing Statistical Yearbook-2000
Zhoushan Statistical Yearbook-2000
Zhuhai Statistical Yearbook-2000

China Statistics Press
Address: No. 75 Yuetan Nanjie, Sanlihe, Beijing 100826, P.R. China
Email: yearbook@stats.gov.cn

content"). Recently, NBS director Liu Hong threatened to crack down on the malpractice of reporting false statistics by local enterprises and local officials.[2] All this inevitably tends to reinforce the public mistrust of the official statistics.

However, virtually all serious China scholars agree that the Chinese government has not been engaged in any deliberate falsification of statistical data, for the simple reason that it is technically and administratively impossible for a government to deliberately manufacture fake statistics. It is now known that the statistics released by NBS are primarily not for foreign consumption, but for use by China's own scholars and planners. But this does not rule out the quality problem of Chinese statistics, i.e., the existence of many gaps and discrepancies.

Reliability of Chinese Statistics

How reliable are official Chinese statistics? Every China scholar has to confront this important question, as every Sovietologist used to have to do the same on the former Soviet Union. It is commonly believed that a Communist government is prone to control information and make use of official data for propaganda purposes; therefore, its statistics cannot be trusted. There is also a technical reason for the abuse of statistics in a centrally planned economy. Central planning sets production targets for enterprises to fulfil, and this naturally creates pressures on the under-performing enterprises to make false reports.

In the case of China, public confidence in its official statistics has indeed been often dented by official revelations of exaggerated reports or false figures, for instance:

- The most startling example of official statistical malfeasance was the ridiculous claim in the Great Leap Forward period of having doubled grain production in 1958 to 375 million tons, from 185

---

[2] See "Statistics: Figure fakers under fire", *South China Morning Post* (January 12, 2000).

million tons in 1957. Premier Zhou Enlai later had to slash the figure by one third, which was still too high.[3]

- As recently as in 1998, some provincial authorities were accused by Beijing of returning inflated GDP figures in order to prove their fulfilment of Premier Zhu Rongji's much-publicized "8% growth target".[4]
- Following the 1995 Industrial Census, NBS had to undertake a 20% downward adjustment of the gross output for the whole "collective sector" (i.e., mainly the township and village enterprises) for the previous four years.[5]
- Every year, NBS reveals numerous statistical regulation violations — e.g., 60,000 cases in 1997 — by local officials and local enterprises, involving either over-reporting or under-reporting.[6] This has prompted NBS to threaten to take action against those who deliberately report fake statistics for political and financial gains.[7]

---

[3] See State Statistical Bureau, *Ten Great Years* (Peking, Foreign Languages Press, 1960). The initial official claim of grain output for 1958 was 375 million tons, up 102% in one year from the 185 million tons of 1957. This is physically impossible as the long-term rate of food production for most countries is normally 2 to 3%. The claim was later slashed by one-third to 250 million tons, still much too high. The adjusted official figure for 1965 was only 195 million tons. In the event, the Great Leap collapsed in 1959, and China begun to import food in 1961.

[4] In early 1998, Premier Zhu Rongji declared his intention to see 8% growth for China. At the end of 1998, most provinces returned with more than 8% GDP growth figures for the year. NBS eventually had to readjust some provincial figures downward to arrive at a 7.8% growth for China for 1998. See "Numbers Lie: Premier Uncovers Lies", *Yazhou Zhoukan* (March 27, 2000). The same problem has repeated itself. In 1999, China's GDP growth was 7.1%. However, only two provinces reported below 7.1% growth while all the others reported over 7.1% growth, with 10 provinces reporting more than 10% growth. Hence the need for NBS to readjust the numbers. See "Beijing has HK$546 b chasm in key data", *South China Morning Post* (February 29, 2000).

[5] Sean Dougherty, "The Reliability of Chinese Statistics", for the Conference Board. (*ChinaOnline*).

[6] "Statistical fraud in China", *Guangming Ribao* (July 24, 1998).

[7] "False-data warning", *South China Morning Post* (January 12, 2000).

Nonetheless, for almost five decades since the formation of the People's Republic, successive generations of China scholars, after their consistency checks, have found no evidence that the central statistical authorities have deliberately and systematically fabricated statistical information. Sovietologists have come to a similar conclusion on statistics from the former Soviet Union.[8] Official mendacity is simply impossible for the following reasons:[9]

- It is technically and politically difficult for any government to systematically manufacture false economic and social statistics on a large scale.
- Deliberate falsification of official statistics would entail the mammoth administrative complications of keeping two separate sets of books (one for the public and one for restricted use) all the way from the central down to the local levels.
- This, in turn, would entail further complications: Who will be privy to the internal information and who will be kept out? Can a government cheat its people all the time?
- Some statistics such as wages, prices, household incomes, and inflation rates, if falsified, can be easily checked out by the people based on their own personal experience. Faking such data then serves no purpose except to discredit all the other official materials.
- Data like foreign trade and foreign investment cannot be easily falsified as they involve foreign countries. It is also dangerous to tamper with growth figures. To inflate a higher percentage increase for this year would make it more difficult to do it again in the following year, as growth is a cumulative process based on the powerful compound interest rate principle.

---

[8] After the collapse of the Soviet Union, Soviet experts can now have access to the archive and they have confirmed the general reliability of the Soviet sources. ("Reliability of Soviet Sources", 10–16 November 1995). (wwwe.h-net.mus.edu/-russia/threads/index/thrdsvser.html). In fact, it was the American CIA that had exaggerated the Soviet economic figures.

[9] See, e.g. Perkins (1966). Also, Chen (1995).

- In short, an authoritarian government, instead of falsifying numbers, could have easily withheld unfavourable information, or just published selective items in a misleading context.

The fact that the Chinese government has not deliberately falsified statistical information does not mean that its statistics are automatically accurate. Inaccuracy and inconsistency still abound because of the deficiencies in the compilation of data caused by under-qualified statistical workers. The same problem has long plagued other large developing countries like India or Indonesia.

With the emergence of the "socialist market economy", NBS is under no political and ideological pressures to produce inflated statistics. In fact, as the Chinese government is getting more technocratic, it demands more accurate figures from NBS for better macroeconomic management. Since targets are no longer set for enterprises to fulfil, there is also no compelling *political* reason for enterprise managers at the lower level to exaggerate output figures, except for some ulterior motives.

However, economic reform has ushered in a different form of statistical abuse. Some enterprises under-report profits to evade taxes while others hide their losses for different reasons. Still more, some under-report imports to avoid paying duties while others over-report foreign investment for certain preferential treatment. But all these abuses do not constitute a systematic problem as long as the central authorities do not countenance such practices. In principle, the mathematical law of large numbers can sometimes reduce, though not entirely eliminate, such discrepancies by balancing under-reporting with over-reporting.

Suffice it to say that reliability is no longer a central issue for the Chinese official statistics today. It is more a problem of uneven quality. Some statistics tend to be more accurate and more consistent than others. Because of China's administrative inefficiency and widespread corruption and smuggling activities, statistics like imports and foreign direct investment inevitably contain higher levels of *shuifen* or inaccuracy. But the situation has been rapidly improving.

China's Changing Statistical System

The State Statistical Bureau (SSB) was set up in August 1952. Before 1949, state statistics organizations in China had an image problem, because Chiang Kai-shek's internal security apparatus operated under the cloak of "statistical investigation".[10] Immediately after its establishment, SSB started to put in place a national statistical system in order to compile data for China's First Five-Year Plan, 1953–57. The successful implementation of this Plan owes a great deal to the good work of SSB, which in 1954, had a huge workforce of 100,000 "statistical workers" at its disposal [Li (1962)].

The SSB's achievements in the 1950s culminated in the publication in 1960 of China's first statistical compendium, *The Ten Great Years* [SSB (1960)]. However, in 1958, as Mao launched the Great Leap Forward movement, the SSB's professional work went haywire under the slogan "Let politics command statistics". This led to the publication in 1958 of absurd production claims for grain and iron and steel, based on the grossly inflated output figures from the people's communes and the many small "backyard steel-making furnaces". Subsequently, the statistical figures for 1958 were discredited and discarded [Chen (1967)].

After the collapse of the Great Leap Forward, SSB's work continued to be compromised by politics, giving rise to a statistical blackout for China for more than a decade. During the Cultural Revolution (1966–76), SSB was merged with other economic agencies; with only a skeleton staff, it ceased to function as a professional organization.

Effective professional work for SSB was resumed only after the start of economic reform in 1978. Economic reform also led to the restructuring and reorientation of the old SSB. Since then, the main role of SSB is no longer to serve central planning, but to "provide regularly the Chinese public and the international community China's growing statistical information" [SSB (2000)].

---

[10] Chiang's two notorious secret policy organizations were called "Military Statistics and Investigation Bureau" (the *Jun Tong*) and "Central Statistics and Investigation Bureau" (the *Zhong Tong*).

In the early 1980s, the restructured SSB's main focus was to re-establish its national statistical reporting system and to start collecting the economic and social data for its annual publication of the "Statistical Yearbook". It had kept on adjusting its various statistical series as more accurate data became available. Since the early 1990s, with China becoming a "socialist market economy", SSB also started to follow international practices in respect of concept, coverage and classification. The most significant change took place in 1993 when SSB gave up its time-honoured socialist concept of national accounts based on material balances in favour of the international national income concept based on the UN's System of National Accounts (SNA).

The SSB today, renamed NBS (National Bureau of Statistics), has become a modern organization, run by professionals and employing modern methodologies and up-to-date computation techniques to handle China's increasing volumes of economic and social statistical information. Its increased operational efficiency is reflected in its prompt publication of comprehensive statistics on a regular basis, as mentioned earlier. It is also much more open and transparent, no longer subject to unwarranted political interference of the past era, as clearly manifested in its independent release of key economic and social statistical information without prior political clearance from its political masters. All this bodes well for its future growth.

Nonetheless, Chinese statistics today are still plagued by many discrepancies. This is more the case of "people cheating the government" rather than the "government cheating the people", as many enterprise managers and lower-echelon statistical officers still manipulate statistics for ulterior motives. To cope with these abuses, NBS from time to time runs additional surveys or dispatch officials to check on the suspected data sources. More significantly, NBS has recently overhauled its old data collection system by requiring China's 5,000 large-scale enterprises to report their figures direct to NBS instead of submitting them through local governments.[11] The Statistics Law was also revised in June 2000

---

[11] See "National bureau to overhaul data collection to prevent distortion", *South China Morning Post* (September 1, 2000).

in order to punish those who make use of their position to distort statistics for political or financial gains.

Improved Usability

China's statistical system has clearly made impressive progress in recent years. As a result of NBS's constant efforts to revise and update its existing statistics whenever more reliable new sources are available, the usability of Chinese statistics has been much improved. NBS's penchant for greater data accuracy, as manifested in its frequent warning to local statistical officers against mis-reporting, represents significant progress by itself. This should add to the user's confidence.

However, this does not mean that Chinese statistics in its present state are easily usable without problems. As stated earlier, quality among different statistical series remains uneven — series like industrial profits, unemployment, migration, or fertility, are particularly problematic. To make the best use of the Chinese official statistical items, one still needs to understand their background and be keenly aware of their limitations.

References

Dwight H. Perkins, *Market Control and Planning in Communist China* (Cambridge, Mass., Harvard University Press, 1966). Nai-Ruenn Chen, "An Assessment of Chinese Economic Data: Availability, Reliability, and Usability", in Joint Economic Committee of US Congress, *China: A Reassessment of the Economy* (US Government Printing Office, July 1995).

Li Choh Ming, *The State Statistical System of Communist China* (Berkeley and Los Angeles, University of California Press, 1962).

State Statistical Bureau, *The Ten Great Years* (Peking, Foreign Languages Press, 1960). Its Chinese version is called *Wei-da de shi-nian*.

Nai-Ruenn Chen, *Chinese Economic Statistics* (Chicago, Aldine Publishing Co. 1967).

State Statistical Bureau, *Zhongguo Tongzhi kailan* (An Overview of Chinese Statistics), Beijing (May 2000).

3

Understanding China's Statistical System

Part Two: China's National Bureau of Statistics: Its Functions and Structure

REN CAIFANG*

The National Bureau of Statistics (NBS) is a sub-ministerial agency directly under the State Council. The NBS operates and co-ordinates China's national statistical system in accordance with China's Statistics Law. Its major functions include:

- To promulgate laws, regulations, rules, and plans for statistical work, and supervise their implementation.
- To set up and maintain the national economic accounts system and national statistical standards, and review and approve statistical plans.
- To organize the national censuses and surveys, and provide statistical information to the Central government.
- To act as the exclusive agency in verifying, managing and publishing basic national statistical data of China.
- To establish and administer the national statistical information system and its database networks.

---

*Mr Ren Caifang is Senior Statistician of State Bureau of Statistics, China.

Chart 1

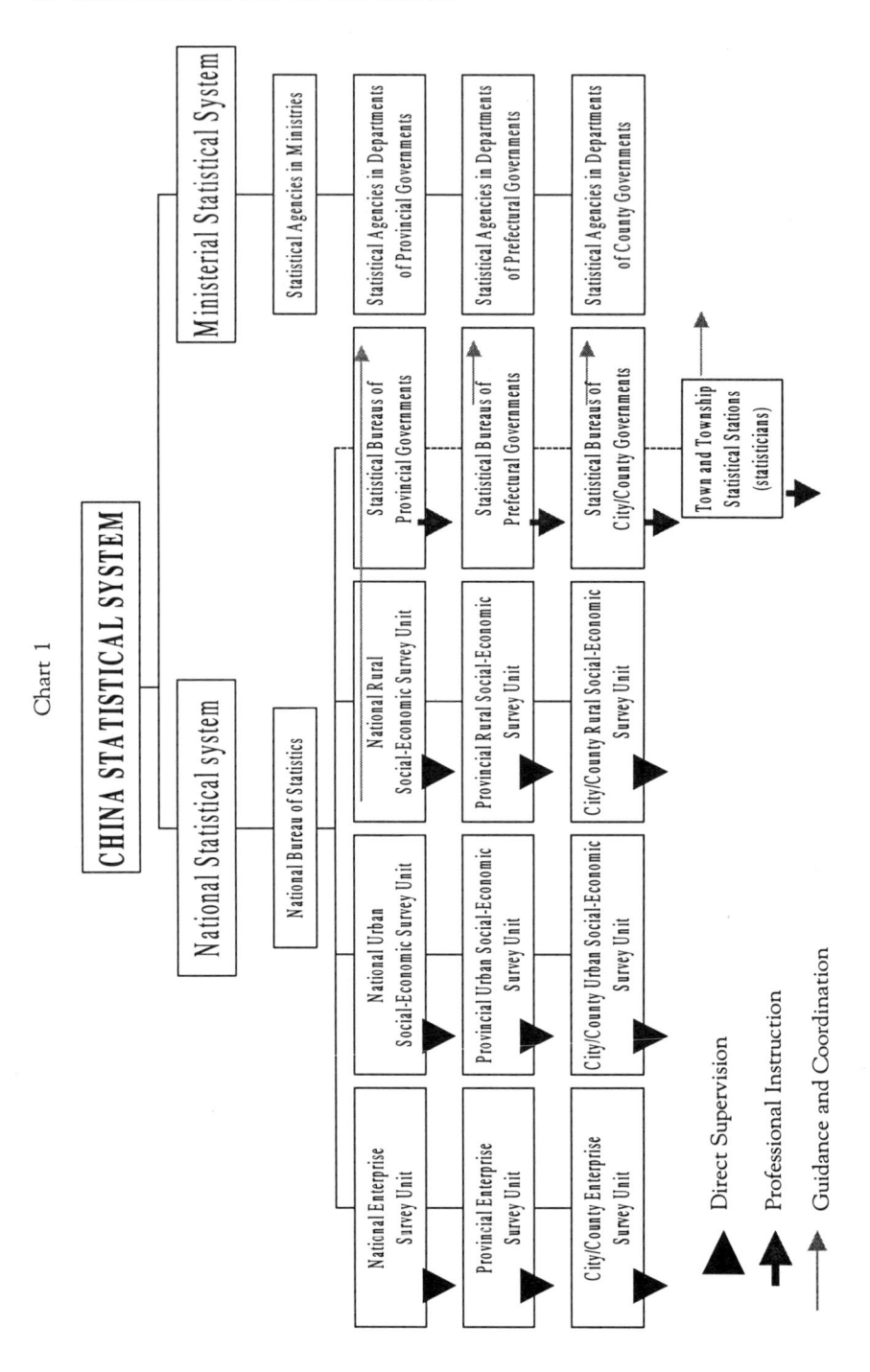

CHINA STATISTICAL SYSTEM

National Statistical system

National Bureau of Statistics

- National Enterprise Survey Unit
  - Provincial Enterprise Survey Unit
    - City/County Enterprise Survey Unit
- National Urban Social-Economic Survey Unit
  - Provincial Urban Social-Economic Survey Unit
    - City/County Urban Social-Economic Survey Unit
- National Rural Social-Economic Survey Unit
  - Provincial Rural Social-Economic Survey Unit
    - City/County Rural Social-Economic Survey Unit

Statistical Bureaus of Provincial Governments
Statistical Bureaus of Prefectural Governments
Statistical Bureaus of City/County Governments
Town and Township Statistical Stations (statisticians)

Ministerial Statistical System

Statistical Agencies in Ministries
Statistical Agencies in Departments of Provincial Governments
Statistical Agencies in Departments of Prefectural Governments
Statistical Agencies in Departments of County Governments

▲ Direct Supervision
↑ Professional Instruction
↑ Guidance and Coordination

- To provide leadership to local statistical agencies, and organize qualification examinations.

China's overall statistical system comprises two major components: (1) The national statistical system, which is managed and co-ordinated by NBS, and (2) The ministerial statistical system. Both operate an extensive four-level network, from the centre to province, to prefecture and to county, as shown in Chart 1. The NBS network collects comprehensive statistical data while the ministerial system is mainly concerned with functional data related to the work of the individual ministries.

The NBS's first duty is to co-ordinate and supervise the professional work of the statistical bureaus at various levels, whose data will be collated and adjusted to form the national statistical series for the national statistical yearbook. The local bureaus are actually administratively autonomous from NBS, which functions more like the final depository of all local statistical data. Besides, NBS is supposed to provide professional guidance and consultation to the administratively independent ministerial network.

However, NBS has under its direct control three key sub-networks: the national enterprise survey unit, national urban survey unit, and national rural survey unit. (Chart 2). These three units generate China's most important and integrated economic data, covering industrial and agricultural production, urban income levels and the consumer price index. Except for foreign trade statistics (from the Department of Customs) and financial data (from the People's Bank of China), NBS's directly-controlled statistics cover the bulk of China's economic activities.

Over the years, NBS has greatly improved its data collection and transmission techniques. Traditionally, reporting was by post. Later, this was supplemented by phone report. Starting in the early 1990s, fax was used in reporting. Recently, reporting is done by email, intranet and internet. Of greater importance, starting from the middle of 2000, large industrial and commercial enterprises are required to submit their statistical reports directly to NBS: This includes: (a) 5,000 large industry enterprises; (b) 3,000 large construction enterprises; and (c) 1,200 large commercial companies.

Chart 2 Three Key National Survey Units

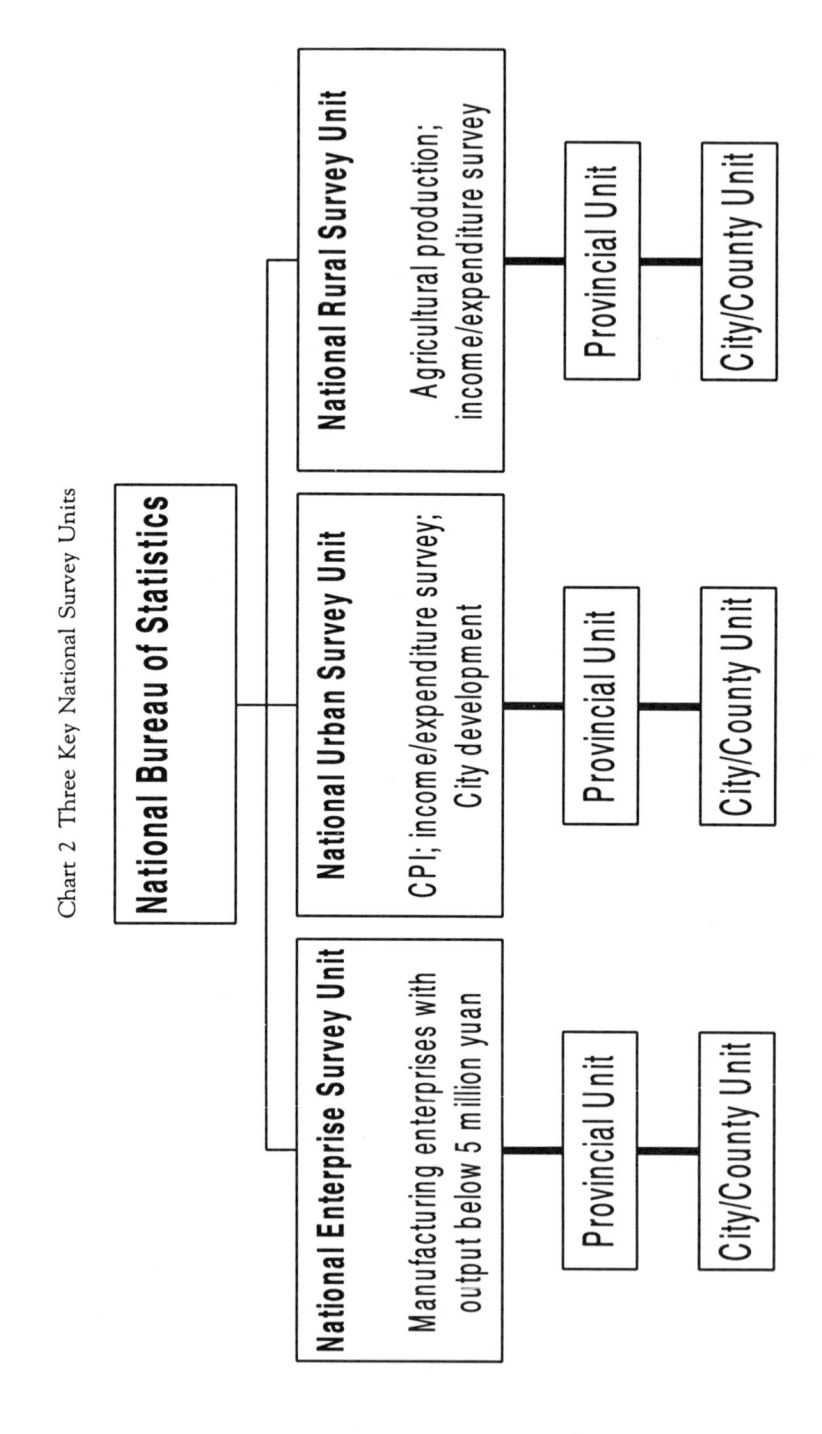

National Bureau of Statistics

- **National Enterprise Survey Unit** — Manufacturing enterprises with output below 5 million yuan
  - Provincial Unit
  - City/County Unit
- **National Urban Survey Unit** — CPI; income/expenditure survey; City development
  - Provincial Unit
  - City/County Unit
- **National Rural Survey Unit** — Agricultural production; income/expenditure survey
  - Provincial Unit
  - City/County Unit

The recent changes not only speed up the processing and publication of these statistics, but also remove unwarranted interference from local officials, thereby reducing the possibility of some irresponsible local officials adding *shuifen* to fudge statistics. In short, these technical and administrative improvements will further improve the operational efficiency and professional standards of China's statistical system.

4

China's Industrial Policy and Long-term Structural Planning

Lu Ding*

1. Contents of Industrial Policy

Industrial policy refers to government attempts to channel resources into sectors that it views as important for future economic growth. According to Johnson (1984), the aim of industrial policy is to create some industries' comparative advantage for a nation. Industrial policy packages usually involve government support or protection of domestic industries that are deemed to have potential comparative advantages but yet to be internationally competitive on their own for the time being. The most common justification for active industrial policy is the "infant industry" argument, which suggests that developing countries could speed up their catching up process by selectively protecting their industries at an early stage of development. Whether or to what extent

---

*Dr. Lu Ding is Associate Professor at Department of Economics, National University of Singapore, and Research Associate at East Asian Institute, National University of Singapore. The author would like to acknowledge the financial support from the Academic Research Foundation of the National University of Singapore for the research presented in this paper.

the active industrial policy is necessary and has been effective in the past to promote development is still an issue subject to debate. Advocates for industrial policy nevertheless stress the positive roles of industrial policy in helping Japan and the newly industrialised economies (NIEs) succeed in achieving rapid economic growth in the past decades (Wade, 1990; Takahashi, 1997).

Various industrial policies pursued by Japan and the NIEs share the feature of active government intervention in resource allocation across industries. They were, however, distinctive from the central planning system that existed in the former Soviet block or pre-reformed China. These differences lie in the fundamental institutions in the economy (Table 1).

In China, an explicit concept of "industrial policy" did not appear in official documents until the late 1980s. By that time, a series of market-oriented reforms started in 1979 had drastically changed the framework and institutions of the Chinese economy. Liberalised market forces gradually dismantled the centrally planned process and replace the latter as the dominant mechanism of resource allocation in daily economic life. The share of the state-owned sector in the national economy was on the wane through the 1980s. At the same time, China was changing itself from a near autarchy in the 1970s to a booming

Table 1. The NIE Industrial Policy Regime vs. the Central Planning System

	Industrial Policy Regime	Centrally Planned Economy
Fundamental mechanism of resource allocation	Market	Central planning
Ownership	Basically private; Public finance may play pivotal role	Public (state or collective)
Decision making	A combination of state and private decisions, with the private de jure right over property use protected	Centrally planned by the state
Information co-ordination	Market transaction guided by state policies	Administrative
Motivation and incentives	Firms: profits State: pragmatic, non-ideological	Firms: fulfilment of plans State: mostly ideological

exporter and an increasingly attractive host to foreign direct investment in the world economy.

Early Policies (1989–1990)

In March 1989, the State Council issued the "Decision on the Gist of Current Industrial Policy", the first explicit and detailed official guideline for a national industrial policy.[1] The document noted four serious problems in China's industrial structure. (1) The production capacity of the manufacturing industries was too big for the relatively underdeveloped agricultural sector, energy and raw material industries, and transportation sector. (2) The production capacity of average-level manufacturing industries was too big and advanced-level manufacturing was in shortage. (3) Inter-regional distribution of industries was not rational and regional (comparative) advantages were not utilised. (4) Inter-enterprise organisation, co-ordination and linkage were not well organised. Industrial concentration was too low to be efficient.

The "Decision" put forward the major principles of China's industrial policy. These include:

- Guiding market development, co-ordinating aggregate demand and aggregate supply, reducing inconsistency between the consumption structure and production structure.
- Reducing production and investment in goods in excess supply, increasing and expanding production and investment in those in shortage. Concentrating on the production of grain, cotton, coal, electricity power supply, transportation, and other light industrial products in shortage.
- Making decisions on priorities and constraints with consideration of market demand, industrial linkage, technology progress, capacity to earn foreign exchanges, and economic efficiency.

According to the above principles, the document gave a list of industries and products that should receive priorities, including:

---

[1] *Zhongguo Jingji Nianjian* (Almanac of China's Economy) 1990, pp. I: 55–59.

- Agriculture and agriculture-service industries.
- A few selected products in light industry and textile industry.
- Infrastructure and basic industries, such as transportation of coal, agricultural input, and passengers, telecommunications, energy supplies (coal, electricity and petroleum), some important raw materials (iron, non-ferrous metal, chemicals).
- Machinery and electronic industries, especially high value-added products;
- High-tech industries, including aerospace products, new materials, and bioengineering technology.
- Exports that earn good profits and foreign exchanges, especially manufacturing goods.

The document also defined the areas of production to be suppressed and constrained. These mainly included low quality products and machinery, consumer durable goods that consumed "excess" electricity, "luxurious" consumer products where the required inputs were in shortage, production modes that were obsolete, energy wasting and environment polluting. There was also a list of products or production activities to be banned. Consistent with the priority industries and products, the document also listed the areas where the state would support investment in capital construction and technology upgrading. In areas subject to suppression and bans, investment would be strictly controlled. On top of that, the Decision specified that exports of high value-added manufacturing goods and domestically abundant commodities should be encouraged. Strict plans should apply to the export of major resource commodities which are vital to national interests. Export of goods in severe shortage in the domestic economy should also be banned.

Later Policies (1991–1995)

In April 1991, the National People's Congress approved the Eighth Five-year Plan (1991–95) and the Ten-year Plan for National Economic and Social Development (1991–2000). Both of the plans regarded the adjustment of industrial structures as the foremost development goal. The Ten-year Plan called for efforts to strengthen agriculture, basic industries and infrastructure facilities. It vowed to restructure and upgrade the manufacturing industry. The Plan gave priority to the development of the electronic industry and urged active promotion of the construction sector and tertiary industry.

Accordingly, the Eighth Five-year Plan (1991–95) stressed the development of 12 sectors and specified output and construction targets for them. These sectors include: agriculture and rural economy, irrigation and water conservancy, energy, transportation and telecommunications, raw material, geological prospecting and weather forecasting, electronic, advanced machinery, defence and research, certain products in light and textile industries, construction, and certain commercial services.

In regard to foreign trade, the Plan took a step further from the Seventh Five-year Plan to promote exports of manufactured goods, in particular machinery products, electrical equipment, light industry products and textile products, and high-tech products. The Plan pledged to increase export quality and adjust the export structure toward one more reliant on higher value-added manufactured goods.

Before China concluded her Eighth Five-year Plan, the State Council promulgated "The Outline of State Industrial Policy in the 1990s" in June 1994.[2] The "Outline" specified the main direction and aspects of China's industrial restructuring during the 1990s as follows:

- Continuously strengthening the status of agriculture as the foundation of the national economy, developing the rural economy in an all-round way.
- Vigorously beefing up basic industries, striving to relieve the strain posed by the slow development of basic industries and infrastructure.
- Accelerating the development of mainstay (pillar) industries to promote overall national economic development. These include the machinery industry, electronic industry, petroleum processing and raw chemical materials industry, automobile industry, and construction industry.

[2] *Renmin Ribao* (People's Daily), Beijing, 23 June 1994.

- Rationally restructuring foreign trade, sharpening the competitive edge of the national industries in the world market. The foreign trade policy should encourage exports of agricultural products with comparative advantages, home electronic appliances, products of high added-value and international competitiveness, and products of new and high technologies. Encouragement was also granted to imports of crucial parts, equipment and technologies. Exports of primary goods and energy intensive goods would, however, be gradually reduced or restricted. Imports of luxurious consumer goods are discouraged.
- Quickening the pace of developing industries using new and high technology, supporting the development of new industries and products.

A remarkable point in the "Outline" was its announcement of a state industrial organisation policy. This policy aims to promote "rational competition", reap economies of scale and exploit co-ordinating specialisation. For industries with strong scale economies the document recommended an approach to support large businesses. For other industries it offered encouragement to small businesses.

This document also defined the authorities of industrial policy making and the procedure of review and approval for industrial policies. The state council was authorised to set the national industrial policies while the State Planning Commission (SPC) was to be in charge of designing and co-ordinating sectoral industrial policies. The "Outline" required the establishment of a formal arrangement for implementing the policies and of a system to evaluate and monitor the outcomes of the policies. All the major state authorities in charge of planning, fiscal budget, banking, taxation, domestic and foreign trade, customs tariffs, security market, state assets, business registration, etc., had to be committed to implementing state industrial policies. They had to consult the SPC for co-ordination before making any major policy decisions that involved industrial development. The SPC would work with relevant authorities to monitor, assess, and analyse the implementation of state industrial policies. Based on that, the SPC would report to the State Council on the effects of implementation and proposes amendments accordingly.

The provincial governments would work out detailed local plans of implementing the "Guideline" and file their plans to the SPC.

Based on the "Outline", the SPC drafted sector-specific industrial policies for telecommunications, transportation, construction, electronics, machinery, petroleum processing and chemical material production. It also masterminded the industrial policies regarding foreign investment, foreign trade, industrial organisation and technology development.

Present Policies (1996–2010)

In March 1996, China's Eighth National People's Congress approved at its fourth session the *Outlines of the Ninth Five-year Plan for National Economic and Social Development and the Long-term Target for the Year 2010*.[3] This landmark document defines the new direction of state intervention and provides a blueprint of national development into the 21st century. The 1996 "Outline" sets the objectives for the year 2010 as follows:

- Double the 2000 GDP figure.
- Control population within 1.4 billion and enable people to live an "even more comfortable life".
- Establish "a relatively complete socialist market economy", a sounder macroeconomic control system with better agility and effectiveness, and a regulatory framework more in compliance with the rule of law.
- Establish a modern enterprise system for state-owned enterprises and develop a number of internationally competitive large enterprises and business groups.
- Optimise industrial structure by:
  - enhancing commercialisation and specialisation in agriculture;
  - building up a group of national infrastructure projects (including the major water control projects in the Yangtze River and Yellow River such as the "Three Gorges" project) and matching

---

[3] Xinhua News Agency Daily Report, 20 March 1996.

development of infrastructure and basic industries to national economic growth;
- promoting pillar industries and making them the major driving force of economic growth; and
- increasing markedly the proportion of the tertiary sector in the national economy and its service functions.
• Promote a more co-ordinated development of regional economies and gradually narrow the gap in development between different regions.

What is noteworthy in these objectives is the emphasis on institution building for a market economy and the development of the so-called "pillar industries". According to the 1996 "Outline", to ensure sustainable and rapid economic growth, the key requirement is to achieve two fundamental transitions. One is the transition from the centrally planned economy to a "socialist market economy", in which the market plays a fundamental role in resource allocation under state macro-control. The other is the transition from an extensive growth mode, which is driven by expansion of production inputs, to an intensive growth mode, which is driven by increasing efficiency and productivity.

The document classifies investment projects into three types, namely "projects of a competitive nature", "projects of a foundation nature", and "projects of a public welfare nature". In the "competitive industries", resources should be allocated primarily by the market. The investment projects in these industries are categorised accordingly as "projects of a competition nature", which should be funded mainly by enterprises and financed through the market. The government, however, will selectively give support to key projects of pillar industries and to high-tech development projects. The pillar industries defined in this document are industries of machinery, electronics, petrochemical, automobile and construction. For these industries, the government may even play a role in "optimising industrial organisations" to promote economies of scale by co-ordinating business regrouping among large enterprises or enterprise groups. The state will continue to play a leading role in "non-competitive industries". The government should be the main fund provider or the leading fundraiser for the "projects of a foundation nature". These projects are likely to be related to infrastructure or "basic industry" (energy supplies and raw materials). Governments "at various levels" should be responsible for funding the "projects of public welfare nature".

2. INSTRUMENTS OF INDUSTRIAL POLICY

From the above review of China's industrial policy since 1989, we observe that, with the transition to a market economy, state intervention in cross-industry resource allocation has gradually moved away from a central planning regime to an industrial policy regime similar to that of NIEs (cf. Table 1). However, legacies of the central planning regime continue to play a role in the government's economic policy making. These legacies characterise the instruments of China's industrial policy.

As summarised by Zhang and Long (1997), China has relied on six types of industrial policy tools: central government financing and planning; empowering key industries with direct financing; preferential interest and tax rates and favourable financing for target industries; infant industry (trade) protection; pricing policies; and administrative means. In addition to these six tools, there are at least two additional important measures. One is the systematic guidelines to channel foreign direct investment into desired industries. Based on these guidelines, the government exercises licensing and approval of investment projects. The other is the various restrictions imposed on foreign ownership, business ranges and geographic scope of foreign-funded enterprises.

All the policy instruments listed in Table 2 have played important roles in implementing the official industrial policy guidelines during the past decade. The relative importance of these instruments, however, has been significantly changed over the years as the whole economy moves towards a more open and market-oriented system. Some of these policy instruments are becoming increasingly difficult to apply in recent years. For instance, since 1997, the Zhu Rongji administration has tried to restructure the state-owned enterprises into modern corporations with tight budget constraints and business autonomy. In this context, the use of policy instruments like direct state price controls and administrative intervention in business organisations is less appropriate.

Table 2. Main Industrial Policy Instruments

Policy instrument	Evidence and examples
1. Central government financing and planning	Central governments: • direct investment in infrastructure projects, • financial assistance to key industries, and • budget assistance to projects in backward regions.
2. Administrative means	Administrative planning measures are used from time to time to implement industrial policy and industrial organisation policy in particular, such as issuing direct orders to close down or merge state-owned enterprises.
3. Pricing policies	• State price controls over power and water supply; • Permitting state telecommunications companies to charge installation fees for new telephone subscribers (1980s to early 1990s);
4. Empowering key industries with direct financing	• Adopting the Building, Operating, and Transferring (BOT) model for infrastructure projects. Local governments or state-owned consortiums have been permitted to issue construction bonds to develop energy and communications industries; • Official approval of stock market listing, IPOs or overseas financing is also influenced by industrial policies.
5. Infant industry (trade) protection	Tariffs and non-tariff measures such as import duties, import quotas, import licensing, and local-content requirements (e.g. car industry).
6. Restrictions on the businesses of foreign-funded enterprises	• The general prohibition on foreign firms from distributing products other than those they make in China, or from controlling their own distribution networks; • Ban on foreign bank branches from operating RMB deposits and loans and restrictions on their business in designated cities.
7. Preferential interest and tax rates and favourable financing	• State banks' low-interest loans and discriminative lending to different industries; • Various industry-oriented tax incentives; • "Co-ordinating tax" for directions of fixed capital in fixed capital investment.
8. Licensing and approval of investment projects	Since 1995, the government has periodically promulgated Direction Guide for Foreign Investment to specify the projects to be encouraged, the ones to be allowed, the ones to be restricted, and the ones to be forbidden.

As a founding member of the Asia-Pacific Economic Co-operation (APEC) and a rising economic power, China has made some important "down-payments" for free trade, including tariff cuts and import quota reductions. In its bid for membership of the World Trade Organisation (WTO), China has gradually cut its average tariff rate from over 40 % to the current 15 % since the early 1990s. As for non-tariff barriers, after the landmark promulgation of the "Law of Foreign Trade of the People's Republic of China" in 1994, China sped up its elimination of license requirements and quotas for most imports and embarked on the transition toward an automatic import licensing system. The Ministry of Foreign Trade and Economic Co-operation, however, promulgated in March 1999 a procedure and a directory for 114 imported commodities subject to non-automatic licensing.[4] Generally, trade-protection as an industrial policy instrument has become less viable in recent years.

Relatively speaking, industry-oriented tax incentives have become more important. In 1994, China launched a comprehensive tax reform unifying all enterprises' corporate income taxes to a flat rate of 33 per cent. The central government, however, announced in March 1994 that it would grant income tax exemptions and concessions to certain businesses and/or categories of incomes, including the following[5]:

- The high-tech enterprises in High-tech Industrial Development Zones would get a reduced corporate income tax rate of 15 per cent. The new high-tech enterprises in these zones were to be exempted from paying income tax for two years after they start operation.
- Most new businesses in the tertiary industry would be granted income tax exemption or reduction for one to two years. These included new firms engaging in consulting services, transportation or telecommunications services, public utilities, health, storage, tourism, foreign trade, commerce, catering, home service, education, culture, etc. The firms providing agricultural service and institutes or colleges doing technological training and

---

[4] *China Economic News*, Beijing, 3 May 1999.
[5] Lu and Tang (1997), pp. 72–73.

technology transfer, consulting and service, would be exempted from paying income tax.
- Firms in production using recycled materials were to be exempted from income tax for five years.
- Incomes from technology transfer with annual income no more than RMB 300,000 were to be exempted from tax.
- Educational institutions' workshops, enterprises specially set up for handicapped persons, and service enterprises specially set up for hiring urban unemployed persons were to get income tax exemption or reduction.
- Township and village enterprises could pay reduced income tax by 10 per cent for community expenses.
- New enterprises in some impoverished areas were to get tax exemption or reduction for three years.

Most of the above income tax benefits (the first 4) are industry-oriented. The rest are mainly for social welfare or equity purposes.

An important tax policy in the early 1990s was the co-ordinating tax for directions of fixed capital investment, which was introduced in 1991, to be levied on the amount of fixed capital investment incurred by indigenous enterprises. A zero tax rate applied to projects "urgently needed by the state". These projects included fixed capital investment in agriculture and water conservancy, energy, transportation, postal and telecommunications, key raw materials, geological prospecting, certain medical research, certain electronic and machinery investment, pollution control, urban public utilities, some storage facilities, etc. For projects encouraged by the state but constrained by energy supply and transportation facilities, the low 5 per cent tax rate applied. For projects that are of an inefficient scale, employing outmoded technologies, or making products already in excess supply, the state policy was to strictly control their development and therefore the highest rate of 30 per cent was applied.[6] All the other projects were taxed at a rate of 15 per cent.[7]

[6] Based on the same principle, the state has also promulgated a list of forbidden projects.
[7] State Council, "The Provisional Regulation on the PRC's Direction-Adjustment Tax on Fixed Capital Investment" (16 April 1991), Zhang and Wu (1994), pp. 584–605.

Another policy instrument that gained greater importance is the guidelines for foreign direct investment. Since China opened its door to foreign direct investment in the early 1980s, Beijing has pursued an official policy to encourage foreign investment in hi-tech manufacturing and infrastructure development such as transportation, telecommunications, and energy resources. Export-oriented projects and import-substitution projects have also been preferred.

After China developed her first set of explicit industrial policies in 1989, the government increasingly used the country's vast market potential as a leverage to lure foreign investment into areas prioritised by the state industrial policies. At the beginning of 1993, China planned a series of measures to attract foreign investment in the areas of finance, communications, information technology, farm products processing, urban infrastructure and housing renovation.[8]

The official guidelines toward foreign investors remained rather obscure until the State Planning Commission, Economic and Trade Commission and MOFTEC jointly promulgated the first explicit direction guide for foreign investment in June 1995.[9] In principle, the government divided foreign-funded projects into four categories: namely, the projects to be encouraged, the ones to be allowed, the ones to be restricted, and the ones to be forbidden.

Projects to be **encouraged** include those that:

- involve new agricultural techniques, comprehensive agriculture development, and development of energy, transportation and major raw materials;
- involve new and/or high-tech and thus can help save energy and raw materials, raise the technical level and economic efficiency;
- can meet the demand of the international market and help upgrade products and thus help open up markets and expand exports;
- involve new technology and equipment for the comprehensive use of natural resources, and recycling of resources, and prevention of environment pollution;

---

[8] Trade and Development Board, *Trade and Investment Guide: China*, Singapore: Arther Andersen, 1993, p. 120.
[9] *China Economic News*, Beijing, 24 July 1995.

- can have a better use of manpower and natural resources in the central and western parts of the country, and are in accord with the state industrial policies; and
- are encouraged by state regulations or policies.

Projects to be encouraged can enjoy a range of preferential treatment as stipulated by state laws and administrative regulations. Besides, if the projects are connected with the construction and operation of energy and transportation infrastructure (coal, electricity, local railways, roads and ports) that require large investment and have long reimbursement periods, the investors can expand their business scope to related areas upon state approval.

Projects to be **restricted** include those:

- with technologies that have been well developed domestically or already introduced from abroad; or projects that would add to a domestic production capacity that has already well satisfied domestic demand;
- in sectors that are only open for foreign investment on a trial basis or are under state monopoly franchise;
- that involve prospecting and exploiting rare and precious mineral resources;
- that involve industries under the state unified planning; and
- that are restricted by state laws and administrative regulations.

According to the State's industrial policies and needs arising from macroeconomic control, restricted foreign-funded projects are divided into sub-category A and sub-category B. The restricted projects shall have a definite operation term. In the case of joint venture, the fixed assets put in by the Chinese side should come from the Chinese firm's own capital or assets (without using bank loans or raising funds).

Foreign investment is **prohibited** for projects that fall into any of the following categories:

- Projects that endanger the country's security or social and public interest;
- Projects that would cause environmental pollution or bring harm to natural resources and human health;

- Projects that have to occupy large tracts of farm land, are harmful to environment protection and development of land resources, and/or endanger the security of military facilities and their effective uses;
- Projects that have to use China's own special craftsmanship or indigenous skills for production;
- Other projects that are banned by the state law and administrative regulations.

Projects not belonging to the categories of being encouraged, restricted or forbidden are those in the **allowed** category. The first catalogue published in June 1995 covered 315 sectors. A more recent catalogue of Major Industries, Products, and Technologies Encouraged for Development in China took effect on January 1, 1998, and covers several hundreds of products and technologies in 29 industries.

Based on the above principles, the State Planning Commission regularly compiles, updates and promulgates the Guiding Catalogue of Industries for Foreign Investment. Government authorities' evaluation and approval of foreign-funded projects should be made in compliance with the Guiding Catalogue of Industries for Foreign Investment. The Catalogue of Industries for Guiding Overseas Investment (December 1997) provides a more detailed list of projects being encouraged, restricted or forbidden.[10]

China's accession to the WTO may remove some of the restrictions specified in these catalogues. For instance, in its 1999 deal with the US on WTO accession, China made commitments to phase out most restrictions in a broad range of services sectors, including distribution, banking, insurance, telecommunications, professional services such as accountancy and legal consulting, business and computer related services, motion pictures and video and sound recording services. It is highly plausible that China will revise rather than abandon these catalogues for guiding foreign investment after its WTO accession.

---

[10] *China Economic News*, Beijing, 2 March 1998.

3. Effects of Industrial Policy

There are different ways to gauge the effects of industrial policy. For instance, Zhang, Zhang and Wan (1998) summarised the features of China's import tariffs as of "high rates, multiple reductions and exemptions, and a narrow base" (pp. 31–34). They also pointed out that the import approval procedure involves high transaction costs and opportunities for rent seeking. Using data of 25 categories of imports, they estimated that trade liberalisation could bring in a static gain of consumer surplus equivalent to 19.5 % of the sum of domestic production and landed value of imports before liberalisation. Netting off the loss of producer surplus and government tariff revenues, the country could still enjoy a net (static) efficiency gain of US$ 5 billion per year through liberalising these imports, or 14% of the consumer-surplus gain.

Taiwan's Chung-Hua Institute for Economic Research published a comprehensive report on China's industrial policy in 1995. The report (CHIER, 1995) found that China's fastest growing five industries from 1991–1993 were all related to the infrastructure, energy and raw material sectors. However, of the four efficiency indicators for industrial enterprises, namely value-added to output value ratio, profit-tax to capital ratio, profit-tax to output value, and total labour productivity (output value to employment) ratio, all but the last one had declined from 1980 through 1993. Finally, the report applied the Data Envelopment Analysis developed by Charnes, Cooper and Rhodes (1978) to work out the rankings of China's industrial sectors from 1987 to 1992. During the researched period, the three pillar manufacturing sectors, namely electronic and telecommunications equipment, raw chemical materials and chemical products, and transport equipment, all ranked very low and did not show much improvement.

Lu and Tang (1997) examined the change of GDP composition by sector from 1980 to 1995 and found that industrial policy had only been partially successful in changing China's industrial structure. The two supposedly prioritised categories, "transportation, postal and telecommunications services" and "other tertiary sectors", saw their shares rise in the late 1980s but the trend was reversed in the first half of the 1990s. Within the heavy industry, the growth of the extraction and raw material sectors lagged behind the growth of the manufacturing sector in terms of output, sales and fixed assets. This phenomenon did not meet the priorities put forward in the Eighth Five-year Plan. In the manufacturing sector, all the three prioritised sub-sectors were outstanding in terms of output growth, asset value and sales.

The view of these mixed effects is shared by some Chinese scholars. Jiang (1996), for instance, pointed out that the state policy to eliminate infrastructure bottleneck had limited effects in the 1980s. Efforts to restrict repeated construction of some over-supplied manufacturing projects in the 1980s were a failure. Promoting textile and light industries in the late 1970s and early 1980s, however, was very successful.

Liu, Yao, and Zhang (1999) used a shift-share method to quantify the components of economic growth and structural changes in employment and investment at both the national and regional levels in China from 1986 to 1994. They found that these structural changes followed a clear regional pattern that favoured some coastal provinces. Their study, however, only analysed shifts in employment and investment among agriculture, industry and service sectors.

In the following analyses, industrial policy impact on business incentives, structural changes, and resource allocation efficiency will be examined in turn.

Impact on Business Incentives

The 1994 tax reform unified nominal corporate income tax rate with some exceptional preferential rates reserved for certain types of foreign investments (see Lu and Tang, 1997 for more details). Most of those preferential rates, however, were gradually phased out in the 1990s. For indigenous firms, the major industry-specific difference in tax burden arises from tax on city maintenance and construction, consumption tax, resource tax and extra charge for education, etc. Table 3A illustrates these differences across manufacturing sectors by displaying the Effective Sales-related Tax Rate on Added Value (ESTR):

$$\text{ESTR} = \frac{\text{Taxes and extra charges on sales of goods}}{(\text{Revenue of sales} - \text{Costs of sales})/(1 + R_{VAT})} \quad (1)$$

where R_{VAT} is value-added tax rate.

In Table 3A, we can observe that, generally, manufacturing industries and the light industry using non-farm products as raw material had tax rates more than 5 percentage points lower than the rate for all industries. The ranking displayed in Table 3B appears to be consistent with official priority policies: The sectors of "electronic and telecommunications equipment", "instruments, meters, cultural and office machinery" and "special purpose equipment" were ranked top in the period. The "transport equipment" sector was in number 1 position in 1991 but dropped to number 9 and 7 in 1995 and 1998 respectively. In contrast, the "ordinary machinery" sector notched up a gain from position 10 in 1991 to position 4 in 1998.

Table 3A. Effective Sales-related Tax Rate on Added Value
(Figures in bold are rated more than 5 percentage points lower than the rate for all industries)

	1991	1995	1998
Light Industry	53.6%	41.6%	42.8%
using farm products as raw material	60.7%	47.6%	51.0%
using non-farm products as raw material	**38.1%**	**29.1%**	**28.1%**
Heavy Industry	45.4%	38.4%	41.2%
mining and quarrying	58.2%	42.2%	48.3%
raw materials industry	52.8%	49.1%	55.6%
manufacturing	**34.1%**	**28.3%**	**28.4%**
-petroleum processing and coke refinery	71.4%	60.7%	77.3%
-raw chemical materials and chemical products	**28.6%**	**29.2%**	**33.6%**
-chemical fibre	**35.9%**	**30.8%**	43.5%
-non-metal mineral products (construction material)	**42.1%**	**35.6%**	**38.0%**
-ordinary machinery	53.0%	**28.1%**	**28.4%**
-special purpose equipment	**36.2%**	**25.3%**	**27.0%**
-transport equipment	**24.4%**	36.6%	**36.1%**
-electronic and telecommunications equipment	**26.0%**	**20.2%**	**20.1%**
-instruments, meters, cultural and office machinery	**30.1%**	**25.0%**	**22.3%**
All industries	49.1%	39.7%	41.9%

Sources: Calculated from China Statistical Yearbook, various issues.

Table 3B. Effective Sales-related Tax Rate Ranking
(from low to high tax rates)

Industrial sector	1991	1995	1998	Mean
-electronic and telecommunications equipment	2	1	1	1.33
-instruments, meters, cultural and office machinery	4	2	2	2.67
-special purpose equipment	6	3	3	4.00
-raw chemical materials and chemical products	3	6	6	5.00
light industry using non-farm products as raw material	7	5	4	5.33
-transport equipment	1	9	7	5.67
-ordinary machinery	10	4	5	6.33
-chemical fibre	5	7	9	7.00
-non-metal mineral products (construction material)	8	8	8	8.00
mining and quarrying	11	10	10	10.33
raw materials industry	9	12	12	11.00
light industry using farm products as raw material	12	11	11	11.33
-petroleum processing and coke refinery	13	13	13	13.00

Sources: Calculated from *China Statistical Yearbook*, various issues.

It is difficult to evaluate the overall impact of trade protection on business incentives since there are so many tariff and non-tariff barriers to trade. On top of that, official intervention towards some domestic prices also has significant incentive impact on business. To capture the combined effects of trade protection and domestic price policy, I compiled the "Protection Index" based on the domestic wholesale and retail statistics:

$$\text{Protection Index} = \frac{\exp.\ (\text{sales margin})}{\exp.\ (\text{import ratio})} \quad (2)$$

in which:
exp. = the constant "e" raised to the power of the number in brackets (The constant e = 2.718282, the base of the natural logarithm.)[11]
Sales margin = (sales revenue − purchase cost)/ purchase cost
Import ratio = import / purchase cost

---

[11] The nominator and denominator are made exponential to encompass the possible negative sales margins and near-zero import ratios.

Table 4. Protection Index in Wholesale Commerce (1998)

Merchandise	Import Ratio	Sales Margin	Protection Index
Machinery and electrical equipment	22.0%	−5.0%	0.76
Natural minerals	29.3%	7.2%	0.80
Wool, cotton and natural fibre	4.0%	−6.1%	0.90
Chemical and allied products	12.0%	7.0%	0.95
Newspapers and books	2.1%	−0.2%	0.98
Metal products	5.0%	5.7%	1.01
Farming producer goods	6.6%	8.5%	1.02
Cars, motorcycles and appliances	0.9%	4.1%	1.03
Of which: cars	0.9%	4.5%	1.04
Energy products	5.1%	9.7%	1.05
Of which: petroleum and products	5.8%	8.7%	1.03
coal and products	1.2%	17.7%	1.18
Recycling industry	0.8%	6.3%	1.06
Handmade fibre, clothing, shoes and hats	12.4%	18.1%	1.06
Building materials	2.9%	10.8%	1.08
Metals, electric power and chemicals	3.7%	11.6%	1.08
Artifacts	12.1%	22.2%	1.11
Daily miscellaneous products	1.7%	12.4%	1.11
Daily merchandise	4.1%	16.1%	1.13
Medicines and medical appliances	1.7%	14.7%	1.14
Food, beverages, tobacco and other Households appliances	2.7%	15.9%	1.14
Of which: food, edible oil	10.3%	3.9%	0.94
tobacco products	0.3%	17.8%	1.19
Timber	3.4%	16.9%	1.14
Products not classified elsewhere	21.6%	36.1%	1.16
Total	5.5%	11.7%	1.06

Sources: Calculated from *Almanac of China's Domestic Trade*, 1999.

According to Table 4, by 1998, some pillar industry products, such as "machinery and electrical equipment", were not well protected from import competition. The car industry enjoyed effective protection as import ratio did not exceed 1% while the wholesalers had a sales margin of 4.5%. This level of protection, however, was much lower than many other merchandise. "Tobacco products" received the most effective protection, followed by "timber" and "medicines and medical appliances". High profit margin and low import ratio indicate huge rents associated with protection. Media reports on smuggling cases seem to be consistent with this indication.

Impact on Structural Changes

Overall, changes in China's economic structure have been largely in line with the industrial policies in the past decade. For instance, in the first half of the 1990s, the three pillar manufacturing sub-sectors, namely the "special purpose equipment", "electronic and telecommunications", and "instruments, metres and office equipment" all grew faster than the industry average in gross output value, fixed assets increment, and sales (Lu and Tang, 1997, pp. 76–77).

Table 5 gives structural changes of foreign direct investment. The share of FDI hosted by the manufacturing sector varied from 45% to 85 % over the years. Starting in 1992, the shares of investment in "construction" and "real estate and public utilities" increased significantly. Another fast growing sector was "Transportation, storage, post & telecommunications". These changes are fairly compatible to the industrial policy guidelines.

In terms of creating some industries' comparative advantage, China's industrial policy has been very successful. The share of exports of goods and services in China's GDP rose from 6 % to over 20 % during 1980–98. China's merchandise trade balance with the rest of the world moved towards surplus in 1990 and grew to over US$ 43 billion in 1998. The composition of trade shifted drastically from primary products to manufactures, which today account for about 90 % of Chinese exports and 80 % of imports (Figures 1A and 1B). As one of the world's top ten trading economies, China now contributes to one fifth of the US trade deficit, equally significant as another source of US trade imbalance — Japan.

Table 5. Percentage Composition of Contracted Foreign Direct Investment (1988–98)

Shares	1988	1989	1990	1991	1992	1993	1994	1995	1996	1997	1998
Farming, forestry, animal husbandry and fishery	3.94	2.17	1.85	1.84	1.17	1.07	1.18	1.90	1.55	2.09	2.31
Mining and quarrying	0.00	0.00	0.00	0.00	0.00	0.00	0.00	0.00	0.00	1.41	1.64
Manufacturing	75.92	83.28	84.43	80.34	56.20	45.92	53.10	67.54	68.90	53.06	59.17
Construction	2.24	1.20	2.75	1.12	3.16	3.48	2.89	2.10	2.73	6.12	3.36
Geological prospecting and water conservancy	0.03	0.00	0.01	0.00	0.00	0.07	0.06	0.01	0.02	0.04	0.00
Transportation, storage, post & telecommunications	1.72	0.93	0.55	0.79	2.66	1.34	2.46	1.86	2.18	5.14	4.42
Commerce & catering	1.21	1.20	1.62	1.45	2.48	4.13	4.74	3.75	3.20	3.61	2.52
Real Estate & public utilities & service	10.01	9.35	6.86	12.56	31.11	39.28	28.86	19.54	17.54	24.60	22.32
Of which: Real Estate										12.20	12.76
Social services (hotels, etc)										5.23	5.78
Healthcare, sporting and social welfare	0.10	0.64	0.58	0.53	0.68	0.43	2.39	0.92	0.48	0.28	0.27
Education & culture	0.84	0.13	0.08	0.47	0.17	0.41	0.74	0.38	0.23	0.14	0.04
Science & Tech	0.14	0.06	0.48	0.15	0.11	0.53	0.33	0.30	0.24	0.27	0.00
Finance & insurance	0.22	0.00	0.00	0.00	0.01	0.07	0.53	0.06	0.00	0.00	0.00
Other	3.62	1.04	0.80	0.74	2.25	3.27	2.72	1.64	2.92	3.25	3.66
Total	100	100	100	100	100	100	100	100	100	100	100

Sources: *Almanac of China's Foreign Economic Relations*, various issues.

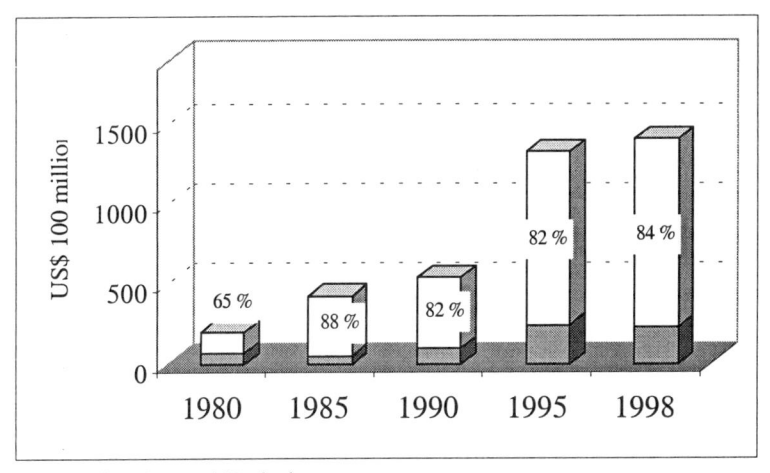

[Figure 1A: Bar chart showing US$ 100 million on y-axis, years 1980, 1985, 1990, 1995, 1998 on x-axis, with percentages 65%, 88%, 82%, 82%, 84%]

Sources: China Statistical Yearbook, various issues.

Figure 1A. Change of Import Structure
(The percentage refers to the share of manufactured goods)

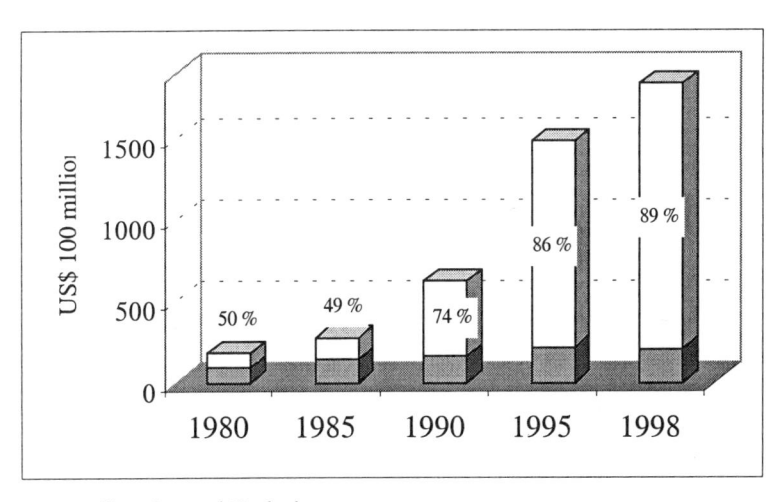

[Figure 1B: Bar chart showing US$ 100 million on y-axis, years 1980, 1985, 1990, 1995, 1998 on x-axis, with percentages 50%, 49%, 74%, 86%, 89%]

Sources: China Statistical Yearbook, various issues.

Figure 1B. Change of Export Structure
(The percentage refers to the share of manufactured goods)

Impact on Allocation Efficiency

To evaluate cross-industry allocation efficiency of the Chinese economy in the 1990s, I will first check the "gross allocation effect", following the methodology developed by Syrquin (1986):

$$A(y) = G_y - \Sigma_i \rho_i G_{yi} \qquad (3)$$

where $A(y)$ is "gross allocation effect" (GAE); G_y and G_{yi} are the growth rate of aggregate labour productivity (real GDP per employee) in the whole economy and in sector i respectively; and ρ_i is the share of sector i in total output (real GDP).

According to Syrquin, the gross allocation effect "measures the growth in aggregate labor productivity that would have taken place with the observed labor shifts, had the relative labor productivities remained constant." The GAE, however, "is a partial measure since it ignores factors other than labor and computes the gains and losses from employment shifts in terms of average and not marginal products" (Syrquin, 1986, p. 252).

To account for the full reallocation effects of both capital and labor, Syrquin also proposes the concept of total reallocation effect (TRE), following the same line of analysis:

$$\text{TRE} = \lambda_a - \Sigma_i \rho_i \lambda_i \qquad (4)$$

which is precisely the amount by which the aggregate growth rate of total factor productivity (λ_a) exceeds the weighted average of the sectoral rates of TFP (λ_i), when the reallocation of resources leads to a reduction in the extent of disequilibrium (Syrquin, 1986, p. 253). A positive TRE indicates that, on the average, sectors with above-average marginal products of capital or labor have increased their share in total capital or employment during the period under investigation.

We apply the above approach to the analysis of six sectors in China's GDP account (Table 6) from 1985 to 1999 using data from *China Statistical Yearbook*. We use the "number of employed persons" as a proxy for labor input (L) and the "consumption of total energy by sector (in tons of

Table 6. Percentage Composition of China's GDP Gross Domestic Product

		Primary Industry	Secondary Industry		Tertiary Industry		
			Industry	Construction	Transportation, post and telecom	Commerce & catering trade	Other tertiary-industry services
Share of GDP	1985	28.4	38.5	4.7	4.5	9.8	14.2
	1990	27.7	37.0	4.6	6.2	7.7	17.4
	1999	17.7	42.7	6.6	5.4	8.4	19.2
Share of jobs	1985	62.4	16.7	4.1	2.6	4.6	9.6
	1990	53.4	15.2	3.8	2.5	4.4	20.8
	1999	47.4	12.8	4.8	2.9	6.7	25.3

Source: China Statistical Yearbook, 2000.

SCE)" (E) for variable capital input.[12] As for a proxy for fixed capital input, the "fixed capital stock" data for the six major sectors are not readily available. We therefore estimate the data by applying the standard perpetual inventory approach. We first find the annual investment amount (I) by summing the "investment in capital construction by sector" and the "investment in innovation and upgrading by sector". Then we sum up the "newly increased fixed assets through capital construction by sector" and the "newly increased fixed assets through innovation and upgrading by sector" to get the annual change rate of fixed capital (ΔK). Since

$$K_t = I_t + (1 - d)K_{t-1} \qquad (5)$$

we have

$$K_{t-1} = I_t - \Delta K_t \qquad (6)$$

Using (6) to estimate the initial-year capital stock, we are able to derive the capital stock series for the consecutive years by adding in the

---

[12] The energy consumption statistics for 1999 is not yet available in the 2000 issue. So we projected the 1999 energy figures based on the previous two years' average growth rate of energy use.

respective ΔK. The resulting estimates for the "industry sector" match very close to the published statistics of the "average net value of fixed assets" for industrial enterprises in the period under study.

With these data, we may apply the neoclassical growth framework to calculate the overall and sectoral rates of total factor productivity (TFP):

$$Y_{ti} = A_i L_{ti}^{\beta_{Li}} K_{ti}^{\beta_{Ki}} E_{ti}^{\beta_{Ei}} \tag{7}$$

and

$$\ln TFP_{ti} = \ln Y_{ti} - \beta_{Li} \ln L_{ti} - \beta_{Ki} \ln K_{ti} - \beta_{Ei} \ln E_{ti} \tag{8}$$

where β_{Li} is (computed) elasticity of labor, β_{Ki} (computed) elasticity of fixed capital, β_{Vi} (computed) elasticity of variable capital and A_i the exogenous technical factor. The TFP growth rate is simply $\lambda_{ti} = \Delta \ln TFP_{ti}$. The length of time series (t = 14 in the first data set and t = 13 in the second data set), however, limits the statistical significance of estimates for the variables in (7). Alternatively, we use the following model to estimate the coefficients:

$$\ln Y_{ti} = \alpha_0 + \alpha_i D_i + \beta_L \ln L_{ti} + \beta_K \ln K_{ti} + \beta_V \ln E_{ti} \tag{9}$$

where D_i is dummy variable (=1 or =0 otherwise) for sector i.

The results of estimated Gross Allocation Effect and Total Allocation Effect among China's six major sectors are displayed in Tables 7. These figures indicate that there was no significant improvement in cross-industry allocation efficiency in the 1990s.

4. Conclusions and Prospects

China's industrial policy regime inherited some legacies from the previously centrally planned economy (such as instruments 1, 2, and 3 in Table 2). As China further restructures its state-owned enterprises and develops the non-state sectors, the relative importance of those instruments associated with administrative measures and central planning features is expected to be diminishing further or relevant only to the provision of public goods and services.

Table 7. Gross Allocation Effect and Total Allocation Effect (1986–99)

	1986	1987	1988	1989	1990	1991	1992	1993	1994	1995	1996	1997	1998	1999	Mean
$\Sigma_i \rho_i G_{yi}$	3.62	7.53	8.04	4.14	-7.56	8.92	13.82	12.64	11.53	9.69	10.33	10.70	19.07	9.77	8.73
G_y	5.82	8.20	7.56	2.10	-9.99	7.67	12.89	12.10	10.89	9.00	7.83	7.30	7.12	5.89	6.74
$A(y)$	2.19	0.67	-0.48	-2.04	-2.43	-1.25	-0.94	-0.55	-0.63	-0.70	-2.50	-3.40	-11.95	-3.88	-1.99
$\Sigma_i \rho_i \lambda_i$	-2.01	1.78	2.55	-2.51	-6.73	4.40	7.22	5.51	4.85	2.70	1.43	-0.98	-1.29	-4.42	0.89
λ_a	-2.42	1.15	1.53	-2.75	-5.56	2.67	5.77	3.92	2.30	1.06	-1.16	-3.01	-4.77	-5.67	-0.50
TRE	-0.41	-0.63	-1.02	-0.24	1.18	-1.73	-1.45	-1.59	-2.54	-1.64	-2.59	-2.03	-3.48	-1.25	-1.39

With China's accession to the WTO, many of the elements that form the foundation of this industrial policy regime will have to be dismantled or phased out in about five years. Most of the trade barriers are expected to be further lowered or removed. Foreign-funded enterprises will have a better chance to gain "national treatment". In its 1999 deal with the US on WTO accession, China committed itself to phase out the remaining import quotas, generally by 2002, but no later than 2005.[13]

Those industrial policy instruments which do not directly conflict with WTO rules may remain. Some of them may become more active and important. For instance, the preferential interest and tax rates and favourable financing for certain industries and the licensing and approval of investment projects may apply to both indigenous and foreign firms as well. However, the domestic demand for such preferential policies may not be as strong as before since the WTO's "national treatment" principle will allow these benefits to be shared by the foreign firms and thus reduce their attractiveness to the indigenous companies. In such a context, it is more difficult to carry out industrial policies specially designed to nurture and protect indigenous firms.

Evidence presented in this paper indicates that the industrial policy in the 1990s was effective in providing business incentives for the desired structural changes to shift comparative advantages towards some favoured industries. It is, however, unlikely that such policies have improved the allocation efficiency across industries. Evidence of the deteriorating GAE (gross-allocation-effect) and TRE (total-reallocation-effect) in cross-industry resource allocation suggests huge potential gains for China to revamp its industrial policy regime in line with the WTO rules.

REFERENCES

Charnes, A., W. W. Cooper, and E. Rhodes. 1978. "Measuring the efficiency of decision making units", *European Journal of Operational Research*, 2 (5): 429–444.

---

[13] US State Department Summary of U.S.-China Bilateral WTO Agreement, 2 February 2000, http://www.chinapntr.gov/bilatsumm.htm.

Chung-Hua Institute for Economic Research (CHIER), 1995. "A Study on the Status of Mainland Industrial Policy and Development" [Research Report 8406-1-185: 0105186(2)]. Taipei: Chung-Hua Institute for Economic Research.

Johnson, Chalmers. 1984. "Introduction: the idea of industrial policy". In Johnson C. ed., *The Industrial Policy Debate*. San Francisco: Institute for Contemporary Studies.

Jiang, Xiaojuan. 1996. *Industrial Policy in the Transition Period: an Analysis of the Chinese Experience*. Shanghai: San Lian Bookstore.

Liu, Aying, Shujie Yao, and Zongyi Zhang. 1999. "Economic growth and structural changes in employment and investment in China, 1985-1994". *Economics of Planning* 32: 171–190.

Lu, Ding and Zhimin Tang. 1997. *State Intervention and Business in China: the Role of Preferential Policies*. London: Edward Elgar.

Syrquin, Moshe. 1986. "Productivity growth and factor reallocation". In Chenery, Hollis B. ed., *Industrialization and Growth*. Oxford: Oxford University Press.

Takahashi, Takuma. 1997. "Industrial policies in developed and developing economies from the perspective of East Asian experience". In Masuyama, S., Vandenbrink, D. and S. Y. Chia, eds., *Industrial Policies in East Asia*. Tokyo: Club Foundation for Global Studies.

Wade, Robert. 1990. *Governing the Market: Economic Theory and the Role of Government in East Asian Industrialization*. Princeton: Princeton University Press.

Zhang, Lianshun and Wu Fang (eds.) 1994. *A Practical Guide to New Tax Laws* (in Chinese), Beijing: China Development Publishing House.

Zhang, Shuguang, Zhang Yansheng, and Wan Zhongxin. 1999. *Measuring the Costs of Protection in China*. Washington: Institute for International Economics.

Zhang, X. and Long. G. 1997. "China's industrial policies in the process of marketization". In Masuyama, S., Vandenbrink, D. and S. Y. Chia, eds., *Industrial Policies in East Asia*. Tokyo: Club Foundation for Global Studies.

Part II

Fiscal Federalism and Reforms

5

Tax Reforms and Government Revenues

LIN SHUANGLIN*

The decline of the government revenue share in GDP has become a major concern for the Chinese government. This paper shows that lowered corporate tax rates, small tax bases, and tax evasions are the main reasons for the decline of government revenue share in GDP. Low budgetary revenues have resulted in low budgetary expenditures and growing budget deficits, stimulated the expansion of extra-budgetary and off budgetary revenues, and made the privatisation of state enterprises more difficult. Although the national data from 1978 to 1996 show that the share of tax revenues in GDP has declined as per capita GDP increases, evidence from thirty Chinese provinces indicates that provinces with higher per capita GDP have higher government revenue shares.

---

*Dr. LIN Shuanglin is Associate Professor of Economics at the University of Nebraska, USA. Dr. LIN was a Visiting Research Fellow at the East Asian Institute, National University of Singapore in 2001. The author thanks Professors John Wong, Jack Hou, and Shufeng Song for their helpful comments.

1. INTRODUCTION

Chinese government budgetary revenues have decreased from 32% of GDP in 1978 to 11.6% of GDP in 1997. Meanwhile the share of central government spending in total government spending accounted for only 27% in 1996. This paper will analyse the reasons for and consequences of the decline in Chinese government revenues, examine the relationship between government revenue and per capita income based on both national and provincial data, and discuss tax reform options for China.

The decline of the Chinese government revenue has been a major concern for Chinese policy makers and economists all over the world.[1] Stiglitz (1998) believed that the Chinese government revenue share in GDP is too small comparing with other countries and is not adequate to fulfill China's ambitious development plan.[2] Brean (1998) argued that, China's economic development and social stability needs a larger government revenue, and warned that, if the government revenue stays low, the end result could be serious weakening of the government's ability to provide essential public goods and services, threatening macroeconomic stability and jeopardising economic transition. Other studies such as Chen (1996) and Huang (1996) also advocated an increase in the Chinese government revenues. The Chinese government vowed to reverse this trend of decline in the share of government revenues in GDP in order to increase the ability of government macroeconomic control.[3] The target share of government revenues in GDP was set at 20% and the target share of central government tax revenues in total government revenues was 60% [See Liu (1998) and Wang (1998), former Ministers of Finance]. However, many fundamental issues have not been fully addressed, such as what are the reasons for and consequences of the

---

[1] In 1997, total government revenues were 865.1 billion yuan, and GDP was 7477.2 billion yuan. See *Statistical Yearbook of China*, 1998.

[2] See Joseph Stiglitz, *China's Reform Strategies in the Second Stage*, A Speech at Peking University, *People's Daily*, November 13, 1998.

[3] See China's People's Congress (1996), *China's Ninth Five-Year Plan for National Economy and Social Development and the Objectives for the Year of 2010*; and Liu (1998), former Chinese Minister of Finance.

decline in government revenues, and how to raise government revenues. To answer these questions, detailed analyses of Chinese government revenues are required.

Our analyses show that lowered corporate tax rates, small tax bases, and tax evasions are the main reasons for the low government revenue share in GDP. Unlike prior studies which blame the decline in the profitability of state enterprises as the major reason for the decline in government revenues, we find that state enterprises, which are benefited from the government's favourable policy in loan markets, pay proportionally much higher taxes than non-state enterprises.

The consequence of a low government budgetary revenue is severe. Low government budgetary revenues are accompanied by low government budgetary expenditures which result in insufficient provisions of public goods, and large government budget deficits which lead to the growth of government debt issuance. Insufficient budgetary revenues also stimulated an expansion of extra-budgetary and off budgetary revenues which may cause misuse of scare resources and corruption. In addition, the small size of government budgetary revenue and its heavy reliance on state enterprises make the privatisation of state enterprises more difficult.

The national data from 1978 to 1997 indicates that the share of government revenues in GDP decreases, as per capita real GDP increases, a phenomena which is contrary to the Wagner Hypothesis. This inverse relationship has resulted from structural changes in China. Surprisingly, the cross-province analysis yields an important result — provinces with high per capita income have high government revenue share in GDP. There have been numerous studies testing the Wagner's hypothesis. Generally, the result from time series analyses supports the hypothesis, while the result based on cross-sectional studies (cross-country studies) refutes the hypothesis.[4] Cross-countries studies are often criticised for

---

[4] Using data from sixty countries for the period of 1957–1960, Hinrichs (1965) showed that although there is a significant correlation between government revenue share and per capita income for all sixty countries, none exists among only developed or developing countries. Musgrave (1969, pp. 122–124) mentioned that time-series data from industrial countries support Wagner's hypothesis but cross-section data from these counties did

ignoring the structural differences among countries. Within one country and under the same tax rule, the problem would be less severe than in a cross-country situation. This cross-province result has a profound implication for Chinese fiscal policy — as the economy develops government revenue share will increase without increasing the tax rate.

Section 2 discusses the government revenue system and tax reforms from a historical perspective. Section 3 discusses factors which determine the decline of the government revenue share in GDP. Section 4 analyses the consequences of a low government budgetary revenue. Section 5 examines the relationship between government revenue share and per capita income by using data from thirty provinces for the period from 1978 to 1996. Section 6 discusses the central and local government revenues. Section 7 provides concluding remarks.

2. Tax Reforms and Government Revenue in China

Like most people in the world, the Chinese do not like the government to overly collect taxes. Here is a story back to 2000 years ago when Confucius was still alive. One day, Confucius travelled to a remote mountain area and saw a lady crying. He went over and asked the lady why. The lady replied that her son was eaten by a tiger recently, and her husband and her father in-law had been also eaten by tigers many years ago. Confucius was puzzled and asked why they chose to live in this dangerous area, instead of an area without tigers. The lady replied that they could not afford to pay heavy taxes in a safe area and tax collectors could not reach this remote mountain area. Confucius was so sad and said, "Heavy tax burden is fiercer than tigers (*ke zheng meng yu hu ye*)!" Many times in Chinese history, heavy taxes resulted in rebellion and even collapse of dynasties.

---

not. Using international 115 countries for the period of 1950–80, Ram (1987) found that, while there is support for the hypothesis in some time series data sets, such support is lacking in most cross-country estimates.

2.1. Tax System before 1978

In 1949, the People's Republic of China was established. Under a centrally-planned economic system, the government controlled the production and allocation of resources. Budgetary principle was collecting revenues and spending them uniformly (*tongshou tongzhi*). State enterprises were required to turn in all their profits to the state. Profits from state enterprises were the major source of government revenues.[5] There existed no competition among firms, and government set prices for almost all products. The government taxed farmers explicitly through the agricultural tax and implicitly through lowering its purchasing prices of agricultural products.

2.2. Tax Reforms

In 1978, China started market-oriented economic reforms. The essence of the reforms has been to decentralise the economy (i.e., shift allocation decisions towards the enterprises) and increase production efficiency. Tax reform is an important part of economic reform, which aimed at providing state enterprises production incentives, cutting off fiscal dependence of state-enterprises on government, equalising tax burdens among enterprises, and promoting fair competition. Tax reforms experienced the following stages.

A. Allow the State Enterprises to Keep Some Profits (*fangquan rangli*)

Major fiscal reforms have occurred since 1979. Three measures were taken by the central government: raised agricultural product prices by 20% which were set by government, raised wages and salaries for employees in state enterprises and government agencies, lowered taxes and allowed state enterprises keep a part of their profits. Experiments of fiscal reforms began in 1979 to allow the state enterprises to keep part of their profit in order to expand production and to issue bonuses and

---

[5] In 1978, tax revenues only accounted for 46% of total government revenues. See *Statistical Yearbook of China*, 1998, p. 273.

awards to workers. These three measures which reduced government tax revenues and increased government spending, immediately resulted in high government budget deficit in 1979 and 1980.

B. Substitute Taxes for Profit (li gai shui)

The success of these experiments in promoting production encouraged the government to pursue further fiscal reform in 1983, i.e., make state enterprises subject to income taxes — a reform which is commonly called substituting taxes for profit (li gai shui). This reform experienced two stages. In the first stage, state enterprises were divided into two groups, large and small. The corporate income (profit) tax rate for the large enterprises was 55%, and it was progressive for small enterprises. The after-tax profits were divided between enterprises and the government.[6] The two main problems were: there was only one single tax, the corporate income tax, which did not allow the government control resource allocation effectively; and enterprises were still required to submit part of their after-tax profits. Thus, government's revenues included both taxes and profits.

The second stage of substituting taxes for profit (li gai shui) began in October 1984. State enterprises were subjected to eleven different taxes if applicable (such as product tax, value-added tax, salt tax, natural resource tax, corporate income tax, adjustment tax or tax on after-income-tax profits, housing tax, land tax, vehicle tax and city construction and maintenance tax), but they no longer had obligation to submit profits to the state. Thus, the process of substituting of taxes for profits was completed. Tax revenue became overwhelmingly dominant in total revenues.[7]

This reform increased state enterprises' incentives to make more profits. The system still comprised some problems: medium and large firms not only needed to pay income tax but also adjustment tax which

---

[6] See Shengming He, *Twenty-year Fiscal Reforms in China* (*Zhongguo Caizheng Gaige Ershi Nian*, Zhengzhou, Zhonggu Chubanshe), 1998, p. 96.

[7] Tax revenues accounted for nearly 100% of total government revenues. See *Statistical Yearbook of China*, 1998, p. 273.

was enterprise-specific; many state enterprises suffered a loss and had to negotiate with the state for subsidies, just as under the profit remittance system; tax rate appeared to be high, but actual exemptions were also large, and tax revenues were not as high as expected; enterprises had strong incentives to expand investment which caused a heavy debt burden, since they could use the before-tax profits from new projects to pay the debt used to finance the projects.

C. The Contract Responsibility System

In December 1986, the Contract Responsibility System (CRS) was introduced on the basis of *substituting profit for tax*.[8] Under the CRS, enterprises were contracted to pay income tax and adjustment tax on a specific level of profit.[9] If they did not achieve that level of profit, they were supposed to make up the rest of the taxes from their own resources. If they exceeded the contract level of profit, they pay taxes at a lower rate on their additional profits. The contract levels were usually based on previous year's profits plus some predicted growth. The CRS provided strong incentives for SOEs to make profits. However, since the contracted profits were not set to grow at sufficiently high rate, the revenue growth from enterprise contracts did not keep pace with economic growth, and the CRS cause the government to loose its revenues. Also, under contract with the central government, different provinces remitted different percentages of local revenues to the central government; and counties also transferred different percentages of revenues to provincial governments.

D. Tax plus Profit System (*li shui fenliu*)

To increase government revenues, a new tax reform began in 1989. SOEs were required to pay corporate income taxes first, and then submit

---

[8] The system was introduced in agriculture first, then expanded to industry, finally used in the area of taxation.

[9] Contracts do not cover product tax, value-added tax, business tax, resource tax, and other taxes.

portion of their profits to the government. The basic idea is that as the owner of SOEs the government should get profits from SOEs. Also, SOEs no longer had the privilegeto use the before tax profits to repay debt caused by investment. To increase firms' ability to repay its debt, the government lowered income tax rate for small firms. The tax rate for large and medium enterprises was still 55%, but for small enterprises the tax rate was set uniformly at 35%.[10] Since the introduction of the CRS, negotiations between enterprises and the state and between central government and local governments had become extensive. Leaders of many SOEs were more concerned about how to bargain with government than how to compete with other firms. This severely subverted the process of enterprise reform.[11] In addition, over the years central government revenue share in total revenues decreased significantly, down to only 22% in 1993. The central government was determined to reverse this trend.

E. Tax Sharing System (*fen shui zhi*)

In 1994, a new tax system — tax sharing system was established. Several significant changes in the tax system took place, including reduction of the types of tax from thirty seven to twenty three; unification of the income tax rate for all enterprises to 33% (joint ventures preserve their preferential tax rates); division of taxes into three categories, namely, national taxes which were paid to the central government, joint taxes which were shared by the central and local governments, and local taxes which were paid to local governments; establishment of a central taxbureau (*guo shui ju*) and local tax bureau (*di shui ju*); and establishment of central to local tax rebate (*shuishou fanhuan*) system.[12]

---

[10] The rate was reduced to 33% in 1991.

[11] Bargaining existed under the old centrally-planned system on the issues concerning resource allocations.

[12] **Central government taxes** include (1) tariff, (2) consumption tax (similar to excise tax in the U.S.), (3) corporate income tax from central government-owned enterprises, (4) income tax from local banks and foreign banks and other financial institutions, (5) income tax from rail road, headquarters banks, headquarters insurance companies

The most important joint tax is the value-added tax, which is levied on all stages and spheres of industrial processing. Currently, there are two rates:[13] for products related to agricultural production (such as fertiliser, feeds, and machines) and basic consumption goods (such as foods, cooking oil, water, and natural gas) the tax rate is 13%; and for most other goods the rate is 17%. Of the value-added tax revenues, 75% are remitted to the central government and 25% remains in the province. The most significant local tax is business tax (*yingye shui*). It is levied on the transfer of intangible assets or sale of immovable properties, primarily "service enterprises" including transportation, communications, financial services, real estate sales, and entertainment. Education institutions and hospitals are exempted from this tax.

As a result of the tax reform, the central government share in total revenue increased from 22% in 1993 to 55.7% in 1994! However, the real tax revenue actually declined from 1993 to 1994.

Tax reforms provided incentives for SOEs to improve their productivity and increase their profits. However, since SOEs faced different production and market conditions, a uniform tax rule towards

---

(including business tax, income tax, profit and urban construction and maintenance tax), (6) profits from central government enterprises. **Local government taxes** include (1) business tax (excluding business tax from rail road, headquarters banks, and headquarters insurance companies), (2) income tax from local enterprises (excluding income tax from local banks and foreign banks and other financial institutions), (3) profits from local enterprises, personal income tax, urban land tax, fixed investment direction adjustment tax, (4) urban construction and maintenance tax (excluding the tax from rail road, headquarters banks, and headquarters insurance companies), (5) housing tax, (6) vehicle license tax, (7) urban real estate tax, (8) vehicle tax, (9) stamp tax, (10) land appreciation tax, (11) slaughtering tax, (12) agricultural (animal husbandry) tax, (13) cultivated land occupation tax, and (14) contract tax. **Taxes shared by the central and local governments** include (1) value-added tax (the share of the central government is 75%), (2) natural resource tax (only ocean oil resource tax belongs to the central government), (3) stamp tax from stock exchange (the share of the central government is 50%).

[13] See Provisional regulations of the People's Republic of China on value-added Tax, December 13, 1993 (In *A collection of Tax Laws and Regulations of the People's Republic of China*).

all of them may not create fair tax burden and fair competition among enterprises. The government still needs to subsidise loss-making SOEs. Moreover, tax reforms resulted in a decline of the share of government revenue in total GDP.

Tax revenues were only part of total government revenues. In 1978, tax revenues were only 51.93 billion yuan, accounting for 46% of total government revenues in 1978. After a series of tax reforms, the levels of tax revenues and total government revenues have been very close. In 1984, tax revenues were 80.49 billion yuan (at 1978 constant price), accounting for 58% of total government revenues. In 1997, tax revenues were 216.2 billion yuan (at 1978 constant price), accounting for 95.2% of total government revenues (which was 227.2 billion yuan).

2.3. Government Revenues from Various Taxes

Table 1 shows revenues from various taxes. Before 1985, taxes can be divided into three major categories, industry and commerce tax (tax imposed upon the gross receipts from sales of products or provision of services), tariff (taxes from imports and exports of goods and services), and agriculture and herdery tax.[14]

Tariff decreased from 16.0 billion yuan in 1985 to 8.0 billion yuan in 1996, a more than 50% drop. Meanwhile, from 1985 to 1996, the volume of trade (exports plus imports) grew at an annual rate of 13.8% and increased from 161.3 billion yuan to 638.8 billion yuan (at the 1978 constant price), a 4 times rise.[15] The decrease in tariff was caused by tax exemptions, the decrease in the tax rate on imported goods and the increase in the rebate rate on exports [see Li (1997)]. Clearly, the decrease in tariff has contributed to the decline in the government revenue.

Corporate income taxes from state enterprises declined by 59.3%, from 46.5 billion yuan in 1985 to 18.94 billion yuan in 1997. Corporate

---

[14] In China, tax laws are made by the National People's Congress and the Standing Committee of the National People's Congress.
[15] *Statistical Yearbook of China*, 1998.

income taxes from collective enterprises declined by 43.4%, from 7.82 billion yuan to 4.43 billion yuan in 1997. In the meantime, industrial output increased considerably. The real output of state owned enterprises grew at 3.65% annually and increased by 54.95% from 1985 to 1997; and the real output of collective owned enterprises grew at 12.83% annually and increased by 3.68 times from 1985 to 1997.[16] In 1997, corporate income taxes accounted for 10.8% of total tax revenues.[17]

Agriculture and herdery taxes increased from 3.28 billion yuan in 1985 to 9.78 billion yuan, a near 200% increase. In 1997, the output of agriculture and herdery accounted for 18.7% of GDP and shared 4.8% of taxes.[18] Product taxes were eliminated in 1994 while value-added tax increased considerably in the same year. From 1985 to 1996, value-added taxes increased considerably from 11.53 billion yuan to 78.42 billion yuan, a 6.8 time increase. Business tax also increased rapidly after its introduction in 1985. In 1994, consumption tax was introduced and sales tax was reduced in an equal amount.

The government is increasingly relying on consumption-related taxes (value-added tax, sales tax and consumption tax). In 1996, the share of value-added tax in total tax revenue reached 42.9%; the share of sales tax was 15.2; the share of consumption tax (introduced in 1994) was 8.0%; the share of corporate income taxes from state enterprises was 11.9%; the share of corporate income taxes from collective enterprises was 2.1%; the share of agriculture and herdery tax was 5.3%; and the share of tariff was 4.4%. China's tariff revenues and income tax revenues are much lower than countries at the same stage of economic development. Personal income tax accounted only for 2.5% of total tax revenues, and its share in GDP is almost negligible.

---

[16] *Statistical Yearbook of China*, 1998, p. 433.
[17] Studies show that in only 16 of 82 developing countries did the corporation income tax account for more than 20% of total taxes in the 1980s.
[18] *Statistical Yearbook of China*, 1998, p. 55.

Table 1. Composition of Real Tax Revenues *

(100 million yuan)

Year	Total	Industry & Commerce Tax	Tariff	Agriculture & Herdery Tax	Corporate Income Taxes State Enterprises	Corporate Income Taxes Collective Enterprises	Product Tax	Value Added Tax	Sales Tax	Consumption Tax
1978	519.28	462.12	28.76	28.40						
1979	527.27	472.85	25.49	28.93						
1980	528.86	472.25	31.02	25.60						
1981	569.01	494.58	48.82	25.61						
1982	620.59	552.46	42.07	26.05						
1983	677.37	601.53	47.06	28.79						
1984	804.89	687.71	87.57	29.60						
1985	1593.12	856.73	160.20	32.83	465.14	78.24	464.17	115.30	164.77	
1986	1539.57	885.27	111.65	32.78	438.44	71.43	402.50	170.98	192.25	
1987	1469.02	880.21	97.71	34.87	386.55	69.67	366.00	174.47	207.28	
1988	1384.17	860.29	89.76	42.67	330.59	60.86	278.48	222.57	230.41	
1989	1340.90	865.53	89.25	41.76	286.92	57.44	260.71	211.81	239.58	
1990	1358.62	895.04	76.56	42.30	290.86	53.87	279.70	192.59	248.31	
1991	1399.24	927.05	87.64	42.42	293.68	48.45	294.53	190.15	263.92	

Table 1 Continued

Year	Total	Industry & Commerce Tax	Tariff	Agriculture & Herdery Tax	Corporate Income Taxes State Enterprises	Corporate Income Taxes Collective Enterprises	Product Tax	Value Added Tax	Sales Tax	Consumption Tax
1992	1463.99	996.54	94.47	52.92	277.43	42.63	307.84	313.47	292.48	
1993	1669.40	1254.90	100.62	49.33	228.68	37.54	322.25	424.28	379.01	
1994	1652.77	1261.84	87.90	74.63	196.57	31.83		744.15	216.00	157.12
1995	1695.60	1288.87	81.95	78.09	213.25	33.43		730.79	243.07	152.06
1996	1828.96	1394.93	79.89	97.79	217.66	38.68		784.23	278.61	164.17
1997	2162.30	1740.29	83.90	104.38	189.41	44.31				

Sources: *Finance Yearbook of China*, 1997, p. 445; *Statistical Yearbook of China*, 1998, p. 274. General retail price index (1978=100) was used to calculate the figures.

* **Industry and Commerce Tax** includes eighteen different taxes, which are value-added tax, consumption tax, business tax, natural resource tax, corporate income tax, income tax on foreign invested and foreign owned enterprises, personal income tax, urban construction and maintenance tax, housing property tax, urban real estate tax, vehicle license tax, vehicle tax, land appreciation tax, urban land tax, stamp tax, fixed investment direction adjustment tax, slaughtering tax, and banquet tax. **Tariff** includes export and import tax and vessel tonnage tax. **Agriculture and Herdery Tax** includes three different taxes, which are agricultural (animal husbandry) tax, cultivated land occupation tax, and contract tax. Currently, there are a total of twenty-three different taxes in China.

3. FACTORS CONTRIBUTING TO THE DECLINE IN GOVERNMENT REVENUE SHARE

In 1978, China's per capita GDP was 379 yuan (about US$200). Since economic reforms started in 1978, the economy has been growing at an annual rate of around 10%. In 1997, per capita GDP reached 1601 yuan at 1978 constant price (6079 yuan at current price), more than four times as large as that in 1978. However, government revenue has not grown at the same pace as GDP. In 1978, total government revenues accounted for 31.2% of GDP, it was 22.36% of GDP in 1985, 10.9% of GDP in 1990, and 11.6% in 1997.[19] Figure 1 shows the share of government revenue in GDP, the share of government spending in GDP, and per capita GDP graphically.[20] It can be seen that, both the share of government revenues in GDP and the share of government spending in GDP were decreasing over time, as per capita real GDP increases.

Generally speaking, the decline in Chinese government revenue share in GDP is the result of economic decentralisation and tax reforms. In order to find ways to increase the government revenue share, an analysis of the specific determinants of government revenue is necessary. The factors which contributed to the decline in government budgetary revenues include lowered corporate income tax rates, declining profitability of the state enterprises, limited tax coverage, and tax evasions.

3.1. Lowered Corporate Tax Rate

Before the economic reforms started, state enterprises submitted all their profits to government, i.e., the corporate profit tax rate is 100%. Government revenues depended largely on profits from state enterprises. In 1978 the ratio of profits to tax revenue was 110%. As discussed in Section 2, over the years, the government has taken significant steps to reform the tax system, from allowing state enterprises to keep a part of

---

[19] See *Statistical Yearbook of China*, 1997.
[20] Similar diagram can be drawn even if we include extra-budgetary revenues and expenditures in government revenues, which accounts for more than 5% of GDP.

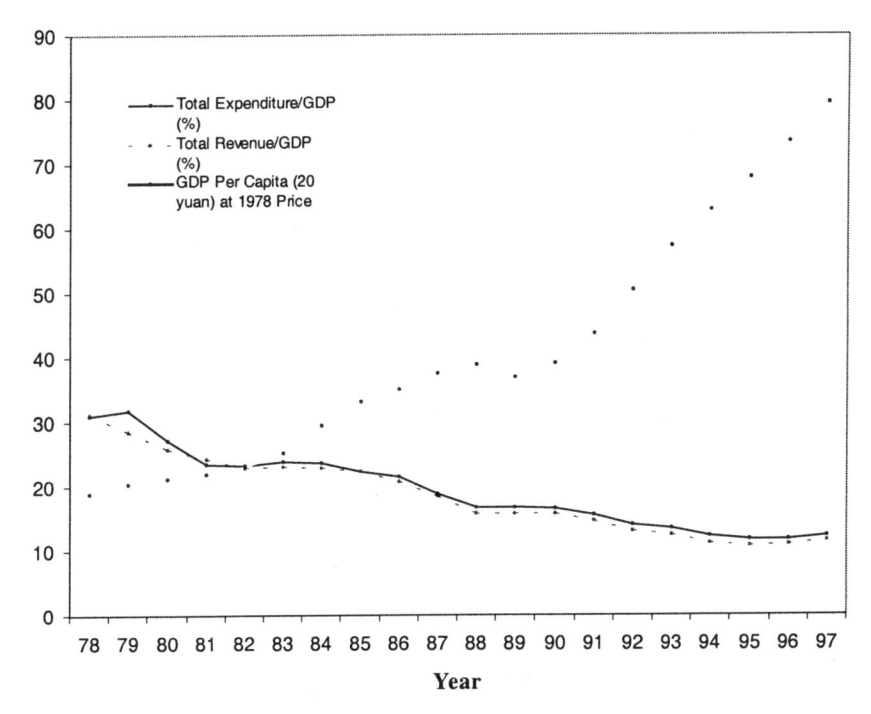

Figure 1. Government Budgetary Revenues and Per Capita GDP (1978–1997)

profits (*fangquan rangli*), to substituting taxes for profit (*li gai shui*), to implementing contract responsibility system, all intending to reduce excess burdens of state enterprises and increase their production incentives. The corporate profit tax rate was 33% since 1994. Corporate income taxes from state enterprises declined by 59.3%, from 46.5 billion yuan in 1985 to 18.94 billion yuan in 1997. Corporate income taxes from collective enterprises declined by 43.4%, from 7.82 billion yuan to 4.43 billion yuan in 1997.[21] Note that we simply point out that a lower corporate income tax rate is a factor contributing to the decline of government revenue share in GDP, but not arguing that the corporate income tax rate is too low.

---

[21] Calculated by the author based on the data from *Statistical Yearbook of China*, 1998.

3.2. Smaller Tax Base

Tax revenues depend on tax rate, as well as the size of taxable income. In China, although tax rates may not be low, the tax bases are small. One example is the agricultural taxation. Agricultural tax rates set in 1958 are different among different provinces, and is around 15%. The tax base is the quantity of agricultural products per unit of cultivated land in an average year. For more than 40 years (particularly since the collapse of the people's commune), despite a large increase in agricultural productivity, the average product per unit of land (*mu*) has never changed. Thus, the actual tax rate is only less than 2.5%! [22]

Small tax base is also caused by tax exemptions and reductions. One example is tariff. China's tax rates on imported goods and services are much higher than those of high-income and middle income countries. However, there exist many exemptions and tax deductions. As a result, tariff revenues have been declining despite that trade expands.

The current tax system does not cover all economic activities, especially new activities. For example, foreign investors enjoy tax exemption for two years, tax reduction for three years, and only pay taxes from the fifth year when they have profits. It is reported that many of them are "losing" money after the fifth year. Investment by overseas enterprises (foreign enterprises and enterprises of Hong Kong, Taiwan, and Macao) accounted for 11.6% of total investment in 1997.[23] Thus, the output produced by overseas enterprises, and therefore taxable income, is considerably large.

The decline in the profitability of state enterprises reduces the base of taxation. For many years, state enterprises overly initiated many investment projects, resulting in extra production capacity. A survey of more than 900 major industrial products producers by the State Statistical Bureau showed that, in half of these enterprises, the capacity utilisation rate was less than 60%.[24] Production cost has been increasing and many

---

[22] See Chinese Tax System (*zhongguo shuishou zhidu*), 1996
[23] *Statistical Yearbook of China*, 1998, p. 189.
[24] See Economic Daily (*Jingji Ribao*), January 21, 1999.

state-enterprises have suffered losses.[25] The percentage of state enterprises suffering from losses were 9.7% in 1985, amounting to 3.2 billion yuan; 27.6% in 1995, amounting to 34.9 billion yuan; and 39.2% in 1997 amounting to 83.1 billion yuan.[26] It should be mentioned that, even though the number of loss-making state enterprises was large, state enterprises as a whole contributed a large amount of revenue to government. In 1995, state enterprises contributed 444.1 billion yuan as revenues to the government, while the government only gave 32.8 billion yuan as subsidies to loss-making enterprises.[27] There exists an illusion that state enterprises were a burden to the government. In fact, state enterprises as a whole are a money machine for the government!

3.3. Tax Evasions

Tax evasion is the act of deliberate failing to pay legally due taxes. Tax evasion is one of the most intractable problems of economic policy in developing countries. Tax evasions are widespread in China. It was estimated that 30% of state enterprises, 60% of joint ventures, 80% private enterprises, and 100% individual street vendors evade taxes [Yu (1997)]. Many enterprises have two accounts, one is real, and the other is fake [see Liu (1998)]. The fake account is used for evading tax payment.

In many cases, income is paid in cash instead of cheque. Hence, there are no legal transaction records, and income is not reported to the tax authorities. For example, a large portion of individual's income is non-wage income (cash awards and subsidies). When people receive payment-in-kind instead of money, it is a taxable transaction by law.

---

[25] The ways to calculate profit is are different in China and Western countries. Many Chinese SOEs have profits, but without money to pay bonuses and other welfare payments. In Western countries, those payments should be part of a firm's production cost. Thus, profits for Chinese SOEs are actually exaggerated [see Zhou and Yang (1992), p. 19].
[26] See Liu (1998).
[27] See *Statistical Yearbook of China*, 1998, pp. 272–273.

However, this part of the income is not reported as income and personal income tax cannot be levied.[28]

Until year 2001, savers were not required to use their real name and resident number in their bank accounts. Thus, it was hard for the tax authority to monitor the interest income tax collection.

Tax delay is also a serious problem. Based on official survey conducted in the Anhui province in 1994 [see Ma (1998)], taxes collected accounted for 74.2% of taxes which should be collected; and in 1995, taxes collected accounted for 79.8% of the taxes supposed to be collected. The situation for corporate income tax collection was worse. In 1995, corporate income taxes collected amounted to 2.9 billion yuan, which was only 47.3% of the taxes to be collected.

4. Consequences of Low Government Revenues

Low government budgetary revenue has resulted in low government budgetary expenditures, growing government budget deficit, and expansion of extra-budgetary budget revenues. Low government budgetary revenues also severely affects state-enterprise reforms.

4.1. Low Government Budgetary Expenditures and Increasing Government Budget Deficits

Government expenditure share in GDP has been also declining as the share of government revenue in GDP decreases. This can be seen intuitively from Figure 1. In 1978, government expenditure share in GDP was 31%. It decreased to only 12.3% in 1997. Low government

---

[28] There may be several reasons for the high proportion of tax evasion. (1) The lack of "rule of law"; (2) The legal concept of taxation has yet to be formed in Chinese society, and tax payers do not have the habit of paying taxes; (3) Some local officials grant reductions or exemptions without proper authorisation from the central government; (4) The lack of efficiency in tax administration and in some cases the acceptance of bribes by tax collectors [See Li (1991)].

revenues limited government's ability to provide needed public infrastructures.[29]

The pressure of increasing government expenditures forced the government to issues debt to raise funds. Table 3 shows *government revenue, expenditure, and deficit* from 1985 to 1996. The government run budget deficit in every year during this period, and budget deficit has been increasing. To finance budget deficit, the government issued a large amount of bonds. From 1958 to 1978, China had no foreign debt

Table 3. Government Revenue, Expenditure, and Deficit *

(billions of yuan)

Year	Revenue	Expenditure	Deficit	GDP
1985	228.3	232.4	4.1	896.4
1986	244.6	262.7	18.1	1020.2
1987	257.6	282.3	25.1	1196.3
1988	280.3	313.7	33.4	1492.8
1989	326.4	363.8	37.4	1690.9
1990	355.0	391.7	36.7	1854.8
1991	367.2	415.2	48.0	2161.8
1992	392.8	453.9	61.1	2663.8
1993	475.9	545.9	70.0	3463.4
1994	558.4	632.4	74.2	4675.9
1995	654.1	751.8	97.7	5847.8
1996	771.9	875.6	103.7	6788.5
1997	..	..	..	7477.2

Sources: World Bank, China 2020, Development Challenges in the new Century, Washington D.C.; *Statistical Yearbook of China*, 1997.

*In calculating government revenue and expenditure, IMF includes subsidies to state enterprises, while the Chinese government treats subsidies to state enterprises as negative revenues. Also, IMF includes interest payment on debt in expenditure, while the Chinese government does not.

---

[29] In a county in the western part of China, which the author visited recently, there is no street light in the downtown area due to the shortage of government revenues.

and domestic debt. As China started economic reforms in 1979, its international and external borrowings began, and its total government debt has been on an increase. Facing slower economic growth, the Chinese government has recently adopted an expansionary fiscal policy by increasing government spending.[30] The bonds issued in one year was 31.5 billion yuan in 1993 and 241.2 billion yuan in 1997, a record high. In 1998, the government issued 280 billion yuan of government bonds in addition to 100 billion yuan of special bonds for infrastructures, the largest bond issue in Chinese history. In 1999, China plans to issue 341.5 billion yuan government bonds (excluding any special bonds). The interest payment on government debt is increasing.

4.2. Expansion of Extra-budgetary Revenues

Limited government revenue forced the government to encourage government agencies and educational institutions to pursue revenues by themselves. Many government agencies and educational institutions (universities, colleges, or even high schools) have their own business enterprises, which provide funds to finance their expenditures.[31] Extra-budgetary revenue, which is not included in the government budget, is the non-tax revenue collected by various levels of government and government agencies by using administrative power (including local fiscal authorities, central and local government branches, state enterprises, and government agencies and institutions).[32] Extra-budgetary revenue emerged along with the centrally-planned economic system. But before 1978, the size of extra-budgetary revenue was relatively small. Extra-

---

[30] China's economic growth in 1998 slowed down to 7.8%, compared to 8.8% in 1997 and an average of 11% during the period of 1993–1997. The target growth rate of GDP for 1999 has been set at 7%.

[31] Until recently, even the People's Liberation Army had their own businesses.

[32] Extra-budget revenues include: revenues from the service provided by government agencies; administrative fees (license fee, etc.); and revenues from business run by colleges, high schools and primary schools. Extra-budgetary revenues are used for investment in fixed assets, for city maintenance, for welfare, for encouragement and awards, for administrative and business activities, and etc.

budgetary revenue was only 7.8% of budgetary revenue in 1952, 4.2% in 1953, 20.6% in 1960, 16% in 1965, and 33.4% in 1978.

Extra-budgetary revenues expanded greatly from 1978 to the 1990s. Local governments and central government branches, and state enterprises explored more and more extra-revenue sources, arbitrarily setting up new fees and increasing the level of fees (*luan shoufee*), arbitrarily raising funds from local enterprises and individuals (*luan jizi*), and arbitrarily adding new fines and increasing the levels of existing fines (*luan fakuan*). Table 4 shows extra-budgetary revenue and expenditure of central and local governments. They also tried to find ways to move the budgetary revenue to extra-budgetary revenue.[33] The extra-budgetary revenue accounted for 97.7% of budgetary revenues in 1992. The coverage of the extra-budgetary revenue has been adjusted largely since 1993. The central government forced the local governments to eliminate some fee collections and to lower some other fee collections, and included some extra-budgetary revenues in the budgetary revenues. More importantly, extra-budgetary revenue no longer included extra-budgetary revenues of state enterprises. As a result, the extra-budgetary revenues and expenditures were considerably reduced. This does not mean that the actual extra-budgetary revenues declined in 1993. In fact, using the definition (or broad coverage) of 1992, the extra-budgetary revenue actually increased by 46.2%, compared to 1992. Moreover, extra-budgetary revenue kept increasing. In 1993, the extra-budgetary revenue and expenditure declined to 56.2 billion yuan, but went back to 67.579 billion yuan in 1995,[34] and rose to 103.05 billion yuan in 1996 (at 1978 constant price). In 1996, the ratio of extra-budgetary revenue to budgetary revenue was 52.6%, with the narrower definition (excluding the extra-budgetary revenues of state enterprises).[35]

---

[33] See Shengming He, *Zhongguo Caizheng Gaige Ershi Nian*, Zhengzhou, Zhonggu Chubanshe, 1998, p. 71.
[34] The total tax revenue was 299.01 billion yuan in 1991 and was 329.69 billion yuan in 1992. It increased to 425.5 billion yuan in 1993.
[35] *Statistical Yearbook of China*, 1991, 1998.

Table 4. Real Extra-Budgetary Revenue and Expenditures of Central and Local Governments (100 million yuan)

Year	Real Extra-Budgetary Revenue	Central Government	Local Government	Real Extra-Budgetary Expenditure	Central Government	Local Government
1982	711.65	239.98	471.67	651.18	201.29	449.89
1983	845.14	314.32	530.81	764.90	262.34	502.56
1984	1009.75	399.78	609.97	947.10	357.04	590.06
1985	1194.40	496.57	697.84	1073.40	438.76	634.64
1986	1279.32	527.71	751.61	1162.28	471.97	690.30
1987	1392.45	568.31	824.14	1263.38	509.00	754.39
1988	1366.98	525.28	841.70	1242.19	488.05	754.15
1989	1307.19	527.18	780.01	1230.63	479.78	750.85
1990	1304.11	516.75	787.37	1303.35	499.61	803.74
1991	1517.69	646.28	871.41	1447.01	591.14	855.87
1992	1711.78	758.32	953.46	1620.74	707.29	913.45
1993	562.00	96.47	465.53	515.61	78.02	437.60
1994	600.43	91.33	509.09	551.38	72.54	478.84
1995	675.79	89.18	586.61	654.66	98.67	555.99
1996	3893.34	947.66	2945.68	3838.32	1034.92	2803.40
1997	2826.00	145.08	2680.92	2685.54	143.91	2541.63

*The coverage of the extra-budgetary revenue and expenditures has been adjusted largely since 1993, and the data may not be comparable with those in previous years.

Source: *Statistical Yearbook of China*, 1997; *Finance Yearbook of China*, 1998. General retail price index (1978 = 100) was used to Calculate the figures.

Furthermore, the existence of extra-budgetary revenues provides the opportunity for many government agencies, state enterprises, and local governments to have off-budget revenues (called "the Little Golden Box," or "third source of finance"). Off-budgetary revenues are revenues collected by local government and enterprises which are out of the central government's control and monitor. In 1995, budgetary revenues were 623.9 billion yuan, and extra-budgetary revenues were about 384.3 billion yuan, accounting for 61.6% of the total budgetary revenues. It was estimated that, in 1995, the off-budget revenues were about 200 billion yuan, accounting for nearly 30% of budgetary revenues [Liu (1998)]. Some observations indicated that the off-budget revenues accounted for 5% of GDP [Lin and Wang (1997)].

The increase in extra-budgetary revenues was a source of corruption. Ironically, many loss-making state enterprises have their own profit-making businesses. For example, a state enterprise may also run a profitable hotel and a restaurant, and the profit may become either extra-budgetary revenue or off-budgetary revenue. Extra-budgetary and off-budgetary revenues are often abused, such as purchasing luxury vehicles for corrupt officials, sponsoring their travels, lending the fund out for high interest income, and speculating in stock and real estate markets, etc. Eliminating extra-budgetary and off-budgetary revenues will reduce corruption among local government, government agencies and institutions, as well as SOEs.

4.3. Slowing State-Enterprises Reforms

In general, private enterprises are more efficient than state-enterprises. Based on Chinese data for the period of 1978-1996, Lin (1998) showed that provinces which invested more in state enterprises grew slower than provinces which invested more in private enterprises. Thus, privatising state enterprises seems desirable for Chinese economic development.

An analysis of government revenue by ownership indicates that state enterprises pay proportionally much higher taxes (see Table 2). In 1978, 87% of the total government revenue was from the state enterprises, 12.6% was from collective enterprises, and 0.4% was from individual enterprises. In 1995, 71.1% of the total government revenue was from the state enterprises, 17.2% was from collective enterprises, and 6.1% was from individual enterprises, and 5.5% was from other enterprises (including foreign enterprises and joint ventures). In 1978, the share of industrial output by state enterprises was 77.6%, and the share by collective enterprises was 22.4%, and there were no individual enterprises at that time.[36] In 1995, the share of industrial output by state enterprises was 34%, the share by collective enterprises was 36.6%, and by individual

[36] The data on GDP by ownership are not available.

Table 2. Real Government Revenue by Ownership*

(100 million yuan)

Year	Total Revenue	State Ownership	Collective Ownership	Individual Economy	Other Types of Ownership
1978	1132.26	984.79	142.40	5.07	0.00
1979	1123.90	982.39	136.31	5.20	0.00
1980	1073.02	931.82	135.31	5.88	0.00
1981	1062.14	919.11	135.01	7.99	0.03
1982	1074.76	915.65	145.27	13.76	0.09
1983	1193.84	1001.62	169.57	13.00	9.64
1984	1395.80	1155.77	210.69	16.07	13.27
1985	1565.04	1214.89	308.45	28.22	13.49
1986	1562.60	1223.86	272.56	36.91	29.27
1987	1509.51	1112.47	282.03	66.55	48.46
1988	1364.93	977.39	268.45	78.66	40.43
1989	1310.18	922.92	258.19	72.02	57.05
1990	1414.11	1008.71	262.47	65.91	77.01
1991	1473.79	1051.01	256.76	82.62	83.40
1992	1546.79	1102.59	264.21	87.97	92.02
1993	1706.14	1222.31	294.53	93.16	96.14
1994	1682.17	1201.62	290.43	93.96	96.16
1995	1752.93	1247.13	302.02	107.27	96.51

*Revenue from both domestic and foreign debts is excluded in this table.
Source: *Statistical Yearbook of China*, 1997. General retail price index (1978 = 100) was used to calculate the figures.

enterprises was 12.9%, and other enterprises was 16.6%.[37] The share of industrial output by state enterprises was down to 25.5% in 1997. It was reported that, in 1998, 54% of total tax revenues was from state enterprises.[38] It can be seen that the government still heavily relies on state enterprises for tax revenues.

[37] See *Statistical Yearbook of China*, 1997, p. 413.
[38] *China Finance and Economic News* (*Zhongguo Caijing Bao*), May 28, 1999.

The Chinese tax system is severely distorted. Since it is difficult to collect taxes directly from private individuals and non-state enterprises, the government collects taxes indirectly.

First, the government subsidises state-enterprises by lending to them at favourable terms. In China, most banks and other financial institutions are owned and controlled by the government. The government has adopted a biased lending policy in favour of the state enterprises. About 70% of loans have been given to state enterprises. For example, in 1995, the government banks made 2800 billion yuan out of total lending of 4000 billion yuan to state enterprises. Also, government loans to state enterprises were at lower interest rates.

Sometimes the real interest rates on loans to state enterprises were even negative. For example, in 1994, the government loans to state enterprises were at an interest rate less than 11%, but the inflation rate was over 20%.[39] All state enterprises have been interested in pursuing loans backed by the government. Some did not use the loans to improve technology and to raise productivity, instead they re-lent the loans out at a higher interest rate to make money [Yi (1996)]. In this case, state enterprises make profits not because they are more efficient, but because they get subsidies from the government through better loan conditions.

Second, loans to individual enterprises have been subjected to higher interest rates and other conditions. For example, in 1993 the interest rate charged to individual enterprises (industrial and commercial households) was 20% higher than the interest rate charged to state enterprises.

Third, private savers pay taxes implicitly through lowed real interest income. The percentage of bank deposits from urban and rural individuals was 55% in 1993, 55.8% in 1994, 57.3% in 1995, 58.2% in 1996, 58% in 1997.[40] The real interest rate were actually negative in 1993, 1994, and 1995. The interest income lost by individuals was a tax paid to the government.

---

[39] See Li and Li (1996).
[40] *Almanac of China's Finance and Banking*, 1998, p. 508.

Fourth, the government allows monopolistic SOEs to make monopoly profits. In China, many production sectors (e.g., telecommunications, natural gas, electric power, and petroleum) are monopolised by state enterprises. Instead of regulating the prices of these monopolistic enterprises, the government has allowed these enterprises to charge monopoly prices. For example, for several years, the fee for installation of a telephone line was about 5,000 yuan (higher than the average nominal wage of staff and workers in 1994). Consumers and non-monopoly firms pay higher prices. The government then taxed the monopolistic enterprises.

Fifth, the government intervenes commodity markets. For example, the government set price floors for some goods recently. With the price floors, non-SOEs can not compete with SOEs by lowering prices. As a result, the SOEs may make profits, the non-SOEs may loose profits, and consumers pay higher prices.

There is a Chinese saying, "the fur of sheep must come from sheep" (*yangmao chuzai yang shenshang*). Taxes are eventually paid by private firms and individuals implicitly, but not explicitly. State enterprises serve as a channel through which the government can get tax revenues. If government cannot find other revenue sources, privatisation of profitable state enterprises would be like "pursuing a tiger's fur (*yu hu mo pi*)." The government may continue to subsidise state enterprises and increase their profits for the simple reason of tax revenues. Thus, low budgetary revenues may slow down the process of privatising state enterprises.

5. Economic Development and Government Revenue

More than a century ago, Wagner (1883) observed that during industrialisation, as per capita income increases, the size of government (represented by either the share of government spending in output and the share of government revenues in total output) increases. For example, the share of U.S. government expenditures in GDP was only 9.9% in 1929, it was 21.3% in 1960, and was 34.4% in 1993. In 1991, the share of government expenditures in GDP was 34.4% in Japan, 37.4% in

Germany, 38.7% in the UK, 43% in Canada, 46.3% in France, 60.6% in Sweden [see Rosen (1995), pp. 16–17]. The Wagner's theory can be used to predict the trend of government size during the process of economic development. It can be seen from Figure 1 that Chinese national data from 1978 to 1997 rendered no support to the Wagner's hypothesis. But, as we discussed before, this is largely due to structural changes in the period of economic reforms.

We now examine the relationship between the share of government revenues in GDP and per capita GDP based on the data for thirty Chinese provinces.[41] We will examine the relationship between the ratio of government revenues to GDP and per capita GDP. We will use the data for the whole period (1978–1996), as well as three sub-periods (1978–1984, 1984–1990, and 1990–1996).

Let R be the ratio of government tax revenues to GDP and Y be the per capita GDP. The regression equation is as follows: $R = a + bY + u$, where a is a constant, b is the coefficient of Y, and u is the stochastic error term. The regression results for periods of 1978–1996, 1978–1984, 1984–1990, and 1990–1996 are as follows:

(1) $R_{7896} = 0.05 + 0.08\, Y_{7896}$
    (4.8) (8.3)   R-square = 0.71

(2) $R_{7884} = 0.05 + 0.19\, Y_{7884}$
    (3.6) (9.2)   R-square = 0.75

(3) $R_{8490} = 0.05 + 0.08\, Y_{8490}$
    (4.6) (6.6)   R-square = 0.61

(4) $R_{9096} = 0.07 + 0.02\, Y_{9096}$
    (9.0) (2.9)   R-square = 0.23

T-values for the coefficients are given in the parentheses. The number of observations used for each regression is 30. The cross-province

---

[41] The data are from a recently published statistical book by China's National Bureau of Statistics, *Twenty Years' Regional Statistics after Reforms and Opening-Up*, Beijing: China Statistical Publishing House, 1997.

regression analysis shows that provinces with a higher per capita GDP had a larger ratio of government revenues to GDP, i.e., provinces with higher per capita income can collect proportionally more revenues. Another equation we estimated is $\log(R) = a + b\log(Y) + u$, where a is the intercept and b is the coefficient. The results remain qualitatively unaltered.[42]

Economists argued that the relative larger government size might be a result of greater productivity of high-income countries, which are able to raise their taxable capacities and leave more for government after essential consumption needs are met [Oshima (1957)], or might be a result of lower productivity and higher operation costs in public sectors [Martin and Lewis (1957)]. How could wealthy provinces collect more taxes relative to their GDP? (1) In the wealthy provinces, people have higher ability to pay taxes. (2) Wealthy provinces may have better facilities and better trained staff to collect taxes. (3) Individuals and enterprises in the wealthier provinces have a higher opportunity cost of evading taxes than people in poor province. The result of the above analysis has a profound implication for Chinese fiscal policy — as the economy develops government revenue share may increase without increasing the tax rate.

6. Central and Local Government Revenues

Most prior studies only focused on a lower central government spending, but neglected the large central government revenues. A major concern has been the decline in the share of central government spending in total government spending. It should be mentioned that the share of central government revenue in total revenue has in fact largely increased since 1978.

Table 5 shows revenues and expenditures by central and local governments. The share of the central government spending in total government spending was 59% in 1970, 47.4% in 1978, and only 27.1%

---

[42] The regression results are available on request.

Table 5. Revenues and Expenditures by Central and Local Governments*
(100 million yuan)

Year	Total	Total Revenues Central Government	Local Government	% of Central Government	Total	Total Expenditures Central Government	Local Government	% of Central Government
1970	662.9	183.0	480.0	27.6	649.4	382.4	267.0	58.9
1975	815.6	96.6	719.0	11.8	820.9	409.4	411.5	49.9
1976	776.6	98.9	677.7	12.7	806.2	377.6	428.6	46.8
1977	874.5	113.9	760.6	13.0	843.5	393.7	449.8	46.7
1978	1132.3	175.8	956.5	15.5	1122.1	532.1	590.0	47.4
1979	1146.4	231.3	915.0	20.2	1281.8	655.1	626.7	51.1
1980	1159.9	284.5	875.5	24.5	1228.8	666.8	562.0	54.3
1981	1175.8	311.1	864.7	26.5	1138.4	625.7	512.8	55.0
1982	1212.3	346.8	865.5	28.6	1230.0	651.8	578.2	53.0
1983	1367.0	490.0	876.9	35.8	1409.5	759.6	649.9	53.9
1984	1642.9	665.5	977.4	40.5	1701.0	893.3	807.7	52.5
1985	2004.8	769.6	1235.2	38.4	2004.3	795.3	1209.0	39.7
1986	2122.0	778.4	1343.6	36.7	2204.9	836.4	1386.6	37.9
1987	2199.4	736.3	1463.1	33.5	2262.2	845.6	1416.6	37.4
1988	2357.2	774.8	1582.5	32.9	2491.2	845.0	1646.2	33.9
1989	2664.9	822.5	1842.4	30.9	2823.8	888.8	1935.0	31.5
1990	2937.1	992.4	1944.7	33.8	3083.6	1004.5	2079.1	32.6
1991	3149.5	938.3	2211.2	29.8	3386.6	1090.8	2295.8	32.2
1992	3483.4	979.5	2503.9	28.1	3742.2	1170.4	2571.8	31.3
1993	4349.0	957.5	3391.4	22.0	4642.3	1312.1	3330.2	28.3
1994	5218.1	2906.5	2311.6	55.7	5792.6	1754.4	4038.2	30.3
1995	6242.2	3256.6	2985.6	52.2	6823.7	1995.4	4828.3	29.2
1996	7408.0	3661.1	3746.9	49.4	7937.6	2151.3	5786.3	27.1

Sources: The Finance Yearbook of China, 1997, p. 461, 462.
*The figures in this table does not include the revenues from issuing internal and external debt, and does not include interest payment on internal and external debt and basic construction expenditures financed by foreign debt.

in 1996. Before 1978, provincial and local governments handed over all their tax revenues to the central government, and the central government reallocated the funds to each province and then to local governments. Since the central government had final control over the allocation of the tax revenue, it did not really matter who collected the tax revenues. Now provincial and local governments can retain and control a large part of the tax revenue. Thus, the central government's role in reallocating resources was reduced. To increase its ability of control, the central government focuses on revenue collections. In fact, the central government's share of total tax revenues now is much larger than that in 1978. In 1978, the share of tax revenues collected by the central government was 15.5%, it reached 40.5% in 1984, decreased to 22% in 1993, jumped back to 55.7% in 1994, and came down to 49.4% in 1996. The government's target is to raise the revenue share to 60%.

The central government wants larger economic power of control over local governments.[43] In China, provincial and local governments have no right to issue bonds to finance their expenditures. As the central government has more tax revenues, all provincial governments demand funds from the central government. Each province submits some funds to the central government and the central government transfers funds to each province. The net transfer from the central government to every province was positive.[44] Thus, large central government revenues have invited bargaining between the central and local governments, which may not be efficient based on economic ground.

7. Concluding Remarks

The central question in public finance is the optimal size of government.[45] China was under a centrally-planned economy, which required a large

---

[43] In China, provincial governments suppose to have rights to make laws concerning local affairs. However, in practice, the central government has emphasised the uniform of tax laws, and local tax laws are rare. See Minister of Finance, *Tax System of China*, 1996, p. 25.

[44] *Finance Yearbook of China*, 1997.

[45] The optimal government size should be determined by comparing the benefits that would flow from government expenditures and the cost of financing those expenditures [see Pigou (1928)]. Feldstein (1997) argued that the deadweight loss must be included when calculating the cost related to an increase in government tax revenues, and the deadweight loss is much larger than people usually think. He believe that a dollar government outlay may have a total cost, including the deadweight loss, that exceeds two dollars.

government. As the economy moves towards a market-oriented system, government size should shrink. Yet it may take time to reduce the government size. If budgetary, extra-budgetary, off-budgetary, and social security contributions are added up, Chinese government should have at least 25% of GDP in its disposal,[46] higher than its target of 20%. On average, developing countries' government size is smaller than developed countries. The size of Chinese government is not small compared to countries at the same level of economic development.[47] Given that it is difficult to reduce the government size in a short period of time, raising revenues is important for the Chinese government. The government should continue to reform its tax system, aiming at fairness and efficiency (transparent, less distortion, and simple). First, the government budget should be unified by merging extra-budgetary revenues and expenditures into budgetary revenues and expenditures. Second, the government should broaden the tax base and eliminate unnecessary tax exemptions and reductions. Third, the government should equalise tax burdens among enterprises, collect more taxes from non-state enterprises, and treat state and non-state enterprises equally in the loan markets. Fourth, the government should reinforce tax laws and reduce tax evasions by training more qualified tax administrators and by setting heavier penalties for tax evasions and higher rewards for firms and individuals who follow the tax laws.

[46] Total social insurance and welfare funds accounted for 4.04% of GDP in 1997 (Calculated by the author based on the data from *Statistical Yearbook of China*, 1998, p. 55 and p. 795).

[47] For instance, in 1997, government total revenue (central and local governments) share in GDP was 20.3 % in India in 1995, 27.8% in Malaysia in 1996, 17.6% in Indonesia in 1993, and 20.2% in Thailand [See IMF, *Government Finance Statistics*, 1998; IMF, *International Financial Statistics Yearbook*, 1998]. In 1992, the share of taxes in GNP was 16.0% for low-income countries (24.3% excluding India), 19.0% for lower-middle-income countries, 21.0% for upper-middle-income countries and 27.0% for high-income countries. See Gillis, Perkins, Roemer, and Snodgrass (1997), p. 331.

REFERENCES

Barro, Robert, "A Cross Country Study of Growth, Saving, and Government," NBER Working Paper #2855, February 1989.

Brean, Donald, Financial Perspectives on Fiscal Reform, In Trish Fulton, Jinyan Li and Dianqing Xu (eds.), *China's Tax Reform Options*, World Scientific, 1998.

Chen, Gong, Some Policy Issues on Boosting Government Revenues (Zhenxeng Guojia Caizheng de Jige Zhengce Wenti), *Finance* (Caizheng), 9, 1996. Also in: Ministry of Finance (eds.), *The Finance Yearbook of China*, Publishing House of Financial Journals, Beijing, China, 1997, pp. 763–769.

China's Ministry of Finance, Tax Division, *Tax System in China*, Beijing: Enterprise Management Publishing House, 1996.

China's Ministry of Finance, *The Finance Yearbook of China*, Publishing House of Financial Journals, Beijing, China, 1997.

China's National Bureau of Statistics, *A Statistical Survey of China*, Beijing: China Statistical Publishing House, 1998.

China's National Bureau of Statistics, *Statistical Yearbook of China*, Beijing: China Statistical Publishing House, 1997, 1998.

China's National Bureau of Statistics, *Twenty Years' Regional Statistics after Reforms and Opening-Up*, Beijing: China Statistical Publishing House, 1997.

China's People's Congress (1996), *China's Ninth Five-Year Plan for National Economy and Social Development and the Objectives for the Year of 2010*. In: Ministry of Finance (eds.), *The Finance Yearbook of China*, Publishing House of Financial Journals, Beijing China, 1997, 22–41.

China's Tax Bureau, *Tax Yearbook of China*, Beijing: China's Tax Publishing House, 1997

Feldstein, Martin, "How Big should Government Be?" National Tax Journal, Vol. 50, No. 2, June 1997, 197–213.

Gillis, Malcolm, Dwight Perkins, Michael Roomer, and Donald Snodgrass, *Economics of Development*, fourth edition, New York: W.W. Norton & Company, 1995.

He, Shengming, *Twenty Years' Fiscal Reform in China* (Zhongguo Caizheng Gaige Ershi Nian), Zhengzhou, Zhonggu Chubanshe, 1998, p. 71.

Hinrichs, Harley H., 1965, "Determinants of Government Revenue Shares among Less-Developed Countries, *Economic Journal* 75, 546–556.

Huang, Kehua, Taking the Opportunity of Reforms and Promoting Government Revenues (Bawo Gaige Jiyu, Zhenxeng Guojia Caizheng), *Finance*

(Caizheng), 9, 1996. Also in: Ministry of Finance (eds.), *The Finance Yearbook of China*, Publishing House of Financial Journals, Beijing, China, 1997, 763–769.

International Monetary Fund, 1998, *Government Finance Statistics Yearbook*, Washington, D.C.

International Monetary Fund, 1998, *International Financial Statistics Yearbook*, Washington, D.C.

Landau, Daniel, "Government Expenditure and Economic Growth: A Cross-Country Study," *Southern Economic Journal*, 49, January 1983, 783–92.

_____, "Government and Economic Growth in the Less Developed Countries: An Empirical Study for 1960–1980," *Economic Development and Cultural Change*, 35, 1, October 1986, 34–75.

Lee, Peng, *A Report on the Ninth Five-Year Plan for National Economy and Social Development and the Objectives for the Year of 2010*, 1996. In: Ministry of Finance (eds.), *The Finance Yearbook of China*, Publishing House of Financial Journals, Beijing, China, 1997, 12–22.

Li, Jinyan, *Taxation in the People's Republic of China*, New York: Praeger, 1991.

Li, Dou, "Lun Zhengxing Caizheng de Renwu ji Duice," *Shandong Jingji*, January 1997.

Lin, Guangfeng, and Fengming Wang, "Dui Caizheng Shouru 'Liangge Bizhong' Wenti de Butong Renshi," *Dangdai Caijing*, No. 10, 1997, 36–39.

Lin, Shuanglin, 1998, "Allocation of Resources and Economic Growth: Evidence from China," Working Paper.

Liu, Xinyi, "Zhonggou Caishi Gaige de Lilun Sikao," *Hubei Caishi*, No. 4, 1998, 4–7.

Ma, Qianli, "Tigao Caizheng Yunxing Zhiliang de Sikao," *Zhongguo Caizheng*, No. 1, 1998, 12–14.

Oshima, Harry T., 1957, Share of Government in Gross National Product for Various Countries, American Economic Review, 381–90.

Ram, Rati, 1987, Wagner's Hypothesis in Time-Series and Cross-Section Perspectives: Evidence from "Real" Data for 115 Countries, Review of Economics and Statistics, 194–204.

Stiglitz, Joseph, A Speech at Peking University, *People's Daily*, November 13, 1998

Tax Bureau, People's Republic of China, 1996, *The Chinese Tax System*, Beijing, Enterprises Management Publishing House.

Wang, Bingqian, "Renzhen Guanche Shwuda Jingshen Kaichuang Caizheng Keyan Xinjumian," *Caizheng Yanjou*, No. 3, 1998, 2–11.

Wagner, Adolf, 1883, *Finanzwissenschaft*, Part I, Third Edition, translated and extracted by Nancy Cooke in R.A. Musgrave and A.T. Peacock, eds., Classics in the Theory of Public Finance, 1–15, London: Macmillan.

Yi, Gang, 1996, Analyses of Chinese Financial Assets and Some Policy Implications, *Working Paper Series*, No. 1996004, China Center for Economic Research, Beijing University.

Yu, Dingcheng, "Jingji Zhuhuo, Shuishou Zhu Kong," *Yiangzhou Daxue Shuiwu Xueyuan Xuebao*, No. 1, 1997, pp. 5–10.

6

Fiscal Decentralisation and Economic Growth[†]

JUSTIN LIN YIFU & LIU ZHIQIANG*

1. INTRODUCTION

The Chinese economy has grown at a record rate of about 10 percent annually since the launching of the economic reforms in the late 1970s. Many factors are shown to have played important roles in the growth process. These include, among others, rural reforms that made the

---

[†] Reprinted with permission from *Economic Development & Cultural Change*, 49:1 (2000) 1–21. © The University of Chicago Press.

*Dr. LIU Zhiqiang was Senior Research Fellow at the East Asian Institute, National University of Singapore from 1999–2000. Dr. Justin LIN Yifu is Professor at Hong Kong University of Science and Technology. The authors would like to thank Hans Binswanger, Jack Hou, Huagang Li, Jun Ma, Suzanne Piriou-Sall, Anwar Shah, Heng-fu Zou, and an anonymous referee for helpful comments and suggestions on early versions of the paper. They are especially indebted to an anonymous referee, whose comments have improved the paper. The authors would also like to acknowledge support from the World Bank and from a DAG grant at the Hong Kong University of Science and Technology. This article is a substantially revised version of a paper presented at the "Third Biennial Pacific Rim Allied Economic Organizations Conference," 13–18 January 1998, Royal Orchid Sheraton, Bangkok, Thailand.

household the unit of agricultural production, enterprise reforms that introduced material incentives to enterprise management, various price reforms, importation of technology, opening up the market to international trade and foreign investment, and a flourishing non-state sector. An important aspect of this multi-faceted reform, the fiscal reform initiated in the early 1980s, has not been examined adequately. The main concern of this paper is to investigate whether fiscal decentralisation has contributed positively to the growth process of the Chinese economy.

In a broad sense, fiscal decentralisation is much the same in China as elsewhere in the world: the central government relinquishes its fiscal controls to subnational governments. According to the proponents of fiscal decentralisation, such a shift of fiscal power and responsibility to lower levels of government may increase economic efficiency because governments at lower levels have informational advantage over the central government concerning resource allocation (Oates 1972).[1] In other words, subnational governments are in better positions to provide the kind of public goods and services that closely meet the local need. Furthermore, when local government officials are responsible for the provision of public services, they are under closer scrutiny by their constituencies and have a greater incentive, as a result, to exercise their fiscal responsibilities in the best interest of the general public (see e.g., Shah and Qureshi 1994). In addition, local governments in China control the majority of the country's enterprises. Fiscal decentralisation may harden the budget constraints of local enterprises (Qian and Roland 1996) and consequently, may improve the local enterprises' efficiency and lead to a higher and more sustainable economic growth. Fiscal decentralisation may also bring about dynamic gains to the economy as well. The recent endogenous growth literature has illustrated that institutional arrangements affect economic growth.[2] It is conceivable therefore that a change from a centralised to a decentralised fiscal system can increase the long-term rate of economic growth (Oates 1993, Liu 1997).

---

[1] The efficiency gain argument is shared by many scholars, such as Bahl and Linn (1992) and Bird (1993).
[2] See, e.g., Barro (1990), King and Rebelo (1990), and Jorgenson and Yun (1990).

Some people have challenged the significance of the efficiency gain that fiscal decentralisation can bring about. First, the alleged informational advantage of the local government may not be in fact significant. The central government can assign its representatives to local offices, who can have sufficient knowledge about the local preferences and can therefore play a role in the resource allocation process under a centralised fiscal system. Second, the central government can involve officials at the subnational level in the decision process as well. Third, there is the question whether local officials are necessarily better informed given that they are not elected in democratic elections as in the case of most developing countries; and even though they are indeed better informed, there is still the question whether they have greater incentive to act upon the information.[3] Moreover, as local governments in China directly own most local enterprises, they may set up trade barriers to protect local enterprises, causing fragmentation of markets, rent seeking and other efficiency losses.

During the 1980s, the Chinese fiscal system underwent some important changes. It was changed from a unitary system, where the central government had absolute control over revenue collection and budget appropriation, to a relatively decentralised arrangement, where revenues were shared by the central and provincial governments. Under this arrangement, most of the provincial governments were required to remit a portion of their budget revenues to the central government. In cases where provincial revenues cannot cover the specified expenditures, the central government might provide some subsidies to those provinces. Similar fiscal arrangements were made between successive tiers of governments at subnational levels.

Understanding the role of fiscal reform in the growth process thus far is important for future reforms in China. If the changes in the fiscal

---

[3] Obviously, whether or not there is any significant efficiency gain associated with fiscal decentralization cannot be settled on theoretical ground alone. The issue must be subject to rigorous empirical tests. There are also cautionary arguments against fiscal decentralization on other grounds, ranging from macroeconomic control to corruption at lower levels of government. Prod'homme (1995) presents an elaborate discussion of the arguments.

system are conducive to economic growth, as the proponents have argued, then future reforms should aim at fortifying and institutionalising the position of the decentralised system. On the contrary, if fiscal decentralisation is ineffective in bringing about economic growth, China may be better off with a more centralised fiscal system, or may implement corresponding reforms in other areas to reap the full benefits of a decentralised fiscal arrangement.

The significance of this study goes beyond an assessment of the economic reforms in China. The World Bank and other international organisations have actively engaged in studying and evaluating various fiscal reform programs implemented in many countries, such as China, Brazil, and Argentina, in the hopes of drawing useful lessons from them for others to follow. The findings of this study therefore have far-reaching practical values for the international community as a whole. At the theoretical level, our study also makes a contribution to the economics literature by providing an empirical test of whether fiscal decentralisation increases economic efficiency.

Studies on China's economic reforms are numerous (see e.g., Perkins 1988), but few focus on evaluating the impacts of fiscal reforms on economic growth. Zhang and Zou (1996) and Ma (1997) are two exceptions.[4] The former finds that fiscal decentralisation has been detrimental to economic growth, whereas the latter reaches an opposite conclusion. However, these scholars' results should be interpreted with caution because in their analyses they either used a problematic measure for decentralisation or failed to take into account other concurrent reforms.

In this study, we examine the effect of fiscal decentralisation on economic growth by using a production-function-based regression analysis framework that has been widely adopted in the empirical literature on economic growth. Our estimation results, based on a province-level panel data set from 1970–1993, suggest that fiscal decentralisation has made a positive contribution to the growth process. We also find that the rural

---

[4] There are quite a number of non-quantitative studies addressing various aspects of fiscal systems in China. See, e.g., Wong (1991, 1992) and Qian and Weingast (1995), among others.

reform, the non-state sector, and capital accumulation along with the fiscal reform are the key driving forces of the impressive growth in China over the past twenty or so years.

The innovation of the current study is two-fold. First, we include separate proxies for major reforms in the empirical investigation, while focusing on the effect of the changes in the fiscal system on the rate of economic growth. Second and more important, we measure, unlike previous scholars, the degree of fiscal decentralisation by a marginal retention rate — the rate at which revenue increments are retained by provincial governments.

The rest of the paper proceeds as follows. In Sec. 2, we provide an overview of the fiscal reforms in China in the 1980s, concentrating on the changes in fiscal relations between the central and provincial governments. We then set out the econometric model in Sec. 3 and briefly discuss the data set in Sec. 4. In Sec. 5, we report the estimation results. In the last section, we summarise the conclusions of the study.

2. FISCAL DECENTRALISATION IN CHINA

The fiscal system in China was highly centralised before the reforms.[5] The financial relation between the central and provincial governments was labelled *tongshou tongzhi* (unified revenue collection and budget appropriation). No subnational governments had a separate budget: the central government collected all revenues and prepared a consolidated budget for governments at all administrative levels. This financial arrangement was extended to state-owned enterprises (SOEs): they were required to remit all profits or financial surpluses to the state and the state would cover all their expenditures by fiscal appropriation. In effect, the financial management of the SOEs was a part of state finance.

The centralised fiscal system was consistent with the centralised production and resource allocation mode adopted in China during the

---

[5] For a detailed discussion on China's fiscal system before the reforms, see Lardy (1975), Oksenberg and Tong (1991), Wong *et al.* (1995), and Lin *et al.* (1997). The last two also contain a detailed account of the fiscal reforms from the early 1980s to the early 1990s.

pre-reform era, but was incompatible with the market-oriented reforms embarked upon in 1979. There are three major driving forces behind the changes in China's fiscal system. The first is that the remarkable growth of non-state-owned enterprises — township and village enterprises, joint ventures and private firms — has undermined the dominance of state enterprises. Loss-making state enterprises have been rising in number and have become a great drain on the fiscal system. The government has been forced to turn to alternative revenue sources. Second, the balance of political power has shifted towards local autonomy as a result of the economic reforms. It is natural for subnational governments to demand a commensurate decision-making power in the fiscal arena as a consequence of their greater political autonomy. The third impetus to decentralise the fiscal system stems from purely economic reasons. As it has become clear that economic interests greatly influence the behaviour of individuals as well as governmental bodies, the centralised fiscal system has to be changed in order to provide local governments with incentives to step up the effort of revenue collection and to promote economic growth.

Like other reforms, fiscal reform started as an experiment. In as early as 1977, Jiangsu province was chosen to try out an alternative fiscal arrangement with the central government. Under this arrangement, the province was contracted to remit a share of its total revenues each year to the central government. The share was determined according to historical records of local revenues and expenditures of the province.

In 1980, the central government enacted revenue-sharing arrangements under the name "dividing revenues and expenditures with each level of government responsible for balancing its own budget." Under this arrangement, revenues were classified by source and divided into central fixed revenues (including customs duties and revenues remitted by centrally owned state enterprises), local fixed revenues (including salt taxes, agricultural taxes, industrial and commercial income taxes, revenues remitted by locally owned state enterprises, and other taxes and levies of a local nature), and central-local shared revenues (including profits of large-scale enterprises under dual leadership by the central and local government, industrial and commercial taxes or turnover taxes).

There were some exceptions to the 1980 arrangement. Guangdong and Fujian were required to remit a lump sum to the central government each year and allowed to retain the rest of their revenues. The five minority autonomous regions (Xizan, Xinjiang, Ningxia, Inner Mongolia, and Guangxi) and the three poor and remote provinces with large numbers of minority people (Qinghai, Yunnan, and Guizhou) received subsidies which were to increase at an annual rate of 10 percent.

However, despite promises to keep the sharing schemes unchanged for five years, there were frequent changes made to the sharing rules especially during 1982–83. The 1980 arrangement was very short lived.

In 1985, a major change occurred with the reform of the tax system and the replacement of state enterprises' profit remittances with income taxes. Although revenues were still divided into three categories — central fixed, local fixed, and shared — the criteria for the divisions were changed. Whereas the previous divisions were based primarily on the ownership of state enterprises, the new divisions were related to tax categories.[6]

To accommodate different local social and economic conditions, four types of revenue-sharing arrangements were introduced. Fourteen provinces, including 3 municipalities, were contracted to remit a specific

---

[6] *Central fixed revenues* were specified as income and adjustment taxes collected from centrally owned state enterprises; business taxes collected from the rail, civil aviation, telecommunications and financial sectors; revenues remitted by national defense industries; special taxes on petroleum fuel; customs duties; turnover and income taxes and use-right fees collected from off-shore petroleum joint ventures; treasury bonds and special levies for energy and transportation development. Seventy percent of turnover taxes collected from enterprises under the Ministry of Petroleum, the Ministry of Electricity, the Petro-Chemical Corporation, and the Nonferrous Metal Corporation were assigned to the central budget.

Local fixed revenue included income and adjustment taxes and contract fees collected from locally owned state enterprises; collective enterprise income tax; agricultural taxes; vehicle and ship license fees; urban real property tax; livestock transaction tax; country fair transaction tax; deed fees; and 30 percent of turnover taxes collected from enterprises. *Central-local shared revenues* included turnover taxes (product, value-added, and business taxes), except those specified as central or local fixed revenues; resource taxes; construction taxes; salt taxes; personal income taxes; the tax levied on state enterprises' bonus payments; and turnover and income taxes collected from joint ventures excluding off-shore petroleum firms.

share of their local fixed and shared revenues. Guangdong and Heilongjiang received the most favourable provisions requiring remittance of a lump sum of revenues to the central government. Five provinces received lump sum transfers from the central government, while the remaining seven provinces received central subsidies that were stipulated to increase at an annual rate of 10 percent in subsequent years.

The 1985 fiscal arrangement ensured that central and local fixed revenues accounted for a relatively small part of the total government budget, the main portion being specified as shared revenue. This meant that the central government now relied on local governments to increase total revenues and to provide resources to the central government. Because local governments could retain some of the shared revenues, it was in their interest to increase these revenues.

In 1988, the arrangements were changed again under fiscal contracting. Five types of sharing schemes were established, as opposed to four types during 1985–87. The sharing formula for each province is reported in Table 1.

3. Econometric Model

To examine the effect of fiscal decentralisation on economic growth, we adopt a production-function-based estimation framework that has been widely used in the empirical literature on economic growth (see e.g., Mankiw et al., 1992). We assume a Cobb-Douglas production function, so production at time t can be described as

$$y(t)=A(t)k(t)^\alpha \varphi^{1-\alpha}, \qquad (1)$$

where y denotes the output per capita, k the capital per capita, A the level of technology, φ the fraction (assumed to be constant) of the population in the labour force, and $0<\alpha<1$. Expressing (1) in log form and taking first-order differentiation with respect to time, we find that the growth rate of output per capita is

$$g(t)=\dot{y}(t) = \dot{A}(t) + \alpha \dot{k}(t). \qquad (2)$$

Table 1. Central-province Fiscal Arrangements and Marginal Retention Rate

	1985–1987		1988–1993	
Province	Sharing Scheme*	FD	Sharing Scheme**	FD
Beijing	a	49.55	b	100.00
Tianjin	a	39.45	a	46.55
Shanghai	a	23.54	c	100.00
Hebei	a	69.00	b	100.00
Shanxi	a	97.50	a	87.55
Liaoning	a	51.08	b	100.00
Heilongjiang	c	100.00	c	100.00
Jiangsu	a	40.00	b	100.00
Zhejiang	a	55.00	b	100.00
Anhui	a	80.10	a	77.50
Shandong	a	59.00	c	100.00
Henan	a	80.00	b	100.00
Hunan	a	88.00	d	100.00
Hubei	a	100.00	a	100.00
Sichuan	a	100.00	a	100.00
Shaanxi	e	100.00	e	100.00
Jilin	e	100.00	e	100.00
Jiangxi	e	100.00	e	100.00
Gansu	e	100.00	e	100.00
Inner Mongolia	f	100.00	e	100.00
Xinjiang	f	100.00	e	100.00
Guangxi	f	100.00	e	100.00
Ningxia	f	100.00	e	100.00
Yunan	f	100.00	e	100.00
Guizhou	f	100.00	e	100.00
Qinghai	f	100.00	e	100.00
Guangdong	c	100.00	e	100.00
Fujian	e	100.00	e	100.00

Sources: * Dangdai Zhongguo Caizheng Editing Committee, 1988, pp. 376–77;
    ** Zhu (1993), pp. 294–96.
Sharing Schemes:
a. Remitting a share of the local revenues;
b. Remitting a share of local revenue in the base year and the total remittance increases at a pre-determined rate in the subsequent years;
c. Remitting a fixed amount of the revenues to the central government;
d. Remitting a fixed amount in the base year and the total remittance increases at a pre-determined rate in subsequent years;
e. Receiving a fixed amount of subsidy from the central government;
f. Receiving a fixed amount of subsidy in the base year and the total subsidy increases at a pre-determined rate in subsequent years.

By Equation (2), the growth rate of output per capita depends on two factors: the growth rate of capital per capita and the rate of technological progress. It should be noted that the $\dot{A}(t)$ term reflects not just technology but also differences in resource endowments and institutions across regions and over time as well as in other unobservable region-specific characteristics. In the present study, we assume that $\dot{A}(t)$ depends on two sets of variables.

The first set includes variables explicitly measuring two of the most important reform programs that have been implemented during the reform period. They are fiscal decentralisation (FD) and the household responsibility system (HRS). The effect of fiscal decentralisation on economic growth is the central concern of the study. However, since fiscal decentralisation constitutes only one aspect of the multi-faceted reform effort in China and is likely to correlate with others, controlling the effects of other reform measures is crucial for evaluating the direct effect of fiscal decentralisation. Previous studies have ignored this point, and their conclusions therefore should be considered with caution. The household responsibility system reform has been the most important source of agricultural growth in the reform period (Lin 1992). This reform has also increased farmers' autonomy and led to the emergence of township and village enterprises, which have been the most dynamic force of China's recent rapid growth. We also include the relative price of farm products to non-farm products (FPMP) to measure the impact of the price liberalisation, which has substantially raised the relative price of agricultural products. The effects of other policy reforms, such as the enterprise reforms, the open door policy, and so on, are not directly measured due to the lack of appropriate proxies. However, the year dummies in the regression models will indirectly capture their effects.

Included in the second group of variables are those that capture regional differences in resource endowments. Fiscal capacity (FISCAP), defined as a three-year moving average of per capita real GDP, reflects the financial strength of a region. The percent of rural population (POPSHR) and the total population (TPOP) are used to ascertain the impacts of urbanisation and the size of the population on economic growth. The relative importance of non-state-owned enterprises in the industrial sector, measured by the share of non-SOEs' output in the total industrial output (NSOESH), is introduced to capture the role of non-SOEs in the growth process.

We use the growth rate of per capita investment, in real terms, in fixed assets as a proxy for the growth rate of per capita capital.

The growth regression equation is thus specified as a two-way error component model:[7]

$$GGDP_{it} = \beta_1 FD_{it} + \beta_2 HRS_{it} + \beta_3 NSOESH_{it} + \beta_4 GI_{it} + \beta_5 \ln(FISCAP)_{it} + \beta_6 FPMP_{it} + \beta_7 POPSHR_{it} + \beta_8 \ln(TPOP)_{it} + \mu_i + \lambda_t + v_{it}, i = 1,...,N; t = 1,...,T \qquad (3)$$

where i denotes province, t denotes time, $GGDP_{it}$ is the growth rate of per capita GDP, GI_{it} the growth rate of per capita investment, μ_i the unobservable individual effect, λ_t the unobservable time effect, and v_{it} the remainder stochastic disturbance term. Note that λ_t is province-invariant and it accounts for any time-specific effect that is not included in the regression. This is particularly important for our analysis because the growth pattern of the Chinese economy has been largely dictated by the central government's macroeconomic policies: expansionary macroeconomic policies result in high growth and high inflation which, in turn, lead to austerity policies and low growth. Failing to account for such time-specific macro environments may result in a biased assessment of the effect of fiscal decentralisation on economic growth.

There is an additional question about the specification of the regression model. If μ_i and λ_t are assumed to be fixed parameters to be estimated and the remainder disturbances stochastic with $v_{it} \sim IID(0, \sigma_v^2)$, then (3) is a two-way fixed effects error component model. If all three components of the error term are stochastic, Equation (3) amounts to a two-way random-effects error component model. Since there is no compelling theoretical argument in favour of one specification against

---

[7] Variables measured in percentage are introduced into the regression equation as level variables, whereas POPT and FISCAP are in log form. It should be noted that such a specification is adopted to facilitate the interpretation of the estimates and has no bearing on the conclusion of the paper.

the other, we choose the fixed-effects over the random-effects model based strictly on the results of Hausman's specification test (see Section 5).

It is important to note that fiscal decentralisation provides local authorities with more resources and thus they can invest and spend more. Therefore, fiscal decentralisation may affect economic growth by raising investments. Part of the effects of fiscal decentralisation on economic growth would consequently be accounted for by GI in Equation (3). Fiscal decentralisation may also contribute to growth by improving the efficiency of resource allocation at the local level. If it results in more investment in infrastructure or more efficient allocation of resources, say, more investment in high productivity sector and less investment in low productivity sector, fiscal decentralisation will influence the long-term rate of economic growth. Such an effect is captured by the coefficient of FD in our growth equation and is the main concern of our empirical investigation.

4. Data

Our empirical analyses are based on province-level panel data from 28 of the 30 provinces (including three municipalities: Beijing, Shanghai, and Tianjin) in mainland China for the period 1970 to 1993.[8] Table 2 contains the list of variables used, their definitions and mean values. Per capita real GDP data are taken from *The Gross Domestic Product of China 1952–95*. Government revenues and expenditures are taken from *Compilation of Historical Statistics for Each Province, Autonomous Region, and the Directly Administered Municipalities 1949–1989* and various issues of the *Statistical Yearbook of China*. Data on fixed asset investment are taken from statistical yearbooks of the sample provinces. All these data are constructed with the actual figures in current prices and indices from 1970–1993 to obtain corresponding figures in real terms (in 1970 prices). The share of non-SOEs' output in the total industrial output and total and rural populations are taken from various issues of the *Statistical*

---

[8] Hainan and Xizan are excluded because of data incompleteness.

Table 2. Definitions and Mean Values of Variables Used

Variable	Definition	Unit	
GGDP	The growth rate of real per capita GDP	Percent	0.071
FD	Fiscal decentralisation: the marginal retention rate of locally collected budgetary revenue.	Percent	0.424
HRS	Household responsibility system: the percentage of production teams in rural areas that adopted the system.	Percent	0.607
FISCAP	Fiscal capacity: the moving average of real per capita GDP in the three years that proceed.	Yuan/person	644
POPSHR	The percent of rural population	Percent	0.760
TPOP	The total population	in thousand	36,568
FPMP	The relative price of farm products to non-farm product: the ratio of state's real procurement price index for farm products to real retail price index of manufacture goods in rural area.	Ratio	1.550
NSOESH	The share of non-SOEs' output in the total industrial output.	Percent	0.290
G_I	The growth rate of per capita fixed asset investment (in real term).	Percent	0.062
FDAVG	An alternative measure for fiscal decentralisation: the average retention rate of locally collected budgetary revenue.	Percent	0.592

Yearbook of China. The relative price of farm products to non-farm products is calculated from the information collected from *Price Statistical Yearbook of China* (*Wujia Nianjian*) and all the aforementioned data sources. The household responsibility system index measures the percentage of production teams in rural areas that adopted the system. It is taken from Lin (1992).

Measuring fiscal decentralisation is a key challenge for our work. Cross-country studies have used the ratio of state spending to federal spending as a proxy for fiscal decentralisation. However, such a measure is not feasible because data on central spending by provinces in China are not available. Alternative measures must be sought. There are two empirical studies on fiscal reforms in China, each using a different decentralisation measure. Ma (1997) measures the degree of fiscal decentralisation by the average share of government budgetary revenue retained by a province. Such a proxy, although appealing, fails to capture the dramatic change in the central-province fiscal relations initiated in the 1980s for two reasons. First, many provinces had been net contributors to the central government's budget even in the pre-reform period, i.e., they collected more revenues than they spent. Thus, by Ma's measure, fiscal decentralisation would have started much earlier even though under the unified-collection-and-budget-appropriation system, central approval was essential for any spending at the provincial level. The second reason has to do with Ma's measure being an average, rather than the marginal, retention rate. It is the rate at the margin that is expected to influence the behaviour of provincial or sub-provincial governments.

The second empirical study of fiscal decentralisation in China is Zhang and Zou (1996). Zhang and Zou measure fiscal decentralisation by the ratio of provincial spending to total central spending (or a variant). This measure is questionable. Since their province-specific decentralisation measure shares a common denominator — the total spending of the central government — the degree of fiscal decentralisation is entirely determined by the local spending of a province. The larger the local spending, the greater the fiscal decentralisation is said to be. Thus, the province with the highest local spending would also be the one that enjoys the highest degree of fiscal latitude. In reality, however, this is hardly the case because the magnitude of fiscal spending in a province reflects the population and economic size of the province instead of its fiscal freedom. For example, Sichun, the province with the highest provincial spending, did not actually enjoy more fiscal leeway than Guangxi, a much smaller province. Similarly, Shanghai, although having a larger fiscal expenditure than Tianjin, did not have more fiscal freedom.

Another important issue that is overlooked by previous studies concerns the effective starting point of fiscal decentralisation in China. It is true, as we noted earlier, that China's fiscal reform started in the early 1980s. But the revenues that were shared by the central and provincial governments were small. Moreover, the changes in the fiscal relations between the central and provincial governments were, to a large extent, experimental and temporary during 1980–1984. The revenue sharing rules were not set for multiple years and were subject to annual negotiations between the two tiers of governments. Some scholars (see, e.g., Wong 1991) have pointed out that many of the fiscal changes planned in this brief four-year period were short-lived. From the viewpoint of provincial governments, there was a great deal of uncertainty about the future fiscal policies of the central government. The best strategy for provincial governments was, quite possibly, to retain the status quo. In contrast, the fiscal reforms from 1985 onwards were much more clearly defined. The revenue sharing rules were fixed initially for three years and then for a longer period of time. Although the agreed-upon sharing formulas were changed in a few instances during the contract period, they were largely followed.

In the present study, we consider fiscal decentralisation to start in 1985 and measure it by the *marginal* retention rate of locally collected budgetary revenues by provincial governments. As discussed in Section II, there were four types of central-province fiscal arrangements in 1985–1987 and five types in 1988–1993. Our fiscal decentralisation measure is determined by how much of the revenue increment is kept by provincial governments. In cases where provinces were permitted to retain a share of their revenues, FD is equal to the share specified. Fourteen provinces in 1985–1987 and five provinces in 1988–1993 were in this category. The remaining types of arrangements imply a 100 percent marginal retention rate.[9] The marginal retention rates for the sample provinces are reported in table 1 in the column titled FD. The fiscal decentralisation measure assumes the value of zero for all provinces prior to 1985.[10]

---

[9] Sharing rules in this category are: 1) remitting a share of local revenue in the base year and the total remittance increases at a pre-determined rate in the subsequent years; 2) remitting a fixed amount of the revenues to the central government; 3) remitting a fixed amount in the base year and the total remittance increases at a pre-determined rate in the subsequent years; 4) receiving a fixed amount of subsidy from the central government; 5) receiving a fixed amount of subsidy in the base year and the total subsidy increases at a pre-determined rate in the subsequent years.

[10] See section II.

5. RESULTS

Table 3 reports the basic regression results on the growth rate of per capita GDP. Table 4 presents robustness tests of the results to alternative specifications of the measure for fiscal decentralisation. Note, first, the test statistics reported at the bottom of Table 3. The row titled HN contains the Hausman statistics for testing the random-effects model against the fixed-effects model. As the χ^2 statistics indicate, the Hausman specification tests reject the random-effects model as a valid specification. The row titled LR shows the results of likelihood ratio tests concerning the hypothesis of no fixed effects. As the χ^2 statistics are greater than the critical values corresponding to the one percent level of significance, the tests argue in favour of the two-way fixed-effects model against the classical regression with no fixed effects. Thus all regressions are specified as two-way fixed-effects models. In the interest of simplicity, the estimates for province and year dummies are not reported in the tables but are available to the reader upon request. Since the Breusch-Pagan Lagrange Multiplier test rejects the null hypothesis of homoscedasticity,[11] we report, in parentheses, the t-statistics that are based on heteroskedasticity-consistent standard errors (White 1980).

A. Basic Results

Model 1 of Table 3 is a straightforward estimation of equation (3). Fiscal decentralisation is shown to have a positive and significant effect on the growth rate of per capita GDP. The estimate, 0.0362, implies that *ceteris paribus* the growth rate of per capita GDP should rise by 3.62 percentage points in response to a fiscal decentralisation that raises the marginal retention rate of budgetary revenue from 0 to 100 percent. The rural reform is also shown to have a positive and significant impact on the growth rate. As expected, the growth rate of fixed capital investment is

---

[11] In addition, the Durbin-Watson tests revealed no evidence that the true error disturbances are auto-correlated in any of the models reported in the tables or discussed in the text.

Table 3. Growth Rate of Per Capita GDP Regressions

Variable	(1)	(2)	(3)	(4)[1]	(5)[2]
FD	0.0362 (2.703)	0.0349 (2.595)	0.0265 (2.049)	0.0259 (1.659)	0.0271 (2.039)
HRS	0.0372 (1.768)	0.0408 (1.951)	0.0448 (2.163)	0.0565 (2.304)	0.0336 (1.685)
G_I	0.0478 (3.819)	0.0493 (3.897)	0.0459 (3.692)	0.0538 (2.879)	0.0237 (1.919)
FISCAP	−0.144 (−5.308)	−0.126 (−4.509)	−0.157 (−5.664)	−0.138 (−3.810)	−0.125 (−3.804)
NSOESH	0.142 (3.163)	0.145 (3.288)	0.203 (4.116)	0.259 (3.811)	0.173 (4.052)
FPMP	0.0107 (1.158)	–	0.00522 (0.575)	−0.0172 (−1.149)	0.00575 (0.576)
POPSHR	0.0446 (0.630)	–	0.0353 (0.509)	−0.0746 (−0.422)	−0.0545 (−0.782)
TPOP	−0.209 (−1.612)	–	−0.310 (−2.366)	−0.405 (−2.634)	0.137 (3.960)
Subsidy Dummy	–	–	0.0275 (3.648)	–	–
HN[a]:	36.31 [8]	34.13 [5]	35.20 [9]	20.24 [9]	37.98 [9]
LR[a]:	289.29 [47]	285.14 [47]	286.40 [47]	181.34 [35]	215.71 [42]
Adj-R^2:	0.52	0.52	0.53	0.56	0.51
Sample size:	534	534	534	294	406

Note: Province and year dummies are included in all models; estimates are corrected for heteroskedasticity according to White (1980); t-statistics are in parentheses; [a] numbers in square brackets are degrees of freedom associated with the χ^2-statistics; [1] estimates based on the subsample excluding provinces that received subsidy from the central government; [2] estimates based on the sub-sample 1979–1993.

positively and significantly associated with the growth rate. The price reform variable is insignificant. The estimate for NSOESH is positive and statistically significant, indicating that the non-state sector has become an important impetus for economic growth. The coefficient for FISCAP is negative and statistically significant, implying that richer provinces tend to grow at a lower rate. This is suggestive evidence of conditional convergence in income levels across provinces in China. Other variables, capturing the differences in initial conditions across different regions, are generally insignificant.

To examine whether the estimated effect of fiscal decentralisation is sensitive to the inclusion of insignificant variables, we estimate model 2. The estimates hardly vary.

Recall that the degree of fiscal decentralisation is measured by the marginal retention rate on the revenue increments by provincial governments. As such, subsidy-receiving provinces have a 100 percent retention rate, similar to provinces that remit a fixed amount of their revenues to the central government. One may question the validity of such an approach. In model 3, we examine whether the estimates of model 1 remain the same when we distinguish between subsidy-receiving provinces and other provinces by introducing a dummy variable. The dummy variable, called subsidy, equals one for subsidy-receiving provinces during the period 1985–93 and zero for all other provinces and for the rest of the sample period. The estimate for fiscal decentralisation reduces from 0.0362 to 0.0265, but remains statistically significant at the one percent level. The coefficient for the newly added dummy variable is positive and significant, indicating that *ceteris paribus* subsidy-receiving provinces grow at a faster rate. The estimates for all other variables are very similar to those of model 1. A second way to deal with the issue is to estimate model 1 using a sub-sample that excludes all subsidy-receiving provinces. This is done in model 4. These estimates are very similar to those in model 3 and are also in line with those in model 1, despite the almost 50 percent reduction in the sample size. There is no compelling evidence, therefore, against our treating subsidy-receiving provinces as having a 100 percent marginal revenue retention rate.

Another potential source of bias is that parameter values in the pre-reform period may be different from those in the reform period. In other words, the estimates may be sensitive to the inclusion of the data from the pre-reform years. In model 5, we report the results of the growth regression applied to the sub-sample covering only the reform period

1979–1993.[12] The estimate for FD remains statistically significant and is similar to its counterparts in models 3 and 4. The most noticeable change happens to the estimate for the total population. Unlike in the previous models, this coefficient is positive and statistically significant, suggesting that larger provinces tend to grow faster than smaller ones. No appreciable changes occur in the rest of the estimates. There is no strong evidence, therefore, that our results are driven by the pre-reform sub-sample.

B. Robustness Tests for the Specification of Fiscal Decentralisation Variable

It is conceivable that a substantial period of time may pass between the initiation of a reform measure and its final impact on the growth rate. To explore such a possibility, we specify the growth rate to be a function of the fiscal decentralisation variable lagged by one or two years. The lag allows for the response time of the growth rate to changes in this reform measure. When the fiscal decentralisation variable lagged by one year is used in model 1 of Table 4, all estimates, especially that for the fiscal decentralisation, are remarkably similar to those of model 1 in Table 3. In model 2 of Table 4, the fiscal decentralisation measure lagged by two years is introduced. Again, the results indicate that fiscal decentralisation has had a positive impact on the rate of economic growth. The only discernible change is with respect to the size of the estimate associated with the fiscal decentralisation variable, which is bigger than its counterparts in any of the models analysed so far. It might be tempting for us to identify what the optimal lag structure is for this variable. However, the presence of high autocorrelation in the fiscal decentralisation variable rules out a meaningful analysis of the distributed lag structure. Nevertheless, when we specify a lag structure that includes

---

[12] An alternative way to address the issue is to test the stability of the parameters in the growth equation between the pre-reform and reform periods. However, because FD and HRS assume the value of zero during the pre-reform period, the Chow's test is not feasible.

Table 4. Growth Rate of Per Capita GDP Regressions

Variable	(1)[1]	(2)[2]	(3)[3]	(4)[4]	(5)	(6)
FD	0.0372 (2.750)	0.0503 (3.633)	0.0217 (2.510)	0.0315 (2.422)	—	0.0254 (1.607)
FDAVG[a]	—	—	—	—	0.0119 (2.358)	0.0082 (1.392)
HRS	0.0387 (1.831)	0.0411 (1.938)	0.0374 (1.774)	0.0379 (1.788)	0.0397 (1.863)	0.0389 (1.839)
G_I	0.0489 (3.865)	0.0484 (3.858)	0.0478 (3.822)	0.0479 (3.829)	0.0483 (3.854)	0.0481 (3.848)
FISCAP	−0.144 (−5.298)	−0.147 (−5.398)	−0.143 (−5.266)	−0.143 (−5.267)	−0.142 (−5.206)	−0.145 (−5.338)
NSOESH	0.145 (3.216)	0.159 (3.433)	0.138 (3.097)	0.138 (3.087)	0.155 (3.313)	0.157 (3.386)
FPMP	0.00974 (1.049)	0.00948 (1.019)	0.0105 (1.136)	0.0106 (1.147)	0.0103 (1.149)	0.0101 (1.117)
POPSHR	0.0417 (0.593)	0.0376 (0.541)	0.0426 (0.601)	0.0416 (0.587)	0.0390 (0.551)	0.0438 (0.618)
TPOP	−0.206 (−1.593)	−0.208 (−1.611)	−0.207 (−1.599)	−0.206 (−1.589)	−0.253 (−1.915)	−0.243 (−1.819)
Adj-R^2:	0.52	0.52	0.52	0.52	0.52	0.52
Sample size:	534	534	534	534	534	534

Note: Province and year dummies are included in all models; estimates are corrected for heteroskedasticity according to White (1980); t-statistics are in parentheses; [1] FD is introduced as a lagged variable (by one period); [2] FD is introduced as a lagged variable (by two periods); [3] FD is introduced in log form; [4] FD is introduced in logistic form; [a] FDAVG is defined as the average rate of budgetary revenues retained by provincial governments.

FD lagged by one year and two years, we obtain positive estimates for both of them but the estimated standard errors become predictably larger because of the presence of multicollinearity.[13]

So far, we have chosen the linear transformation of the marginal retention rate as our standard fiscal decentralisation measure. However,

[13] We have also conducted regression analyses in which HRS is introduced in lag forms. The results are not sensitive to alternative specifications of the lag structure for this variable.

it is possible that the relationship between the degree of fiscal decentralisation and the growth rate is non-linear. To examine the robustness of our results to alternative specifications of FD, we therefore rerun the regression model 1 of Table 3 using a logarithm transformation and a logistic transformation of this variable.[14] The results are reported in models 3 and 4 of Table 4, respectively. The estimates for FD are still positive and statistically significant. The estimate from the logarithm specification, 0.0217, implies that a switch from a centrally controlled fiscal system to a fully decentralised one should raise the rate of growth by about 10 percent. A similar interpretation obtains from the estimate pertaining to the logistic transformation of FD. The estimates for all other variables hardly change.[15]

We next examine the robustness of our results to an alternative, but less pertinent, measure for fiscal decentralisation. In model 5 of Table 4, the average revenue retention rate is used.[16] The results are generally consistent with the findings in the previous regression models. The only noticeable change is that the estimate for FD is much smaller than the estimates obtained from other models where fiscal decentralisation is defined as the marginal retention rate of budget revenue by a province. This indicates that the growth rate is more responsive to a change in the marginal retention rate than in the average retention rate. Put differently, two provinces that are allowed to keep the same proportion of their budget revenues may experience different growth rates of per capita GDP just because they are subject to different retention rates at the margin. In this case, the growth rate is higher in the province facing a

---

[14] For a general logistic function, FD={1+exp[(−X+a)/k]}$^{-1}$, the mean is a, and the standard deviation is kπ/3$^{0.5}$. We assign the inflection point of the function to 50 percent marginal retention rate (i.e., a = 0.5) and set the standard deviation to 0.25 so that the marginal retention rate variable (X) falls within two standard deviations of the mean.

[15] In principle the same specification issue applies to HRS. We focus on testing the robustness of the estimate associated with FD to alternative specifications because fiscal decentralization is the central concern of the study. However, when HRS is also introduced in log or logistic form, its estimate as well as that of FD remain positive and statistically significant.

[16] See our criticism of the average revenue retention rate in the previous section.

higher marginal retention rate than in the one having a lower marginal retention rate. In fact, when we introduce both measures (the marginal and the average retention rates) in model 6 of Table 4, the estimate associated with the marginal retention rate remains positive and significant at the 10 percent level, whereas the estimate for the average retention rate (albeit positive) loses significance. This may suggest that the marginal retention rate is a superior measure for fiscal decentralisation. Furthermore, the estimate is larger for the former (0.0254) than for the latter (0.0082), consistent with the results from the models where the two measures are introduced separately.

C. *Testing the Exogeneity of the Fiscal Decentralisation Measure*

Although the results of our regression analysis show that fiscal decentralisation is strongly associated with the growth rate of per capita GDP, it is arguable that the direction of causality may go from the latter to the former: poor provinces with low growth rates tend to be receivers of fiscal transfers from the central government whereas rich provinces with high growth rates are more likely to be given greater fiscal freedom. If this is the case, all our estimates will suffer from endogeneity bias and hence will be inconsistent. There are several indications, however, that fiscal decentralisation is exogenously determined. First, we find that our measure for fiscal decentralisation, FD, is quite stable. It assumes the value of zero in all provinces before 1985 and shows little within-province variation over time during the remainder of our sample period. The central-province fiscal arrangement was changed only once after it was first introduced in 1985. The adjustment was made in 1988 and was implemented accordingly till 1993, the last year of our sample period. Second, we have conducted a Hausman test of the potential endogeneity of the fiscal decentralisation variable. This test fails to reject the hypothesis that the marginal retention rate on budget revenue is exogenous to the model.[17]

---

[17] We have also tested the exogeneity of HRS jointly with FD. Hausman test reveals no strong evidence that HRS and FD should be treated as endogenous variables.

D. Investment and Other Dimensions of Fiscal Decentralisation

We have argued in Section 3 that fiscal decentralisation may raise the growth rate in two ways. First, fiscal decentralisation can lead to an increase of capital investment at the provincial level, which, in turn, brings about economic growth. For provincial governments, the incentives to invest are stronger under a decentralised fiscal system than under a centralised one, because the former affords provincial governments a greater share of returns that additional investment may generate. Indeed, if there exists a positive relationship between fiscal decentralisation and the amount of provincial government investment, the estimates for fiscal decentralisation reported in Tables 3 and 4 would understate the total effect of fiscal decentralisation on economic growth. We examine this issue through an independent regression analysis, in which the growth rate of per capita investment (GI) is regressed against FD and other independent variables included in the growth regressions. The result shows that fiscal decentralisation and investment are positively correlated. However, the correlation is not statistically significant.[18] Thus, based on our sample, there is no compelling evidence suggesting that fiscal decentralisation promotes growth by raising total capital investment.

The second channel through which fiscal decentralisation increases the growth rate is the enhancement of efficiency of resource allocations. As we have noted in section 1, provincial governments may have an informational advantage vis-à-vis the central government about the local needs and, as a result, are able to deliver public goods and services that are sensitive to local economic conditions. For example, a province can increase its total output by allocating more resources, or reallocating

---

[18] The regression model (province and time dummies are included but not shown) and results are: G_I = 0.00245 (0.038) * FD + 0.0247 (0.317) * HRS – 0.0834 (-0.875) * FISCAP – 0.0451 (-0.242) * NSOESH + 0.00369 (0.091) * FPMP – 0.0388 (-0.148) *POPSHR – 0.580 (-1.768) * LPOPT, where the numbers in parentheses are t-statistics and all variables are as defined in table 2. The adjusted R^2 = 0.41. Furthermore, the relationship between G_I and FD appears to be insensitive to alternative regression specifications. For example, the estimated coefficient for FD remains positive and insignificant in a simple regression of G_I against FD.

resources from low-productivity, to high-productivity areas. It is important to note that such efficiency gains due to fiscal decentralisation, similar to technological changes, can have long-lasting effects on the growth rate of per capita GDP. Our econometric model allows us to isolate such effects. And the estimation results show, unequivocally, that fiscal decentralisation has made significant contributions to the rate of economic growth among provinces in China.

However, the paucity of relevant data precludes a detailed analysis on how fiscal decentralisation has brought about efficiency gains in China. Nevertheless, there is some evidence from aggregate provincial statistics suggesting that in the wake of fiscal decentralisation provincial governments have allocated a bigger portion of their revenues to high productivity areas. For example, we find a positive and significant association between the share of budgetary expenditure on infrastructure investment and the degree of fiscal decentralisation.[19] One possible interpretation of this result is that provincial governments have tried to improve the efficiency of resource allocation by spending more on infrastructure, which increases the productivity of all other forms of capital, and less on low productivity areas, such as the agricultural sector.[20] Perhaps, the most telling evidence is the active involvement of county governments in the development of township and village enterprises (TVEs). Fiscal decentralisation was not confined to central-provincial fiscal relations. Similar decentralised fiscal arrangements were introduced between provincial and county governments. This has changed the investment behaviour of county governments, who now can keep a greater share of locally generated revenues. As a result, they have stronger

---

[19] The regression model (province and time dummies are included but not shown) and results are: BESHINF = 0.0486 (3.033) * FD – 0.0569 (-3.401) * HRS + 0.0249 (2.694) * G$_I$ + 0.119 (5.371) * FISCAP – 0.138 (-3.794) * NSOESH – 0.00344 (-0.398) * FPMP – 0.132 (-1.981) * POPSHR – 0.419 (-0.510) * TPOP, where BESHINF is the share of budgetary expenditure on infrastructure investment, the numbers in parentheses are t-statistics, and explanatory variables are as defined in Table 2. A simple regression of BESHINF against FD yields an estimate of 0.0655 for FD with a t-statistic of 3.986.
[20] The relationship between the shares of budgetary expenditure on agriculture related activities and fiscal decentralization is statistically insignificant albeit positive.

incentives not only to invest more but also to invest more in high productivity rural industrial sector: building more TVEs. A fuller analysis of the role played by county governments is beyond the scope of the current study.[21]

Our use of the marginal retention rate as a measure of fiscal decentralisation is an improvement over the measures used in previous studies. But it is not a perfect indicator. The level of fiscal decentralisation also depends on the degree to which the central government can interfere in local government's financial affairs through other channels. For example, the central government may grant a province some preferential policies, such as permission to set up special economic zones and the power to approve investment projects. However, to the extent that such policies are province specific, their effects are captured by province dummies, which we have introduced in all the growth regressions.

6. Conclusion

In this paper, we investigate the effect of fiscal decentralisation initiated in the mid-1980s in China on the growth rate of per capita GDP. We find that fiscal decentralisation has made a significant contribution to economic growth, consistent with the hypothesis that fiscal decentralisation can increase economic efficiency. In addition, we also find that the rural reform, capital accumulation and non-state sector development are the key driving forces of the economic growth in China over the past twenty or so years.

These results allow us to draw two conclusions. First and more general is that institutional arrangements matter. Besides fiscal decentralisation, other reforms (the household responsibility system in the rural sector and the "privatisation" of the industrial sector by way of expanding the

---

[21] There is some preliminary evidence suggesting a positive linkage between the development of TVEs and fiscal decentralization. When we regress provincial per capita TVE investment on our fiscal decentralization measure and other control variables, we obtain a positive estimate for FD. However, the estimate is not statistically significant.

non-state-owned enterprises) have also been conducive to economic growth in China. Second, according to the data set, fiscal decentralisation has raised the growth rate in China mainly by improving the efficiency of resource allocation rather than by inducing more investment.

It should be noted that the changes in the fiscal relationship between the central and provincial governments in China since the 1980s are much more intricate. The marginal rate of budget revenues retained by provincial governments, which we have adopted as the measure of fiscal decentralisation in the empirical investigation, will not fully capture the intricacy. A better understanding of the factors and mechanisms that are crucial to the central-province negotiation process is important. For this reason, the results of this study should be viewed as tentative and further investigation is most desirable.

References

Bahl, Roy W. and Linn, Johannes F., *Urban Public Finance in Developing Countries*, New York: Oxford University Press, 1992.

Barro, Robert J., "Government Spending in a Simple Model of Endogenous Growth," *Journal of Political Economy* 98, vol. 5, pt. 2, 1990, S103–25.

Bird, Richard M., "Threading the Fiscal Labyrinth: Some Issues in Fiscal Decentralisation," *National Tax Journal* XLVI, vol. 2, 1993, 207–27.

China Ministry of Finance, *Ten Years Reform in Finance and Taxation (Caishui Gaige Shi Nian)*, Department of System Reforms, Beijing: Chinese Finance and Economics Publishing House, 1989.

China Ministry of Finance, *China Fiscal Statistics 1950–91*, Beijing: Chinese Finance and Economics Publishing House, 1992.

China Statistical Bureau, *Compilation of Historical Statistics for Each Province, Autonomous Region, and the Directly Administered Municipalities 1949–1989*, Beijing: Statistical Publishing House, 1990.

China Statistical Bureau, *Price Statistical Yearbook of China (Wujia Nianjian)*, Beijing: Statistical Publishing House, various years.

China Statistical Bureau, *Statistical Yearbook of China*, Beijing: Statistical Publishing House, various years.

China Statistical Bureau, *The Gross Domestic Product of China, 1952–1995*, Liaoning: Dongbei University of Finance and Economic Press, 1997.

Dangdai Zhongguo Caizheng Editing Committee, *Public Finance in Modern China (Dangdai Zhongguo Caizheng)*, Beijing: China Social Sciences Press, 1988.

Jorgenson, Dale W. and Yu, Kun-Yong, "Tax Reform and U.S. Economic Growth," *Journal of Political Economy* 98, vol. 5, pt. 2, 1990, S151-93.

King, Robert G. and Rebelo, Sergio, "Public Policy and Economic Growth: Developing Neoclassical Implications," *Journal of Political Economy* 98, vol. 5, pt. 2, 1990, S126-50.

Lardy, Nicholas, "Centralisation and Decentralisation in China's Fiscal Management," *The China Quarterly* 61, March 1975, 26-60.

Lin, Justin Yifu, "Rural Reforms and Agricultural Growth in China," *American Economic Review* 82, 1992, 34-51.

Lin, Justin Yifu; Liu, Zhiqiang; and Zhong, Funning, "Fiscal Decentralisation and Rural Development in China," a Report Submitted to the World Bank, June 1997.

Liu, Zhiqiang, "Fiscal Decentralisation and Rural Growth," manuscript, December 1997.

Ma, Jun, *China's Economic Reform in the 1990s*, 1997.

Mankiw, Gregory N.; Romer, David; and Weil, David N., "A Contribution to the Empirics of Economic Growth," *The Quarterly Journal of Economics*, May 1992, 407-37.

Oates, Wallace E., *Fiscal Federalism*. New York: Harcourt Brace Jovanovich, 1972.

Oates, Wallace E., "Fiscal Decentralisation and Economic Development," *National Tax Journal* XLVI, vol. 2, 1993, 237-43.

Oksenberg, Michel and Tong, James, "The Evolution of Central-Provincial Fiscal Relations in China, 1971-1984: The Formal System," *The China Quarterly* 125, March 1991, 1-32.

Perkins, Dwight H., "Reforming China's Economic System," *Journal of Economic Literature* 26, June 1988, 601-45.

Prud'homme, Remy, "The Dangers of Decentralisation," *The World Bank Research Observer*, August 1995, 210-26.

Qian, Yingyi and Weingast, Barry R., *China's Transition to Markets: Market-preserving Federalism, Chinese Style*, Stanford, CA: Hoover Institution on War, Revolution and Peace, Stanford University, 1995.

Qian, Yingyi and Roland, Gerard. "The Soft Budget Constraint in China," *Japan and the World Economy* 8, June 1996, 217-23.

Shah, Anwar and Qureshi, Zia, "Intergovernmental Fiscal Relations in Indonesia," 239 World Bank Discussion papers, 1994.

Zhang, Tao and Zou, Heng-fu, "Fiscal Decentralisation, Public Spending, and Economic Growth in China," manuscript, Policy Research Department of the World Bank, 1996.

White, Herbert, "A Heteroskedasticity-Consistent Covariance Matrix Estimator and a Direct Test for Heteroskedasticity," *Econometrica* 48, May 1980, 817–38.

Wong, Christine P.W., "Central-Local Relations in an Era of Fiscal Decline: The Paradox of Fiscal Decentralisation in Post-Mao China," *China Quarterly* 128, 1991, 691–715.

Wong, Christine P.W., "Fiscal Reform and Local Industrialisation," *Modern China* 18, 1992, 197–227.

Wong, Christine P.W.; Heady, Christopher; and Woo Wing T., *Fiscal Management and Economic Reform in the People's Republic of China*, Oxford University Press, 1995.

Xie, Danyang; Zou, Heng-fu; and Davoodi, Hamid, "Fiscal Decentralisation and Economic Growth in the United States," *Journal of Urban Economics* 45, 1999, 228–39.

Zhu, Xingmin (ed.), *Reform and Practice of Financial System and Management in Jiangsu Province (Jiangsu Sheng Caizheng Guanli Tizhi Gaige Yu Shijian)*, Beijing: China Financial and Economic Publishing House, 1993.

7

Too Many Fees and Too Many Charges: China Streamlines Fiscal System

LIN SHUANGLIN*

LUAN SHOUFEI: A RUNAWAY HORSE IN CHINA

Luan Shoufei (亂收費, illicit collection of fees and other charges) has been one of the most noticeable economic phenomenon in China since the start of its economic reform. Government administrative and operating fees, government service charges, and various government funds amounted to about 400 billion yuan in 1996, accounting for 54% of total budgetary revenue and 35.4% of total government revenue (budgetary plus extra-budgetary revenue). No other government in the world has such a high proportion of fee in its total revenue. There are more than 1000 types of fees authorized by the government, compared

---

*Professor Lin Shuanglin is Professor of Economics at the University of Nebraska, USA. He was Visiting Senior Research Fellow of East Asian Institute in 2000. He would like to express his deep appreciation to Professor John Wong, EAI Research Director, for bringing his attention to this important subject, and for Professor Wong's helpful comments and suggestions. Thanks also go to Mr. Gu Qingyang, Miss Nah Seok Lin, and Mr. Aw Beng Teck for their valuable help.

to only 23 taxes! [Gao (1999)] In 1997, the total number of administrative and operating fees reportedly reached 6800 (authorized and unauthorized).[1] As an old Chinese saying goes, "Tyranny is fiercer than a tiger (*ke zheng meng yu hu* 苛政猛於虎)." Today, many Chinese are saying, "Excessive fees are fiercer than a tiger (*ke fei meng yu hu* 苛費猛於虎)!"

Fee collection emerged along with the establishment of the People's Republic of China. There are mainly two different types of fees, namely, administrative fee (*xingzheng xing shoufei* 行政性收費) and operating fee (*shiye xing shoufei* 事業性收費). Government branches and institutions are all involved in fee collection, such as state-owned banks, customs, all commissions (e.g., education, economic and trade, and birth control), all bureaus (price control, foreign exchange, environmental protection, industry and commerce, etc.), and all ministries (e.g., public security, civil affairs, justice, labor, finance, culture, health, transportation, construction, light industry, agriculture, forestry, etc.).

Administrative fees are collected by government branches and authorized organizations using administrative power. Administrative fees include: fees for certificates, registration, and permits (e.g., permits for producing a product or operating a business, fee for visa application, fee for holding a weapon, export or import permit, driver's license), fees for application forms (e.g., application forms for importing goods and vehicle number application), fees for resource management (e.g., land management fee, and mineral resource compensation fee); fund-raising (road maintenance fee, port construction fee, bridge fee, extra education fee, and old-age and retirement funds); and various fines.

Operating fees are collected by government branches and institutes for providing monopolistic services. They include examination and inspection fees (e.g., examination of a product, evaluation of an invention, driver's test, and examination for self-learners); education or information fees (e.g., tuition, consulting fees, boarding expenses, and weather forecasts); and fees for health services (hospital fees, immunization fees, and examination of epidemic disease).

---

[1] *People's Daily*, April 25, 1999.

Explosive Growth

Most fees are included in extra-budgetary revenues collected by local fiscal authorities, central and local government branches, state enterprises, and government agencies and institutions.[2] The data on the revenue from fee collection is not available annually. However, the data on the total extra-budgetary revenue is available. Table 1 shows the real extra-budgetary revenue, its ratio to budgetary revenue, and its composition from 1952 to 1996. The ratio of extra-budgetary revenue to budgetary revenue was 7.8% in 1952, 4.2% in 1953, 20.6% in 1960, 16% in 1965, and 31% in 1978. Extra-budgetary revenues expanded greatly since 1978. While extra-budgetary revenue accounted for 76% of budgetary revenue in 1985, it reached 111% of budgetary revenue in 1992! The coverage of extra-budgetary revenue has been largely adjusted since 1993. Currently, extra-budgetary revenue only includes the extra-revenue of local fiscal authority, and the administrative and operating units of government but not the extra-budgetary revenue of state enterprises. Thus, figures of total extra-budgetary revenue after 1993 were incomparable with the figures before 1993.

Table 1 also shows the real extra-budgetary revenue of local government, administrative units and institutions from 1952 to 1997, which is equal to total extra-budgetary revenue minus extra-budgetary revenue of state enterprises and are comparable throughout the whole period. It can be seen that the real extra-budgetary revenue of local government, administrative units, and institutions has been increasing rapidly since 1978, from 7 billion yuan in 1978 to 65 billion yuan in 1996 at 1950 constant price, a nine-fold increase in 16 years.

---

[2] Extra-budget revenues include: revenues from the service provided by government agencies; administrative fees (license fee, etc.); and revenues from business run by colleges, high schools and primary schools. Extra-budgetary revenues are used for investment in fixed assets, for city maintenance, for welfare, for encouragement and awards, for administrative and business activities, etc.

Table 1. Composition of Real Extra-Budgetary Revenue
(100 Million Yuan, 1950 = 100)*

Year	Total Extra-Budgetary Revenue	Extra-budgetary Revenue/ Budgetary Revenue	Extra-Budgetary Funds of Local Government & Administrative Units and Institutions	Local Fiscal Authority	Administrative Units & Institutions
1952	12.18	0.08	11.21	11.21	0.00
1955	14.39	0.07	5.82	2.74	3.08
1960	93.11	0.21	36.77	18.49	18.28
1965	56.14	0.16	20.96	7.04	13.92
1970	76.76	0.15	31.52	10.23	21.29
1978	255.42	0.31	69.54	22.88	46.66
1979	326.73	0.40	78.35	28.82	49.54
1980	379.44	0.48	78.48	27.81	50.67
1981	399.65	0.51	83.91	27.46	56.45
1982	523.64	0.66	95.51	29.53	65.98
1983	621.90	0.71	105.19	32.00	73.19
1984	742.80	0.72	123.59	34.52	89.08
1985	878.82	0.76	159.28	25.32	133.96
1986	941.63	0.82	182.88	23.41	159.47
1987	1024.65	0.92	203.55	22.53	181.02
1988	1006.30	1.00	207.96	20.86	187.10
1989	961.95	1.00	200.80	19.67	181.14
1990	959.83	0.92	225.92	21.47	204.45
1991	1116.84	1.03	263.69	23.68	240.01
1992	1259.78	1.11	309.26	29.70	279.56
1993	413.55	0.33	413.55	33.11	380.44
1994	441.88	0.36	441.88	33.22	408.66
1995	497.31	0.39	497.31	35.47	461.84
1996	703.58	0.53	654.26	40.60	613.66
1997	506.68	0.33	453.65	20.78	432.87

Sources: Statistical Yearbook of China, 1989, 1998, and 1999.

*The coverage of the extra-budgetary revenue and expenditures has been adjusted largely since 1993, and the data may not be comparable with those in previous years. Since 1997, the extra-budgetary revenue does not include the government funds (fees) that are included in the budgetary revenue.

Excessiveness

The Chinese economy is inundated by too many fees.[3] From the State Council to village and neighborhood committees, fee collection exists wherever administrative power exists. There are 340 administrative and operating fees authorized by the State Council, involving more than 50 ministries, commissions and bureaus. In addition, there are several hundred items of fees authorized by provincial government (autonomous regions and municipality directly under the central government). There also exist 421 items of various funds and additional charges. Foreign investors also need to pay fees. A survey indicated that in Weihai city of Shandong province, there existed 5000 fees related to foreign investment, of which 3971 are at the province level.[4]

The revenue from fee collection is enormous. It was reported that the administrative and operating fees amounted to 195.8 billion yuan in 1996, of which 56.2 billion yuan and 139.6 billion yuan were from administrative fees and operating fees, respectively. Various funds and additional charges came up to 217.2 billion yuan (not including social security funds of 101.4 billion yuan). All these added up to about 400 billion yuan [Wang (1999)], accounting for 54% of total budgetary revenue (which was 740.8 billion yuan in 1996).

Every country in the world collects fees, in addition to collecting taxes; for example, passport fee, marriage license fee, business registration fee, and so on. In most countries, fees are only a small part of government revenue. However, no country in the world has such high fees in government revenue as China. Table 2 shows the ratio of fees, service charges, non-industrial and incidental sales, fines and forfeits to total government revenue for selected countries. The ratio was only 3.51% in the U.S. in 1996, 2.93% in the UK in 1995, 7.67% in Australia in 1997, 6.75% in India in 1995, and 2.12% in Thailand in 1996, compared to 38.8% in China.

In Shiyan city of Hubei province, there were 26 government agencies and units collecting 79 different types of fees from private enterprises

---

[3] After the tax reform in 1994, the number of taxes was reduced to only 23.
[4] *Cangao Xiaoxi* (Reference News), December 17, 1998.

Table 2. Administrative Fees, Charges, Nonindustrial and Incidental Sales, Fines and Forfeits as Percentage of Total Government Revenues (FEE) in Selected Countries*

Country	Year	Fee (%)
China	1996	35.4
U.S.	1996	3.5
U.K.	1995	2.9
France	1997	6.3
Australia	1997	7.7
Mexico	1996	1.5
India	1995	6.8
Indonesia	1993	1.8
Malaysia	1997	6.4
Thailand	1996	2.1

*The figures are calculated by the author based on *Government Finance Statistics Yearbook*, IMF, 1998.

and industrial and commercial households [Zheng (1994)]. In Suzhou city of Jiangsu province, the number of fees imposed on farmers reached 56, and the number of collectors amounted to 20 [Suzhou Price Bureau (1993)]. In Fujian province alone, in 1997, there were 22,542 administrative and operating units to collect fees. The revenue from fee collection was 6.7 billion yuan in 1997 [Cheng (1999)]. One enterprise in Shanghai was "invited" to join 120 associations and pay membership fee of 110,000 yuan, besides registration fee, document fee, and travel fee for each meeting.[5]

Fees are multifarious. In Fuzhou prefecture of Jiangxi province, industrial and commercial households and private enterprises were subjected to more than 30 kinds of fees: industrial and commercial management fee, facility renting fee, various license fees, various management fees, various registration fees, public security fee (*zhi an fei* 治安費), security insurance fee (*bao an fei* 保安費), joint defense fee (*lian fang fei* 聯防費), tea fee, road occupation fee, sanitation fee, physical

[5] *Jingji Cankao Bao* (Economic Reference News), December 22, 1994.

examination fee (*ti jian fei* 體檢費), garbage clearance fee (*laji qingsao fei* 垃圾清掃費), garbage moving fee (*laji daiyun fei* 垃圾代運費), garbage disposal fee (*laji chuli fei* 垃圾處理費), anti-pollution fee (*paiwu fei* 排污費), sanitation supervision and examination fee (*weisheng jiandu jiance fei* 衛生監督監測費), newspaper and magazine fee (*shubao zazhi fei* 書報雜誌費), greening fee (*luhua fei* 綠化費), various sport game judgment fee (*jingsai pingbi fei* 競賽評比費), secrecy guarantee fee (*baomi baozheng jin* 保密保證金), security responsibility deposit (*zhi an zeren zhuang yajin* 治安責任狀押金), road and market construction fund-raising, education and electricity fund-raising, single-girl family sterilization fee (*chun nu hu jiezha fei* 純女戶結扎費), Madame Song Qingling foundation contribution (*Song Qingling jijin* 宋慶齡基金), contribution to the foundation for taking up the cudgels for a justice (*Jianyiyongwei jijin* 見義勇爲基金), and so on [Wu (1997)].

In the urban area, real estate development firms had to pay 48 to 172 types of fees, along with 12 types of taxes. In Hunan province in 1998, fees collected from individual and private enterprises amounted to more than 140 types, involving 40 government administrative and operating units. According to a survey of 100 industrial and commercial households conducted by Zhangjiajie city of Hunan province, the fees paid was 10 times as high as taxes.[6] In Wuxi city of Zhejiang province, the number of fees reached nearly 4000 [Jia (1999)].

Irregularity

According to State Council documents, the Price Control Bureau of both central and local governments are responsible for the management and supervision of administrative and operating fee collection, and should set the standard of fees in consultation with other related branches of government.[7] Later, the State Council specified clearly that the right to

---

[6] *People's Daily*, June 21, 1999.
[7] The State Council of the People's Republic of China, *Zhonghua renmin gongheguo jiage guanli tiaoli* (Price Control Regulations of the People's Republic of China), November 1987.

set up a new item of administrative and operating fee would belong to the Ministry of Finance, in consultation with the Price Control Bureau, while the right to set the level of fees would belong to the Price Control Bureau, in consultation with the Ministry of Finance.[8] Recently the government announced that only the central government and provincial government have the right to establish an administrative or operating fee. Despite the rulings, in reality, fee collection (including charges and fund-raising) is in a state of disorder, characterized by the arbitrary setting up of new fees and increases in the level of fees (*luan shoufee* 亂收費), the arbitrary raising of funds from local enterprises and individuals (*luan jizi* 亂集資), and the arbitrary additions of new fines and increases in the levels of existing fines (*luan fakuan* 亂罰款).

First, raising the level of fees without the government's permission. Some areas raised market fees (such as market management fee, economic contract evaluation fee, industrial and commercial household registration fee, and market exchange fee) by 15–40%. For example, in Hebei province, the fee for a one-child birth permit was set at 1.5 yuan by the provincial birth control agency. However, the actual fee for the permit was between 20 to 60 yuan.[9]

Second, enacting fees without authorization. In 1998, there were 204 kinds of fees collected from township enterprises by more than 60 agencies and units, of which 46% were inappropriate and unauthorized fees [Research Group (1998)]. According to a survey by Guangdong Bureau of Pricing, one-third of the total fee collected from firms was set by the central and provincial government, while two-thirds were unlawfully enacted by lower level of government and its branches [Liu (1996). In some areas, a young couple needs to pay more than 20 kinds of fees to get a marriage licence [Pan (1993)].

Third, continuing to collect fees already abolished by the government. Hunan province eliminated market management fee for the book market. However, with the authorization of the city's Price Bureau and Finance Bureau, the News and Publishing Bureau of Changsha city continued to

---

[8] The State Council, May 1991.
[9] *People's Daily*, June 21, 1999.

collect market management fees of 380,000 yuan from 242 individual booksellers in Dingwangtai book market.[10]

Fourth, collecting fees and fines in advance. Some local governments force firms to pay cash pledge for security. Some schools even ask their students to deposit money in school to pay for fines (students are fined for failure in an exam, absence, being late, and so on) [Chen (1993)]. In January 1999, Dapozhen Public Security Bureau in Yushu City of Jilin Province collected a fine of 5000 yuan from each village in advance for potential illegal gambling activities. The revenue was spent by the Public Security Bureau.[11] Normally, fines are used to punish unlawful activities. However, in this case, fines were collected as a form of revenue. The fines became the permit fee for gambling, and thus, actually encouraged gambling activities.

PROLIFERATION OF FEES — A PRODUCT OF ECONOMIC TRANSITION

There are several reasons for the rapid expansion of fee collection. These include fiscal decentralization, the decline in government budgetary revenue, the increase in government branches and institutions, and the lack of rule of law.

Fiscal Decentralization

Before 1978, the Chinese government's fiscal policy was "*tongshou tongzhi* (collecting revenues uniformly and paying expenditures uniformly 統收統支)". While the central government financed all public projects and public welfare, the government branches and institutions managed their own budget, strictly following the central government's regulations; they only issued basic wages and salaries to their employees and had no incentive to collect fees. Administrative branches and operating units

---

[10] *People's Daily*, June 21, 1999.
[11] *Zhongguo Caijin Bao* (China's Financial and Economic News), June 16, 1999.

only collected limited fees, such as business registration fee, marriage license fee, tuition fee in high schools and elementary schools.

Fiscal decentralization is an important component of economic reform which started in 1978. Local governments were given the right to make their own investment decisions. Central government branches and institutions, as well as local governments, were allowed to dispose the revenue they earned, such as issuing bonuses and awards to their employees. The principle of managing self-earned revenues is as follows, "putting them into special savings account, managing them with a plan, using them with the authorization of fiscal authorities (*caizheng shenpi* 財政審批), accepting government banks supervision, self-collect and self-use". The last principle is the key, all the others exist only in name. This is understandable since with higher revenue, they can increase wages and salaries, issue more bonuses and awards to their employees, improve office conditions, purchase other facilities (such as luxury cars). Thus, there exist strong incentives for government agencies and local government to reap more revenue from fee collection.

Decline in Government Budgetary Revenue

Tax reform is an important aspect of economic reform.[12] Tax reforms in China have resulted in a continuous decline in government budgetary revenue. As a share of GDP, this revenue decreased from 34% in 1978 to 23.4% in 1980, 14.7% in 1992, and 11.6% in 1996. Facing limited revenue and growing demand for expenditures, the central government allowed central government branches and local governments to collect their own revenues. In 1980, the government started the "fiscal responsibility system (*caizheng baogan* 財政包幹)", calling on every government institution with potential for fund-raising to actively expand

---

[12] Tax reforms have experienced the following stages: allowing the state enterprises to keep some profits (*fenquan rangli* 分權讓利) in 1979, substituting taxes for profit (*li gai shui* 利改稅) in 1983, the Contract Responsibility System in 1986, tax plus profit system (*li shui fenliu* 利稅分流) in 1989, and eventually, tax sharing system (*fen shui zhi* 分稅制) in 1994.

services and pursue revenues, in order to solve the problem of fund shortage. In 1989, the Ministry of Finance announced clearly that government institutions should only rely on government fully or partially for some expenditures, and on themselves for other expenditures [Wu (1997)]. The government did not have enough money, instead it set favorable policies to facilitate revenue collection.

Government branches and institutions were forced to pursue revenues (chuangshou 創收). Many government branches and institutions began to start their own businesses. Most of them failed either because of poor management skills or government regulations. They however finally found their own "comparative advantage" in pursuing revenue — collecting fees (including service charges and fines)!

Expansion of Government Administrative Branches and Institutions

Government branches and institutions have greatly expanded. From 1984 to 1990, the number of government branches increased by 55,000.[27] Workers and staff in government agencies, party agencies and social organizations increased from 4.17 million in 1978 to 10.74 million in 1997.[13]

Not only is the number of government employees increasing, their salaries are also increasing as income for non-government employees rises. The average wages and salaries for employees in government agencies, party agencies and social organization are generally higher. For example, the average annual salary for a staff working in a government or party agency or any social organization in 1998 was 7,776 yuan, while it was 7,668 yuan for an average employee in the entire state sector (including SOEs). Thus, the government faces pressure to raise revenues to pay for the increased salaries. Limited government budgetary revenue has so far forced government agencies and educational institutions to pursue revenue by themselves.[14]

---

[13] *Statistical Yearbook of China*, 1998, p. 139.
[14] *Statistical Yearbook of China*, 1999, p. 165.

Lack of Rule of Law

Unlike taxes, which must be approved by the National or Provincial People's Congress, fees are not governed by law. Fees are set by the Price Control Bureau and Ministry or Bureau of Finance of the central and provincial governments. The legal concept has yet to be formed in Chinese society, and the administrative and operating units at various levels of governments do not yet have the habit of following the rules of fee collection. There is no specific law on how to punish the behavior of arbitrary fee collection, which is currently light. When a fee collection violation is determined, the administrative or operating unit will be asked to return the fees, and the officials are usually subjected to self-questioning and public confession. In extreme cases, the leader of the unit can be removed from office.[15] There exists a perception that fee revenue is used for public expenditure or welfare, and thus, officials should not be punished for their arbitrary fee collection.

CONSEQUENCES OF EXCESSIVE FEE COLLECTION

Normally, fee collection can provide the urgently needed funds for public goods and public infrastructure, increase the local governments' fiscal autonomy, and improve resource allocation through explicitly relating benefit to cost. However, three major consequences of excessive fee collection exist, namely, the rise in business cost, the expansion of government size, and the increase in corruption.

Increase in Business Cost

Firms and industrial and commercial households must pay numerous fees to operate a business. These fees are added to firms' production cost directly. For example, in 1996, township enterprises paid 204 different kinds of fees to over 60 government branches and units.[16]

---

[15] *People's Daily*, June 29, 1999.
[16] *Jingji Cankao Bao* (Economic Reference News), April 18, 1996.

Paying fees also increases firms' transaction cost, as they need to use scarce resources to deal with fee collectors. Instead of improving production technology and management, they may even need to use resources to bribe fee collectors and to avoid paying fees. Large production cost may force firms to lower output or even leave the business. In November 1995, Tianjin Yasiya Commercial Center started operation. In the first two months, the firm spent 300,000 yuan on fees, fines, mandatory contributions, and entertaining guests. High operating cost forced the firm to close down — after only four months.[17]

The irregular and arbitrary nature of fee collection increases uncertainties and risks faced by business enterprises. With so many hidden costs, it is difficult for firms to estimate production cost. The unpredictability of cost may reduce profit expectations, and therefore dampen firms' incentive to invest.

Expansion of Government Size

Excessive fee collection, which is caused by the expansion of government, may also lead to an expansion of government size. Without revenue from fee collection, it would be difficult for government to expand. More revenue from fee collection makes the expansion of government possible. Table 3 shows composition of real extra-budgetary expenditure. Administrative and operative expenditures of government grew at an annual rate of 12.8%, from 3.9 billion yuan in 1982 to 20.9 billion yuan in 1995 at 1978 constant price. Administrative and operating expenditures accounted for 32% of total extra-budgetary expenditure in 1995.

Increase in Corruption

Fee collection also causes corruption. Fee revenues are often treated as off-budget revenues (called "小金库 the Little Golden Box", or "third source of finance") by government agencies, state enterprises, and local governments. Off-budgetary revenues, which are revenues collected by

---

[17] *Jingji Ribao* (Economic News), April 11, 1996.

Table 3. Composition of Real Extra-Budgetary Expenditures*
(100 Million Yuan)

Year	Total Extra-Budgetary Expenditure	Investment in Fixed Assets	Expenditure for City Maintenance	Administrative & Operating Expenditures
1982	651.18	324.49	21.62	39.14
1983	764.90	327.02	25.00	33.92
1984	947.10	381.80	24.69	38.50
1985	1073.40	445.96	22.17	50.53
1986	1162.28	424.48	23.03	59.91
1987	1263.38	508.19	26.69	73.83
1988	1242.19	472.08	26.19	78.14
1989	1230.63	425.20	16.57	75.59
1990	1303.35	445.79	17.06	90.08
1991	1447.01	493.43	18.18	103.55
1992	1620.74	596.64	22.14	122.42
1993	515.61	113.80	26.86	145.10
1994	551.38	194.87	27.59	178.53
1995	654.66	251.47	29.44	208.51
1996	1015.97	..	..	332.02
1997	705.24	..	..	336.18

Sources: *Statistical Yearbook of China*, 1998, p. 283; 1999, p. 276; *Finance Yearbook of China*, 1998.
*The coverage of the extra-budgetary revenue and expenditures has been adjusted largely since 1993, and the data may not be comparable with those in previous years. General retail price index (1978 = 100) was used to calculate the figures.

local governments, government branches and institutions, as well as state enterprises, are out of the control and supervision of fiscal authorities. It has been estimated that in 1995, off-budgetary revenues accounted for nearly 30% of budgetary revenues [Liu (1998)] and 5% of GDP [Lin and Wang (1997)].

Off-budgetary revenues are often abused and used for lavish pursuits, such as purchasing luxury vehicles, sponsoring tourists, lending the fund for high interest income, and purchasing stocks and real estate, etc. Fee collection hence becomes an important source of money in the "Little Golden Box". The money in the Box has been arbitrarily disposed, where 80% of the money has been reported to be used for treating guests, purchasing presents, personal uses, and paying bribes. The money in the "Little Golden Box" is sometimes saved in personal bank accounts. Corruption in government branches and agents negatively affects people's incentive to work, and may also cause social unrest.

A Bumpy Road to Fee Reform

The government has made efforts to reform fee collection. In July 1996, the State Council passed a resolution on strengthening the management of extra-budgetary revenue, attempting to merge fee revenues into government budget. At the Second Session of the National People's Congress in March 1999, Xiang Huaicheng, Minister of Finance, promised to speed up the reform of the fee collection system, focusing on eliminating unreasonable fee, changing some fees to prices, merging some fees into taxation, and keeping some necessary fees and strengthening their management. The target is to complete fee reforms within three to five years. He announced that the starting point was to reform the fee collection for traffic and vehicles [Xiang (1999)]. Currently, fees on traffic and vehicles account for 39% of total fee revenues and unlawful fees for traffic and vehicles account for 46%.[18]

At the Third Session of the Ninth National People's Congress on March 6, 2000, Xiang Huaicheng assured that the Ministry of Finance would continue to carry out fee and tax reforms (*fei shui gaige* 費税改革). He announced that the preparation of fuel tax and vehicle purchasing tax had been completed and the two taxes would be collected when other conditions were ready [Xiang (2000)].

The reform of rural fee collection is also on the top of the government agenda. Xiang Huaicheng emphasized that rural fee reform is a major event in rural China, just like the land reform in the early 1950s and

---

[18] See *Zhongguo Caizheng* (China's Public Finance), May 1999, p. 1.

the reform of the people's commune in the early 1980s. A pilot project will be conducted in the entire Anhui province and some counties of other provinces in 2000.

Fee reform will affect the size of the Chinese government. The centrally-planned system adopted by China for many years has resulted in an oversized government. There is no way for the public to avoid the real tax burden if the government size remains unchanged. To solve the fiscal problem, China must reduce the size of its government, such as getting rid of unnecessary government branches and reducing administrative personnel. Fee reform will reduce government's total revenue (the sum of fees and taxes) in the short run and force the government to reduce its expenditure.[19]

Fee reform will affect the fiscal relationship between the central and the local government, and that between the central government and its agencies. Currently, fees are not only collected but also disposed off by local governments and government agencies. If fees are converted into taxes, an issue arising would be the allocation of taxes between the central and local governments. If the central government gets part of the new tax revenue, then the central government's position in the allocation of tax revenue will be strengthened while the local governments' position weakened. Thus, the process of converting fees into taxation may become a process of fiscal centralization. China is a large country and fiscal centralization may involve inefficient use and misallocation of resources. On the other hand, decentralization may cause over-expansion of local governments and corruption. China needs a decentralized fiscal system (e.g., giving local government the right to issue bonds and introducing tax laws), along with an effective monitoring system to make local officials accountable to the people they serve and prevent them from being corrupt.

Fee reform requires the establishment of new tax laws or revising existing ones. Fees are determined by administrative and operating branches of government, instead of legislative branches. Thus, the process

---

[19] In the long run, the reduction in fee and tax burden will increase the incentives to invest and work, and therefore, increase output and taxable income.

of fee reform is also a process of legalization. Law enforcement is another issue in China. Besides inadequate training and low quality of tax officials, many taxpayers do not have the habit of paying taxes. Occasionally, incidence of tax revolts occur in China, in addition to tax avoidance and tax evasion.[20] Thus, the success of tax and fee reform relies very much on the improvement of the entire legal environment in China.

REFERENCES

Chen, Jicai, "Dui geti siying qiye fiyong qingkang de diaocha (A Survey on the Fee Burden of Individual Enterprises)", *Jiage Yuekan* (Price Monthly), No. 12, 1993.

Cheng, Qinggong, and Pan Guohong, "Xingzheng Shiye xing shoufei xianzhuang ji jiaqiangguanli duice" (the Current Status of Administrative Fee Collections and the Strategies for Management), *Zhongguo Wujia* (China Prices), 1999, No. 4, 15–20.

Fee, Zhengming, "Gaijin fangdichan shui shou and zhengdun zhuzhai jiansheshoufei", *Zhongguo Wujia* (China Prices), 1996, No. 12, 20–22.

Jia, Kang, "Feigaishui xiangguan wenti fenxi ji jiben duice silu tantao (Problems and solutions of transforming from fees to taxation)", Gao, in Peiyong (ed.), *Fi Gai Shui* (Converting Fees into Taxation), Economic Science Publishing House, 1999.

Liu, Yali, "Shoufei, bugai chulong de menghu (Fee Collection: the Tiger Which Should Not Be Released)", *Zhongguo Caijing Bao* (China Finance News), April 2, 1996.

Lu, Xiaoping, "Taozhu tuojiang de yema (Trapping the Runaway Horse)", *Zhongguo Caijing Bao* (China Financial and Economic News), March 27, 1996.

Pan, Xining, "Nongmin fudan duowei toushi (Farmers' Burdens from Various Perspectives)", *Jiage Yuekan* (Price Monthly), No. 10, 1993.

Gao, Peiyong, *Fei Gai Shui* (Transformation from Fee to Taxation), Economic Science Publishing House, 1999.

Research Group on Arbitrary Fee Collection Control, Social Science Foundation of Hebei province, "Zhengzhi luan shoufei duice yanjou (Strategies for

[20] *Minpao*, July 30, 1999.

Controlling Arbitrary Fee Collections)", *Zhongguo Wujia* (China Prices), No. 3, 1998.

Suzhou Price Bureau, "Suzhou shi sheji nongmin de xingzheng shiyexing shoufei qingkang diaocha (Surveys on Fee Collections from Farmers in Suzhou City)", *Zhongguo Wujia* (China Prices), 1993, No. 3.

Wang, Shijun, "Fei gai shui wenti yanjou zongshu (Summary of the research on transforming from fees to taxation)", *Jingjixue Dongtai*, May 1999, 34–36.

Wu, Shi-an, *China's Fee Collection Research, Zhongguo Caizheng Jingji Chubanshe*, China Finance and Economics Publishing House, 1997, p. 213.

Wu, Shi-an, *China's Fee Collection Research, Zhongguo Caizheng Jingji Chubanshe*, China Finance and Economics Publishing House, 1997, p. 228.

Xiang, Huaicheng, "Guanyu 1998 nian zhongyang he difang yusuan zhixing qingkang ji 1999 nian zhongyang he difang yusuan caoan de baogao", *Gazette of the Standing Committee of the National People's Congress of the People's Republic of China*, No. 2, 1999.

Xiang, Huaicheng, "Guanyu 1999 nian zhongyang he difang yusuan zhixing qingkang ji 2000 nian zhongyang he difang yusuan caoan de baogao", *Chong Caizheng*, April 2000.

Zeng, Qing, Liu Zhengbin, Luo Huicheng, "Geti gongshanghu he siyingqiye fudan qingkang diaocha (The Burden of Industrial and Commercial Households)", *Zhongguo Wujia*, 1994, No. 3.

Zhang, Manying, et al., "Muqian shoufei ji fangdichan jiage qingkang diaocha (Survey on fee collection and housing and real estate pricing)", *Zhongguo Wujia* (China Prices), 1998, No. 10, 19–23.

Zhang, Wei, *Jigou Gaige Da Xieyi (On Price Reforms)*, *Price Monthly*, 1993, No. 11.

8

From the Helping Hand to the Grabbing Hand: Fiscal Federalism and Corruption in China

KANG CHEN, ARYE L. HILLMAN & QINGYANG GU*

1. INTRODUCTION

The distinction between grabbing and helping hands of government officials has arisen in explaining outcomes in transition economies. In Russia, the Ukraine, and elsewhere, government officials have been described as having grabbing hands in their dealing with the private sector (see Frye and Shleifer 1997, Shleifer 1997, Gelb et al. 1998, Levin and Satarov 2000, Blejer and Škreb, 2001). In China government officials have been described as providing a helping hand to private investment and initiative (see Oi 1992, 1994; McKinnon 1992; Montinola et al. 1995; Qian and Weingast 1996, 1997; Jin et al. 1999). In Russia, local governments did not benefit from an expansion in the local tax base,

---

*Dr. Chen Kang is Associate Professor and Head of Division of Applied Economics at the Nanyang Business School, Nanyang Technological University. He is also Research Associate of the East Asian Institute, National University of Singapore. Dr. Arye L. Hillman is Professor of the Department of Economics, Bar-Ilan University, Israel. Mr. Gu Qingyang is Assistant Professor at Nanyang University, Singapore and was Research Officer of the East Asian Institute, National University of Singapore in 2000.

because increases in tax revenues of local government were offset by obligations to remit taxes to the center. Local government officials therefore had no incentive to adopt helping hand behavior that could help expand the local tax base and increase tax revenue (Zhuravskaya 2000). The grabbing hand grabbed where possible through extortion and unofficial payments, before the central government could stake its claim. The helping hand in China also reflected self-interest of local government officials, who personally benefited from taxes on the profits of local businesses, because regional or local government was the residual claimant under the revenue-sharing rule with the central government. Blanchard and Shleifer (2000) propose that the helping hand in China was also attributable to the authority of the center to appoint provincial governors and fire those with grabbing hands.

This praise for the helping hand in fiscal federalism in China contrasts, however, with other studies that have observed problematical aspects of inter-government relations. The problems include regional protectionism, self-interested intervention by local government officials in local business, and erosion of central government authority (see Chen 1991, 1995; Wong 1987, 1991). The existence of these problems led the central government of China to change the structure of central-local fiscal relations in 1994. The changes meant that local government was no longer the residual claimant to tax revenue and that restrictions were placed on the benefits that local government could provide to local business.

In this paper we investigate how the change in fiscal relations between central and local government affected the choice of local government between helping and grabbing hand behavior. Section 2 sets out the background for the change in central-local fiscal relations. In Section 3, helping or grabbing hand behavior is measured by the relation between local government off-budget revenue that local governments keep for themselves and budgetary revenue that is subject to the revenue-sharing rule with the center. The measure of helping and grabbing hand behavior applied to the individual Chinese provinces confirms the presence of a significant change from helping hand to substantive grabbing hand behavior in local government after the fiscal re-centralization in the 1990s. The benevolent helping hand that had distinguished the experience of local government in China from the grabbing hand of local government in Russia and other former socialist European countries was no longer present.

The empirical estimates moreover indicate that the change in revenue sharing by the central government of China from high to low shares of budgetary tax revenue for local government led to Pareto-inefficient changes. The center did benefit from the fiscal centralization, but at the expense of local government. Moreover, budgetary revenue and economic growth declined because of the change from helping to grabbing hand behavior by local government.

2. Taxation and Fiscal Federalism in China

Before the introduction of market-oriented economic reforms in China in the late 1970s, local governments were not responsible for their expenditures, which were financed through the national budget. There was no incentive for local government to seek to increase revenue, because all revenues were sent to the center for redistribution. Confronted with declining revenues, the Ministry of Finance (MOF) introduced a center-local government revenue-sharing system in 1977. Local government entered into long-term revenue-sharing contracts with the central government. The contract specified the total revenues to be remitted to the central government, and left local government as the residual claimant to revenues collected in the local jurisdiction. The MOF moved cautiously at first. There were experiments with revenue sharing in Jiangsu and a few other provinces. The system was declared as a success by MOF, because it brought more certainty to the central government budgetary revenue, and was subsequently extended to all provincial-level governments in 1980 (Chen 1998a).

The new revenue-sharing contract changed the incentives of local government officials. Rather than seeking rents from the center, the local officials now had an incentive to enhance the local tax base.

The new revenue-sharing procedure also had an unintended political-economy consequence. Revenue sharing was identified as a reform measure that had been introduced by reformist leaders at the center.

Since local government officials were beneficiaries of the perceived economic reform, reformist leaders at the center had pro-reform support from regional politicians. The balance of pro-reform and anti-reform forces was changed, and the reformists were able to proceed with broad reform measures (Chen 1995). Regional governments also became more sensitive to spontaneous local calls for policy changes, and played a pivotal role in state-society interactions that were very important in China's reform process (Chen 1998b). Regional governments had incentives to promote market reform and economic growth, and China became an example of successful "market-preserving federalism" (Jin et al. 1999).

In the early 1980s, the new revenue-sharing system satisfied the needs of the central government. The assured revenue for the center satisfied the conservatives at the MOF. The reformist leaders at the center were also satisfied, because the tilt in the balance of political dominance allowed a strategy of "playing to the provinces" as a counterbalance to vested interests of line ministries in the central government (see Shirk 1993).

The revenue-sharing system was, however, not sustainable under conditions of substantial economic change. As in many early-transition economies (see Bogetić and Hillman 1995), the Chinese government relied principally on the state sector for tax revenue, but revenues of state-owned enterprises were in decline because of overall decline in the state sector and because of competition from new non-state competitors. The familiar circumstance of decreasing tax revenues soon emerged. Tax revenue collected by local governments to be shared with the center declined.[1] Tax revenue collected directly by the central government and not shared with the provinces declined even more.

At the same time, the richer provinces, which were net remitters of tax revenue to the center, increased their share of tax revenue.[2] This

---

[1] Total budgetary revenue declined from 23.7% of GDP in 1985 to 13.5% in 1993 (See Table 1). Budgetary revenue shared between the center and provinces declined from 14.4% of GDP to 10.8% during the same period.
[2] From 61.8% in 1985 to 85.8% in 1993.

Table 1. Shares of Provincial Budgetary Revenue (in percentage).

Year	Share of remitting provinces	Share of provinces receiving subsidies from the center	Share of all provinces	Shared budgetary revenue as % of GDP	Total budgetary revenue as % of GDP
1985	61.8	131.7	96.4	14.4	23.7
1986	67.1	141.7	104.3	15.7	22.2
1987	70.1	140.8	107.1	15.1	19.7
1988	75.9	126.1	102.8	13.5	17.8
1989	79.8	122.2	103.0	14.1	18.0
1990	79.4	122.0	104.4	13.1	17.9
1991	81.0	118.8	102.6	12.3	16.0
1992	81.3	118.2	101.4	10.6	14.2
1993	85.8	112.7	98.5	10.8	13.5
1994	78.7	96.0	88.5	9.7	11.8
1995	76.5	95.3	87.0	8.9	11.2
1996	77.9	94.5	87.3	8.9	11.3
1997	66.1	89.2	79.6	8.7	12.0
1998	61.8	86.3	74.4	9.6	12.8

Sources: Calculated by the authors based on data from various issues of *China Statistical Yearbook* and *China Fiscal Yearbook*.

Notes: (a) All budgetary revenue figures have been adjusted so that subsidies to loss-making state-owned enterprises are no longer counted as revenue-negating items as practiced by the Chinese statistical authorities. (b) Provincial revenues are revenues collected by the province adjusted for remittance to and subsidies from the center. The post-1994 figures also include tax repayment (*shuishou fanhuan*) from the center.

increase reflected the revenue sharing rule, which obliged regional governments to provide stipulated tax remittances, but allowed them to keep tax surpluses.

The central government consequently had less income to redistribute to poorer provinces, and the revenue share of the provinces receiving subsidies from the center declined.[3] The central government was, in this period, on the verge of bankruptcy, and frequently sought to renegotiate the revenue-sharing agreements with local governments. Richer provinces were asked to make additional "contributions" to the central government.

Since the center did not have its own tax collection administration, there was no alternative but to rely on tax revenue remittances from regional governments. The regional governments, however, had ready means of avoiding tax remittance obligations. They could withhold tax remittances by diverting tax revenues from budget to off-budget items, which were not subject to sharing with the center. Revenue could also be withheld from the center by giving regional enterprises tax holidays and exemptions (Wong 1991). These activities by regional government were consistent with their residual claimant status for tax revenues. The tax exemptions increased resources for local investment and expanded the local tax base.

Local government officials had, in these circumstances, incentives to offer a helping hand to local enterprises. However, the helping hand could create inefficiencies. Local government officials protected their participation in local investment through local protectionist policies that prevented free movement of goods across regional boundaries. With regional banks under their close supervision, local government officials could also selectively direct credit to local enterprises. The regions became, in effect, independent economic fiefdoms (Chen 1991). With the local protectionism and directed bank credits, a proliferation of small-scale high-cost activities was inefficiently duplicated across localities.

Regional government was now an impediment to change and resisted attempts at re-centralization (see Chen, 1991). By the early 1990s, the central government sought to re-centralize the fiscal system, but only succeeded in 1994 with the introduction of a new tax-sharing system (TSS) that distinguished between exclusive central and local government

---

[3] From 142% in 1986 to 113% in 1993. Shares were more than 100% because of subsidies received from the center.

tax bases. Shared taxes were instituted, including the value-added tax. A central tax bureau was set up to collect the center's taxes.

Local tax bureaus at the same time continued to collected local taxes. As an incentive for local government, the center agreed to a special transfer payment (*shuishou fanhuan* or tax repayment) to provinces to ensure that local revenues did not decline. The reference point was provincial government revenue in 1993. However, the objective of the central government was to increase its share of total tax revenues from 40% to 60%.

The new system ended the downward trend of the budgetary revenue to GDP ratio and increased the share of the center in total budgetary revenue.[4] At the same time, the revenue shares of the regional governments significantly declined.[5] Local government is no longer the residual claim to local tax revenues.

Regional government also lost discretion to grant tax reductions and exemptions to their local enterprises. Banks were re-organized and re-centralized.[6] The center also tightened control over extra-budgetary funds, which were re-channeled into budget items.[7] Extra-budgetary charges and *ad hoc* levies were also placed under central government scrutiny.

The re-centralization took place at a time when the central leadership felt that political support from the provincial governments was not

---

[4] In 1998 total budgetary revenue was 12.8% of GDP, only slightly below the 13.5% in 1993.

[5] Budgetary revenue shares for remitting provinces fell from 85.8% in 1993 to 61.8% in 1998. The provinces that were recipients of subsidies from the center also experienced revenue losses. Their share of revenue declined from 112.7% to 86.3% in the same period (Table 1). Since their share dropped below 100% after 1994, these provinces also became net contributors to the center's budget revenue.

[6] The branches of the People's Bank of China were re-organized with regional headquarters following the Federal Reserve System of the United States. Managers of state owned bank are no longer under the supervision of local governments, and major bank loans have to go through the Credit Approval Committee in which local governments have no representation.

[7] See Zhang (1999).

important,[8] and the re-centralization measures were implemented despite unpopularity at the regional level. Discontented provincial leaders were rotated or replaced.[9] Local governments were also given additional expenditure responsibilities while being compelled to give up revenue sources. The central government set annual growth targets for central tax revenue and threatened to remove tax bureau chiefs if targets were not met.[10] Compliance by local government officials was in general based on such coercion and administrative orders, and not on compatible incentives and budgetary laws. Tax revenue targets were based on pre-achieved levels and were subject to ratchet effects, so that high tax collection in one year implied a higher target for the following year. Officials at the tax offices therefore had no incentive to collect revenue beyond the tax target. Local government revenue targets could also be achieved by simultaneously inflating tax revenue and expenditure.[11] The central tax bureau resorted to various means of meeting the tax-revenue targets, even if the achievements were only notional, and did not provide actual revenue for the central budget.[12]

The central government reacted by directing to itself yet more tax revenue from the regions or from outside the budget. Uncertainty and

---

[8] After the Communist Party formally adopted the "socialist market economy" as the objective of economic reform at its 14th congress in 1992 and with the old generation of revolutionary leaders passed the scene, there were no major political obstacles for market reform in China. Nor were there major challenges to the new leadership at the center.

[9] See Blanchard and Shleifer (2000).

[10] When the center wanted to increase its tax revenue by an additional 100 billion yuan in 1998, it just held a telephone/video conference to mobilize tax collection.

[11] The center actually made it easy for local governments to do so. In an effort to promote certain sectors of the economy, the central government started the practice of *xianzheng houfan, lieshou liezhi* – taxes collected from enterprises in privileged sectors were returned to these enterprises while the amount was recorded under both revenue and expenditure. The practice proliferated because local governments found it very useful. They could effectively grant tax exemptions and inflate budgetary revenue and expenditure at the same time.

[12] For example, 13 types of extra-budgetary revenues were brought into the budget to boost the budgetary revenues in 1997, but the spending plans is still determined by the administrative agencies that collect the funds. This means that this part of budgetary revenue is not available for normal government expenditure and the increase in the budgetary revenue is artificial.

mistrust spread in the tax sharing system, as the center repeatedly and arbitrarily used administrative orders to redefine tax-sharing rules. Regional governments in turn responded by finding additional means of hiding revenues from the center. Since the central government and its departments were collecting additional extra-budgetary revenues, it was difficult to prevent local governments from doing the same. Financial resources overall thus increasingly came outside budgetary control (Zhang 1999).

Extra-budgetary revenue had been prevalent in the pre-reform era, and was expanded under the fiscal system of the post-reform period. Local governments were permitted to collect fees and charges outside the budget when government revenue was inadequate to cover expenses. This eroded the tax base, led to more budget deficits, and to the imposition of yet more off-budget fees and charges. The vicious cycle was reinforced by the post-1994 re-centralization.[13] In 1998, the central government outlawed more than 20,000 different types of *ad hoc* fees and charges that were being collected by government departments (Wang 1999). Other fees and charges were however invented and collected.

Shleifer and Vishny (1993) have proposed that disorganized corruption is more averse to economic development than organized corruption. When corruption is disorganized, different ministries, agencies and levels of local governments independently seek personal revenue through bribes without accounting for the adverse effects of their independent appropriation activities. The cumulative burden of corruption therefore increases. The change that took place at China's local government level in response to the center's re-centralization policy was from organized to disorganized corruption. The organized corruption that provided a helping hand was replaced by the disorganized corruption of a grabbing hand.

The change from helping to grabbing hand was also a change from the behavior of stationary bandits to roving bandits (see Olson 1993,

---

[13] For example, fees and charges were twice taxes in 1996 in Guangdong, Sichuan and Xian City of Shaanxi Province (An and Yue 1999). Gao (1999) estimated taxes to be no more than around one-third of total government revenue.

2000). The stationary bandit that provided a helping hand had a broad interest in the long-run development of the local tax base. The roving bandit had a narrow personal interest in extracting revenue through the grabbing hand. The roving bandit takes and moves on, and does not care for what can be taken tomorrow.

3. The Empirical Evidence on the Significance of the Helping and Grabbing Hand

The change by the center from low to high tax shares in the 1990s is established from the published data in Tables 1 and 2. We require a measure of the magnitudes of the helping and grabbling hand to show that local government responded to the fiscal re-centralization by switching from helping to grabbing hand and thus the increases in disorganized corruption and roving-bandit behavior. The relation between the components of government revenue provides such a measure.

China's government revenue is composed of (1) budgetary revenue, (2) extra-budgetary revenue (*yushuanwai shouru*) and (3) extra-establishment revenue (*zhiduwai shouru*). Extra-budgetary revenue is in principle under control of the central government, with collection of revenue taking place through official documents issued by the State Council, the State Planning Commission or Ministry of Finance. Extra-budgetary revenue is however under decentralized management and allocation of funds is by different agencies and organizations at various levels of the government. As a consequence extra-budgetary revenue is not well controlled by the central government, and many extra-budgetary revenue items are not recorded in official statistics. A study by the central government in 1996 suggested that the actual extra-budgetary revenue for 1995 was 1.6 times that recorded in the official statistics (Zhang 1999).

Extra-establishment revenue is the revenue collected by government departments and organizations at the discretion of the officials themselves. No rules govern collection of extra-establishment revenue and there are no official statistics. The collection of extra-establishment revenue has

Table 2. Shares of Provincial Budgetary Revenue (in percentages).

Province	1985–1993	1988–1993	1994–1998
Anhui	122.4	117.5	92.0
Beijing	86.6	91.3	75.7
Fujian	119.4	113.0	95.1
Guangdong	99.1	96.7	80.4
Gansu	135.2	126.7	114.1
Guangxi	136.4	126.0	109.5
Guizhou	142.4	130.8	107.1
Hainan	204.8	185.6	117.5
Hebei	98.0	98.8	86.9
Henan	112.9	108.5	89.2
Heilongjiang	126.5	120.2	87.5
Hubei	105.1	101.2	89.4
Hunan	109.5	106.2	90.4
Jilin	139.1	135.0	100.5
Jiangsu	72.1	73.4	70.6
Jiangxi	149.9	138.0	113.2
Liaoning	83.1	86.5	79.5
Inner Mongolia	203.6	178.1	130.2
Ningxia	244.9	213.9	137.1
Qinghai	246.8	208.9	168.8
Sichuan	118.0	112.8	88.3
Shandong	99.4	102.6	76.7
Shanghai	43.9	52.9	53.4
Shaanxi	132.9	123.7	103.4
Shanxi	116.9	107.4	85.8
Tianjin	74.8	79.7	65.6
Xinjiang	237.3	205.9	118.7
Yunnan	109.8	111.3	71.7
Zhejiang	76.5	79.4	76.2
Average of remitting provinces	75.8	80.5	72.2
Average of provinces receiving subsidies	126.0	120.0	92.2
National Average	101.7	101.8	82.5

Sources: Calculated by the authors based on data from various issues of China Statistical Yearbook and China Fiscal Yearbook.

Note: In this study, Guangdong, Zhejiang, Jiangsu, Shanghai, Tianjin, Beijing, Liaoning and Hebei are classified as the remitting provinces based on the net remittance data, and the rest of classified as subsidy receiving provinces.

been described as "san luan" (three times arbitrarily): collecting fees arbitrarily, imposing fines arbitrarily, and raising funds arbitrarily.

Extra-budgetary revenue and extra-establishment revenue are associated with the grabbing hand through the use of the authority of government to impose a variety of predatory regulations on business. Various government departments and agencies collect different off-budget revenues under different names and justifications, and the revenues are principally used for privileged consumption by local government officials, or sent to foreign bank accounts.

Budgetary revenue on the other hand provides finance for helping hand activities such as provision of public goods, infrastructure, and law and order. We can accordingly use the proportion of budgetary revenue to total government revenue to measure the helping against grabbing hand. The higher is the proportion of government revenue that is outside the budget, the weaker is the helping hand and correspondingly the greater is the grabbing hand.

While official statistics on budgetary and extra-budgetary revenue are readily available, there are no official statistics for extra-establishment revenue. There are, however, a number of estimates of extra-establishment revenue at the national level. Three of these estimates are listed in Table 3, together with our own estimate. Column A is from Zhang (1999), who assumes that extra-establishment revenue is entirely absorbed by fixed asset investment within the state-owned enterprises. This assumption would result in underestimation, especially in the post-1994 period. Column B is taken from the State Planning Commission Study Team (1999). This study makes conservative assumptions about ratios of tax to non-tax revenue, but does not explain the rational behind these assumptions. Column C is derived by Yang (1999), who uses the residual method by deducting the budgetary revenues and extra-budgetary revenue from the estimated total government expenditure. Many assumptions are made when estimating total government expenditure, including values of investment expenditure and transfer payments.

Our estimation is in Column D. Since we know that extra-establishment revenue was not significant in the mid-1980s, we begin with no extra-establishment revenue in 1985. We take budgetary revenue

Table 3. Estimated Extra Establishment Revenue (in billion yuan)

Year	A	B	C	D
1985	27.4			0.0
1986	36.9			6.9
1987	34.6		66.6	13.1
1988	52.1		83.2	28.4
1989	51.2		86.1	33.7
1990	65.0		105.1	62.2
1991	179.1	27.1	149.1	82.5
1992	273.5	15.6	218.7	145.4
1993	291.6	17.6	314.1	196.8
1994	370.7	61.0	497.1	326.8
1995	415.3	101.2	536.6	471.6
1996		182.7	598.0	575.8
1997		266.8		680.8
1998		288.1		653.4

Sources: Column A is from Zhang (1999); Column B from State Planning Commission Study Team (1999); Column C by Yang (1999); and Column D is the estimate of the authors.

and extra-budgetary revenue as adequate to cover government expenses, and use the revenue to GDP ratio of 1985 as a constant revenue-adequacy ratio throughout the sample period. Multiplying the ratio by GDP gives the adequate-revenue level. The extra-establishment revenue is derived by subtracting the budgetary revenue and the extra-budgetary revenue from the estimated adequate revenue. While the adequacy ratio might understate the actual value of adequate revenues, this method allows us to use extra-establishment revenue to estimate measures of the helping hand and the grabbing hand by provinces.

In Table 4 we see that, for most provinces, the helping hand index decreased between 1985 and 1993, as local governments shifted resources outside the budget in order to avoid sharing with the center. There was an acceleration in the grabbing hand after 1994.

Our estimates show significant changes. The national helping hand index decreased by more than 30% from 0.67 in 1988–1993 to 0.43 in 1994–1998. The same pattern is observed for most of the provinces. The

Table 4. The Helping Hand Index by Provinces

Province	1985–1993	1988–1993	1994–1998
Anhui	0.72	0.64	0.44
Beijing	0.83	0.80	0.68
Fujian	0.68	0.59	0.32
Guangdong	0.80	0.72	0.60
Gansu	0.74	0.67	0.45
Guangxi	0.70	0.60	0.32
Guizhou	0.78	0.73	0.48
Hainan	0.72	0.68	0.53
Hebei	0.69	0.63	0.40
Henan	0.76	0.69	0.46
Heilongjiang	0.80	0.72	0.40
Hubei	0.72	0.62	0.33
Hunan	0.73	0.65	0.41
Jilin	0.89	0.83	0.45
Jiangsu	0.61	0.52	0.33
Jiangxi	0.76	0.66	0.42
Liaoning	0.61	0.54	0.38
Inner Mongolia	0.78	0.70	0.48
Ningxia	0.70	0.61	0.42
Qinghai	0.73	0.63	0.40
Sichuan	0.80	0.75	0.40
Shandong	0.73	0.70	0.43
Shanghai	0.92	0.92	0.61
Shaanxi	0.73	0.66	0.50
Shanxi	0.67	0.60	0.40
Tianjin	0.65	0.59	0.33
Xinjiang	0.63	0.51	0.30
Yunnan	0.76	0.78	0.58
Zhejiang	0.73	0.69	0.44
National Average	0.73	0.67	0.43

Source: Estimated by the authors.

significant decline in the helping hand and increase in the grabbing hand suggest why the central government should become pre-occupied with corruption at the regional and local government level.

Helping Hand and Investment

In order to understand how the helping hand helps, we can consider the relationship between the helping hand index and investment. We specify the investment equation:

$$\log(inv_{st}) = \alpha_s + \beta \log(gdp85_{st}) + \gamma_t \log(help_{st}) + \varepsilon_{st}$$

where s and t indicate province and year, *inv* is fixed asset investment in 1985 prices, *gdp85* denotes GDP in 1985 prices, *help* is the helping hand index, and e is the error term. This is a fixed effect model with the varying coefficient for the helping hand index. In order to estimate the varying coefficient, we make use of the time trend variable t and the dummy variable *dummy*, which equals to 1 in 1994–1998 and 0 elsewhere. The estimation results are presented in Table 5.

Table 5. Helping Hand

Dependent Variable: logarithm of fixed investment in 1985 prices

Variable	Total	State Owned Enterprises & Urban Collectives	Township & Village Enterprises	Other Types of Ownership
Ln(GDP85)	0.8001	0.7217	0.8011	0.2268
	(13.7761)	(13.7238)	(9.1310)	(2.1324)
Ln(help)	0.5558	0.2729	0.8323	1.8675
	(5.3057)	(2.5318)	(6.3113)	(9.9793)
Ln(help)*t	−0.0359	−0.0203	−0.0522	−0.1508
	(−3.2073)	(−1.7877)	(−3.2967)	(−7.4021)
Ln(help)*dummy	−0.1392	−0.0479	−0.2537	−0.4970
	(−3.0705)	(−1.0211)	(−3.8754)	(−6.2671)
Number of Obs.	406	406	406	406
Adjust R-square	0.9931	0.9921	0.9613	0.9790
Residual SS	12.7388	12.9871	60.0536	67.4016
S.E. of Regression	0.1848	0.1866	0.4013	0.4251

Notes: (a) Provincial fixed effects are included in all models that are estimated by GLS from 1985 to 1998. (b) t-statistics are given in parentheses.

The equation is estimated with four different dependent variables according to ownership types. The results confirm the role of the helping hand in promoting investment. We observe that the coefficient of the helping hand index, which is significantly positive in all four equations, is greatest for investment by firms with ownership that includes private firms and foreign investment. The coefficient on the helping hand is also significantly greater for Township and Village Enterprises (TVEs) than for State Owned Enterprises (SOEs) and urban collectives. The helping hand is thus more effective for private investment and less so for the state-owned enterprises and urban collectives. The declining coefficient of the helping hand index in TVEs and other ownership indicates that the helping hand becomes less important as market reforms progress. Since the dummy variable is significantly negative, regional government became less effective in helping investment in the post-1994 period after the implementation of the re-centralization measures.

High Taxes and the Grabbing Hand

We can examine the relationship between high center taxes and the grabbing hand of local government through the equation:

$$\log(grab_{st}) = \alpha_s + \beta \log(cpi_t) + \gamma \log(local_{st}) + \theta \log(staff_{st}) + \varepsilon_{st}.$$

Here s and t indicate province and year, and *grab* is the grabbing hand index (*grab* = 1 - *help*), *cpi* is a corruption perception index, *local* is the local revenue shares summarized in Table 2, *staff* is the number of government officials and administrative staff, and e is the error term. We estimate three models using different definitions for *staff*. *Staff1* is the number of government officials and administrative staff, *Staff2* equals to *Staff1* divided by population, and *Staff3* equals to *Staff1* divided by non-agricultural population.

Table 6 shows the estimation results. The coefficient of *local* is significantly negative in all three models, which confirms that the lower is the tax shared by the local government (the higher tax remittances to the center), the stronger is the grabbing hand. The coefficients of *local* in (2) and (3) are less than −1, which means that the grabbing hand index would increase by more than 1% if the local share decreases by 1%. Thus, a large proportion of reduction in the helping hand indices in the 1990 (see Table 4) was due to the decrease of the local shares of budgetary revenues (see Table 2). Thus, the fiscal recentralization has a significant adverse effect on investment (see Table 5) and on the budgetary tax base.

Higher values of the corruption perception index value indicate a less corrupt government.[14] The coefficient of *cpi* is significantly negative for all three equations, which confirms our expectation that more corrupt governments grab more. Since the coefficients for the *staff* variables are all significantly positive, an increase in the number of government officials leads local governments to grab more.[15]

In order to assess the dynamic impact of fiscal recentralization, Gu (2002) includes the estimated relationships between local share, grabbling/helping hand and investment in an economy-wide multiregional model which endogenizes GDP, investment and other relevant variables. The model is run in a counter-factual simulation from 1994 to 1998 to study the impact of the fiscal recentralization, and the key results are provided in Table 7. It shows that the center benefited from high revenue share and fiscal recentralization, but at the expense of local governments. It also shows that fiscal centralization was inefficient, because it led to lower budgetary revenue and lower economic output.

4. Conclusions

We have investigated the change from helping hand to grabbing hand behavior in China. The change is associated with fiscal recentralization.

---

[14] The source of the Corruption Perception Index is *Transparency International*. We use interpolation to fill in the values for four years in which the index is not available.
[15] On the general theory of bureaucracy, and consequences of the expansion of bureaucracy, see Niskanen (1971). Niskanen looks at self-interested behavior of bureaucracy under democracy. Our empirical results point to the same principles of self-interested behavior under autocracy.

Table 6. The Grabbing Hand

Dependent Variable: logarithm of grabbing hand index

Variable	(1)	(2)	(3)
Ln(CPI)	–0.2901	–0.3576	–0.7103
	(–6.0841)	(–6.8765)	(–12.7860)
Ln(local)	–0.8682	–1.1524	–1.4515
	(–11.1028)	(–14.3106)	(–15.6348)
Ln(staff1)	1.7522		
	(18.1464)		
Ln(staff2)		1.9685	
		(13.9793)	
Ln(staff3)			1.0745
			(5.1807)
Number of Obs.	406	406	406
Adjust R-square	0.9441	0.9354	0.8787
Residual SS	25.8903	31.1938	36.2403
S.E. of Regression	0.2631	0.2888	0.3113

Notes: (a) Provincial fixed effects are included in all models that are estimated by GLS from 1985 to 1998. (b) t-statistics are given in parentheses.

Table 7. Changes in Budgetary Revenue and GDP due to Fiscal Centralization

Year	Center Billion yuan	Center As % of GDP	Local Billion yuan	Local As % of GDP	Center & Local Billion yuan	Center & Local As % of GDP	GDP (%)
1994	29.0	0.6	–39.0	–0.8	–10.0	–0.2	–0.6
1995	37.3	0.6	–51.4	–0.9	–14.1	–0.2	–1.0
1996	46.2	0.7	–66.8	–1.0	–20.6	–0.3	–1.3
1997	118.7	1.6	–173.1	–2.3	–54.4	–0.7	–3.1
1998	178.0	2.3	–283.9	–3.6	–105.9	–1.3	–6.3

Source: Gu (2002).

The evidence confirms that local government switched from helping to grabbing hand when the center altered budgetary tax shares to increase the center's share at the expense of local government. The change from helping to grabbing hand in China has eliminated the difference that was previously observed between the helping hand of local government in China and the grabbing hand in Russia (and other post-socialist European countries).

We have shown that the helping hand help investment most effectively for private firms and least effective for state-owned enterprises. The helping hand becomes less effective with the fiscal re-centralization. We have also shown that the grabbing hand grabs more when (1) the center takes more from the revenue pool, (2) the government is more corrupt, or (3) the size of the government bureaucracy expands.

The general conclusion is that fiscal federal relations can affect growth and investment, and efficiency, through incentives that affect the form of corruption by local government officials. Our study shows that when local government can choose between helping and grabbing hands, revenue maximization by the center might not be an appropriate objective. As in the case of China, the corruption of the helping hand when taxes are decentralized can be socially preferable to the corruption of the grabbing hand when taxes are centralized.

Local governments lost from the fiscal re-centralization because they are worse off with a low local budgetary tax share and a grabbing hand. Many local government officials acknowledge that more than two thirds of China's counties have been in budget deficit in recent years.[16] As a result, many township governments are running on "the neutral gear" (*kongzhuan*) fiscally, which means that the county government provides little or no fiscal income to township governments. Since the township government is the lowest level of government in China and does have its own tax revenue sources, may township government officials, including school teachers, have to be paid by fees and charges collected from rural households. In many cases, government officials confiscated and sold

---

[16] From authors' personal communication with local government officials from Heibei and Shangdong provinces.

farmers' assets because they failed to pay their dues. The grabbing hand grabs, literally!

Local government in China provided a helping hand when the center was politically weak and there was pre-commitment to a low remittance rate from local government to the center. When the center felt politically capable, it chose high tax remittances from local government, which led to an inefficient equilibrium with the grabbing hand of local government. The helping hand was corrupt, but nonetheless socially preferable to the corruption of the grabbing hand. Under the disorganized grabbing hand, growth slowed, since illegally diverted revenue was not used for investment but was used for consumption or was diverted abroad.[17]

In choosing high tax remittance from local governments, the central government in China may have hoped to eliminate local government discretion, or organized corruption, by fiscal control from the center. With the personal benefits from being a local government official reduced, the officials might leave local politics or the local bureaucracy and move to the socially more productive private sector. Our results show, however, that it may have been naïve for the central government to believe that redirection of taxes to the center would make being a local government official sufficiently unattractive to entice departure from political and bureaucratic positions. The bandits become roving rather than stationary. The grabbing hand of disorganized roving bandits takes more, and is more inhibiting for private sector development than the organized helping hand of stationary bandits, who consider the future tax base when deciding when and how to take — and to give.

References

An, Tifu, and Yue, Shuming. "Analysis, Judgement and Adjustment on China's Macro Tax Burden." *Jingji Yanjiu (Economic Research)*, (No. 3, 1999): 41–47.

Blanchard, Olivier, and Shleifer, Andrei. "Federalism With and Without Political Centralization: China versus Russia." *NBER Working Paper 7616*, 2000.

---

[17] Capital flight in 1997 is estimated to have been 40 billion US dollars, which is 90% of utilized foreign direct investment for China in the same year (Song 1999).

Blejer, Mario, and Marko Škreb, eds., *Ten Years of Transition: The Lessons and the Prospects*. New York: Cambridge University Press, 2001.

Bogetić Željko and Hillman, Arye L., eds. *Financing Government in Transition, Bulgaria: The Political Economy of Tax Policies, Tax Bases, and Tax Evasion*, The World Bank, Washington, D.C., 1995. Reprinted by Avebury Publishing, Brookfield, Vermont, 1996.

Chen, Kang. "The Failure of Recentralisation in China: Interplay among Enterprises, Local Governments, and the Centre," in Arye L. Hillman, ed., *Markets and Politicians: Politicized Economic Choice*. Holland: Kluwer Academic Publishers, 1991, pp. 209–229.

———. *The Chinese Economy in Transition: Micro Changes and Macro Implications*. Singapore: Singapore University Press, 1995.

———. "Accidental Freedom: Economic Development Experience in Post-Mao China," in K. T. Liou, ed., *Handbook of Economic Development (Public Administration and Public Policy Series/69)*. New York: Marcel Dekker, 1998a, pp. 611–630.

———. "Administrative Decentralisation and Changing State-Society Relations in China." *International Journal of Public Administration*, 1998b, 21(9), pp. 1223–1255.

Frye, Timothy, and Shleifer, Andrei. "The Invisible Hand and the Grabbing Hand," *American Economic Review*, May 1997, 87(2), pp. 354–358.

Gao, Peiyong. China's Tax and System of Taxation under Market Economic Condition, in Gao Peiyong, ed., *Economists on Tax for Fees*. Beijing: Economics Science Press, 1999.

Gelb, Alan; Hillman, Arye L. and Ursprung, Heinrich W. "Rents as distractions: Why the Exit from Transition is Prolonged," in Nicolas C. Baltas, George Demopoulos, and Joseph Hassid, eds., *Economic Interdependence and Cooperation in Europe*. New York: Springer Verlag, 1998, pp. 21–38.

Gu, Qingyang. Interprovincial Relations in China's Decentralized Economy: A Multiregional Model Ad Its Applications, PhD Dissertation, Nanyang Technological University, Singapore, 2002.

Jin, Hehui; Qian, Yingyi and Weingast, Barry R. "Regional Decentralization and Fiscal Incentives: Federalism, Chinese Style." *Stanford University Working Paper*, SWP-99-013, 1999.

Levin, Mark and Satarov, Georgy. "Corruption and institutions in Russia." *European Journal of Political Economy*, March 2000, 16(1), pp. 113–132.

McKinnon, Ronald. "Spontaneous Order on the Road Back from Socialism: An Asian Perspective." *American Economic Review*, May 1992, 80(2), 31–36.

Montinola, Gabriella; Qian, Yingyi and Weingast, Barry. "Federalism, Chinese Style: The Political Basis for Economic Success in China," *World Politics*, October 1995, 48(1), pp. 50–81.

Naughton, Barry. "Chinese Institutional Innovation and Privatization from Below." *American Economic Review*, May 1994, 84(2), pp. 266–270.

Niskanen, William, *Bureaucracy and Representative Government*. Aldine, Chicago, 1971.

Oi, Jean. "Fiscal Reform and the Economic Foundation of Local State Corporation in China," *World Politics*, October 1992, 45(1), pp. 99–126.

_____. *Rural China Takes Off: Incentives for Reform*. Berkeley: University of California Press, 1994.

Olson, Mancur. "Dictatorship, Democracy, and Development." *The American Political Science Review*, September 1993, 87(3), pp. 567–576.

_____. *Power and Prosperity: Outgrowing Communist and Capitalist Dictatorships*. New York: Basic Books, 2000.

Qian, Yingyi and Weigast, Barry R. "China's Transition to Market: Market-Preserving Federalism, Chinese Style." *Journal of Policy Reform*, 1996, 1(2), pp. 149–185.

_____. "Federalism As a Commitment to Market Incentives." *Journal of Economic Perspectives*, 1997, 11(4), pp. 83–92.

Shirk, Susan L. *The Political Logic of Economic Reform in China*. Berkeley: University of California Press, 1993.

Shleifer, Andrei and Vishny, Robert W. "Corruption." *Quarterly Journal of Economics*, August 1993, 108(3), pp. 599–617.

Shleifer, Andrei. "Government in Transition." *European Economic Review*, 1997, 41(3), pp. 385–410.

Song, Wenbing. "A Study of China's Capital Flight Problem: 1987–1997." *Jingji Yanjiu (Economic Research)*, May 1999, pp. 39–48.

State Planning Commission Study Team. "An Empirical Study of China's Macro Income Distribution in the 1990s." *Jingji Yanjiu (Economic Research)*, November 1999, pp. 3–12.

Wang, Chengyao. "Reform the Irrational Distribution Structure That Has Small Tax but Large Fees," in Gao Peiyong, ed., *Economists on Tax for Fees*. Beijing: Economics Science Press, 1999.

Wong, Christine P.W. "Between Plan and Market: The Role of the Local Sector in Post-Mao China." *Journal of Comparative Economics*, 1987, 11, pp. 385–398.

———. Central-Local Relations in an Era of Fiscal Decline: The Paradox of Fiscal Decentralization in Post-Mao China. *China Quarterly*, 1991, pp. 691–715.

Wong, Christine P.W., Heady, Christopher and Woo, Wing T. *Fiscal Management and Economic Reform in the People's Republic of China.* Hong Kong: Oxford University Press, 1995.

Yang, Bin. "A Theoretical Study and Empirical Analysis of Government Non-Tax Charges," in Gao Peiyong, ed., *Economists on Tax for Fees.* Beijing: Economics Science Press, 1999.

Zhang, Le-Yin. "Chinese Central-Provincial Fiscal Relationships, Budgetary Decline and the Impact of the 1994 Fiscal Reform: An Evaluation." *China Quarterly*, 1999, pp. 115–141.

Zhang, Tao and Zou, Heng-fu. "Fiscal Decentralization, Public Spending, and Economic Growth in China." *Journal of Public Economics*, 1998, 67, pp. 221–240.

Zhuravskaya, Ekaterina V. "Incentives to Provide Local Public Goods: Fiscal Federalism, Russian Style." *Journal of Public Economics*, 2000, 76, pp. 337–368.

Part III

Inter-regional Policy

9

China's Inter-Provincial Disparities: 1952–1995

TIAN XIAOWEN & RON DUNCAN*

INTRODUCTION

From 1952 to 1995, China's inter-provincial disparities in measures of output and livelihood witnessed two opposite U-shaped patterns with the turning points for both around the late 1970s and the early 1980s (Figures 1, 2, and 3).[1] Why did the two kinds of indicators of economic development move in opposite directions in the pre-reform and the reform periods? The answer to this question can help to clarify the recent controversy over whether market-oriented reforms have led to a widening of regional economic disparities in China. To address the question, we first discuss the inter-provincial measures of output and livelihood. Then we discuss in turn the reasons for the opposite patterns observed in these economic indicators. The final section concludes.

---

*TIAN Xiaowen is Research Fellow at the East Asian Institute, National University of Singapore. Ron DUNCAN is Professor at the National Centre for Development Studies, Asia Pacific School of Economics and Management, Australian National University.
[1] This paper focuses on inter-provincial disparities, leaving aside coastal-interior disparities for another paper.

OUTPUT AND LIVELIHOOD MEASURES

In the development literature, the relationship between economic development and income equality is usually assumed to take an inverted U-shaped pattern (Kuznets 1955). That is, as a country develops, income inequality increases at first, and then decreases after some point. Considerable empirical work has been carried out to test the Kuznets hypothesis using data on both personal income and regional income distributions. As far as regional income distribution is concerned, the hypothesis passed some of the tests but failed others. In studies on China's inter-provincial disparities, the test results were even more confusing. For the pre-reform period, for instance, some found that 'China successfully avoided the widening of inter-provincial disparities frequently associated with the early stages of growth — or, in other words, that China's development path differs markedly from the classic inverted U', while others concluded that 'Maoism increased regional inequality' (Lyons, 1991, p. 472). A similar controversy also occurred with regard to the change in inter-provincial disparities in China in the reform period (Tsui, 1991; Lee, 1995; Jian, Sachs, and Warner, 1996).[2]

Limited data were no doubt an important reason for the confusion, but the lack of interest in distinguishing between measures of output and livelihood was also partly responsible. On the basis of data on output (national income and GDP), for instance, Chen and Fleisher (1996) found a narrowing of inter-provincial disparity in post-1978 China. On the basis of data measuring livelihood (income of rural residents and income of urban residents), however, Lin, Cai, and Li (1994) illustrated a widening of inter-provincial disparities over the same period. It is crucial to note that output and livelihood indicators may differ owing to government regional income transfer policy in China's case. Pioneer work was done by Lyons (1991) to distinguish between output and livelihood (represented by per capita consumption) measures. Unfortunately, owing to data constraints that study was confined to the pre-1987 period and the estimated changes in inter-provincial disparities were not accurate.

---

[2] For detailed information on the debate, see Lyons (1991).

Thanks to new data sets released by the China Statistical Bureau in recent years, such work can be now improved considerably. Output indicator can be examined upon data on real per capita national income before 1978 and data on real per capita GDP after 1978.[3] Livelihood indicators can be examined using data on real per capita consumption of all residents, real per capita consumption of agricultural residents, and real per capita consumption of non-agricultural residents. As shown in Figures 1 and 2, the two kinds of economic indicators moved in opposite directions in the pre-reform and the reform periods, i.e., they displayed two opposite U-shaped patterns.[4]

To confirm the finding, we can also use data on real per capita income of all residents, real per capita income of rural residents, and real per capita income of urban residents as measures of livelihood. Here, income of urban residents refers to so-called 'total income' of urban residents in Chinese terms, and is the 'total actual cash income, including regular or fixed income and one-off income. Circulating income such as withdrawals from bank deposits, loans borrowed from relatives or friends, repayment of loans received and various temporary collection of money is excluded'. Income of rural residents refers to so-called 'net income' of rural residents in Chinese terms, and is the 'total income after the deduction of expenses, which can be spent for investments for production and non-production construction and for improvement of daily life, while loan income borrowed from banks or friends and relatives is not included'

---

[3] National income is net material product (NMP) in the socialist accounting framework, and is equal to gross value of output minus material consumption. It is, therefore, an output indicator, as suggested by its strong correlation with GDP. It is different from 'income' of residents which is a livelihood indicator, as explained below.

[4] Regional disparities are, as is the case in most studies, measured here in relative terms. The most commonly used relative measures are the coefficient of variation and the Gini coefficient. We use the former which is calculated upon the equation: $CV = \frac{\sqrt{\frac{\Sigma(X_i - \mu)^2}{N}}}{\mu}$, where X stands for the indicator, i for the region to be measured where $i = 1,2,3...N$, and μ for the arithmetic mean of the indicator for all the regional units. The estimated Gini coefficients for both the output and livelihood indicators confirmed the findings we reached by calculation of the coefficient of variation.

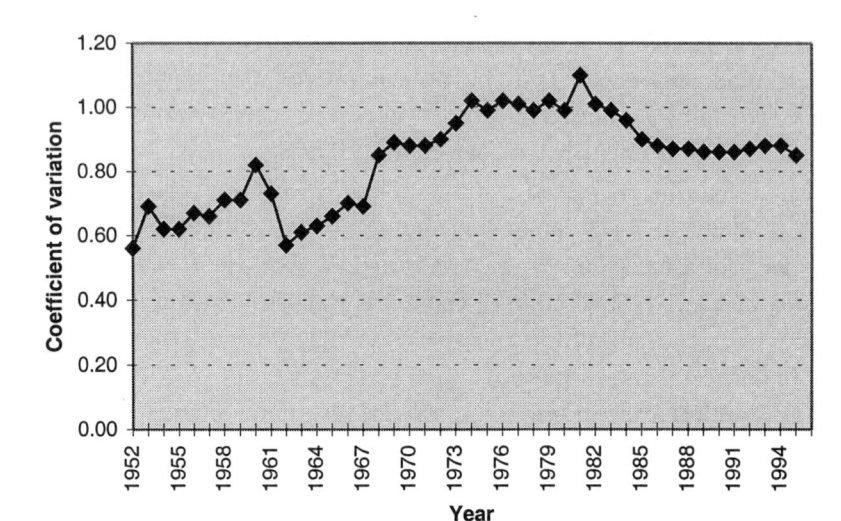

Note: Inter-provincial output disparity is measured here by per capita national income before 1978, and per capita GDP after 1978, in real terms.
Sources: *Statistical Yearbook of China 1983–1997*, Beijing; Statistical Yearbooks of the 30 provinces and metropolitan cities in China.

Fig. 1. Inter-provincial Output Disparities in China, 1952–1995

Sources: *Statistical Yearbook of China 1983–1997*, Beijing; Statistical Yearbooks of the 30 provinces and metropolitan cities in China, China.

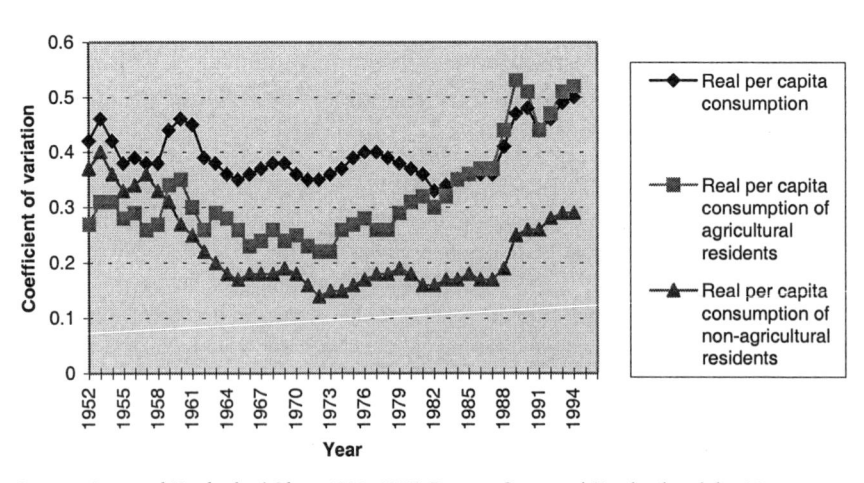

Fig. 2. Inter-provincial Consumption Disparity in China, 1952–1994

(*Statistical Yearbook of China 1994*, p. 291). Per capita income of all residents, *Ia*, is calculated using the formula:

$$Ia = \frac{IrPr + IuPu}{P} \quad (1)$$

where *Ir* stands for per capita income of rural residents, *Iu* for per capita income of urban residents, *P* for population, *Pr* for rural population, and *Pu* for urban population. Data on per capita income (rural and urban residents alike) are available only for the post-1978 period, and they also show a rising trend over the period (see Figure 3) similar to that shown by per capita consumption, as suggested by Lin, Cai, and Li (1994).

The Kuznets hypothesis holds, therefore, only for output, not for livelihood indicators of development, and the underlying factors behind the two opposite U-shaped patterns in measures of output and livelihood have to be found to resolve the controversy over China's inter-provincial disparities.

Sources: Statistical Yearbook of China 1983–1997, Beijing; Statistical Yearbooks of the 30 provinces and metropolitan cities in China, China.

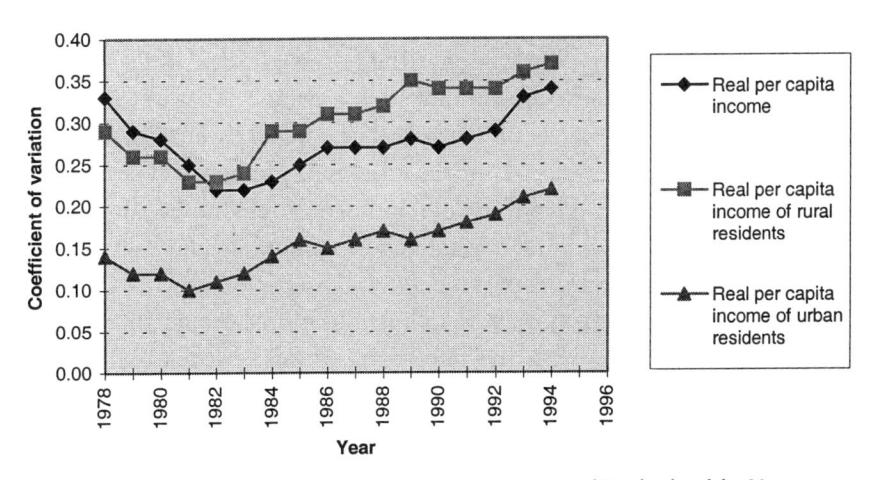

Fig. 3. Inter-provincial Income Disparity in China, 1978–1994

CHANGES IN INTER-PROVINCIAL OUTPUT DISPARITIES

An explanation for the inverted U-shaped pattern in China's inter-provincial output disparities can be found in the different characteristics of industrialisation in the pre-reform and the reform periods.

Industrialisation was inward-looking in the pre-reform period while it was outward-looking in the reform period. After taking national power, the Communist Party pursued a balanced regional development policy and focused upon the backward interior regions of the 'Third Front' in its industrialisation program.[5] Provinces of the Third Front witnessed, therefore, the fastest growth in per capita output value of industry in that period. Due to an extreme self-reliance doctrine, however, industrialisation in interior regions in that period had to rely mainly upon the most advanced 'old industrial' regions (especially Shanghai, Beijing, Tianjin, and Liaoning) for capital goods, technology, and services. As shown in Table 1, industrialisation in that period did not bring about corresponding rapid economic growth in the backward 'newly-industrialised' regions. Instead, it led to the rapid economic growth of the most advanced 'old industrial' regions, and thereby to a widening inter-provincial output disparity. In that period, Ningxia, Qinghai, Shanxi*, and Gansu were the fastest-growing in terms of per capita output value of industry, but were not the fastest-growing in terms of per capita national income.[6] Ningxia ranked, for instance, first in the growth of per capita output value of industry but ranked twenty-first in the growth of per capita national income. Beijing, Shanghai, Tianjin, and Liaoning as the most advanced 'old industrial' regions in that period grew the fastest by providing capital goods, technology, and services for industrialisation in interior provinces.

From 1978 onward, however, industrialisation became increasingly outward-looking along with the deepening of market-oriented reforms,

---

[5] The 'Third Front' included the provinces of Sichuan, Guizhou, Shanxi (in western China), Gansu, Qinghai, Ningxia, Quangxi, Hubei, Hunan, and Shanxi (in central China).

[6] Shanxi* is the province in western China.

Table 1. Industry Growth and National Income Growth in China's Provinces, 1952–1978

Order	Region	Per capita national income in 1952 (yuan in current prices)	Region	Growth rate of per capita national income (%)	Region	Growth rate of per capita output value of industry (%)
1	Shanghai	584.15	Beijing	7.30	Ningxia	13.90
2	Tianjin	261.96	Shanghai	6.00	Qinghai	12.70
3	Beijing	250.80	Tianjin	5.30	Gansu	12.00
4	Heilongjiang	207.92	Liaoning	5.00	Shanxi*	11.10
5	Liaoning	193.58	Shanxi*	4.50	Neimenggu	10.80
6	Xinjiang	157.20	Qinghai	4.40	Hunan	10.60
7	Neimenggu	149.58	Shandong	4.10	Guangxi	10.50
8	Jilin	142.87	Jiangsu	3.80	Henan	10.30
9	Hebei	109.47	Hebei	3.60	Sichuan	10.10
10	Ningxia	104.23	Zhejiang	3.60	Hebei	10.00
11	Jiangxi	103.26	Henan	3.50	Shandong	10.00
12	Zhejiang	101.81	Yunnan	3.50	Jiangsu	9.70
13	Jiangsu	95.29	Gansu	3.50	Shanxi	9.60
14	Fujian	95.06	Hunan	3.40	Beijing	9.50
15	Qinghai	94.41	Sichuan	3.30	Anhui	9.40
16	Gansu	93.43	Hubei	3.10	Hubei	9.30
17	Shanxi	93.25	Guangdong	3.10	Guizhou	8.80
18	Guangdong	88.13	Shanxi	3.00	Yunnan	8.70
19	Shandong	84.73	Guangxi	2.80	Zhejiang	8.50
20	Hubei	82.73	Jilin	2.70	Fujian	8.50
21	Hunan	77.07	Fujian	2.60	Guangdong	8.30
22	Anhui	76.87	Ningxia	2.50	Tianjin	8.20
23	Henan	75.96	Guizhou	2.30	Jiangxi	8.10
24	Shanxi*	75.46	Heilongjiang	2.20	Liaoning	7.60
25	Yunnan	62.42	Neimenggu	2.00	Xinjiang	7.60
26	Guangxi	61.35	Jiangxi	2.00	Shanghai	7.40
27	Sichuan	57.31	Xinjiang	1.90	Jilin	7.30
28	Guizhou	54.77	Anhui	1.70	Heilongjiang	5.80
29	Hainan	..	Hainan	..	Hainan	..
30	Xizang	..	Xizang	..	Xizang	..

Notes: a Growth rates are calculated at 1978 constant prices;
b .. denotes that data are not available.
Sources: *Statistical Yearbook of China 1983–1997*, Beijing; Statistical Yearbooks of the 30 provinces and metropolitan cities in China, China.

and coastal regions were given many special policy deals in relation to terms of foreign investment, management of foreign trade, and exemption from taxes, etc. The outward-looking industrialisation implied unbalanced regional development in favour of the coastal regions and was responsible for the rise of five 'newly-industrialised dragons' in southeast coastal China (i.e., Guangdong, Jiangsu, Zhejiang, Fujian, and Shandong). The five dragons relied, however, mainly upon advanced foreign countries for capital goods, technology, and services; Shanghai, Beijing, Tianjin, and Liaoning, as the 'old industrial' regions lost advantage in this regard, and thereby declined in relative terms. As shown in Table 2, industrialisation in the reform period led to rapid economic development in the initially backward southeast coastal five 'dragons' and, therefore, to a narrowing of inter-provincial output disparities. The five 'dragons' were the fastest-growing regions not only in terms of per capita output value of industry but also in terms of per capita GDP.

It is an irony that the balanced regional development policy before reforms widened inter-provincial output disparities whereas the policies of unbalanced regional development in the reform period narrowed inter-provincial output disparities. The irony resulted from the different orientations of industrialisation as shown above, but it was also determined by the different driving forces of industrialisation in the two periods.

Industrialisation was driven by state-owned enterprises in the pre-reform period while it was driven by non-state owned enterprises in the reform period. Immediately after taking national power, the Communist Party leaders pursued a radical nationalisation policy. Throughout the entire pre-reform period, nationalisation was the dominant policy. State-owned enterprises were established throughout the nation and became the main driving force of industrialisation. As shown in Table 3, state-owned enterprises grew faster than non-state owned enterprises in most regions, particularly in 'newly industrialised' interior regions. State-owned enterprises established in backward interior regions on the Third Front were mainly munitions industries under the direct control of the central government. As a result, they did not have much linkage with regional economic needs and, therefore, could not contribute much to economic development in the 'newly industrialised' regions.

Table 2. Industry Growth and GDP Growth in China's Provinces, 1978–1993

Order	Region	Per capita GDP in 1978 (yuan in current prices)	Region	Growth rate of per capita GDP (%)	Region	Growth rate of per capita output value of industry (%)
1	Shanghai	2483.97	Guangdong	11.26	Zhejiang	20.33
2	Beijing	1280.92	Zhejiang	10.80	Guangdong	19.81
3	Tianjin	1141.57	Jiangsu	9.44	Fujian	18.27
4	Liaoning	666.47	Fujian	9.31	Jiangsu	17.87
5	Heilongjiang	553.59	Shandong	9.11	Shandong	17.68
6	Jiangsu	427.22	Xinjiang	8.90	Anhui	15.63
7	Qinghai	425.75	Jilin	8.17	Xinjiang	15.09
8	Jilin	381.43	Anhui	8.16	Henan	15.03
9	Guangdong	364.78	Yunnan	8.13	Jiangxi	14.59
10	Shanxi	363.05	Henan	8.11	Sichuan	14.52
11	Hebei	361.99	Sichuan	7.74	Hebei	14.27
12	Ningxia	348.88	Beijing	7.60	Hubei	13.97
13	Gansu	346.15	Shanxi*	7.46	Neimenggu	13.87
14	Hubei	330.06	Jiangxi	7.44	Guangxi	13.80
15	Zhejiang	326.69	Neimenggu	7.41	Yunnan	13.76
16	Shandong	319.97	Guizhou	7.38	Jilin	13.10
17	Xinjiang	312.49	Liaoning	7.33	Guizhou	13.02
18	Neimenggu	307.46	Gansu	7.33	Hunan	12.91
19	Shanxi*	292.55	Hebei	7.28	Shanxi	12.65
20	Hunan	284.54	Hubei	7.24	Shanxi*	12.64
21	Jiangxi	273.33	Ningxia	7.06	Liaoning	12.35
22	Fujian	270.59	Shanghai	6.64	Ningxia	12.25
23	Anhui	239.57	Hunan	6.53	Beijing	11.82
24	Sichuan	237.21	Guangxi	6.16	Qinghai	11.53
25	Henan	230.54	Shanxi	6.04	Heilongjiang	11.22
26	Yunnan	223.39	Tianjin	5.61	Tianjin	11.21
27	Guangxi	223.25	Heilongjiang	5.01	Gansu	10.90
28	Guizhou	173.57	Qinghai	4.54	Shanghai	10.00
29	Hainan	..	Xizang	..	Xizang	..
30	Xizang	..	Hainan	..	Hainan	..

Notes: a Growth rates are calculated at 1978 constant prices;
b .. denotes that data are not available.
Sources: Statistical Yearbook of China 1983–1997, Beijing; Statistical Yearbooks of the 30 provinces and metropolitan cities in China, China.

Table 3. Uneven Growth between Forms of Industry Ownership in China's Provinces, 1952–1978

Order for growth of output value of state-owned enterprises	Region	Growth rate of output value of state-owned enterprises (%)	Growth rate of output value of non-state owned enterprises (%)
1	Qinghai	19.70	6.40
2	Ningxia	17.90	7.40
3	Gansu	16.10	3.90
4	Henan	14.60	6.40
5	Guangxi	14.60	5.60
6	Hunan	13.60	7.00
7	Sichuan	13.20	5.40
8	Anhui	13.10	4.60
9	Fujian	13.00	3.50
10	Shanghai	12.70	.05
11	Hebei	12.60	6.60
12	Neimenggu	12.30	7.90
13	Yunnan	12.20	3.80
14	Xinjiang	11.80	.10
15	Shandong	11.70	7.80
16	Shanxi*	11.60	9.10
17	Beijing	11.40	5.30
18	Hubei	10.20	7.70
19	Tianjin	9.90	4.40
20	Jiangxi	9.80	4.80
21	Jiangsu	9.50	10.10
22	Shanxi	9.30	11.00
23	Guizhou	8.50	9.60
24	Guangdong	8.20	8.30
25	Zhejiang	8.10	9.10
26	Liaoning	7.80	6.90
27	Jilin	7.00	8.70
28	Heilongjiang	6.30	4.00
29	Hainan	..	..
30	Xizang	..	..

Notes: a Growth rates are calculated at 1978 constant prices;
   b .. denotes that data are not available.
Sources: *Statistical Yearbook of China 1983–1997*, Beijing; Statistical Yearbooks of the 30 provinces and metropolitan cities in China, China.

After 1978, however, market-oriented reforms triggered a process of de-nationalisation. Non-state owned enterprises rose rapidly in a market competition context and became the main driving force of industrialisation. In the reform period (see Table 4), non-state owned enterprises grew faster than state-owned enterprises in almost every region, particularly in the 'newly industrialised' five 'dragons' in southeast coastal China. Non-state owned enterprises are not under the control of the central government and can easily adjust to the changing demand in domestic and international markets according to regional comparative advantage. They can, therefore, serve regional economic needs well and led to rapid development in the 'newly industrialised' regions.

Changes in Inter-provincial Livelihood Disparities

Although the balanced regional development policy adopted by China did not lead to a narrowing of inter-provincial output disparities before 1978, it did lead to a narrowing of inter-provincial disparities in living standards owing to government intervention in the form of regional income redistribution.

Communist equalitarianism required that residents in all regions enjoy a living standard as equal as possible. To this end, the Chinese government requisitioned a large share of income from richer and faster-growing regions (especially Shanghai) to subsidise residents in more backward and more slowly-growing regions (especially the western provinces). As shown in Tables 1, 2, and 5, Shanghai, Tianjin, and Liaoning were among the richest and fastest-growing regions in the period between 1952 and 1978, and contributed the most to the requisitioned regional income. They together contributed 62 per cent of the total requisitioned regional income, while most of the backward interior provinces were net recipients of it. An exception was Beijing, the capital city with all the central government institutions, which did not contribute very much to the requisition though it was the fastest-growing region. Due to the government intervention in the form of regional income redistribution, therefore, residents in backward regions

Table 4. Uneven Growth between Forms of Industry Ownership in China's Provinces, 1978–1993

Order for growth of output value of non-state owned enterprises	Region	Growth rate of output value of non-state owned enterprises (%)	Growth rate of output value of state-owned enterprises (%)
1	Guangdong	38.09	14.02
2	Shandong	37.10	12.10
3	Fujian	24.46	11.99
4	Zhejiang	24.12	13.15
5	Jiangsu	22.24	11.55
6	Anhui	22.08	11.72
7	Gansu	21.73	9.31
8	Shanghai	20.85	6.52
9	Xinjiang	20.27	13.99
10	Guizhou	20.00	12.16
11	Hebei	18.80	10.01
12	Henan	18.62	11.34
13	Tianjin	18.58	7.45
14	Beijing	18.54	8.89
15	Sichuan	18.38	11.66
16	Jiangxi	18.18	12.07
17	Liaoning	17.83	9.30
18	Neimenggu	17.77	12.45
19	Hubei	17.67	11.80
20	Shanxi*	16.89	10.49
21	Guangxi	15.29	12.22
22	Yunnan	15.28	13.05
23	Shanxi	15.24	10.15
24	Hunan	15.18	10.69
25	Jilin	14.42	11.84
26	Ningxia	14.20	11.37
27	Heilongjiang	13.74	10.54
28	Qinghai	9.09	11.73
29	Hainan	..	..
30	Xizang	..	..

Notes: a Growth rates are calculated at 1978 constant prices;
     b .. denotes that data are not available.
Sources: *Statistical Yearbook of China 1983–1997*, Beijing; Statistical Yearbooks of the 30 provinces and metropolitan cities in China, China.

Table 5. Redistribution of Regional Income in China's Provinces 1952–1992
(100 million yuan)

Region	1952–1978 Inflow	1952–1978 Outflow	1952–1978 Net Inflow (+) and Net Outflow (−)	1979–1992 Inflow	1979–1992 Outflow	1979–1992 Net Inflow (+) and Net Outflow (−)
Beijing	58.90	164.30	−105.40	297.46	119.06	178.40
Tianjin	.00	381.00	−381.00	18.56	258.89	−240.33
Hebei	44.00	119.20	−75.20	.00	429.20	−429.20
Shanxi	16.40	50.60	−34.20	144.19	27.61	116.58
Neimenggu	61.30	58.80	2.50	438.38	.00	438.38
Liaoning	.00	737.80	−737.80	.00	707.85	−707.85
Jilin	22.70	47.00	−24.30	202.76	.00	202.76
Heilongjiang	.00	301.30	−301.30	.00	249.38	−249.38
Shanghai	.00	1757.40	−1757.40	.00	1619.62	−1619.62
Jiangsu	.00	321.70	−321.70	.00	924.23	−924.23
Zhejiang	.00	89.90	−89.90	.00	361.00	−361.00
Anhui	9.60	39.80	−30.20	44.72	42.00	2.72
Fujian	72.70	1.60	71.10	123.99	1.78	122.21
Jiangxi	65.10	13.30	51.80	153.85	1.20	152.65
Shandong	1.20	190.40	−189.20	.00	569.16	−569.16
Henan	67.30	26.80	40.50	.00	188.85	−188.85
Hubei	65.60	95.20	−29.60	.00	329.80	−329.80
Hunan	.00	132.20	−132.20	35.04	96.80	−61.76
Guangdong	11.60	94.20	−82.60	63.50	374.94	−311.44
Guangxi	86.30	.20	86.10	190.57	.00	190.57
Hainan	.00	.00	.00	73.11	.00	73.11
Sichuan	191.60	10.50	181.10	197.38	9.48	187.90
Guizhou	161.70	1.90	159.80	161.72	.00	161.72
Yunnan	138.70	1.40	137.30	274.69	.00	274.69
Xizang	.00	.00	.00	89.67	.00	89.67
Shanxi*	103.40	.60	102.80	504.98	.00	504.98
Gansu	74.40	23.60	50.80	205.82	12.30	193.52
Qinghai	11.40	.00	11.40	198.53	.00	198.53
Ningxia	30.00	.00	30.00	122.09	.00	122.09
Xinjiang	129.50	.10	129.40	548.81	.00	548.81

Notes: National income minus national income actually utilised; the positive is outflow and the negative is inflow.

Sources: Statistical Yearbook of China 1983–1995, Beijing; Statistical Yearbooks of the 30 provinces and metropolitan cities in China.

enjoyed a relatively high living standard as compared with the output level in these regions (see Table 6). To encourage residents to stay in backward interior regions (especially Tibet and Qinghai), the central government even offered them a wage level higher than that in most other regions.[7] As a result, inter-provincial livelihood disparities narrowed remarkably despite the widening inter-provincial output disparities in the pre-reform period. As shown in Figures 4, up to 1978 inter-provincial livelihood inequalities were much narrower than inter-provincial output inequalities.

After 1978, market-oriented reforms led to increasing competition between regions, which was even encouraged by the Communist Party. As a result, regional autonomy strengthened and central government's intervention in regional income redistribution weakened. In the period between 1952 and 1978, for instance, about 11 per cent of provincial income was requisitioned by the central government for regional income redistribution. In the period between 1979 and 1992, the share fell to about 5 per cent.

Given the remarkable relaxation of government intervention in regional income redistribution, the widening of regional livelihood

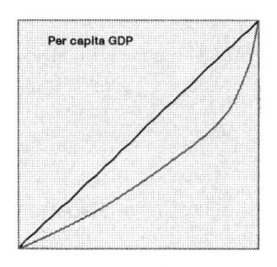

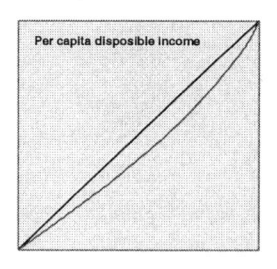

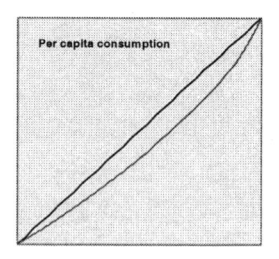

Note: Per capita disposable income is estimated upon per capita net income of rural residents and per capita total income of urban residents.
Sources: Statistical Yearbook of China 1983–1995, Beijing; Statistical Yearbooks of the 30 provinces and metropolitan cities in China, China.

Fig. 4. Lorenz Curves for Provincial Output and Livelihood in China in 1978

---

[7] In 1978, for instance, the average wage in Tibet was higher than in most other provinces in China.

Table 6. Regional Development Indicators for China in 1978 and 1994 (Shanghai = 100)

Region	Per capita GDP 1978	Per capita GDP 1994	Per capita real income of rural residents 1978	Per capita real income of rural residents 1994	Per capita real income of urban residents 1978	Per capita real income of urban residents 1994
Beijing	51.57	55.19	80.09	71.29	74.62	86.75
Tianjin	45.96	41.34	54.51	66.04	73.72	82.73
Hebei	14.57	15.40	40.61	47.97	56.36	62.83
Shanxi	14.62	12.61	36.20	36.06	58.46	47.57
Neimenggu	12.38	12.49	46.31	40.21	55.88	51.16
Liaoning	26.83	26.78	65.91	61.09	70.04	55.11
Jilin	15.36	17.34	64.72	54.05	56.44	45.97
Heilongjiang	22.29	15.78	61.15	52.59	69.00	44.49
Shanghai	100.00	100.00	100.00	100.00	100.00	100.00
Jiangsu	17.20	27.80	40.97	66.97	58.81	68.10
Zhejiang	13.15	26.89	58.78	77.98	76.48	81.06
Anhui	9.64	12.25	40.38	37.40	66.45	59.97
Fujian	10.89	18.57	49.00	59.59	69.32	58.41
Jiangxi	11.00	12.96	50.13	47.81	66.28	51.90
Shandong	12.88	18.91	40.81	60.12	73.76	76.24
Henan	9.28	11.35	37.41	41.92	73.29	58.72
Hubei	13.29	14.54	39.37	46.39	67.35	60.42
Hunan	11.45	10.77	50.79	36.16	66.14	58.75
Guangdong	14.69	29.67	62.85	72.18	68.39	100.18
Guangxi	8.99	9.14	42.75	37.63	59.02	60.65
Hainan	..	26.49	..	33.15	..	56.74
Sichuan	9.55	10.86	45.28	35.61	66.58	56.85
Guizhou	6.99	7.03	38.83	31.58	52.48	57.00
Yunnan	8.99	9.99	46.67	30.24	64.33	69.43
Xizang	..	14.34	..	41.12	..	83.51
Shanxi	11.78	11.66	47.74	30.58	59.22	49.41
Gansu	13.94	12.70	35.96	28.49	70.49	53.08
Qinghai	17.14	11.73	42.40	36.60	67.18	52.37
Ningxia	14.05	12.07	41.33	34.40	65.43	54.95
Xinjiang	12.58	15.94	42.40	36.45	85.56	57.42

Notes: a   Growth rates are calculated at 1978 constant prices;
      b   .. denotes that data are not available.
Sources: Statistical Yearbook of China 1983–1997, Beijing; Statistical Yearbooks of the 30 provinces and metropolitan cities in China, China.

disparities in the reform period can be taken as caused by two regional forces. On the one hand, it has been a result of the strengthening autonomy of the most advanced 'old industrial' regions. Although these regions, such as Shanghai, Tianjin, and Liaoning, were still among the main contributors to the requisitioned regional income in the period, the share of their contribution fell remarkably.[8] The most obvious case is Shanghai. In the period between 1952 and 1978, Shanghai contributed 38 per cent of all the requisitioned regional income. In the period between 1979 and 1992, its share fell to about 26 per cent. On the other hand, it has been a result of the strengthening autonomy of the fastest-growing regions (especially Guangdong and other Southeast coastal provinces). Although these regions have contributed an increasing share of the requisitioned regional income in the period, the amount of the requisitioned income was rather small in relation to their rapid economic growth. In the period, for instance, Guangdong ranked first in per capita GDP growth, but its contribution to the requisitioned regional income was even less than Hebei and Hubei which were much poorer and grew much more slowly!

Residents in backward interior regions are the main losers from the relaxation of government intervention in regional income redistribution. Relative to the richest region, Shanghai, residents of most backward interior regions witnessed a declining living standard in the reform period while those of most coastal regions witnessed a rising living standard. The widening regional livelihood disparities are potential sources of social instability challenging the Chinese government.

Conclusion

It is crucial to distinguish between output and livelihood indicators in the examination of China's inter-provincial disparities. The inverted U-

---

[8] Their share fell from 62 percent in the pre-reform period to 41 percent in the post-reform period. Beijing, one of the richest regions, became a net recipient of the requisitioned regional income in the post-1978 period.

shaped pattern of inter-provincial output disparities was determined mainly by the different characteristics of industrialisation in the pre-reform and the reform periods, and it suggests that outward-looking and de-nationalisation oriented industrialisation in the reform period narrowed inter-provincial output disparities. The U-shaped pattern of inter-provincial livelihood disparities was determined mainly by the degree to which government intervened in regional income redistribution, and it suggests that the intervention weakened along with the strengthening of regional autonomy in the process of transition to market systems. If regional equity is a goal, therefore, China should find appropriate approaches to strengthen governmental transfer to prevent regional livelihood disparities from widening.

REFERENCES

Chen, J. and Fleisher, B.M. (1974) "Regional Income Inequality and Economic Growth in China," *Journal of Comparative Economics* **22**:141–64.
Kuznets, S. (1955) "Economic Growth and Income Inequality," *American Economic Review* **45**,1–28.
Jian, T.L, Sachs, J.D and Warner, A.M. (1996) "Trends in Regional Inequality in China," *China Economic Review* **7** (1), 1–21.
Lee, J. Ch. (1995) "Regional Income Inequality Variations in China," *Journal of Economic Development* **20** (2), 99–118.
Lin, J.Y.F., Cai, F. and Li, Zh. (1994) *China Miracle: Development Strategies and Economic Reforms*, Sanlian Press, Shanghai.
Lyons, Thomas P. (1991) "Inter-provincial Disparities in China: Output and Consumption, 1952–1987," *Economic Development and Cultural Change* **4**, 471–505.
Tsui, K.Y. (1991) "China's Regional Inequality, 1952–1985," *Journal of Comparative Economics* **17**, 1–21.

10

China's Drive to Develop Its Western Region (I): Why Turn to This Region Now?

TIAN XIAOWEN*

FROM EAST TO WEST

On 19 January 2000, an Inter-ministerial Committee for Developing the Western Region of the State Council was set up in Beijing, with Premier Zhu Rongji as the Chair (Table 1). The formation of this high-powered committee showed the determination of the Chinese government to develop the poor and backward interior, and signified the beginning of a shift in focus of economic development from the eastern (coastal) to the western region.

China's 31 provinces and metropolitan cities are currently divided into eastern (coastal), central and western regions.[1] The western region

---

* TIAN Xiaowen is research fellow at East Asian Institute. He would like to express his thanks to Professor John Wong for his comments and suggestions, and Mr Aw Beng Teck for his editorial assistance.

[1] The eastern region includes Liaoning, Beijing, Tianjin, Hebei, Shandong, Jiangsu, Shanghai, Zhejiang, Fujian, Guangdong, Hainan and Guangxi. The central region includes Heilongjiang, Jilin, Inner Mongolia, Shanxi, Henan, Anhui, Hubei, Hunan and Jiangxi. The western region includes Xinjiang, Gunsu, Qinghai, Ningxia, Shaanxi, Tibet, Sichuan,

Table 1. The Inter-ministerial Committee for Developing the Western Region of the State Council

Chair:	
Zhu Rongji	(Premier)
Deputy Chair:	
Wen Jiabao	(Vice Premier)
Director of General Office:	
Zeng Peiyan	(Director of Commission of National Development and Planning)
Members:	
Sheng Huaren	(Director of National Commission of Economy and Trade)
Chen Zhili	(Minister of Education)
Zhu Lilan	(Minister of Science and Technology)
Liu Ji	(Director of National Defence Industry and Science)
Li Dezhu	(Director of Minority Nationality Affairs)
Xiang Huicheng	(Minister of Finance)
Fu Zhihuan	(Minister of Railway)
Huang Zhendong	(Minister of Transportation)
Wu Jichuan	(Minister of Information Industry)
Chen Yaobang	(Minister of Agriculture)
Sun Jiazheng	(Minister of Culture)
Dai Xianglong	(Director of the Chinese People's Bank)
Liu Yunshan	(Executive Minister of Propaganda of the Central Committee of the CPC)
Tian Congming	(Minister of Broadcasting and Television)
Wang Zhibin	(Director of the National Bureau of Forestry)
Wang Xueyuan	(Director of the National Bureau of Foreign Experts)
Tian Fengshan	(Minister of Land and Resources)

Yunnan, Guizhou and Chongqing (see Map 1). The eastern region is along the coast and, therefore, is also called the coastal region. The central and western regions are in the interior and, therefore, are also called interior regions.

includes nine provinces and one metropolitan city. It accounts for 56 percent of China's land area, but only 23 percent of China's population and 14.5 percent of China's GDP (Table 2). Here the physical environment is very harsh, and most of the land areas are covered by mountains, hills, plateaus, deserts and dry lands. Transportation and telecommunication facilities are extremely underdeveloped. Up to 1998, for instance, railway coverage was 26 km per sq km in this region while it was 153 km per sq km in the eastern region. Until now there is no railway at all in Tibet. The poor telecommunication facilities is shown in the low number of telephone sets and internet subscribers. In 1998, for instance, there were 411 telephones and one internet subscriber in every 10,000 persons in the western region, while the figures were 1,002 and 10 in the eastern region, respectively.

Owing to the harsh physical environment and poor infrastructure, the western region could not make full use of its abundant natural resources and tourist resources (see Part II), and has been the poorest region in China for centuries. Up to now, 90 percent of Chinese living under the poverty line are in the western region. Illiteracy rate is much higher in the western region (27 percent) than in the east coast region (14 percent). In Tibet and Qinghai, illiteracy rates are as high as 54 percent and 43 percent, respectively. The poverty and backwardness of the western region has been a major concern for Chinese leaders, even in the early years of economic reform when they focused their attention primarily on the east coast region.

In as early as the early 1980s, Deng Xiaoping proposed the idea of two stages of regional development, that is, the coastal provinces were to make use of their location advantage to develop first, and they could then help the development of the interior provinces. During his southern tour in 1992, Deng further proposed that China should move from the first stage to the second, that is, shift the focus of reform and development from the coast to the interior, by the end of the 20th century. The shift of focus of reform and development from the coast to the western region was, therefore, a well-planned move that had been under deliberation for more than a decade.

Table 2. Basic Statistics of Western Provinces, 1998

Province	Area 1,000 Sq.km	Population 10,000	GDP 100 million Yuan	GDP Per capita Yuan	GDP Growth (1979–1998) (%)	Fixed Asset Investments 100 million Yuan	FDI US $ million	Exports US $ million
Chongqing	82	3,060	1,429	4,684	11.9	493	431	484
Sichuan	485	8,493	3,580	4,339	9	1,145	373	1,214
Guizhou	176	3,658	842	2,342	8.6	278	45	425
Yunnan	394	4,144	1,794	4,355	9.3	660	146	1,014
Tibet	1230	252	91	3,716	8.2	41	0	29
Shaanxi	206	3,596	1,382	3,834	9	518	300	1,094
Gansu	454	2,519	870	3,456	8.4	301	39	385
Qinghai	721	503	220	4,367	6.9	109	0	117
Ningxia	66	538	227	4,270	8.8	107	19	235
Xinjiang	1660	1,747	1,117	6,229	10.1	515	22	655
West Region	5475	28,510	11,552	4,052	9	4,168	1,374	5,653
All China	9600	124,810	79,396	6,392	9.3	28,406	45,463	183,757
Share of West Region (%)	56	23	15	-	-	15	3	3

Sources: *China Statistical Yearbook*, 19981–1999; provincial statistical yearbooks for western provinces.

When Deng Xiaoping proposed reorienting development to the interior, his main concern was to "resolve the problem of widening disparities between coastal and interior regions."[2] Since then, however, other concerns have developed and further motivated the current westward drive, such as the separatist movements in minority nationalities that threaten national unity and security, the sluggish domestic demand that became worse during the Asian financial crisis, and the deterioration of the ecological environment that caused devastating disasters along the Yangtze River and the Yellow River in recent years. China's current drive for developing its western region has, therefore, been initiated and promoted to achieve multiple goals.

Narrowing Regional Disparities

The primary goal of the westward drive is no doubt to narrow regional economic disparities. Following the adoption of the reform and opening-up policies in 1978, China encouraged the coastal areas to utilize their location advantage to achieve more rapid economic growth than other parts of the country. To this end, a series of preferential policy treatments was granted to coastal areas with regard to foreign investment, foreign trade, taxation and the establishment of the Special Economic Zones. As a result, coastal areas developed faster than their interior counterparts, and the disparities between coastal and interior regions widened quite consistently in the last two decades.

From 1978 to 1998, as shown in Figure 1, the ratio of GDP per capita of the coastal region to that of the central region rose from 1.50 to 1.84, and the ratio of GDP per capita of the coastal region to that of the western region rose from 1.84 to 2.53. Particularly in the 1990s, the disparities between coastal and western regions widened remarkably. Looked at in greater detail, the widening of the gap between coastal and western regions is even more astonishing. GDP per capita of the Qinghai Province as a percentage of that of Shanghai — the richest coastal

---

[2] See *Selected Works of Deng Xiaoping* (Beijing: People's Press, 1993), Vol. 3, p. 374.

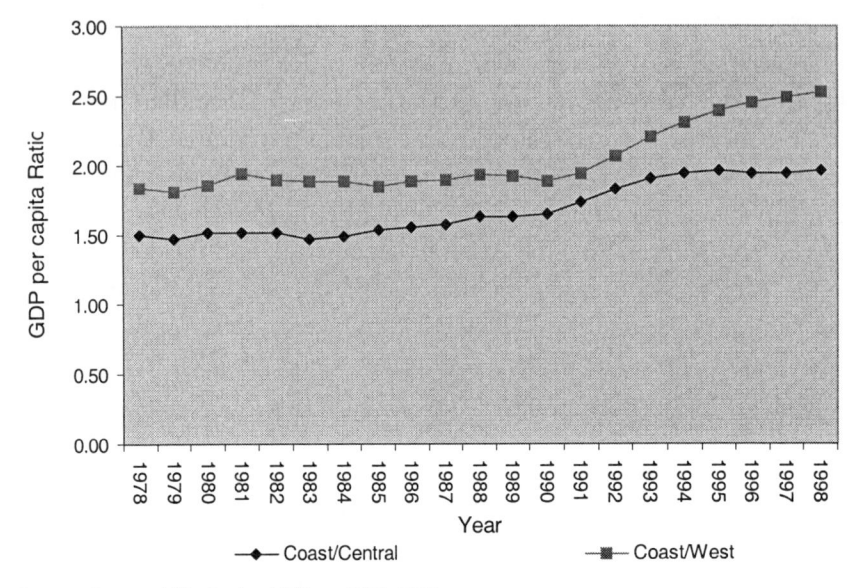

Sources: *Statistical Yearbook of China,* 1983–1999.

Fig. 1. Disparities between Coastal and Interior Regions, 1978–1998

metropolitan city — was, for instance, 17 percent in 1978, but it fell to 10 percent in 1998. Consumption per capita of the Qinghai Province as a percentage of that of Shanghai fell from 54 percent in 1978 to 25 percent in 1998! By 1998, as shown in Figures 2 and 3, all western provinces were below the national average in terms of GDP per capita and consumption per capita.

Compared with the fastest-growing provinces like Guangdong, Zhejiang, Jiangsu, Fujian and Shandong in the east coast region, as shown in Tables 3 and 4, all interior provinces fell well behind in terms of the growth of both GDP per capita and consumption per capita. In 1978, four of the five coastal provinces lagged behind Qinghai in terms of GDP per capita, and all of them lagged behind Qinghai in terms of consumption per capita. From 1978 to 1997, however, GDP per capita in the five coastal provinces increased by about 7–9 times while that in Qinghai increased only by about 3 times. Over the same period, consumption per capita in the five coastal provinces increased by about

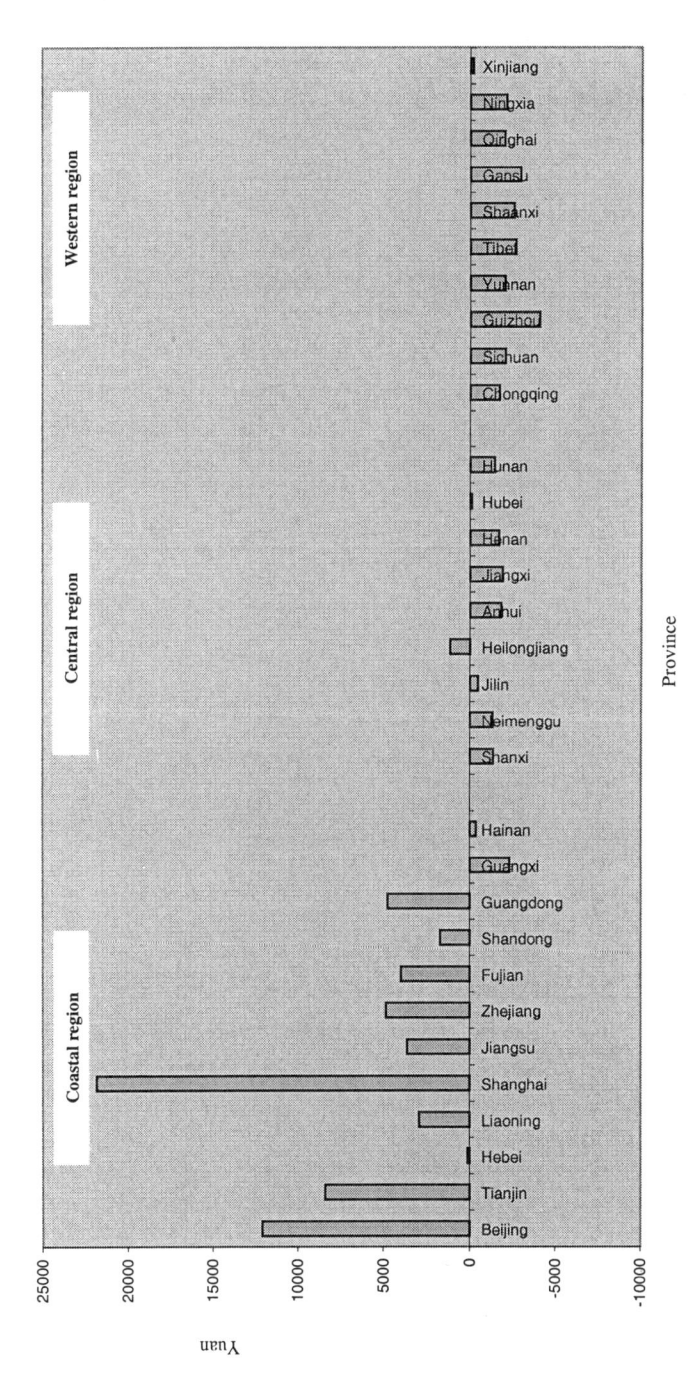

Fig. 2. GDP per Capita of Individual Provinces Minus GDP per Capita of National Average in China, 1998

Sources: Statistical Yearbook of China, 1980–1999.

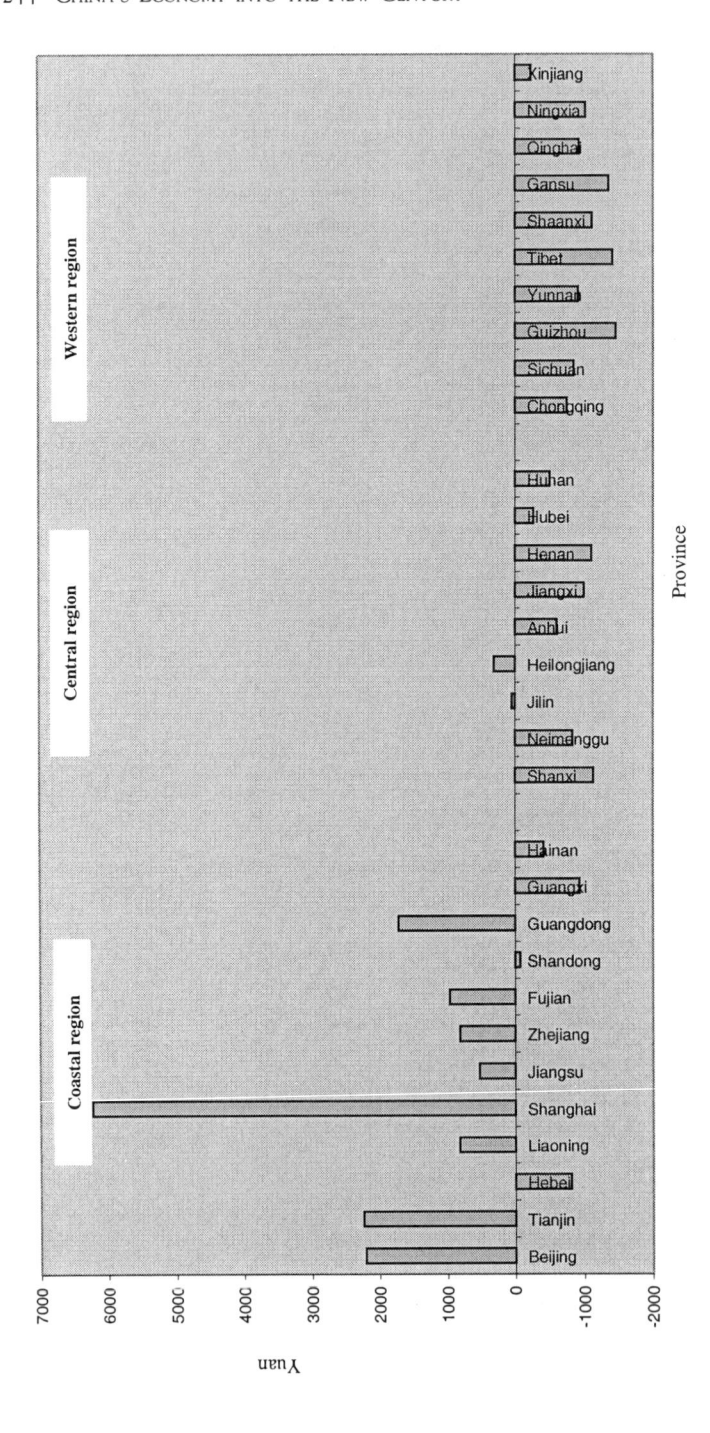

Fig. 3. Consumption per Capita of Individual Provinces Minus Consumption per Capita of National Average in China, 1998

Sources: Statistical Yearbook of China, 1980–1999.

Table 3. GDP per Capita in China's Provinces, 1978–1997

Region	GDP per capita in 1978 at current price (Yuan)	GDP per capita in 1997 at 1978 constant price (Yuan)	GDP per capita index in 1997 calculated at 1978 constant price (1978=100)
Coastal			
Beijing	1,281	5,831	455
Tianjin	1,142	4,830	423
Hebei	362	1,760	486
Liaoning	667	2,677	402
Shanghai	2,484	11,610	468
Jiangsu	427	3,183	745
Zhejiang	327	3,098	948
Fujian	271	2,198	810
Shandong	320	2,128	664
Guangdon	365	3,198	877
Guangxi	223	988	443
Hainan	..	2,368	..
Central			
Shanxi	363	1,335	368
Neimenggu	308	1,311	427
Jilin	381	1,835	481
Heilongjiang	554	1,655	299
Anhui	240	1,409	588
Jiangxi	273	1,457	533
Henan	231	1,275	553
Hubei	330	1,659	503
Hunan	285	1,167	410
Western			
Sichuan	237	1,556	656
Guizhou	174	697	402
Yunnan	223	1,048	469
Tibet	..	1,635	..
Shaanxi	293	1,209	413
Gansu	346	1,299	375
Qinghai	426	1,165	274
Ningxia	349	1,280	367
Xinjiang	313	1,569	502
National average	379	1,742	460

Note: .. denotes data are not available.
Sources: *Statistical Yearbook of China* 1983–1999, Beijing; statistical yearbooks of the 30 provinces and metropolitan cities in China.

Table 4. Consumption per Capita in China's Provinces, 1978–1997

Region	Consumption per capita in 1978 at current price (Yuan)	Consumption per capita in 1997 at 1978 constant price (Yuan)	Consumption per capita index in 1997 calculated at 1978 constant price (1978=100)
Coastal			
Beijing	347	1,387	400
Tianjin	368	1052	286
Hebei	160	599	374
Liaoning	252	867	344
Shanghai	416	1,892	455
Jiangsu	187	843	451
Zhejiang	193	839	434
Fujian	183	695	380
Shandong	169	621	368
Guangdon	196	992	506
Guangxi	131	332	254
Hainan	..	..	..
Central			
Shanxi	144	474	328
Neimenggu	194	502	259
Jilin	227	649	286
Heilongjiang	250	577	231
Anhui	142	457	321
Jiangxi	186	544	301
Henan	126	527	418
Hubei	145	558	385
Hunan	159	407	256
Western			
Sichuan	138	540	392
Guizhou	125	310	248
Yunnan	141	329	234
Tibet	..	541	..
Shaanxi	155	419	271
Gansu	143	342	239
Qinghai	226	479	212
Ningxia	185	393	212
Xinjiang	215	534	248
National average	175	667	381

Note: .. denotes data are not available.
Sources: *Statistical Yearbook of China*, 1983–1998, Beijing; statistical yearbooks of the 30 provinces and metropolitan cities in China.

4–5 times while that in Qinghai increased only by about 2 times. By 1997, therefore, GDP per capita in the five fastest-growing coastal provinces had been already twice or three times as high as that in Qinghai, and consumption per capita in the five coastal provinces had all surpassed that in Qinghai!

The current gap between the coastal and interior regions becomes more vivid if a comparison is made between an interior province and the "open" areas in southeast coastal China. In 1997, for instance, per capita GDP and per capita savings in Qinghai province were 4,074 yuan and 2,300 yuan, respectively. In that year, by contrast, GDP per capita and per capita savings of 14 open coastal cities were 21,987 yuan and 18,034 yuan, five times and 7.8 times as high as those in Qinghai, respectively. Per capita GDP and per capita savings of the four special economic zones were 49,791 yuan and 27,599 yuan, 12.2 times and 12 times as high as those in Qinghai, respectively!

The widening regional disparities is antagonistic to the Communist ideology that still dominates the Party and the government, and has caused a great deal of unhappiness from those living in the interior, who complain about the fairness of the on-going reform and opening-up programme [Hu et al. (1995)]. The discontent gained in strength in the years immediately following the Tiananmen Square Incident in 1989.[3] Were the increase in regional inequality not brought under control, not only would the on-going reform and opening-up programme but also the legitimacy of the current regime be under threat. The primary goal of the westward drive is, no doubt, to narrow the disparities between the east coast and the interior regions.

Ensuring National Security

Another motivation behind the westward drive is to ensure national security. The west is a region where China's minority nationalities live in compact communities. Fifty of the 54 minority nationalities in China,

---

[3] See *People's Daily*, 23 February 1992.

including the Uighur, the Tibetan, the Hui, the Yi, the Bai, the Hani, the Zhuang, the Dai and the Miao, live in the western region. In fact, three of the nine provinces in the western region are autonomous regions dominated by minority nationalities, that is, the Xinjiang Uighur Autonomous Region, the Tibetan Autonomous Region, and the Ningxia Hui Autonomous Region. Owing to the ethnic diversity, the western region experienced frequent ethnic conflicts in Chinese history, and has been a main concern in China's national security for centuries.

After 1978, the Chinese central government relaxed its control over local affairs in order to provide incentive for local authorities at various levels to accelerate reform, opening-up and economic development. The Chinese central government also adopted a more liberal policy allowing the freedom of religious beliefs among minority nationalities. Along with the process of decentralization and liberalization, the movement toward greater autonomy or even full independence gained momentum in some of the minority areas in the western region. China's opening-up to the outside world presented an opportunity for the separatists to work in concert with their supporters abroad [Pomfret (2000)].

In the Xinjiang Uygur Autonomous Region, for instance, Muslim extremists have been demanding that Xinjiang become a separate Muslim state, independent of China. In February 1997, hundreds of Uighurs took to the streets in *Yining*, a city near the border between China and Kazakhstan, shouting "God is supreme" and "independence for Xinjiang". They turned violent when the Chinese government tried to crack down on the demonstration. The Chinese official media reported that 10 people were killed, but Uighur exile groups put the death toll at more than 100. After the crackdown, the Muslim extremists went on with murder, bombing and violent rampage against Beijing, and they were provided with weapons from the Uighur exile groups in China's neighboring countries. This January, in Aksu, an isolated town in Xinjiang, several separatist militants were killed by the police [Pomfret (2000)].

In the Tibetan Autonomous Region, separatist movements have posed an even greater threat. Ever since the Tibetan government led by the spiritual leader Dalai Lama fled abroad in 1959, the Tibetan Buddhism separatist movement has never stopped its demand for independence.

The exile Tibetan government tried to make use of international forces against the Chinese government, and gained considerable support from extremist Tibetan Buddhists both inside and outside China. In September 1987, for instance, after the exiled Dalai Lama called for an independent statehood for Tibet, riots broke out in Lhassa in support of the spiritual leader. In the following two years, a series of protests in various forms was reported in Lhassa. The Tibetan separatist movements staged a violent rebellion in March 1989, in which scores of people were killed. The Chinese government had to declare martial law in Lhassa for more than one year. After that, although open violent opposition against the Chinese government subsided, covert separatist activities did not stop, as indicated by the escape of the 14-year-old Karmapa Lama, leader of the Kargyu sect of Tibetan Buddhism, to India in early January this year.

Faced with the pressure from separatist movements, the Chinese government believes the best solution to the problem is to further integrate the minority nationalities into the rest of the nation. That is to say, the central government will help the backward western region catch up with other parts of the nation in economic reform and development. The Chinese government hopes that along with the rise in the living standard and the increased flow of commodities, resources and personnel across regions, the minority nationalities in the western region will become less and less dissatisfied with the government, and consider themselves, more and more, as part of a unified nation [Zheng (2000)].

Providing New Sources of Growth

A third motivation behind the westward drive is to provide new sources of growth. In the 1990s, the Chinese economy had changed from a "shortage economy" to a "surplus economy" characterized by over-capacity in production and low levels of private consumption. Excessive investment and increasing polarization contributed to the change. With few exceptions, for instance, more than half of the production capacity in domestic appliances lay idle; yet, more investments were pouring into this sector (Table 5). On the other hand, most residents in poor areas could not afford to buy these commodities due to low income. As a

Table 5. Production Capacity of Domestic Appliances, 1995

Product	Production Capacity (10,000 Units)	Utilization Ratio (%)	Additional Production Capacity from Further Investment At Year End (10,000 Units)
Washing Machine	2183	43.4	228
Vacuum Cleaner	1284	43.2	20
Electric Fan	14253	65.1	255
Fridge (10000)	1821	50.5	217
Air Conditioner	2035	33.5	380
Color TV	4468	46.1	260
Oil Fume Extractor	892	40.2	17
Video Recorder	517	41.7	190
Video Camera	35	12.3	1
Microwave	259	38.6	--

Source: China Industrial Development Report 1999, Beijing.

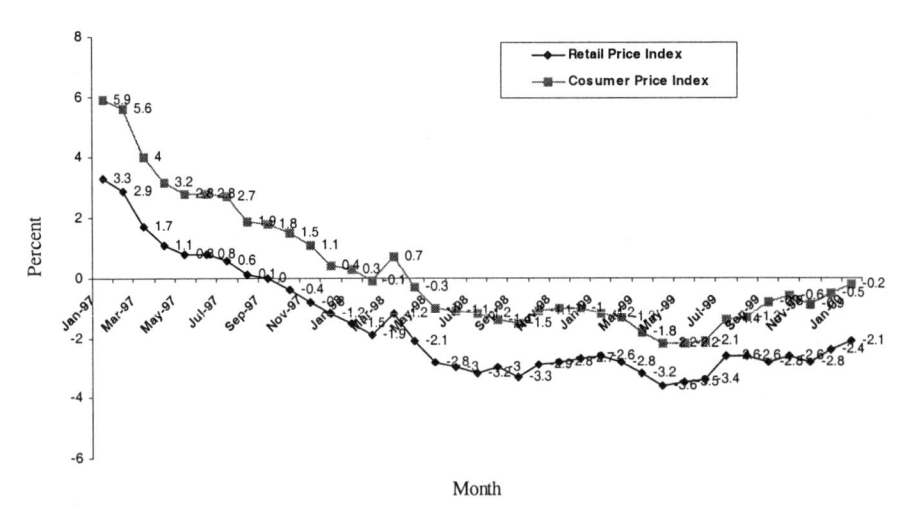

Source: Statistical Yearbook of China, 1999.

Fig. 4. Deflation in China since October 1997

result, overstocked goods increased enormously. The overstocked TV sets numbered, for instance, more than 3 million in the late 1990s.

The problem became worse during the Asian financial crisis. China's exports became less competitive due to the currency devaluation in neighboring countries. China's foreign trade growth rate turned negative in 1998, the first time in 16 years, and only picked up in late 1999 and early 2000. Goods that could not be sold in international markets flooded domestic markets, which were already under the pressure of weak consumer demand. Consumer price fell for more than 28 successive months after October 1997, and only showed signs of a bottom-out in February 2000 (Figure 4). China had suffered from its most serious deflation in the reform period.

China adopted expansionary fiscal and monetary policies to boost domestic demand during the Asian financial crisis, but the policies did not achieve as much effect as was expected.[4] The decrease in both domestic and international demand led to a slowdown in economic growth, and the growth rate of GDP fell continuously in the late 1990s (Figure 5). The growth slowdown exerted pressure on employment,

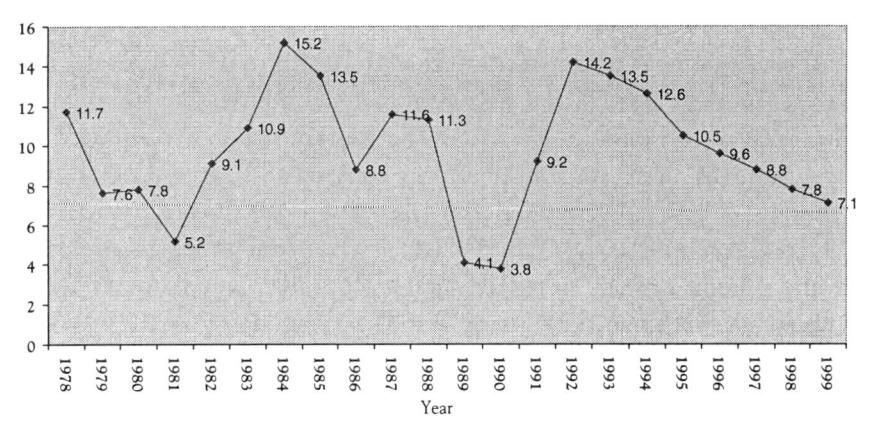

Source: Statistical Yearbook of China, 1999.

Fig. 5. GDP Growth Rate in China, 1978–1999

---

[4] For a detailed analysis, see John Wong, "China's Economy in 1998," *EAI Background Brief*, No. 25, 1998.

Table 6. Consumption of Durable Goods among Rural Residents in Coastal and Western Regions, 1998

Goods	Out of 100 Rural Households in Western Region	Out of 100 Rural Households in Coastal Region
Bicycle	92	191
Colour TV	19	45
Electric Fan	32	166
Washing Machine	14	38
Refrigerator	2	24
Camera	1	5
Motor Bicycle	5	21

Source: *China Industrial Development Report 1999*, Beijing.

causing increased concern among policymakers. To resolve the problem of sluggish demand and growth slowdown, new policy initiatives had to be made.

Through the westward drive, China is trying to provide new sources of growth. The westward drive would increase the consumption capacity of residents in the most backward areas of the country. It has been estimated that nearly 90 percent of the Chinese people living under the poverty line are located in the western region, and they have extremely low levels of consumption capacity. The western region accounts for 23 percent of China's population, but only consumes 13 percent of China's consumer goods. Rural residents in the western region are particularly poor, and consume, as shown in Table 6, much less than their counterparts in the coastal region in major durable consumer goods, particularly domestic appliances. If the living standard of residents in the western region were raised to the same level as their coastal counterparts, domestic demand would certainly increase considerably.

The westward drive would also entail a large number of public projects in infrastructure construction, which would not only yield employment opportunities but also provide a solid basis for sustainable economic development in the long run. A consensus has, therefore, been reached among Chinese leaders: the "grand strategy of developing the western region" will become an important measure to boost domestic demand and promote coordinated, sustained, rapid and healthy development of the national economy.

Tackling Ecological Problems

Finally, the westward drive was initiated to tackle deteriorating ecological problems in the western and the central regions arising from China's rapid economic development. China was so eager to achieve rapid industrialization and economic growth that it did not pay much attention to environmental protection. Under the policy of "taking grain as the key link," for instance, rural residents were encouraged to turn hillsides and grasslands into farmlands, causing ecological imbalances. The deterioration of the ecological environment has been particularly severe in the interior, and has led to serious consequences such as desertification of lands, floods and dry-up of rivers. In particular, the soil erosion and water losses in the upper and middle reaches of the Yangtze River and the Yellow River have caused frequent disasters in recent years.

In the Yangtze River floods in 1998, for example, about 3,000 people died, and 3 million people were left homeless. The floods also did tremendous damage to crops, and made subsequent summer crop planting on some of the most fertile farmlands along the Yangtze River virtually impossible. In addition, the floods killed thousands of livestock, inundated hundreds of thousands of hectares of farmland, and destroyed both farm machinery and irrigation infrastructure. In the three provinces of Hunan, Hubei and Jiangxi alone, the floods completely destroyed more than 3 million hectares of crops and aquaculture, and severely affected 7 million hectares of cultivated land.[5]

The Yellow River is more of a threat than the Yangtze River, although it has not caused serious floods in recent years. The River remains a potential source of the most devastating floods due to its high silt content

---

[5] For a detailed analysis, see John Wong, "Explaining China's Floods," *EAI Background Brief*, No. 21, 1998.

accumulated over the years. Millions of tons of yellow mud choke the channel, causing the River to overflow its banks and change its course. In the lower reaches of the Yellow River, the riverbed has actually become higher than the level of the surrounding countryside. Unlike the Yangtze River, the water of the Yellow River is only held by its levees shielding 120,000 sq km of land. This means that more than 7.3 million hectares of farmlands and a population of about 78 million are exposed to possible devastating floods. If the levees were broken in the rainy seasons, the damage could be much greater than that caused by the fateful floods of 1931, in which the death toll hit almost 4 million.

As a result of the water loss in its upper and middle reaches, in the meantime, the Yellow River has begun to run short of water in its lower reaches in the dry seasons in recent years. In 1972, the water level fell so low that for the first time in China's long history, the River dried up before reaching the sea. It failed to reach the sea for 15 days that year, and did so intermittently in the years that followed. Since 1985, it has run dry each year, with the dry-up periods becoming progressively longer. In 1996, it dried up for 133 days. In 1997, it failed to reach the sea for 226 days, and for a long stretch of time, it did not even reach the Shangdong province, the last province it flows through en route to the sea. The dry-up of the Yellow River has seriously affected agricultural and industrial facilities located along its lower reaches.

The Chinese government has spent huge amounts of effort and money to fight these disasters each year, but little progress has been made in easing the threat. A fundamental solution to the problem is to protect the ecological environment of the upper and middle reaches of both the Yangtze River and the Yellow River. Both rivers have, as shown in Map 1, their sources in Qinghai, a western province, and their upper and middle reaches in other western and central provinces. By pursuing ecologically sound development of the western region, the Chinese government hopes to eradicate the roots of disasters.

As can be seen from the above discussion, most of the goals in developing the western region are by far not easy to achieve. The westward drive is, therefore, not a temporary policy move, but a long-term strategic reorientation that will continue well into the 21st century. The Chinese

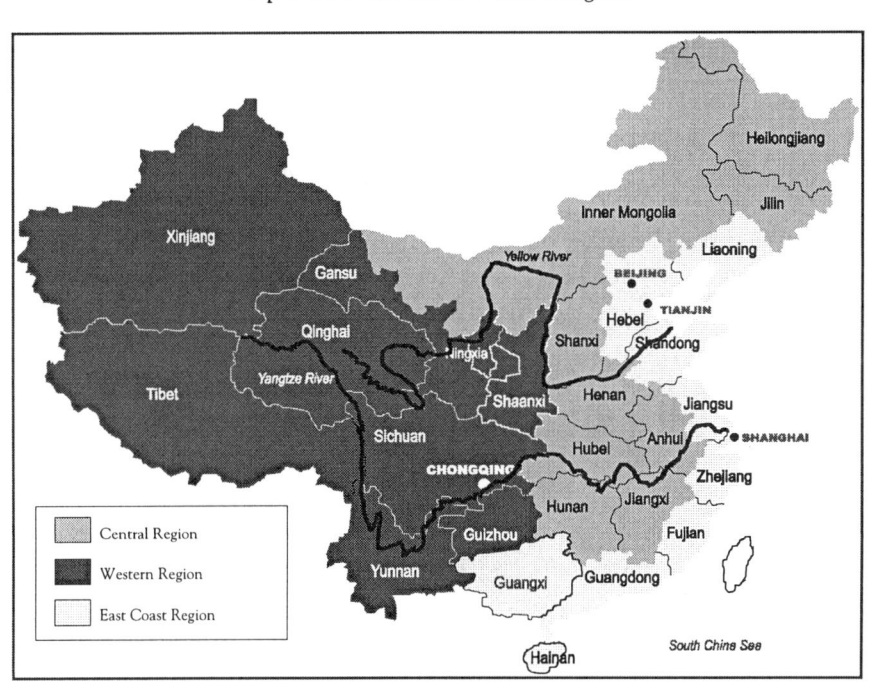

Map 1 Classification of China's Regions

government is prepared to "spend decades or even a whole century of effort to build a western region marked by economic prosperity, social progress, stable lifestyle, national unity, and beautiful mountains and rivers."[6]

---

[6] This is a quotation from a talk by President Jiang Zemin during his visit to Xi'an on 17 June 1999. See Xinhua News Agency, 18 June 1999.

References

Hu Angang et al, *China Regional Disparities Report* (Liaoning: Liaoning People's Press, 1995).

John Pomfret, "Separatists Defy Chinese Crackdown: Persistent Islamic Movement May Have Help From Abroad," *Washington Post*, 26 January 2000.

Zheng Yongnian, "The Development of the Western Region and the Problem of Minority Nationalities," *Hong Kong Economic Journal*, 15 February 2000.

10

China's Drive to Develop Its Western Region (II): Priorities in Development

TIAN XIAOWEN*

REPRIORITIZING DEVELOPMENT

In the past, the Chinese government gave first priority to resource exploitation in the richly endowed western region.[1] In the planning period, industrialization in the western region was based on the development of resource-related industries, particularly mining, metallurgy and defense industries. In agriculture, the exploration of land resources focused on reclaiming waste lands, and rural residents were encouraged to build terraced fields up the hillsides following the model of Dazhai, a village in Shanxi Province once glorified in Mao's era. After 1978, along with the shift in focus of industrialization to the coastal region, China tried to turn the western region into the supplier of natural

---

*Dr Tian Xiaowen is Research Fellow at East Asian Institute. He would like to express his thanks to Professor John Wong for comments and suggestions, and Mr Aw Beng Teck for editorial assistance.

[1] For instance, 50 percent of China's reserve of minerals are located in the five provinces in the western region, that is, Xinjiang, Gansu, Ningxia, Qinghai and Shaanxi.

resources and raw materials for the coastal region. As a result, resource-related industries bloomed, and the previous policy of land exploitation was not corrected. For various reasons, however, such resource-oriented development did not much benefit the western region, and at times even did more damage to the regional economy.

First, domestic prices were distorted. The domestic commodity prices of raw materials, grains, minerals and metals were brought down to a very low level to facilitate rapid industrialization in the planning period, and were among the last to be liberalized in the reform period. The coastal region benefitted very much from the "unfair price" structure, but the resource-based western region was the loser. Second, international prices of the products of raw materials, grains, minerals and metal have been falling for many years (Figure 1), and the western region has faced

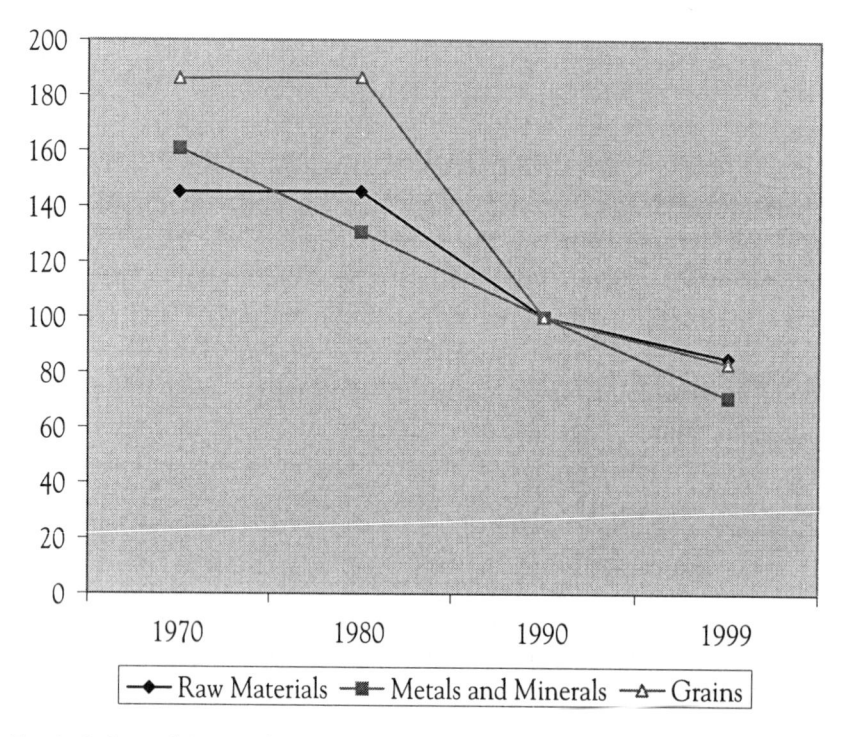

Fig. 1. Indices of Commodity Prices of Raw Materials, Grains, Metals and Minerals in International Markets, 1970–1999

increasing competition since China's opening up to world market.[2] Third, the Chinese economy has already turned from a "shortage" to "surplus" economy since the mid 1990s, and the decrease in domestic demand drove the domestic prices down. In 1998, for instance, the supply of metals and minerals well surpassed the demand, and domestic prices of these products fell 4–7 percent, a fall which was much greater than the prices of other products. In fact, the oversupply of grains also posed similar problems. The western region has suffered tremendously.

On top of that, the exploration of resources in the western region was carried out without careful consideration of resource conservation and environmental protection. Hundreds and thousands of small-scale mines were built in the rural areas; and they produced mineral products of low quality to be sold at rock-bottom prices. Trees were chopped down, and hillsides and grasslands were turned into farmlands. Water loss and soil erosion became worse year after year. As the Yangtze River and the Yellow River rise in the western region, the deteriorating environment in the western region has resulted in devastating floods hitting provinces in the lower reaches of the rivers.[3]

Faced with these problems, China had to reconsider the previous resource-oriented policy, and reprioritize development of the western region. As early as in October 1999, Premier Zhu Rongji proposed four new priorities in developing the western region, that is, infrastructure construction, ecological protection, industry-structure adjustment, and the development of sciences, technology and education. Zhu's proposal was reconfirmed at the first meeting of the Leading Committee of

---

[2] Calculated at 1990 constant prices in US dollars, for instance, the commodity price of raw materials, minerals, and grains in 1999 were only 59 percent, 44 percent, and 45 percent, respectively, of those in 1970. Although the falling prices were accelerated by a decrease in demand during the Asian financial crisis, the long-run movement of changes in commodity prices was clearly not in favor of the products of raw materials, grains, minerals and metals. Most of China's exports of raw materials, grains, and minerals and metals were from the western region directly or indirectly, and the falling prices for these products hit the western region badly.

[3] For a detailed discussion, see TIAN Xiaowen, "China's Drive for Developing Its Western Region (I): Why Turn to This Region Now," EAI Background Brief, No. 71, 2000.

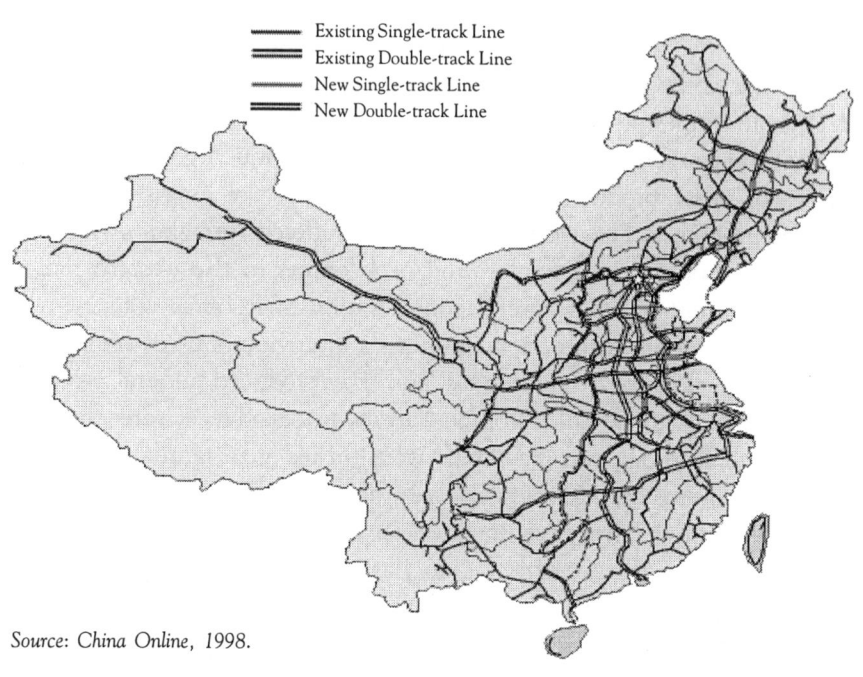

Map 1 China's Railway Construction Projects, 1998–2002

—— Existing Single-track Line
═══ Existing Double-track Line
—— New Single-track Line
═══ New Double-track Line

Source: China Online, 1998.

Developing the Western Region of the State Council on 16–19 January 2000. The four priorities have become the main targets in China's drive to develop the western region in the years to come and, therefore, they deserve particular attention.

INFRASTRUCTURE CONSTRUCTION

The first priority is given to infrastructure construction, which is believed to be the "foundation" (*jichu*) in the development of the western region.[4] The decision was made in consideration of the extremely poor infrastructure in the region. As shown in Maps 1 and 2, for instance,

---
[4] *People's Daily*, 1 November 1999; *People's Daily*, 23 January 2000; *People's Daily*, 5 April 2000.

Map 2 China's National Highway System

Source: *China Online* November 10, 1998.

transportation networks are most underdeveloped in the western region. Up to 1998, railway coverage was 26 km per sq km in this region, compared to 153 km per sq km in the coastal region. Until now there is still no railway in Tibet. The poor telecommunication facilities are shown in Map 3, and can also be illustrated by the number of telephone sets and Internet subscribers. In 1998, for instance, there were 411 telephones and one Internet subscriber for every 10,000 persons in the western region, while the figures were, respectively, 1,002 and 10 in the coastal region. With such poor infrastructure, the western region is hard to access. To develop the western region, China has to first make the region accessible to investors.

According to the Chinese government, infrastructure construction will, first of all, focus on highways and roads at three levels. The first

Map 3 China's Postal Service Network

全国干线邮运网络结构示意图
(CHINA'S POSTAL SERVICE NETWORK)

includes 15,000 main national highways and trans-provincial main roads linked to the western region (Table 1). The second level involves 185,000 km of roads connecting cities in the western region. The third level includes 149,000 km of roads in rural areas connecting 452 towns, 41,530 villages, and 972 production and construction corps in the western region that are currently not accessible by roads. All the highways and roads will be completed in 10 years, and a total of 700 billion yuan will be invested.

In the meantime, the infrastructure of railways and airports will be strengthened. In the next five years, a total of 100 billion yuan will be invested in the construction of railways. The focus will be on railways linking individual provinces within the western region, railways linking the western region to the coastal region, and railways linking the western region to neighboring countries in central Asia such as Kirghizia and

Table 1. 8 National Highways and 8 Main Trans-provincial Roads linked to the Western Region

Links in The 8 National Highways	Links in The 8 Main Trans-provincial Roads
1. Erlianhaote (Inner Mongolia) to Hekou (Guangxi);	1. Lanzhou (Gansu) to Mohan (Yunnan);
2. Southwest provinces to Beihai (Guangxi);	2. Baotou (Neimenggu) to Beihai (Guangxi);
3. Dandong (Liaoning) to Lhasa (Tibet);	3. Yinchuan (Ningxia) to Wuhan (Hubei);
4. Qingdao (Shandong) to Yinchuan (Ningxia);	4. Xiàn (Shaanxi) to Hefei (Anhui);
5. Lianyungang (Jiangsu) Huoerguosi (Xinjiang);	5. Changsha (Hunan) to Chongqing;
6. Shanghai to Chengdu (Sichuan);	6. Altay (Xinjiang) to Hongqilapu (Xinjiang);
7. Shanghai to Ruili (Yunnan);	7. Xining (Qinghai) to Korla (Xinjiang);
8. Hengyang (Hunan) to Kunming (Yunnan).	8. Chengdu (Sichuan) to Zhangmu (Tibet).

Uzbek.[5] In particular, a railway connecting Kunming and Singapore is currently under consideration. In addition, 5 billion yuan will be invested in the construction of 11 new airports and the upgrading of nine airports in the western region.[6]

---

[5] The railways under construction include, for instance, 1) the double track line between Baoji of Shaanxi and Lanzhou of Gansu, the double track line between Xi'an of Shaanxi and Hefei of Anhui, the double track line between Zhuzhou of Hunan and Liupanshan of Ningxia and Gansu; 2) the single track line between Suining of Sichuan and Chongqing, the single track line between Da County and Wan County of Sichuan, the single track line between Wan County of Sichuan and Zhicheng of Hubei, the single track line between Taiyuan of Shanxi and Zhongwei of Ningxia, the single track line between Shenmu and Yanan of Shaanxi and the single track line between Xi'an and Ankang of Shaanxi.

[6] The 11 new airports are in Guangyuan, Mianyang, Panzhihua, Jiuzhaigou, Wanzhou, Tongren, Simao, Lincang, Zhongchuan, Erletai and Kuche. The nine airports to be upgraded include Chendou Airport, Kunming Airport, Urumqi Airport, Xianyang Airport, Geermu Airport, Dunhuang Airport, Luzhou Airport, Beihai Airport and Qimo Airport.

Map 4 The Project of Piping the Gas in the West to the East

The gas pipeline project

Fast facts about project:
Project cost: 120 billion yuan
Total length: 4,200 km
Starting date: 2001
Start point: Tarim Basin, Xinjiang
End point: Shanghai
Provinces included: Gansu, Ningxia, Shaanxi, Shanxi, Henan, Anhui and Jiangsu

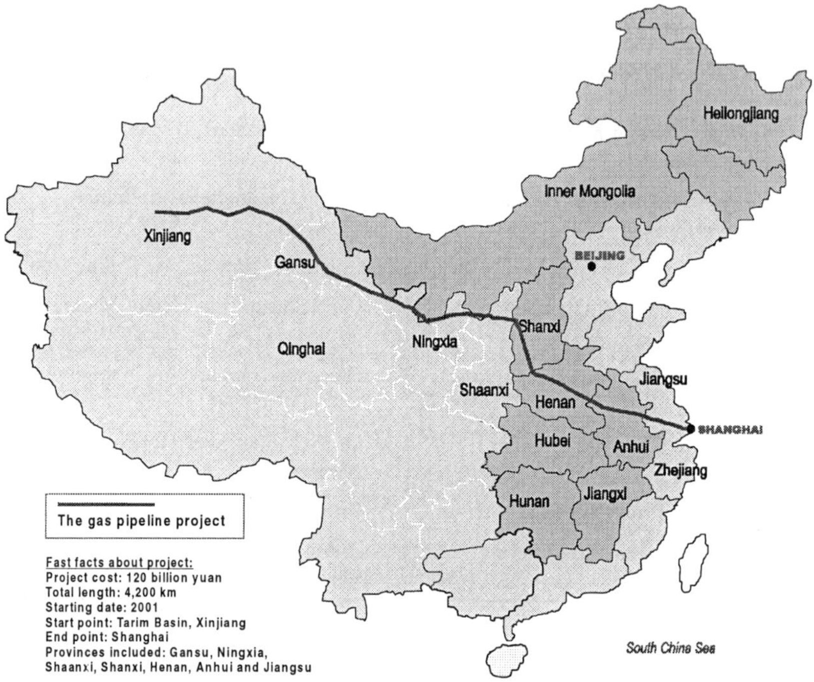

Efforts will also be made to construct natural gas pipelines. For instance, a mega project called "piping the gas in the west to the east" will commence in 2001, with a total investment of more than 120 billion yuan. The gas pipelines (Map 4) will connect the Tarim Basin in Xinjiang Province, which accounts for 22 percent of China's reserve of natural gas, with Shanghai. The gas pipelines, spanning some 4,200 km, will cut across seven provinces (Gansu, Ningxia, Shaanxi, Shanxi, Henan, Anhui and Jiangsu).

Furthermore, attention will be given to power networks, post and telecommunication networks, broadcasting and television stations, and water resource facilities. For instance, 17 million small-scale or miniature "rain containers" will be built in the western region, particularly in the upper reaches of the Yellow River, to resolve the problem of water loss.

In the next three years, 190 billion yuan will be invested in the construction and renovation of power networks in the rural areas, particularly those in the western region.

Ecological Protection

The second priority is given to ecological protection, which is considered as the "fundamental" (*genben*) in the development of the western region.[7] In the next 10 years, an estimated 200 billion yuan will be invested in various projects of ecological protection; most of the investment will be in the western region, particularly in the upper and middle reaches of the Yangtze River and the Yellow River. These projects will focus on constructing and protecting forests and grasslands to prevent soil erosion, water loss and desertification.

The most important project is the so-called "turning farmlands back into grasslands" (*tuigeng huancao*) or "turning farmlands back into forests" (*tuigeng huanlin*) project. Two thirds of the silt (sediment) that have accumulated in the Yellow River and the Yangtze River are from the hillside farmlands. Currently, there are nearly 20 million hectares of hillside farmlands in the country, 70 percent of which are in the western region. To encourage farmers to turn these hillside farmlands back into forests or grasslands, the Chinese government is offering 100 kg of grains, 50 yuan worth of nursery-grown plants, and 20 yuan worth of education and health subsidies for every *mu* of farmland that is converted back into grasslands or forests. This project is, therefore, also called "exchanging grains for forests and grasslands." In 2000, the project is carried out on a trial basis in 174 counties in the upper and middle reaches of the two rivers (located in the western region).

Another project is the so-called "enriching people by establishing eco-homelands." In the past, more than 30 percent of the firewood used by residents in the western region were obtained by cutting down trees,

---

[7] *People's Daily*, 1 November 1999; *People's Daily*, 23 January 2000; *People's Daily*, 5 April 2000.

causing widespread deforestation. In addition, crop straws were used as a source of energy and, therefore, could not be used to fertilize farmlands. This has resulted in deterioration of the quality of farmlands. The new project involves the introduction of the technology and know-how of renewable energy resources developed in the coastal region, such as marsh gas, into the rural areas of the western region. Such alternative forms of energy are aimed at reducing reliance on firewood and thus preventing deforestation and soil deterioration. Currently, a number of villages in seven western provinces (Shaanxi, Gansu, Ningxia, Qinghai, Yunnan, Guizhou and Sichuan) have been selected as experimental units for this project.

A third project is to build nature reserves and ecological protection zones. In the next five years, a total of six million hectares of nature reserves and ecological protection zones will be built in the western region, particularly in the Qinghai-Tibet Plateau, the headstream areas of the Yangtze River and the Yellow River, the mountain and valley areas in the southwest provinces, and the highland and desert areas in Xinjiang and Inner Mongolia. By 2005, the number of the nature reserves and ecological protection zones in the western region will increase from the present 776 to 1,000, and account for 8.5 percent of China's total land area.

Besides these projects, a number of policy measures will be taken to ensure the preservation and protection of the ecological environment in the western region. In the upper and middle reaches of the Yangtze River and the Yellow River, for instance, mountain passes will be sealed, logging will be forbidden, and lumber markets will be closed down. To promote afforestation, the government plannns to develop forestry under various forms of non-state ownership, such as share-holding system, joint-stock cooperative system and private enterprises. In particular, the government will promote the household contract responsibility system in afforestation. Any juridical persons will be encouraged to turn wastelands into forests, and entitled to obtain the right to use the forest according to terms stimulated in the contract. The rights to use the forest will be inheritable and transferable. The holder of the rights will be entitled to receive income from the forest.

Industry-Structure Adjustment

The third priority is given to industry-structure adjustments. This is considered as the "key" (*guanjian*) to developing the western region.[8] The outdated industrial structure is responsible for, among other things, the poor income of rural residents, the lack of economic advantage, and the low level of competitiveness in the western region. The western provinces have been asked to adjust their industrial structure in accordance to both their own natural conditions and the demand of domestic and international markets. In so doing, they have to develop their own geographically-specific industries or geographically-advantageous industries so that they can become more competitive in domestic and international marketplace. Structure adjustments in industry will focus on the following areas.

In agriculture, emphasis will be on geographically-specific crops and plants, such as cotton, sugar, fruits, vegetables, herbs, and tobacco leaves. The production of "green" food and "health" products will be given particular attention. In the meantime, greater efforts will be made to develop animal husbandry, particularly cattle and sheep husbandry. Processing industries for geographically-specific farm products and animal husbandry products will become key players in the western region. Given the ethnic diversity of the western region, the processing of ethnically-specific products, such as Muslim food, also offers great potential for growth.

In resource exploitation, conventional resources with weak market demand, such as minerals and raw materials, will give way to new resources with strong market demand, such as natural gas and hydroelectricity. Currently, the western region accounts for 87 percent of China's reserve of natural gas, which are mainly located in the gas fields in the Tarim Basin, the Qaidam Basin, the Shanganning Basin and the Sichuan Basin. The four gas fields will become centers of gas exploitation once the "piping the gas in the west to the east" project

---

[8] *People's Daily*, 1 November 1999; *People's Daily*, 23 January 2000; *People's Daily*, 5 April 2000.

takes off. The western region also accounts for 70 percent of China's reserve of hydroelectricity, which are mainly located in Sichuan, Yunnan, Tibet and Guizhou. These provinces have great potential to become centres of hydroelectricity exploitation. As for minerals and raw materials, the new strategy calls for "rational exploration and resource reservation," emphasising a more sober and cool-headed approach in utilizing the resources.[9]

In the meantime, greater effort will be made to phase out traditional industrial enterprises that use excessive resources, employ backward technology, have small capacity of production, produce goods of low quality, and that pollute environment. In addition, similar enterprises in the coastal region will not be allowed to relocate to the western region. Instead, industrialization in the western region will focus on the development of new industrial sectors and the transformation of the traditional industrial sectors with the help of new technology. In particular, the western region is encouraged to actively develop high-tech industries, including IT industries, new materials science, aerospace, and machinery and equipment.

Finally, and most importantly, the western region is asked to make use of their geographic advantage to develop tourism and related tertiary industries. There are seven world-class cultural heritage sites in this region earmarked by UNESCO. These sites include the Mogao Grottoes in Gansu, the Qin Shi Huang Mousoleum in Shaanxi, the Valley of Nine Stockaded Villages in Sichuan, Huanglong in Sichuan, the Emei Mountain in Sichuan, the Li River in Yunnan and the Potala Palace in Lhasa, Tibet. In addition, the Three Gorges of the Yangtze River, the Figurines of Soldiers and Horses, and the Silk Route in this region are also well-known tourist sites. On top of that, 50 of China's 56 minority nationalities, such as the Uighur, the Tibetan, the Hui, the Yi, the Bai, the Hani, the Zhuang, the Dai, and the Miao, live in compact communities in this region. Because of its cultural-historical sites, breathtaking scenery and ethnic diversities, the western region has attracted millions of tourists all over the world. Currently, the region

---

[9] *People's Daily*, 24 January 2000.

accounts for about 30 percent of foreign tourists in China, and has enormous potential to develop tourism and related tertiary industries.

DEVELOPMENT OF SCIENCE, TECHNOLOGY AND EDUCATION

The fourth priority is given to the development of science, technology and education. This is considered to be the "important condition" (*tiaojian*) for the development of the western region.[10] Apart from a few exceptions such as Shaanxi Province, Sichuan Province and Chongqing City, science, technology and education are extremely underdeveloped in the western region. In 1998, for instance, most western provinces were below the national average in terms of number of patents produced, number of articles on science and technology published, share of high-tech products in exports, and number of university students (Table 2). In the poorest provinces of Tibet and Qinghai, the illiteracy rate went as high as 54 percent and 43 percent, respectively. With the dawn of the knowledge-based economy, the western province will certainly be hampered by a lack of dynamics in its long-run growth. Due to its unique historical background, the region is asked to focus on the following areas in the development of science, technology and education.

In areas with a large number of defence industries, such as Shaanxi Province, Sichuan Province, Guizhou Province and Chongqing City, emphasis will be placed on making full use of the technology developed in the defence industries over the past few decades. The technology in aerospace, electronics, ship-building and automobile production in the defence industries in the western region is considered among the most advanced in the country, and can be used in a wide range of civil industries. These western areas are, therefore, asked to develop the defence industries into high-tech centres, and promote the transfer of advanced technology from the defence industries to the civil industries.

In big cities with a large number of universities and research institutes, such as Xi'an in Shaanxi Province, Chengdu in Sichuan Province and

---

[10] *People's Daily*, 1 November 1999; *People's Daily*, 23 January 2000; *People's Daily*, 5 April 2000.

Table 2. Development of Science, Technology and Tertiary Education in the Western Region, 1998

Province	Patents (per 100,000 persons)	Articles on Sciences and Technology Published in Domestic Journals (per 100,000 Persons)	Articles on Sciences and Technology Published in International Journals (per 100,000 Persons)	Share of High-Tech Products in Exports (%)	Number of University Students (per 100,000 persons)
Chongqing	1.2	..	..	..	2.7
Sichuan	1.9	8.2	1.2	2.4	1.8
Guizhou	0.9	3.1	0.1	0.6	1.2
Yunnan	1.7	4.0	0.5	3.2	1.5
Tibet	0.2	1.0	0.0	0.0	1.4
Shaanxi	2.7	19.3	3.6	3.9	4.1
Gansu	1.2	8.1	1.9	1.8	2.1
Qinghai	1.1	4.1	0.2	0.0	1.7
Ningxia	1.6	3.8	0.1	0.5	2.1
Xinjiang	1.9	5.4	0.3	0.5	2.6
Nation	3.4	9.8	2.0	5.3	2.7

Notes: .. indicates that data are not available.
Source: Statistical Yearbook of China 1999.

Lanzhou in Gansu Province, attention will be given to making full use of the human resources in these academic institutions. In Xi'an, for instance, there are more than 60 universities, including the famous Xi'an Transportation University, more than 4,000 research institutes, and more than 800,000 personnel in various science and technology fields. With these academic institutions and trained personnel, Xi'an enjoys unique advantage in developing science, technology and tertiary education. The Software Park in Xi'an has, for example, developed into a software park of national grade, and has the potential to become the largest base for software development, software production and software services in China.

In small cities, towns and vast rural areas with a large number of the less educated, emphasis will be placed on making primary and secondary education universal. A number of projects will be started to achieve this goal. In June 2000, one project was initiated to encourage schools in the coastal region to help schools in the poorer areas of the western region; another project was initiated to get schools in big cities in the western region to help schools in the rural areas within the region. In the meantime, distance education programme will be started in the western region, and a total of 70 million yuan will be invested in this project this year. In addition, a number of existing projects will be strengthened to train teachers in the poor areas in the western region.

Finally, but not exclusively, greater efforts will be made to introduce talents and advanced technology from other parts of the nation, as well as from foreign countries, into the western region. To encourage talents from the central and coastal regions to go to the western region, the central government has adopted a new policy of "no change in permanent residence, no change in identification, and freedom to go back." In the meantime, the central government has initiated a project to provide financial support for returned overseas scientists and technicians to conduct research in the interior. Individual western provinces have also begun to adopt special policies to attract domestic and foreign talents. A number of projects will be initiated to promote the cooperation in science and technology between the western region and other parts of the nation as well as foreign countries.

Zhu Rongji's four priorities in developing the western region are well designed, and they fit in quite well with the needs of the western region.

The projects involved are, however, very demanding both financially and technically. Even with the full support of the central and local governments, the successful implementation of these projects will have to depend on how financial and other resources are mobilized in a rapidly commercialising society. The government can no longer rely on political mobilization, as it did in the past through political movements and campaigns, and has to increasingly turn to market forces.

11

Economic Openness and Implications for Chongqing's Development

JOHN WONG*

The development landscape of Asia over the past 50 years has yielded valuable insights into the success and failure of economic development, particularly pertaining to the critical relationship between economic openness and economic development.[1]

The East Asian (EA) region is commonly defined to comprise Japan, China, the four Newly Industrialized Economies (NIEs) of South Korea, Taiwan, Hong Kong and Singapore, and the four Association of Southeast Asian Nations (ASEAN) of Indonesia, Malaysia, the Philippines, and Thailand. Situated on the western rim of the Pacific, all these East Asian economies (EAEs) have displayed a strong capacity for dynamic growth, with many having experienced high growth for a sustained period

---

*Professor John Wong is Research Director at East Asian Institute, National University of Singapore. This paper was presented at the "Chongqing International Symposium on the Development of Western Part of China", June 8–10, 2000, Chongqing, China. The event was organised by the Chongqing Municipal Government and the Chinese Academy of Social Sciences.

[1] For a good summary of the past development thinking and the changing development landscape, see World Bank, *World Development Report 1999/2000: Entering the 21st Century*.

until 1997 when they were hit, in varying degrees, by the regional financial crisis. In fact, several of the EAEs had one after another broken the past world growth records, so much so that the World Bank, in its well-known study, referred to the high growth phenomenon of East Asia as the "East Asian Miracle".[2] (Table 1)

According to the World Bank, it took Britain about 58 years to double its per-capita income from 1780–1838; 34 years for Japan (1885–1919); and 11 years for South Korea (1966–77); but only 9 years for China (1978–87) and another 9 years for it to double again (1987–96).[3] If the World Bank could also single out Guangdong, a province of China, for separate consideration, it would find Guangdong's growth performance even more impressive. Guangdong, with a population of 70 million (equal to France and Belgium combined) increased its per-capita income by 8 times from 1978 to 1997, or doubling it every few years.[4] This suggests that latecomers, once having successfully taken off, can achieve faster economic growth and take a shorter time span to double their per-capita income, because they can take advantage of the backlog of technological progress and surplus capital created by the forerunners.

Japan today is a world-class economic superpower, second only to the United States. In 1998, Japan's nominal per-capita income, at US$32,400, was more than 40 times of China's and more than 20 times that of the ASEAN-four. However, the income gaps between Japan and the four NIEs have been closing, narrowing as the NIEs have graduated to become "NDEs" or "newly developed economies". South Korea, with the lowest per-capita income of the four NIEs, is already a member of the OECD. For political reasons, Singapore has chosen not to join the OECD, even though Singapore's per-capita income in 1998 was slightly higher than that of the United States. More significantly, the ASEAN-four (which were originally resource-based economies, depending heavily on the export of natural resources and primary commodities for growth) have all become industrialized in the sense that their overall economic

---

[2] *The East Asian Miracle* (New York, Oxford University Press, 1994).
[3] *China 2020: Development Challenges in the New Century* (World Bank 1997).
[4] *Statistical Yearbook of Guangdong* 1998 (Statistical Bureau of Guangdong).

Table 1. Performance Indicators of East Asia Economies

	Population (Millions) 1998	GNP per capita, (US$) 1998	PPP estimates of GNP per capita, (US$) 1998	Growth of GDP (%) 1960-70	1970-80	1980-90	1990-98	1998(a)	1999(a)	Consumer Price Inflation (%) 1999(a)	Annual Export Growth (%) 1990-98	Mfg exports as % of total exports 1997	Export-GDP Ratio (%) 1998	Gross Domestic Savings as % of GDP 1990-98	1998	Gross Domestic Investment as % of GDP 1990-98	1998
China	1,239	750	3,220	5.2	5.8	10.2	11.1	7.8	7.1	-0.6	14.9	85	22	43	43	39	39
Japan	126	32,380	23,180	10.9	5.0	4.0	1.3	-3.6	0.9	-0.7	3.9	95	9(b)	34	32(b)	30	29
NIEs
South Korea	46	7,970	12,270	8.6	9.5	9.4	6.2	-6.8	12.3	1.2	15.7	87	38	36	34	37	35
Taiwan	22	12,040(a)	17,495(a)	9.2	9.7	7.1	6.5	4.7	5.1	-0.9	8.1	98	23	26	25	23	21
Hong Kong	7	23,670	22,000	10.0	9.3	6.9	4.4	-7.0	4.5	-4.2	9.5	93	125	32	30	31	30
Singapore	3	30,060	28,620	8.8	8.5	6.4	8.0	-0.7	6.7	1.5	13.3	84	187(b)	48	51	36	37
ASEAN - 4
Indonesia	204	680	2,790	3.9	7.6	6.1	5.8	-17.4	0.5	1.6	8.6	42	28	33	31	33	31
Malaysia	22	3,600	6,990	6.5	7.8	5.2	7.7	-8.6	8.1	2.1	13.2	76	118	39	47	38	32
Philippines	75	1,050	3,540	5.1	6.3	1.0	3.3	-0.1	3.1	3.9	11.0	85	56	17	15	22	25
Thailand	61	2,200	5,840	8.4	7.2	7.6	7.4	-6.0	3.5	-0.5	11.1	71	47	34	36	39	35

Notes: (a) *Asiaweek* Dec. 31, 1999–Jan. 7, 2000. (b) The data refers to 1997.
Sources: *World Development Report 1999/2000*; *Taiwan Statistical Data Book 1999*; *Asian Development Outlook 1999*.

growth is now primarily fuelled by the growth of their manufacturing sector, particularly manufactured exports.[5] The same is true for China. When it started the open-door policy 20 years ago, half of China's exports still made up of primary products, compared to only 16% today. Suffice it to say that as a result of their sustained economic growth, the EAEs have also become industrialized.

A noticeable feature of these EAEs is their growing economic interdependence. The EAEs, despite their inherent political, social and economic divergences, can actually integrate economically quite well as a regional grouping. This is essentially what the Japanese economists often refer to as the "flying geese" principle. Thus, Japan is obviously the natural economic leader of the group and has in fact been the prime source of capital and technology for other EAEs. The resource-based ASEAN-four complement well with the manufacturing-based NIEs, and both are also complementary to the more developed Japanese economy. The huge potential of China, with its vast resource base and diverse needs, offers additional opportunities for all.

Not surprisingly, the EA region has already developed a significant degree of economic interdependence, not out of any formal or institutionalized cooperative arrangements (such as the ASEAN organization) but as a result of market forces — commonly called "open regionalism". Growing regional economic interdependence is manifested in its fairly high level of intra-regional trade. The EA region in 1997 absorbed 54% of China's total exports; 53% of the average of the four NIEs', 50% of the average of the ASEAN-four's, though only 41% of Japan's — still unusually high for Japan as a global economic power.[6]

Apart from a high level of intra-regional trade, intra-regional foreign direct investment (FDI) flows have increasingly operated as a strong

---

[5] Oil and gas used to constitute 80% of Indonesia's exports; Malaysia's exports used to be dominated by rubber, tin and palm oil; Thailand used to depend heavily on exports of rice and sugar; and for the Philippines, export of coconut products. See John Wong, *ASEAN Economies in Perspective: A Comparative Study of Indonesia, Malaysia, the Philippines, Singapore and Thailand*. (London, Macmillan Press, 1979).

[6] Computed from data from IMF, *Direction of Trade Statistics Yearbook 1998*; for Taiwan, country source.

integrating force, especially since a great deal of regional FDI is trade-related in nature. The EAEs are essentially open and outward-looking in terms of being heavily dependent on foreign trade and foreign investment for their economic growth. In particular, China and ASEAN have devised various incentive schemes to vie for FDI, which is generally treated not just as an additional source of capital supply but, more importantly, as a means of technology transfer and export market development. This is particularly the case for China, which in recent years, has become the most favoured destination of all developing economies for FDI.

Explaining East Asian Economic Growth

Why have the EAEs been able to sustain dynamic growth for such a long period? Development economists can easily explain this within the neo-classical framework. On the supply side, rapid economic growth in the EAEs, especially in their early phase of industrialization, was the outcome of their rising labour force and increasing productivity. Growth of labour productivity is associated with the shift of labour from low-productivity agriculture to high-productivity manufacturing. This has happened to Japan, South Korea, Taiwan and China.

Viewed from the demand side, the high growth of the EAEs stemmed from their high levels of domestic investment, which were generally matched by the equally high levels of domestic savings. As can be seen from Table 1, the NIEs on average earmarked 36% of their GDP for domestic investment during the 1990–98 period; while Japan and the ASEAN-four, 34% and 31% respectively. But China had invested even more in the same period, at 43%. High savings and high investment in the EA region created what may be called the "virtuous circle of growth": high savings, high investment, high export growth, high GDP growth and then high savings. In short, the ability of an economy to put aside a larger share of its rising income as savings for the purpose of investment is probably the most convincing explanation of the arithmetic of economic growth in the region.

To create wealth, capital must be combined with labour in terms of both quantity and quality. But continuing high economic growth cannot be sustained by just dumping more and more capital to an increasing size of the labour force. What is more crucial to the process of sustained economic growth is the condition of technological progress resulting from the acquisition of knowledge. Such is the "endogenous growth theory", which emphasizes improvement in productivity and investment in human capital.

Paul Krugman has argued that East Asian growth has been based exclusively on the accumulation of capital per worker rather than increases in output per worker, i.e., productivity growth. Accordingly, East Asian growth could be a flawed strategy of growth without "total factor productivity" (TFP) — the amount of measured overall growth that cannot be explained by such factors as capital or labour — and would eventually bring about a collapse in growth, as in the former Soviet Union [Krugman (1994)]. His observation has since stirred up lively debate among economists and commentators. Several researchers have argued that Krugman has exaggerated the TFP problem of East Asia, and that many EAEs have in fact experienced TFP growth [Young (1995)].

In the case of China, for instance, its high growth during the last 20 years has indeed been accompanied by substantial productivity gains. In accounting for China's 9.4% growth in the period 1978–95, the World Bank has identified 8.8% (elasticity: 0.4) for physical capital growth, 2.7% (elasticity: 0.3) for human capital growth measured by years of education per worker, and 2.4% (elasticity: 0.3) for labour force increases, leaving the unexplained share of growth at 46%. This means that of China's 9.4% GDP growth, 4.3% is the unexplained residual, which is unusually large, compared to South Korea and Japan for the appropriate periods. A substantial part of the residual portion could be the TFP, which was generated from economic reform and the open-door policy.[7] In other words, China's high growth for the past two decades has indeed been sustained by a productivity boom.

High savings and high investment alone would not have generated such sustained high growth for China. Operating under socialist planning before 1978, China also had relatively high savings and high investment

---

[7] *China 2020*, World Bank op cit.

because of controlled consumption. But China's average annual growth during 1952–78 was only 5.7%, which was achieved with gross inefficiency coupled with a great deal of fluctuation. After 1978, with the introduction of economic reform and the open-door policy, China's economy started to take off, chalking up consistently near-double digit rates of growth. Economic reform, by introducing market forces to economic decision making, had brought about greater allocative efficiency. The open-door policy, by reintegrating China into the global economy, had also exposed China to greater external competitive pressures. Hence, higher TFP for China [Hu & Khan (1997)].

This brings to the fore the importance of export orientation in East Asian economic development. All EAEs share the salient common feature of operating an export-oriented development strategy, as reflected in their generally high export-GDP ratios and high export growth as shown in Table 1. Not just for Singapore and Hong Kong on account of their entrepot trade role in the region, South Korea and the ASEAN-four also have high export-GDP ratios. As a result of following the export-oriented strategy, the EAEs were able to reap the gains from trade and specialization and to attract more FDI. It also enabled them to capture a rising share of the world market for their manufactured exports.

Specifically for China, as a result of the open door policy, China's exports grew at the hefty annual rate of about 16%, from US$13.7 billion in 1979 to US$190 billion in 1999. China is now the world's 9th largest exporting country. China's success in attracting FDI has been even more impressive. For the period 1979–99, total FDI inflow to China amounted to US$306 billion, making China the second-largest recipient of international capital in the world after the United States. In all, more than 200 of the world's largest global multinationals have invested in China.[8]

In short, all the EAEs have, in varying degrees, exploited the export-oriented development strategy for their economic growth. China since its open-door policy has been particularly successful, even though it is a late convert to this strategy.

[8] Xinhua News Agency (March 6, 2000).

Table 2. Asia's Economic Laggards

	GNP per-capita (US$) 1998	Growth of GDP (%) 1980–90	Growth of GDP (%) 1990–98	Total exports (US$ million) 1983	Total exports (US$ million) 1998	Exports of goods & services (%) as % of total exports 1980–90	Exports of goods & services (%) as % of total exports 1990–98	Foreign direct investment (US$ million) 1990	Foreign direct investment (US$ million) 1997	Gross domestic investment as % of GDP 1980	Gross domestic investment as % of GDP 1998	Gross domestic savings as % of GDP 1980	Gross domestic savings as % of GDP 1998
Bangladesh	350	4.3	4.8	725	3,778	7.7	13.7	3	135	22	21	13	15
Cambodia	280	-	5.5	15	330	-	-	0	203	-	16	-	4
India	430	5.8	6.1	9,148	33,210	5.9	12.4	162	3,351	20	23	17	18
Laos	330	-	6.7	41	359	-	-	6	90	-	29	-	11
Myanmar	-	0.6	6.3	378	866	1.9	8.8	161	80	21	13	18	12
Nepal	210	4.6	4.8	94	402	3.9	16.8	6	23	18	21	11	19
Pakistan	480	6.3	4.1	3,077	8,370	8.4	3.2	244	713	18	17	7	13
Sri Lanka	810	4.0	5.3	1,066	4,770	4.9	9.0	43	430	34	24	11	17
Vietnam	330	4.6	8.6	616	8,980	-	27.7	16	1,800	-	29	-	21

Source: World Bank, *World Development Report 1999/2000.*

Economic Openness and Development

On the other hand, Asia's economic laggards such as Cambodia, Laos, Myanmar and Vietnam as well as countries in the Indian subcontinent, have generally registered long-term growth at the lower rates of around 4% on account of their low levels of physical and human capital investment. As shown in Table 2, these economies have invested much less and also saved much less, particularly in comparison to the EAEs. Furthermore, these poor economic performers are, on the whole, less open in terms of foreign trade and foreign direct investment than the dynamic EAE economies.

Among their many structural and historical reasons, one of the major explanations of the poor performance of these Asian laggards (at least until recent years) is the fact that they have generally followed policies and developed institutions which have typically obstructed their integration with the global economic system. This in turn slowed down their transition from import substitution industrialization to export expansion, which has been the main economic growth engine of the EAEs. In countries like Laos and Nepal, their self-imposed economic isolation was further aggravated by physical isolation due to their geographic land-locked nature.

In short, economic isolation, due to either the choice of inward-looking development policies or geographic isolation or both, has been the single most important factor for their late economic take-off. Their "policy isolation" self-limits their export expansion while at the same time discourages FDI inflow. "Physical isolation" further hampers their trade and investment in terms of additional time and transportation costs. Not surprisingly, these economies have failed to develop a viable, internationally competitive manufacturing sector.

China's economic development over the past 50 years is an example showing how economic openness is crucial to economic development. China's economy under Mao's self-reliant development strategy during 1952–78 grew at less than 5%. However, following the introduction of economic reform and the open-door policy by Deng Xiaoping, it achieved spectacular growth of 9.6% during 1978–99. But most of the growth in the past two decades has been confined to the coastal region, which was

Table 3. Basic Economic Indicators of China's Western Region

Province	Area (1998)	Population (1998)	GDP (1998)	GDP Growth (1992–98)	GDP Per capita (1998)	Total Fixed Asset Investment (1992–98)	Total FDI (1992–98)	Total Exports (1992–98)
	1000 sq. km	Million	Billion Yuan	%	Yuan	Billion Yuan	US$ million	US$ million
Chongqing	82.4	30.6	143	11.9	4,684	200	2,258	4,271
Sichuan	485.0	84.9	358	10.8	4,339	479	1,800	7,303
Guizhou	176.2	36.6	84	8.4	2,342	119	310	2,391
Yunnan	394.1	41.4	179	10.2	4,355	275	665	6,363
Tibet	1,230.0	2.5	9	12.7	3,716	20	0	287
Shaanxi	205.6	36.0	138	9.8	3,834	223	2,097	6,161
Gansu	454.0	25.2	87	10.2	3,456	131	334	2,161
Qinghai	721.0	5.0	22	8.7	4,367	45	22	732
Ningxia	66.4	5.4	22	9	4,270	49	54	1,072
Xinjiang	1,660.4	17.5	112	9.1	6,229	239	277	3,285
Western Region	5,475.1	285.1	1,155	10.1	4,052	1,580	7,817	34,027
All China	9,600.0	1,248	7,940	10.5	6,392	13,453	250,796	964,067
Share of West (%)	57.0	22.8	14.5	--	--	11.7	3.1	3.5

Sources: *Statistical Yearbook of China*, 1993–99; Provincial statistical yearbooks for western region, 1993–99.

the primary target of the open-door policy. Consequently, the development of the western region lags behind the rest of China and its per-capita GDP in 1998 was well below the national average of 6,392 yuan. (Table 3).

Why has the development of China's western region been lagging behind the coastal region? The western region clearly suffers from all the economic disadvantages of physical isolation on account of its landlocked nature. But its "policy isolation" has also been the major problem. From the outset, as Deng has realized, economic development everywhere cannot take place in all sectors and all regions and that "some have to get rich first". Hence Deng's coastal-biased development strategy. Of the total FDI of US$251 billion that flowed into China during 1992-98, only a trifle 3% found its way to the west. In the same period, the western region captured only 12% of China's total domestic investment and accounted for just 4% of China's total exports. (Table 3). Deng's development strategy, in bringing about rapid economic growth in China, has also led to widening economic disparities between coastal and interior regions.[9] This problem is now crying out for attention.

IMPLICATIONS FOR CHONGQING'S DEVELOPMENT

After the establishment of the People's Republic in 1949, Mao made a conscious effort to start industrialization in China's Northeast and Northwest, away from the strategically vulnerable coastal region. In the 1960s, eager to implement his self-reliant development strategy and fearful of the possible spillover of the Vietnam War into China, Mao located industry (particularly defence-related industries) further inward into China's interior, including Sichuan, Guizhou and Yunnan, under his grand san-*xian* ("third line") development plan. This was done with scant regard to the principle of comparative advantage.

---

[9] This issue has been widely discussed among China scholars. See, e.g., Tian Xiaowen, "Deng Xiaoping's *Nan Xun:* Impact on China's Regional Development", paper presented at the Conference on "Deng's Nan Xun Legacy and China's Development", East Asian Institute, Singapore, April 11-13, 2000.

As economic reform started in 1978, development focus shifted back to the coastal region. With market forces substituting central planning as a guide for resource allocation, capital and human resources are increasingly moving in accordance with the principle of comparative advantage, which naturally favours the historically more developed coastal region over the interior. Furthermore, the open-door policy, in more concrete terms, was actually associated with the establishment of the 5 Special Economic Zones and the 14 "open cities", all of which are located in the coastal region. This has inevitably led to a widening in income inequality between the coastal region and the interior. Initially, economic disparities was not a problem to the Chinese leadership because it was precisely Deng's idea of encouraging some sectors, some regions or some social classes to "get rich first". However, with faster economic growth since the early 1990s, regional economic disparities rapidly widened.[10] Rising inequalities among the provinces became a political problem.

The year 1999 was a turning point in China's economic development. Faced with serious over-investment and over-production in the coastal region, Chinese policy makers were forced to undertake a radical review of China's basic development strategies. In their search for new sources of economic growth, they would naturally set their focus on new development opportunities in the country's less developed interior. In the meantime, China has regrouped its former administrative regions and provinces into three economic regions: the eastern region, the inland region, and the western region.[11]

On January 19, 2000, the State Council set up a high-level inter-ministerial Western Development Committee, headed by Premier Zhu

---

[10] The issue of income inequality in recent years has become a popular topic of research among China scholars. See, Tian Xiaowen, "China's Regional Economic Disparities Under Economic Reform", *EAI Background Brief No. 33* (Singapore, 14 May 1999).

[11] The Eastern region comprises Liaoning, Beijing, Tianjin, Hebei, Shandong, Jiangsu, Shanghai, Zhejiang, Fujian, Guangdong, Hainan, and Guangxi. The Inland region comprises Heilongjiang, Jilin, Inner Mongolia, Shanxi, Henan, Anhui, Hubei, Hunan and Jiangxi. The Western region comprises Xinjiang, Gansu, Qinghai, Ningxia, Shaanxi, Tibet, Sichuan, Yunnan, Guizhou, and Chongqing.

Rongji. The Committee was charged with the mission of mapping out long-term strategies to guide the development of China's western provinces over the next 15 years.

The basic rationale for China's new Westward drive is therefore quite easy to follow. As the coastal region is "over-invested", the marginal efficiency of capital for new investment in the western region, China's last frontier, should be much more favourable. Apart from providing an immediate boost to economic growth, successful economic development of the western region over the long run will satisfy a host of other important objectives, including reduction of over-capacity pressures on the coast, reduction in poverty and ethnic tensions, protection of the environment and the demand of the western region for parity. Accordingly, at the 9th NPC in March 2000, the development of the western region (or "revival of the west") was an important item on its agenda. Zhu called for a "comprehensive plan" with a "sense of urgency".[12] In the Budget 2000, Finance Minister Xiang Huaicheng earmarked 60 billion yuan or 70% of total fixed asset investment for developing the infrastructure for the western region.

It may be stressed that the development of such a huge region half the size of China, with poor communications and inadequate infrastructure, is set to be a massive, long-term undertaking. Many western provinces are landlocked, not easily accessible from the outside. The overall socio-economic profile of the region, as shown in Table 4, is one of extensive backwardness, particularly in respect to its human resources. The central government is expected to take the lead in building up basic infrastructure. This will then be followed by the provision of appropriate incentives to attract domestic and foreign capital.

Furthermore, the western region is not a homogeneous entity. Some parts are more developed than the others. Some provinces are rich in certain natural resources while others have already built up a good defence-related heavy industry. Yunnan is fast developing its economic links with Southeast Asia while while some landlocked provinces like Gansu and Ningxia will remain trapped in economic backwardness for

---

[12] "Nation moves boldly forward", *China Daily* (March 6, 2000).

Table 4. Basic Social Indicators of China's Western Region

Province	GDP Per capita (1998)	Population Natural Growth Rate (1998)	No. of Live Births Per Woman (1998)	Population Per Doctor[a] (1998)	Adult Literacy Rate[b] (1998)	Student Enrollment In (1998) Primary Schools	All Secondary Schools	Institutions of Higher Education
	Yuan	%	Persons	Persons	%	As % of Provincial Population		
Chongqing	4,684	0.55	1.25	712	85	9.43	4.13	0.27
Sichuan	4,339	0.75	1.23	669	84	9.94	3.94	0.18
Guizhou	2,342	1.43	1.57	832	71	13.81	3.98	0.12
Yunnan	4,355	1.21	2.25	702	75	11.73	4.22	0.15
Tibet	3,716	1.59	1.67	500	40	12.41	1.99	0.14
Shaanxi	3,834	0.71	1.50	571	83	13.79	5.93	0.41
Gansu	3,456	1.00	1.50	663	71	12.27	4.75	0.21
Qinghai	4,367	1.45	1.47	500	57	9.73	4.39	0.17
Ningxia	4,270	1.31	1.57	491	74	12.08	5.85	0.21
Xinjiang	6,229	1.28	1.57	407	89	14.30	6.24	0.27
Western Region	4,159	1.13	1.56	644	73	11.66	4.97	0.22
All China	6,392	0.95	1.38	624	84	11.18	5.88	0.27

Notes: [a] is derived from dividing the provincial population by the number of doctors.
[b] is the inverse of adult illiteracy rate.

Sources: Statistical Yearbook of China, 1993–1999 with own calculations; Provincial statistical yearbooks for western region, 1993–1999.

a longer period.[13] It may be pointed out that even the developed US economy with a functioning market mechanism still contains pockets of relative poverty.

Chongqing is poised to take advantage of the new wave of economic openness for more rapid growth. Geographically, Chongqing is less isolated than the other land locked western provinces, and it is also socially more developed than the others, as can be seen from Table 4. Chongqing can develop itself as a regional hub by linking up with the on-going development activities of the Yangtze basin [Liu & Tam (2000)]. Chongqing therefore holds great promise for more successful economic development in the future, particularly after the completion of the Three Gorges Dam project in 2008.

REFERENCES

Hu, Zuliu and Khan, Mohsin, *Why Is China Growing So Fast?* (International Monetary Fund, Economic Issues No. 8, 1997).

Krugman, Paul, "The Myth of Asia's Miracle", *Foreign Affairs* (November/December, 1994).

Liu, William and Tam, Chen Hee, "Chongqing: Pivot to China's Regional Development", *EAI Background Brief No. 56* (Singapore, 17 February 2000).

Young, Alwyn, "The Tyranny of Numbers: Confronting the Statistical Realities of the East Asian Growth Experience", *Quarterly Journal of Economics* (Vol. 110, No. 3, 1995): Barry Bosworth, Susan Collins, and Yu-Chin Chen, *Accounting for Differences in Economic Growth* (Brookings Discussion Papers in International Economics, No. 115, 1995).

---

[13] See the survey in *Liao-Wen News Weekly* (Beijing, No. 48, November 29, 1999).

Part IV
Infrastructure – Hard and Soft

12

China's Infrastructure Development

LIN SHUANGLIN*

1. INTRODUCTION

This paper analyzes China's infrastructures by comparing the country's infrastructure development before and after the economic reform. It also compares China's infrastructures with other countries, as well as infrastructure development among different regions in China. The paper examines the reasons for slow infrastructure growth, discusses the perspective of infrastructure construction in the near future and alternative ways to finance public infrastructures, and provides some policy suggestions.[1]

---

* Dr. Lin Shuanglin is a professor in the Department of Economics, University of Nebraska, USA. An earlier version of the paper was presented last year at the International Symposium on the Reform of China's Public Utilities and Infrastructure, Hainan, China, and the East Asian Institute of the National University of Singapore. Part of the research was accomplished while the author was a visiting fellow at the EAI. The author thanks Professor John Wong and other participants at an EAI research seminar for their helpful comments. Any remaining errors are the author's responsibility.

[1] Economic infrastructures include public utilities (i.e., power, telecommunications, piped water supply, sanitation and sewerage, solid waste collection and disposal, and piped

The positive role of economic infrastructure in economic development has been emphasized in economics. Ashauer (1989) argued that public expenditures were quite productive, and the slowdown of productivity in the U.S. was related to the decrease in public infrastructure investment. Munnell (1990) explored the impact of the stock of public capital on economic activity at the state and regional levels in the United States. She concluded that those states that had invested in infrastructure tended to have greater output, more private investment, and higher employment growth. Eisner (1991) pointed out that public infrastructures not only serve as an intermediate good in physical goods production, they can also be final consumption goods. For example, water and sewage systems benefit the environment, better transportation saves time spent on traveling, public parks give people pleasure, etc. Canning, Fay, and Perotti (1994) found substantial effects of physical infrastructure on economic growth based on the international data set. Easterly and Rebelo (1993) found that public investment in transportation and communication is consistently correlated with economic growth. Thus, infrastructure is vital to a nation's prosperity.

Historically in many countries, such as the U.S., private companies built and operated turnpikes and waterworks. Gradually, the government became the main provider of infrastructures.[2] There are several justifications for this. First, infrastructures are usually subject to economies of scale, i.e., average cost of production decreases as output increases (e.g., electricity, natural gas and water, and mass transit), and thus, infrastructure services are best produced and delivered by monopolies. Since private monopolies may not produce a socially optimal output, government needs to regulate the private monopolies, and the regulation

---

gas), public works (i.e., roads and major dam and canal works for irrigation and drainage), and other transport sectors (i.e., urban and interurban railways, urban transport, ports and waterways, and airports). See the World Bank, 1994. A broad definition of infrastructure also includes human capital (e.g., education and health).

[2] In the U.S., most highways and water and sewer systems are owned by the government. In Japan, the national government, local governments, or public corporations have, directly or indirectly, financed most infrastructures [see Kuninori (1997)]. In South Korea, the government also owns and operates most of the public infrastructures.

cost may be too high. Second, some infrastructures may have external effects (spillover benefits to the parties who do not pay for the projects), and thus, the private rate of return is smaller than the social rate of return. In this case, the infrastructure provision may be unprofitable and private enterprises are not willing to provide infrastructures. Third, environmental consequences and safety issues of infrastructure provision are unlikely to be fully anticipated and incorporated in the market allocations. Fourth, infrastructure projects usually involve large investment that might be difficult for private firms to raise. Fifth, private provision may prevent the poor from getting needed infrastructure services. Governments often redistribute income through the provision of infrastructures. Sixth, it would be difficult for private firms to have nationwide and long-term planning on some infrastructure constructions. All these can be the justifications for the government to be the infrastructure provider. In China, the government at various levels has almost exclusively provided infrastructures.

This paper shows some very interesting results about China's infrastructure development. Several major infrastructures in China grew at a much slower pace after the economic reform (1978 to 1998) than before the economic reform (1952 to 1978). China's infrastructure development has lagged behind its economic growth in the last two decades. The level of some major infrastructures is low compared with countries at the same stage of economic development. China's infrastructure development is quite uneven across regions. Many local infrastructures, especially those in rural areas, are far underdeveloped. In addition to the slow construction of new infrastructures, many existing infrastructures need maintenance and repair. Infrastructures remain as the bottleneck of the economy. The reasons for the slower infrastructure growth include low government spending on infrastructures, as well as insufficient investment from state and private enterprises.

Recently, the Chinese economy has slowed down. The economy grew 7% in 1999, 7.8% in 1998, 8.8% in 1997, compared to an average of 11% during the period 1993–1997. The Chinese government has made great efforts to stimulate economic growth by emphasizing infrastructure development. The main way to finance infrastructure is through government bond issues. It is necessary for the Chinese government to pay more attention to local and rural infrastructures and give local governments more fiscal freedom for infrastructure financing.

Section 2 analyzes China's infrastructures from a comparative perspective. Section 3 examines the reasons for the slow infrastructure development. Section 4 discusses the perspective of infrastructure construction in the near future. Section 5 discusses alternative methods for infrastructure finance. Section 6 concludes the paper with some policy recommendations.

2. China's Infrastructures from a Comparative Perspective

Modern infrastructures emerged in China with railroad construction. In 1876, China began to build a railway, with the Song-Hu (Wusong-Shanghai) railroad being the first. The length of railroads was 360 kilometers in 1894 (of which 79% was controlled by foreign investors); 9,600 kilometers in 1911 (of which 95.1% was controlled by foreign investors); and 13,000 kilometers in 1927 (of which 92% was controlled by foreigners).[3] Since then, continuous wars had hindered China's infrastructure development.

2.1 China's Infrastructure Development from 1952 to 1998

A new wave of infrastructure construction started in China in the early 1950s. Table 1 shows some key infrastructures in China, including roads (for motor vehicles), railways, electricity, telecommunication, aviation routes, petroleum and natural gas pipelines, from 1952 to 1998. The length of railways increased from 22,900 kilometers in 1952 to 57,600 kilometers in 1998. The length of roads increased from 126,700 kilometers to 1,278,500 kilometers in 1998, a ten-fold increase. The length of paved roads increased from 55,300 kilometers to 1,190,100 kilometers in 1998, a twenty-one-fold increase. Electricity output increased from 7.3

---

[3] See Editorial Group, Department of Economics, *Modern Chinese Economic History*, The Chinese People's University, People's Publishing House, Beijing, 1979.

Table 1. China's Infrastructures*

Year	Electricity Output (billion kwh)	Roads Total (1000 km)	Roads Paved Roads (1000 km)	Railways Total (1000 km)	Railways Double-Tracking (1000 km)	Telecommunication Subscriber of Local Phone at Year-end (1000 households)	Telecommunication lines per 1,000 persons	Aviation Routes (1000 km)	Petroleum & Gas Pipelines (1000 km)
1952	7.3	126.7	55.3	22.9	1.4	353.7	0.62	13.1	..
1957	19.3	254.6	..	26.7	..	664.5	1.03	26.4	..
1962	45.8	463.5	..	34.6	..	1552.1	2.31	35.3	0.2
1965	67.6	514.5	..	36.4	..	1263.3	1.74	39.4	0.4
1970	115.9	636.7	..	41.0	..	1311.5	1.58	40.6	1.2
1975	195.8	783.6	..	46.0	..	1692.0	1.83	84.2	5.3
1978	256.6	890.2	651.1	48.6	7.6	1925.4	2.00	148.9	8.3
1979	282.0	875.8	..	49.8	..	2033.0	2.08	160.0	9.1
1980	300.6	883.3	..	49.9	..	2140.7	2.17	195.3	8.7
1981	309.3	897.5	..	50.2	..	2220.9	2.22	218.2	9.7
1982	327.7	907.0	..	50.5	..	2342.5	2.31	232.7	10.4
1983	351.4	915.1	..	51.6	..	2507.6	2.45	229.1	10.8
1984	377.0	926.7	..	51.7	..	2774.3	2.68	260.2	11.0
1985	410.7	942.4	750.3	52.1	10.0	3120.3	2.95	277.2	11.7
1986	449.5	962.8	780.4	52.5	10.6	3503.8	3.26	324.3	13.0
1987	497.3	982.2	..	52.6	..	3907.2	3.57	389.1	13.8
1988	546.7	999.6	..	52.8	..	4726.9	4.26	373.8	14.3
1989	586.5	1014.3	..	53.2	..	5680.4	5.04	471.9	15.1
1990	621.2	1028.3	883.5	53.4	13.0	6850.3	5.99	506.8	15.9
1991	677.6	1041.1	905.9	53.4	13.4	8450.6	7.30	559.1	16.2
1992	753.9	1056.7	926.5	53.6	13.7	11469.1	9.79	836.6	15.9
1993	839.5	1083.5	960.2	53.8	14.3	17331.6	14.62	960.8	16.4
1994	928.1	1117.8	998.1	54.0	15.5	27295.3	22.77	1045.6	16.8
1995	1007.7	1157.0	1043.4	54.6	16.9	40705.6	33.61	1129.0	17.2
1996	1080.0	1185.8	1077.6	56.7	18.4	54947.4	44.90	1166.5	19.3
1997	1135.5	1226.4	997.5	57.6	19.0	70310.3	56.87	1425.0	20.4
1998	1167.0	1278.5	1190.1	57.6	19.6	87420.9		1505.8	23.1
1999	1239.3								

Sources: China's National Bureau of Statistics, *Statistical Yearbook of China*, 1986, 1998, 1999; *People's Daily*, February 29, 2000.
*The figures are calculated by the author.

billions of kilowatt-hours in 1952 to 1,293.3 billions of kilowatt-hours in 1999, an increase of one hundred seventy-seven times!

Table 2 shows the growth rate of several key infrastructures in the periods 1952 to 1978, 1978 to 1990, and 1978 to 1998. Surprisingly, most of the infrastructures grew slower from 1978 to 1998 than from 1952 to 1978. From 1952 to 1978, the average annual growth rate of the length of roads was 7.5%, while from 1978 to 1998, it was only 1.8%. From 1952 to 1978, the annual growth rate of the length of paved roads was 9.5%; while from 1978 to 1998, it was only 3.0%. From 1952 to 1978, the annual growth rate of electricity output was 13.7%, while from 1978 to 1998, it was 7.6%. From 1970 to 1978, the annual growth rate of the length of petroleum and gas pipelines was 24.2% while from 1978 to 1998, it was 5.1%. In the meantime, GDP growth from 1978 to 1998 was much faster than that from 1952 to 1978. From 1952 to 1978, the average annual growth rate of real GDP was 5.7%; while from 1978 to 1998, it was 8.9%.[4] Clearly, most infrastructures failed to grow as fast as the whole economy after 1978.

China's aviation route and telecommunication grew faster from 1978 to 1998 than from 1952 to 1978. From 1952 to 1978, the annual growth rate of the length of aviation routes was 9.4% while from 1978 to 1998, it was 11.6%. Nevertheless, China's airports are still crowded and obsolete. China needs to build large modern airports to meet the growing demand, as Singapore and Taiwan did in the 1970s.[5] From 1952 to 1978, the annual growth rate of telephone line per thousand persons was 4.5%; while from 1978 to 1998, it was 17.6%!

---

[4] From 1952 to 1978, the average annual growth rate of per capita real GDP was 3.3%, while from 1978 to 1998, the average annual growth rate of real GDP was 7.6% (calculated based on *Statistical Yearbook of China*, 1999).

[5] In 1975, Singapore began to develop a new airport and it opened in 1981. Two-thirds of the required funds came from government and one-third came from private companies such as Singapore Airline Group and Changi International Airport Services for the construction of their own facilities. In 1973, Taiwan launched seven infrastructure projects and three industrial development initiatives considered vital for economic development, including Chiang Kai-Shek International Airport (opened in 1979). See Reinfeld (1997).

Table 2. Growth of Some Key Infrastructures, 1952–1998

	1952–1978	1978–1998	1978–1990	1990–1998
Electricity	13.69	7.6	6.58	7.88
Roads	7.5	1.8	1.2	2.7
Paved Roads	9.4	3	2.5	3.7
Railways	2.89	0.85	0.8	0.95
Double Tracking Railway	6.5	4.74	4.47	5.13
Petroleum & Gas Pipeline	24.17 [#]	5.1	5.42	4.67
Aviation Routes	9.35	11.57	10.2	13.66
Subscribers of Local Telephone	6.52	19.08	10.58	31.83
Telephone Line per Thousand Person	4.5	17.62[ξ]	9.14	32.15*
Real GDP per Capita	3.28	7.57	6.09	9.80

Sources: China's National Bureau of Statistics, *Statistical Yearbook of China*, 1986, 1998, 1999. *People's Daily*, February 29, 2000.

[#] Growth from 1970–1978.
[ξ] Growth from 1978–1997.
* Growth from 1990–1997.

Also, it is found that all these infrastructures, except for petroleum and gas pipeline, grew faster from 1990 to 1998 than from 1978 to 1990. However, even from 1990 to 1998, none of these infrastructures grew as fast as from 1952 to 1978. Thus, the slow growth of some key infrastructures during the economic reform period is an indisputable fact.

2.2 International Comparison of Infrastructure Development

Table 3 compares infrastructures between China and other countries and regions based on the data compiled by Canning (1998).[6] In 1995,

---

[6] Csernok, Ehrlich, and Szilagyi (1973) provided evidence on infrastructure development for 15 European countries and the United States, which showed that the U.S. led infrastructure development from 1925 to 1968.

Table 3. Comparison of Infrastructures among Countries *

Country	Electricity kw/per capita in 1995	Paved Road per km^2 in 1993	Rail Road per km^2 in 1991	Telephone line 1000 persons in 1995
Algeria	210.48	28.17	1.7	41.22
Botswana	..	6.65	1.52	42.71
Egypt	256.76	..	4.74	43.55
Ethiopia	8.52	..	0.64	2.62
Namibia	..	2.89	2.89	50.84
Reunion	448.9	..	..	328.38
South Africa	878.45	48.36	18.01	95.91
Canada	3826.59	..	8.71	589.39
Grenada	95.25	..	..	245.54
Guatemala	69.25	32.09	10.46	26.18
Mexico	474.23	45.12	13.4	94.31
U.S.A.	2907.84	389.36	20	625.85
Argentina	562.26	..	12.27	158.61
Brazil	361.93	..	3.55	74.07
Chile	412.1	16.32	9.07	132.68
Peru	155.97	5.91	1.71	45.16
Bangladesh	27.55	59.86	19.23	2.4
China	169.61	..	5.59	33.83
Hong Kong	1624.16	1556.51	113.03	527.38
India	100.46	..	19	12.83
Indonesia	99.75	78.02	3.12	16.17
Japan	1812.34	..	53.66	487.94
Korea, Rep.	785.36	524.8	31.26	413.17
Malaysia	540.41	133.31	5.35	169.89
Mongolia	367.16	..	1.22	31.68
Philippines	105.98	88.56	1.26	19.35
Singapore	1356.97	4965.81	..	429.67
Sri Lanka	85.02	..	22.28	11.17
Thailand	301.23	86.57	7.51	59.79
Austria	964.64	..	75.66	207.37
Bulgaria	1439.1	305.71	38.76	305.15
France	1850.59	..	61.48	557.19
Italy	1156.61	..	27.66	365.53
Poland	763.54	..	12.43	703.37
Switzerland	2320.63	270.64	24.56	681.15
U.K.	1200.7	63.59	10.69	215.3
U.S.S.R.	..	1489.67	67.72	502.91
Australia	2195.49	..	..	..

Sources: Canning, "A Database of World Stocks of Infrastructure, 1950–95," *The World Bank Economic Review*, Vol. 12, No. 3, 1998, 529–547.
*The figures are calculated by the author.

the electricity generating capacity per capita was 169.6 kilowatts for China. It was 2907.8 kilowatts for the U.S., 785.36 kilowatts in South Korea, 301.2 kilowatts for Thailand, and 100.5 kilowatts for India. Most of the power producers (about 75%) in China use coal as fuel, which leads to heavy pollution. The areas relying on hydropower often experience shortages of electric power in dry seasons. The severe shortage of electricity in the 1980s resulted in a dramatic increase in electricity generated by firms of various types. However, the delivery network of electricity is weak, which affects the stability and safety of electricity supply and causes the heavy loss of electricity during the delivery process. Also, the price of electricity is strictly regulated. Thus, there existed a surplus of about 20 million kilowatts in 1998. Still about ten counties in China are without electricity (all of them are in the central and west regions).

The construction of paved roads in China lags behind other countries at the same stage of economic development. In China, paved roads per square kilometer were only 108.6 meters in 1995 and 124 meters in 1998. In 1985, paved roads per square kilometer were 239 meters for India. Paved road construction in industrial and newly industrialized countries is way ahead of China. In 1995, paved roads per square kilometer were 406 meters in the U.S. and 467 meters in South Korea.

China's railroad construction also lags behind many other countries. The length of railroad per square kilometer in China was 5.7 meters in 1991 and 6 meters in 1998. It was 20 meters for the U.S., 25.6 meters for South Korea, 7.5 meters for Thailand, and 19.0 meters for India in 1991. The five major routes, Jinghu (Beijing-Shanghai), Jingguang (Beijing-Guangzhou), Hada (Harbin-Dalian), Jingshen (Beijing-Shenyang), and Longhai (Lanzhou-Lianyungang), are all over utilized at their capacities.

The telecommunication industry has developed rapidly in China. The number of telephone main lines per thousand persons was 33.6 in 1995 and 70.04 in 1998. This compares favourably with the number of telephone main lines per thousand persons of 625.9 in the U.S., 413.17 in South Korea, 59.79 in Thailand, and 12.83 in India in 1995. The demand for telephone service in China is growing, and the potential market for telephone service is huge.

2.3 A Comparison of Infrastructure across Chinese Provinces

Infrastructure development is rather uneven among provinces. Table 4 shows the length of transportation route by region by the end of 1998. It is not easy to compare transportation infrastructures across provinces because the size of the provinces, as well as the population density of provinces, is quite different. Table 4 presents two indexes, the length of transportation route per square kilometer and the length of route per capita. Beijing, Shanghai, and Tianjin led the nation in the length of modern roads (i.e., railroads and highways) per square kilometer in 1998, along with Zhejiang, Fujian, Shandong, Guangdong and Henan. The less populated areas including Tibet, Qinghai and Xingjiang had less modern roads per square kilometer, although the length of roads per capita was rather high. The length of modern roads in provinces such as Guizhou, Ganxu, and Sichuan was low based on both criteria. Table 4 also shows the sum of three transportation routes (i.e., railroad, highway, and waterway) per square kilometer in each province. Shanghai, Beijing, and Guangdong led the nation in the length of total transportation route.

Table 5 shows the length and the growth rate of highways in thirty Chinese provinces from 1986 to 1998. Shanghai, Shandong, Guangdong, and Shanxi led the nation in highway expansion, with the average annual growth rate of highways above 4%. Provinces such as Gansu, Qinghai, Heilongjiang, Hubei, Tianjin, and Jiangxi experienced slow growth of highways from 1986 to 1998, with an annual growth rate around 1%. In seven out of thirty provinces, the growth rate of highways was lower from 1992 to 1998 than that from 1986 to 1992.

The development of telecommunication and internet service is also uneven among provinces (see Table 6). Three municipalities directly under central government control, Beijing, Tianjing and Shanghai, along with Guangdong, Liaoning, Zhejiang, and Fujian, led all other regions in the number of subscribers of local telephone, internet service, and mobile phone. The development of telecommunication service is much slow in the central and west regions, particularly Tibet, Guizhou, Sichuan, and Gansu.

Table 4. Length of Transportation Routes by Region (End of 1998)

Region	(Meters per square kilometer)					(Kilometers per 100,000 persons)			
	Railways in Operation	Extension of the Trunk line	Navigable in land Waterways	Highways	Total Transportation Route	Railways in Operation	Extension of the Trunk lines	Navigable in land Waterways	Highways
National	6.00	8.22	11.49	133.17	158.88	4.61	6.32	8.83	102.43
Beijing	63.63	103.39	0.00	743.93	910.95	8.58	13.94	0.00	100.30
Tianjin	47.91	87.18	8.18	394.09	537.36	5.51	10.02	0.94	45.30
Hebei	19.07	32.02	0.39	301.38	352.87	5.52	9.26	0.11	87.17
Shanxi	16.69	25.69	1.13	323.73	367.25	7.89	12.15	0.54	153.09
Neimenggu	4.62	5.59	0.87	53.12	64.19	21.65	26.22	4.06	249.17
Liaoning	23.72	33.21	3.39	296.55	356.87	8.56	11.98	1.22	107.01
Jilin	19.30	21.24	7.06	187.84	235.44	13.14	14.46	4.81	127.88
Heilongjiang	10.76	14.34	0.00	108.19	133.28	13.11	17.48	0.00	131.90
Shanghai	42.76	68.97	362.07	707.59	1181.38	1.69	2.73	14.34	28.03
Jiangsu	7.57	14.40	239.08	273.31	534.36	1.05	2.01	33.29	38.05
Zhejiang	9.42	14.30	104.08	385.33	513.13	2.11	3.21	23.36	86.47
Anhui	14.12	21.58	46.17	302.03	383.90	2.97	4.54	9.71	63.49
Fujian	8.90	9.00	31.04	400.18	449.12	3.24	3.27	11.29	145.56
Jiangxi	13.28	19.04	30.86	230.42	293.60	5.07	7.27	11.78	87.97
Shangdong	15.67	24.43	9.43	427.63	477.17	2.66	4.15	1.60	72.58
Henan	14.72	27.85	6.90	357.33	406.79	2.53	4.78	1.19	61.38
Hubei	11.27	16.34	40.31	294.38	362.30	3.43	4.98	12.28	89.71
Hunan	10.95	15.45	47.86	286.05	360.30	3.54	4.99	15.46	92.39
Guangdong	4.30	8.09	60.04	515.07	587.51	1.08	2.04	15.13	129.80
Guangxi	8.76	10.28	19.66	222.06	260.75	4.31	5.06	9.67	109.25
Hainan	6.44	6.53	12.18	497.65	522.79	2.91	2.95	5.50	224.70
Chongqing	7.12	7.12	21.13	327.83	363.20	1.93	1.93	5.73	88.92
Sichuan	4.09	4.30	10.87	145.80	165.06	2.70	2.84	7.17	96.13
Guizhou	9.69	10.06	11.17	197.67	228.60	4.51	4.68	5.19	91.86
Yunnan	4.88	5.09	3.48	202.52	215.97	4.48	4.66	3.19	185.71
Tibet	0.00	0.00	0.00	18.71	18.71	0.00	0.00	0.00	891.07
Shaanxi	10.22	12.12	5.25	222.12	249.71	5.40	6.40	2.78	117.36
Gansu	5.95	8.41	0.56	91.96	106.88	9.22	13.02	0.87	142.38
Qinghai	1.52	1.53	0.00	24.91	27.95	21.71	21.83	0.00	356.58
Ningxia	10.79	11.95	6.02	143.74	172.50	13.23	14.67	7.38	176.34
Xinjiang	0.84	1.31	0.00	20.48	22.63	7.68	12.01	0.00	187.53

Source: China's National Bureau of Statistics, *Statistical Yearbook of China*, 1999, p. 503, p. 113.

Table 5. Growth of Highways in Chinese Provinces, 1986–1998 *

	Length (km) 1986	Length (km) 1992	Length (km) 1998	Growth Rate (%) 86–92	Growth Rate (%) 92–98	Growth Rate (%) 86–98
North						
Beijing	8995	10827	12498	3.09	2.39	2.74
Tianjin	3825	4088	4335	1.11	0.98	1.04
Hebei	41161	47034	57263	2.22	3.28	2.75
Shanxi	29263	31554	48560	1.26	7.18	4.22
Inner Mongolia	40380	43704	58430	1.32	4.84	3.08
North East						
Liaoning	35362	41548	44483	2.69	1.14	1.91
Jilin	24625	27192	33812	1.65	3.63	2.64
Heilongjiang	45659	47880	49766	0.79	0.64	0.72
East						
Shanghai	2348	3625	4104	7.24	2.07	4.65
Jiangshu	23152	25325	27331	1.50	1.27	1.38
Zhejiang	24669	30281	38533	3.42	4.02	3.72
Anhui	28158	30571	39264	1.37	4.17	2.77
Fujian	37175	41882	48021	1.99	2.28	2.13
Jiangxi	31857	33986	36867	1.08	1.36	1.22
Shandong	37005	43134	64145	2.55	6.61	4.58
Central						
Henan	39286	45049	57172	2.28	3.97	3.13
Hubei	46083	47892	52989	0.64	1.69	1.16
Hunan	56636	58110	60071	0.43	0.55	0.49
South						
Guangdong	65589	55883	92713	.	8.44	.
Guangxi	33322	37291	51073	1.88	5.24	3.56
Hainan	.	12937	16920	.	4.47	.
South West						
Sichuan	91551	98920	108856	1.29	1.60	1.44
Guizhou	28383	31889	33604	1.94	0.87	1.41
Yunnan	49866	60045	76957	3.10	4.14	3.62
Tibet	21662	21842	22455	0.14	0.46	0.30
North West						
Shaanxi	37668	38318	42202	0.29	1.61	0.95
Gansu	33574	34822	35865	0.61	0.49	0.55
Qinghai	16189	16854	17936	0.67	1.04	0.85
Ningxia	7181	8200	9487	2.21	2.43	2.32
Xinjiang	22227	26024	32762	2.63	3.84	3.23

Sources: China's National Bureau of Statistics, *Statistical Yearbook of China*, 1987, 1993, and 1999.
*Hainan province was split from Guangdong province in 1987 and Chongqing City was split from Sichuan in 1998. The figure for Guangdong in 1986 includes that for Hainan and all of the figures for Sichuan include that for Chongqing.

Table 6. Telecommunication by Regions in 1998
(Number of subscribers per 10,000 persons)

Region	Paging	Mobile Telephone	Email Service	Internet Service	Total Local Telephone*	Urban Telephone	Rural Telephone	Public Telephone
Beijing	191.17	797.51	3.09	26.49	2514.16	2267.44	246.72	43.00
Tianjin	459.35	497.28	0.10	14.91	1731.71	1605.53	126.19	38.70
Hebei	331.45	139.38	0.04	2.54	614.21	420.57	193.64	15.93
Shanxi	216.02	132.85	0.00	1.30	488.88	391.92	96.96	13.32
Neimenggu	179.15	110.41	0.03	0.62	534.92	443.54	91.37	13.84
Liaoning	824.59	309.81	0.25	5.55	1146.94	881.28	265.66	46.84
Jilin	425.72	226.89	0.05	2.39	913.85	728.27	185.58	21.57
Heilongjiang	387.04	278.82	0.00	2.93	903.96	754.33	149.64	20.26
Shanghai	533.95	860.45	1.43	69.95	2944.81	2329.04	615.77	40.35
Jiangsu	423.21	195.07	0.45	9.73	1043.70	537.60	506.10	27.52
Zhejiang	416.43	338.24	0.06	8.47	1127.33	630.49	496.83	32.60
Anhui	238.70	94.28	0.18	1.06	443.73	308.69	135.05	11.39
Fujian	0.39?	443.98	0.37	9.39	1053.24	621.48	431.76	41.96
Jiangxi	278.07	103.25	0.01	1.84	459.36	347.80	111.56	14.03
Shandong	274.13	169.00	0.16	4.51	595.47	393.78	201.69	19.57
Henan	212.51	127.36	0.03	4.63	475.32	339.20	136.12	14.89
Hubei	335.30	140.92	0.27	5.71	685.52	478.70	206.82	27.49
Hunan	311.73	115.81	0.30	2.09	485.45	346.39	139.06	25.26
Guangdong	518.03	507.76	0.24	17.96	1341.81	880.45	461.36	26.48
Guangxi	346.14	108.53	0.02	2.26	356.53	288.93	67.60	14.31
Hainan	744.36	258.83	0.03	12.17	576.41	478.14	98.27	34.70
Chongqing	232.81	121.63	0.00	1.92	504.09	397.04	107.05	12.14
Sichuan	230.25	100.33	0.01	0.29	329.38	266.91	62.46	17.64
Guizhou	172.83	51.23	0.02	0.27	218.41	192.84	25.57	7.67
Yunnan	316.05	105.14	0.03	0.98	453.91	363.44	90.47	13.92
Tibet	62.70	45.63	0.05	0.58	234.79	233.60	1.19	12.26
Shaanxi	206.54	103.39	0.05	3.88	505.77	419.09	86.69	14.29
Gansu	181.22	56.41	0.02	1.26	378.03	339.32	38.71	10.00
Qinghai	115.51	70.18	0.00	0.83	442.57	413.45	29.12	12.08
Ningxia	348.51	92.94	0.00	1.14	696.02	623.94	72.09	19.10
Xinjiang	245.22	89.58	0.00	0.80	683.25	504.30	178.94	21.68

Source: China's National Bureau of Statistics, Statistical Yearbook of China, 1999, pp. 532–533.
*Total Local Telephone = Urban Telephone + Rural Telephone.

2.4 Local and Rural Infrastructures

Local infrastructures have drawn less attention than inter-province infrastructures. Many cities in China have shortages of water supply (particularly in the North). As many as 100 cities are believed to be suffering from water shortage. Many rivers in the North, including the famous Yellow River, are frequently dried up. In addition, most of the inland rivers and lakes are polluted. One third of the reservoirs currently in use is estimated to be working under damaged conditions. Urban transportation is crowded. It has been estimated that the average speed of vehicles has decreased to 12 km per hour in some large cities and suburbs, which severely affects urban life.[7] Urban facilities for sewage and garbage disposal are in urgent need of improvement. Some cities, particularly cities in the central and west regions, still remain at the stage of "letting the wind clean the garbage and letting the sun dry up the sewage."

Rural infrastructures are the weakest in China. In the vast majority of rural areas, there is no running water or sewage system; the roads connecting villages and towns are in poor condition in many provinces, especially in the central and west regions. The electricity delivery net is not well developed and rural residents still use stalks and firewood as fuel for cooking and heating.

A widely neglected issue is the maintenance and repair of existing infrastructures. The problems include unsafe dams, crumbling roads, obsolete airport and port facilities, aging public buildings, and damaged streets. The new constructions are visible achievements of the investors, while the maintenance and repair of existing facilities are less visible. The lack of maintenance will shorten the life of existing infrastructures and result in higher expenditures in the future for repair or replacement. This maintenance problem not only exists in the infrastructure area but also in other areas.

The above analysis has shown some interesting results about China's infrastructure development. Several major infrastructures in China grew slower after than before the economic reform, the levels of some major

---

[7] China Institute for Reform and Development (1999).

infrastructures were low compared with countries at the same level of development; infrastructure development was quite uneven among provinces; and local infrastructures, especially in rural areas, are in poor condition. Thus, infrastructures are still the bottlenecks in the Chinese economy.

3. REASONS FOR SLOW INFRASTRUCTURE DEVELOPMENT

There are three major reasons for the slow development of infrastructures in China, namely, low government spending, insufficient investment by state enterprises, and the lack of private investment.

3.1 LOW GOVERNMENT SPENDING ON INFRASTRUCTURES

Low government spending on infrastructures is the main reason for the slow infrastructure development. The Chinese government's GDP share in expenditure has declined significantly since 1978. In 1978, government expenditure share in GDP was 31%, decreasing to only 12.3% in 1997.[8] The share of government spending on infrastructures in its total spending has also declined. For example, the central government expenditure shares on fuel and energy, as well as transportation and telecommunication, decreased from 1990 to 1996. In 1990, the figures were 4.6% for transportation and telecommunication and 9.4% for fuel and energy; while in 1996, the share was reduced to only 0.6% for transportation and telecommunication and 2.1% for fuel and energy. Local government spending on infrastructures was also low. In 1996, the share of local government's spending on transportation and telecommunication was 0.7% and on fuel and energy, 1.5%.[9] Low

---

[8] In 1999, total government expenditures were 1313.6 billion yuan and GDP was 8205.4 billion yuan [see Zeng (2000)]. Thus, government expenditure share in GDP was 16%.
[9] See International Monetary Fund, *International Financial Statistics*, 1998; International Monetary Fund, *Government Finance Statistics Yearbook*, 1998. All the percentages are calculated by the author.

government expenditures in GDP and low spending share of total government expenditures imply that the share of government expenditures on transportation and communication in GDP is even lower.[10]

Table 7 shows the share of central government expenditures on transportation and communication in relation to total government expenditures for all countries using available data. In China, the share of government spending on transportation and communication in 1995 was only 0.59%, one of the lowest in the world. In contrast, the average share of government expenditure on transportation and communication is 3.9% for industrial countries and 5.8% for developing countries. The average share for Asian developing countries, excluding China, was 8.78%. The share of government spending on transportation and communication was 2.4% in the U.S. in 1996, 10.0% in South Korea in 1997, 14.5% in Thailand in 1996, and 1.3% in India in 1996. Low government spending on infrastructures has slowed the speed of infrastructure development.

3.2 Insufficient Investment from State Enterprises

For a long time, state enterprises in China played an important role in infrastructure investment. Economic reform has changed the economic relationship between the government and state enterprises. State enterprises, including those engaged in infrastructure construction, are no longer subject to *Tongshou Tongzhi* (i.e., state enterprises to submit all their revenues to the government and the government to cover all their production costs). Now they have to pay taxes to the government and as well as their own production costs. They have become profit-oriented and are not willing to invest in unprofitable projects. This has resulted in an under-allocation of resources to infrastructure construction.[11] At the moment, the government does not have sufficient

---

[10] In a county in the western part of China, which the author visited recently, there were no street lights in the downtown area due to the shortage of government revenue.

[11] Some state enterprises in infrastructure even run other profitable businesses, such as hotels and restaurants.

Table 7. The Share of Central Government Expenditures on Transportation and Communication

Country	Year	Trans. & Com.	Country	Year	Trans. & Com.
United States	1996	2.40	Singapore	1995	3.32
Canada	1994	2.98	Sri Lanka	1996	5.76
Australia	1996	1.92	Thailand	1996	14.53
Japan	1993	0.30	Albania	1995	4.70
New Zealand	1996	2.58	Belarus	1992	6.97
Austria	1995	3.62	Bulgaria	1996	1.60
Denmark	1995	2.46	Croatia	1996	6.96
Finland	1995	3.64	Cyprus	1995	5.70
Greece	1995	4.49	Czech Rep.	1996	4.75
Iceland	1995	7.50	Estonia	1996	5.94
Ireland	1994	4.74	Latvia	1996	3.82
Luxembourg	1995	10.35	Lithuania	1996	5.04
Netherlands	1996	3.41	Malta	1994	7.04
Norway	1995	4.77	Poland	1996	1.75
Spain	1994	3.39	Romania	1994	4.56
Sweden	1996	3.48	Turkey	1996	4.11
Switzerland	1995	6.27	Bahrain	1996	3.66
United Kingdom	1995	1.67	Egypt	1994	3.39
Industrial Countries	Average	3.89	Iran	1996	5.22
			Israel	1996	2.10
Botswana	1995	5.11	Jordan	1995	4.14
Burkina Faso	1992	2.18	Kuwait	1996	1.28
Burundi	1996	2.23	Lebanon	1995	4.81
Cameroon	1995	5.33	Oman	1996	1.22
Congo Dem. Rep.	1995	0.06	Syria Arab	1995	2.26
Ethiopia	1993	4.57	United Arab	1994	0.29
Ghana	1993	9.77	Yemen Rep.	1995	2.41
Lesotho	1992	10.4	Argentina	1995	3.65
Madagascar	1996	1.29	Bahamas	1993	1.28
Mauritius	1996	3.68	Belize	1994	9.82
Morocco	1992	5.32	Bolivia	1996	11.79
Seychelles	1995	4.60	Brazil	1993	0.74
Tunisia	1996	2.26	Colombia	1993	6.49
Zambia	1996	9.00	Costa Rica	1995	4.89
Bhutan	1995	12.72	Dominican	1995	12.18
China	1995	0.59	Elsalvador	1996	9.75
Fiji	1996	7.98	Guatemala	1995	11.74
India	1996	1.28	Grenada	1995	14.08
Indonesia	1966	7.34	Mexico	1995	3.86
Korea	1997	9.96	Netherlands Antilles	1995	7.40
Malaysia	1997	9.89	Nicaragua	1994	8.02
Maldives	1996	7.79	Panama	1994	4.03
Myanmar	1995	11.92	Paraguay	1993	8.50
Nepal	1996	11.93	St. Vincent & Grens	1996	6.64
Papua New Guinea	1993	7.18	Trinidad and Tobago	1995	3.38
Philippines	1995	11.96	**Developing Countries**	Average	5.80

Source: International Monetary Fund, *Government Finance Yearbook*, 1998.

funds for infrastructures, and it requires the state enterprises to engage in infrastructure construction, maintenance, and repair. For example, the Ministry of Railroad is required to build new railways (such as the railroad in Tibet).[12] Since the project is most likely unprofitable, the incentive for the state enterprises to build and operate the railroad is just not there.

3.3 Lack of Private Investment

Private enterprises were prohibited from 1957 to 1978, and re-emerged in China from 1980. However, until recently, they were considered supplementary to state enterprises. The lack of legal protection, bank credit, and advanced technology have restricted the development of private enterprises. Infrastructure projects usually involve large investment that would be difficult to raise by private firms. Although private enterprises have developed rapidly in the past 20 years, large-size private enterprises are still limited. By the end of 1998, of the 1.2 million private enterprises (excluding the commercial and industrial households), only 17,000 had registered capital larger than 5 million yuan (about US $0.6 million). Still in their early stage of development[13] and faced with the uncertainty of long-run business conditions, private enterprises have concentrated on production that enables them to make profits in the short run. As mentioned earlier, infrastructures usually require large investment in the short run and yield returns only in the long run. Thus, it is difficult for private enterprises to finance infrastructures. In addition, many infrastructures are necessities for all the people, including those in the low-income group. The government sets the price lower than the cost and uses its revenues to subsidize the state enterprises that provide them. That is to say, the government redistributes income through these infrastructures. Hence, private enterprises will not be able to make any profits from the provision of these infrastructures without raising prices.

---

[12] The Qing-Zang railroad is still 1,200 kilometers to Lhasa (the capital of Tibet). *Peoples Daily*, March 13, 2000.
[13] See Yu (1999).

4. Perspective of Infrastructure Development

The Chinese government has decided to increase infrastructure investment. An increase in infrastructure will stimulate private investment; in addition, the increase demand for goods and services will pull the economy out of a downturn. The government plans to initiate and invest in a large number of infrastructure projects in the near future. This section discusses the perspectives of infrastructure construction in the near future.

Gas and Oil Pipelines. In 2000, construction of the gas pipeline from Chaidamu to Xining to Lanzhou started. The construction of a major gas pipeline from Talimu of Xinjiang province to Shanghai (the so-called "Xiqi Dongshu" project) will begin in 2001. The double-track pipeline will pass through 10 provinces and its total length will be 4,112 kilometers. The estimated project cost is 100 billion yuan and it will be ready in 2003. The pipeline will reduce the energy shortage in the east region of China and stimulate the economic development of the west region. The construction of the oil pipeline from Lanzhou to Chengdu to Chongqing has begun. As one of the nation's major projects, this pipeline will pass through Gansu, Shaanxi, Sichuan, and Chongqing, totaling 1,200 kilometers. It will cost about 4 billion Chinese yuan, and will be completed by June 2002.[14]

Highways. In 2000, the construction of the ongoing national highways such as Jingzhu (Beijing to Zhuhai) highway continued. Provinces will build new local highways. The Ministry of Transportation is reportedly prepared to build eight major roads, Lanzhou to Yunnan, Baotou to Beihai, Aletai to Hongqilapu in Xingjiang, Xinchuan to Wuhan, Xi'an to Hefei, Xining to Kuerle, Chengdu to Zhangmu in Xizang, and Changsha to Chongqing.[15]

Railways. According to the Ministry of Railways, approximately 357 billion yuan will be spent on railway infrastructure and equipment by 2002.[16] The new major projects initiated in 2000 were the railroad from

---

[14] *People's Daily*, March 20, 2000
[15] *Lianhe Zaobao*, February 18, 2000.
[16] China Institute for Reform and Development (1999).

Nanjing to Xi'an and the railroad from Chongqing to Huaihua.[17] In 2000, the government had plans to accelerate the preparation work of the high-speed railroad from Beijing to Shanghai.[18] Also, it was reported that a major railroad from the east to the west along the Yangtze River would be constructed in five years. This road will cut across Sichuan, Chongqing, Hubei, Jiangxi, Anhui, Jiangsu, and Shanghai, totaling 2,024 kilometers.[19] With this road, one can travel from Shanghai to Chongqing in one day by train, rather than seven days and nights by ship.

Airports. The government plans to construct new airports in the Middle and West regions, as well as improve the efficiency of the existing airports. The major new airport project inaugurated in 2000 was the Guangzhou New Airport.[20]

Electric Power and Rural and Urban Electricity Supply Network. Improving the urban electricity delivery network has been the government's top agenda. In 1998, 62 urban electricity delivery network projects were initiated in 20 cities, including Beijing, Shanghai, Chongqing, Tianjing, Taiyuan, Chengdu, Zhenzhou, and Shenyang. The government has also decided to renovate the rural electricity delivery network and reform the rural network management system by establishing a unified price of electricity in the rural area. In 2000, the government accelerated the preparation work for the Guangxi Longtan Hydrogen Power Station and Asia-Pacific Sea Cable.[21] Each province will focus on the renovation of the electricity supply network.

Irrigation System. In the next two to three years, investment will be channeled to ongoing projects [such as the Three Gorges project (*Sanxia Gongcheng*)], new small- and medium-size irrigation and new water conservation projects, and the reconstruction of damaged reservoirs. The major new project to be initiated in 2000 was the Chengdu Zipingpu Water Control Project.[22]

---

[17] See Zeng (2000).
[18] *ibid.*
[19] *People's Daily* (Overseas Edition) March 23, 2000.
[20] *ibid.*
[21] *ibid.*
[22] *ibid.*

Urban Public Utilities. Investment in urban public utilities will dramatically increase in the next few years. The focus will be on improving the urban sewage system and garbage disposal system, increasing the water supply for 100 cities suffering severe water shortage, and introducing an express transportation system to release the urban traffic burden. Last year's major new transportation projects were Shanghai Mingzhu Line (second round) and Nanjing Subway.[23]

While the emphasis is on large inter-province projects, insufficient attention has been paid to local infrastructures. It might be argued that the central government should focus on big and inter-province projects, and local governments should concentrate on small and local projects. The problem is that in China, local governments do not have much fiscal freedom (e.g., they have no right to issue bonds and have limited power to make tax laws) and their sources of financing infrastructures are rather limited.

5. Public Financing of Infrastructures: Alternative Sources

It is widely recognized that private firms are more efficient than state enterprises.[24] However, various concerns, such as high regulation costs, safety, environment protection, large capital requirement, income redistribution, and nationwide planning, have caused the government to be engaged in many infrastructure developments. This section discusses alternative ways of financing China's public infrastructures, namely, taxes, fees and user charges, domestic debt, foreign capital, profits from state enterprises, and labor services.

5.1 Taxes

Tax finance can avoid transferring the burden of infrastructure finance to future generations. As argued, infrastructures that benefit the current

---

[23] *ibid.*
[24] Lin (2000a) showed that, in China, provinces investing more in private enterprises grew faster than provinces investing more in state enterprises.

generation should not be a financial burden to future generations. However, if tax revenues are used to finance infrastructures that last for a long period of time, those who benefit in the future from the facilities will not need to contribute to the cost of the facilities. In reality though, current tax revenues are usually not sufficient to pay for large infrastructure expenditures.

China's government budgetary revenues have decreased from 32% of GDP in 1978 to 11.6% of GDP in 1997, 12.4% in 1998, and 13.9% in 1999.[25] This decline in the government's revenue share in GDP is the result of economic decentralization and tax reforms.[26] Facing an economic downturn, it would be very difficult for the government to increase its budgetary revenues. As was mentioned, government spending on infrastructures such as transportation and fuel has been rather low. Thus, extensively relying on taxes for infrastructure financing appears unlikely in China now.

Many countries finance infrastructures by special taxes. In the United States, the Highway Trust Fund was created whereby proceeds from a federal tax on gasoline, tires, and other motor vehicle parts would be deposited with the government to be used solely for highway construction. In Japan, the government established several special accounts to finance major projects by user fees and earmarked taxes. Japan's national budget currently includes eight special accounts for infrastructure development. The accounts for road, airport, and harbor improvement are the largest. The major sources of revenue earmarked for infrastructure expenditures include a gasoline tax for road improvements and three-quarters of an automobile weight tax for road construction. In China, gas and fuel taxes are yet to be established. Based on other countries' experience, China needs to establish special accounts to finance major projects by earmarking, for example, gas and fuel taxes for highway construction and maintenance.

---

[25] The total national government revenue in 1999 was 1137.7 billion yuan and GDP was 8205.4 billion yuan. See Zeng (2000).

[26] See Lin (2000b) for a discussion of the reasons for the decline in government budgetary revenues and the distortion of China's tax system.

5.2 Fees and User Charges

Fees and user charges can be used to finance infrastructures, such as highways, bridges, water and sewage facilities, and city transportation. The government collects fees and user charges from the people who use these facilities, and then uses the revenue to construct and maintain the infrastructures. This way of financing relates benefits to costs by forcing the user to pay the cost of infrastructure provision.

Fees and user charges are widely utilized in China for infrastructure provisions. For example, fees are used to finance the construction and maintenance of the airport operation system. Domestic airlines paid 10% before 1999 and 5% since 1999 of their total revenue. International airlines paid 4–6% before 1999 and 2% since 1999 of their revenues to the Air Transportation Construction Fund. The money is used for airport infrastructure construction.[27] The airport fee is 50 yuan for domestic passengers and 90 yuan for international passengers. Water fees are used to finance water supply, and the construction and maintenance of new highways are widely financed by tolls.

China currently faces serious problems in fee collection. Fees are excessive. There are over 6,000 types of fees, compared to only 23 taxes. Fees are arbitrary and irregular. Many government agencies, government institutions, and local governments engage in fee collection. Fees are not closely related to the costs of providing public good. For some infrastructures, particularly consumption types of infrastructures, the government sets a low price and subsidizes low-income households. For example, running water is heavily subsidized by the government.[28] For other infrastructures, extra fees may be collected.[29] Fees and user charges

---

[27] See Xia (1999).

[28] Prices vary over regions. For example, on September 20, 1998, water price per ton was 0.7 yuan in Beijing, 0.68 in Shanghai, 0.88 in Tianjin, 0.8 yuan in Taiyuan, 1.1 yuan in Shenyang, 1.2 yuan in Dalian, 1.0 yuan in Nanjing, 0.88 in Guangzhou, 1.20 yuan in Qingdao, 0.5 yuan in Xining, 1.12 in Xiamen, 0.58 in Lanzhou, and 1.36 yuan in Xi'an. See Wang (1999).

[29] For example, in Fuzhou of Jiangxi, individual industrial and commercial households and private enterprises are subjected to more than 30 kinds of fees, including industrial and commercial management fee, public security fee (*zhi an fei*), security insurance fee

are often misused, for example, for paying the salaries and bonuses of government officials. There is thus rising sentiment against excessive fee collection in China.

Fee reform is occurring in China. Some fees will be converted into taxes, while some will be regulated or altogether eliminated. As the first step of the fee reform, the government plans to convert fees on vehicle and transportation fees into a single fuel tax. Despite encountering various problems, using fees and user charges to finance public infrastructures is necessary for China. To reduce distortions, fees and user charges collected in the name of infrastructure development should be used solely for the purpose.

5.3 Domestic Debt

Debt financing allows government to acquire large funds in a short period of time. Unlike taxes, fees and user charges, debt financing can spread the cost of infrastructures over successive generations of service users or beneficiaries. The main cost of debt issuance is the interest payment which encumbers future revenues (i.e., potential tax revenues are dedicated to the repayment of debt and are not available for other uses).[30] Many types of bonds can be issued for infrastructure financing. Based on the repayment method, bonds can be classified as general obligation bonds and revenue bonds. General bonds are backed by future tax revenues, and only those governments with tax authority may issue general obligation bonds. Revenue bonds are secured by the revenue of particular enterprises, such as sewage charges, and highway or bridge

---

(*bao an fei*), joint defense fee (*lian fang fei*), road occupation fee, sanitation fee, physical examination fee (*ti yan fei*), garbage clearance fee (*laji qingsao fei*), garbage moving fee (*laji daiyun fei*), garbage disposal fee (*laji chuli fei*), anti-pollution fee (*paiwu fei*), sanitation supervision and examination fee (*weisheng jiandu jiance fei*), greening fee (*luhua fei*), secret guarantee fee (*baomi baozheng jin fei*), security responsibility deposit (*zhi an zeren zhuang yajin*), road and market construction fund-raising, contribution to the foundation for taking up the cudgels for justice, and so on. See Wu (1997).

[30] Despite a long history of debate, the long-run effect of government debt is still controversial. See Diamond (1965) and Barro (1974).

tolls. Bonds have been widely used for infrastructure financing in other countries. In the U.S., federal, state and local governments have issued bonds to finance public capital projects, including schools, roads, water and sewer systems.[31] In Japan, since the early 1970s, bond issuance for public works has become an important financing instrument, especially during periods of economic recession.

The shortage of government revenue has forced the Chinese government to issue debt. Table 8 shows government debt issue in China from 1950 to 1999. From 1958 to 1978, China did not issue new debt. When China began economic reform in 1979, government debt started increasing. Faced with slower economic growth, the Chinese government has recently adopted an expansionary fiscal policy by increasing government spending. In 1999, China issued 401.5 billion yuan of government bonds, including 50 billion yuan of long-term debt for infrastructure, and 60 billion yuan for infrastructures, technology improvement of large state enterprises, environmental protection, and education. In 2000, the government planned to issue bonds of 438.8 billion yuan, including 100 billion yuan of long-term government debt for infrastructures, science, technology and education, environmental protection and ecology reconstruction, and upgrading the technology of state enterprises.[32] Recently, the government issued an additional debt of 50 billion yuan. China's total debt was 220 billion yuan at the end

---

[31] From 1790 to 1840s, state governments were the most active level of American government. They invested widely in transportation and financial infrastructures (such canals and as banks) and the level of debt is a rough indicator of infrastructure investment. From 1842 to 1933, local infrastructure investments rose steadily relative to state investments (such as water, sewage, curb, and paving projects), as indicated by the rise in local government debt. After 1933, the federal government had by far the largest level of government in debt issue [See Wallis (2000)]. But the state and local government continued to play an important role in infrastructure financing. For example, in 1967, of total state government long-term debt, 27.2% was for education and 36.1% for highways; of total city government long-term debt, 15.2% was for water, 9.2% for sewerage, 5.4% for electricity, and 12.2% for transit [See Fisher (1996), p. 244].

[32] See Zhu (2000).

Table 8. Government Debt Finance in China (100 million yuan)

Year	Total Debt Incurred*	Domestic Debts	Foreign Debts	Total Payment for the Debts**	Payment for the Principal and Interest of the Domestic Debts
1950	3.02	3.02	..	0.03	0.03
1951	8.18	0.01	5.49	0.42	0.40
1952	9.78	0.00	9.78	3.92	0.58
1953	9.62	0.00	9.62	0.91	0.65
1954	17.2	8.36	8.84	2.21	0.89
1955	22.76	6.19	16.57	6.56	1.58
1956	7.24	6.07	1.17	7.22	1.25
1957	6.99	6.84	0.15	8.26	2.18
1958	7.98	7.98	..	9.04	1.81
1979	35.31	0.00	35.31	..	..
1980	43.01	0.00	43.01	28.58	..
1981	73.08	0.00	73.08	62.89	..
1982	83.86	43.83	40.03	55.52	..
1983	79.41	41.58	37.83	42.47	..
1984	77.34	42.53	34.81	28.91	..
1985	89.85	60.61	29.24	39.56	..
1986	138.25	62.51	75.74	50.16	7.98
1987	169.55	63.07	106.48	79.83	23.18
1988	270.78	92.17	138.61	76.75	28.44
1989	282.97	56.07	144.06	72.36	19.30
1990	375.45	93.46	178.21	190.40	113.75
1991	461.4	199.30	180.13	246.80	156.69
1992	669.68	395.64	208.91	438.57	342.42
1993	739.22	314.78	357.90	336.22	224.30
1994	1175.25	1028.57	146.48	499.36	364.96
1995	1549.76	1510.86	38.90	878.36	779.46
1996	1967.28	1847.77	119.51	1311.91	1223.17
1997	2476.82	2412.02	64.80	1918.37	1820.40
1998	3310.98	3228.77	82.16	2352.92	2245.79
1999	..	4015.00	..	..	..
2000	..	4380.00	..	..	..

Sources: China's Ministry of Finance, *Financial Statistical Yearbook of China*, 1997, p. 457; 1998, p. 291; 1999, p. 284; and Xiang (2000).
* Total debt incurred also includes borrowing from banks in 1951 and specific borrowing after 1988.
** Total payment for the debt also includes payment for the principal and interest of foreign debts, and payment of the loans from People's Bank and their interest.

of 1994,[33] and it increased to 330 billion yuan at the end of 1995.[34] Government debt has increased drastically since 1995. The debt-GDP ratio was 5% in 1994, 6% in 1995, and is at least 15% now. Nevertheless, the debt-GDP ratio is still not high compared to many other countries.[35]

Debt will have to be eventually repaid with interest, and thus, it is postponed taxes and fees and user charges. The effect of government debt on the economy depends on how the government spends the funds generated from the debt issue. If the government can use the funds in a productive way, then the government debt will help economic development; if the government uses the funds inefficiently, then the government debt will hurt economic development. China hence needs to emphasize the efficient use of the revenue from bond issues.

5.4 Foreign Capital

Utilization of foreign capital is mainly through foreign direct investment and foreign borrowing. Most foreign direct investment by multinational firms is in the manufacturing industries, instead of infrastructures. International organizations (such as the World Bank, International Monetary Fund, the regional development banks) and the governments of developed countries provide low interest rate loans to developing countries. Most of the loans are used for poverty relief and for infrastructure development. Commercial banks in developed countries also provide loans to developing countries. Foreign borrowing increases

---

[33] See Liu, Liu, and Wang (1997).
[34] See Zhang (1997).
[35] In the U.S., the ratio of government debt to GNP was 0.18 in 1800, 0.05 in 1900, 1.07 in 1945, 0.41 in 1960, 0.23 in 1970, 0.23 in 1980, 0.41 in 1990, and 0.45 in 1996. The debt-GDP ratio was heavily affected by wars. There was a dramatic response to the Great Depression, where the ratio rose from 0.14 in 1929 to 0.38 in 1933. Similar behavior applies to less severe recessions; for example, the ratio rose from 0.23 in 1979 to 0.31 in 1983 [see Barro (1999)]. In the U.S., state and local government can also issue bonds. In 1991, state and local government debt as percentage of GDP was 16.1% (of which state share of debt was 37.7% and local share of debt was 62.3%), while it was 14.5% in 1964 (of which state share of debt was 27.1% and local share of debt was 72.9%). See Fisher (1997).

a country's total resource and total investment by making use of the lender's savings. However, unlike the domestic debt, the future interest payment will go to foreigners. Thus, foreign borrowing is a double-edged sword. Many developing countries have been active in utilizing foreign capital for infrastructure development since 1960s. For countries such as South Korea, foreign borrowing helped economic development before 1990s, showing the importance of the efficient use of foreign funds to augment economic development.

Since China's door was reopened in 1978, foreign direct investment and foreign debt have increased significantly. The total amount of foreign debt actually utilized in China increased from US$1.3 billion in 1984 to US$45.5 billion in 1998. Of the total foreign direct investment in 1998, US$3.1 billion were in electric power, gas and water production and supply, and US$1.6 billion were in transportation, storage, postal and telecommunications.[36] The historical data on foreign debt can be found in Table 8. In 1998, China's foreign debt accumulation reached US$146 billion, making China one of the largest debtors among developing countries.[37] The ratio of China's foreign debt to GDP is still low, and most of the debt is long-term. In other words, the degree of risk of China's foreign debt is still lower than many other developing countries.[38]

Efficient utilization of foreign capital is crucial for developing countries. China should continue to encourage foreign direct investment in infrastructures and to improve the utilization of international loans. It is important that China examines its infrastructure projects financed by international loans carefully, and to make sure that the expected returns from these projects outweigh the principals and interest of the loans.

5.5 Profits from State-Owned Enterprises

Many countries establish public corporations (i.e., state enterprises) to

---

[36] See China's National Bureau of Statistics, *Statistical Yearbook of China*, 1999.
[37] See China's National Bureau of Statistics, *A Statistical Survey of China*, 2000.
[38] See Lin (1999) for a discussion of China's foreign debt.

assume some of the burden for financing and constructing infrastructures. In the U.S., the state and local governments are most commonly involved in water, sewer and local mass transit, while privately regulated enterprises are more common for electricity, natural gas and inter-metropolitan transit. Fisher (1996) reported that cities in 46 out of 50 states operated electric utilities, and cities in 34 states gas utilities in 1996.[39] In Japan, to alleviate the burden on general tax revenue, the government undertook several measures. It created public corporations that charged user fees and issued corporate bonds to borrow from public and private financial institutions.

In the past, China's infrastructure construction was under the charge of various ministries, which in turn controlled many state enterprises. After the reform began, some of the ministries were converted to corporations and state enterprises have become profit-oriented. In general, state enterprises which produce goods and services with positive externality (with public goods features) are losing money, while the natural monopolistic enterprises are making considerable profits. For example, postal and telecommunication enterprises as a whole are very profitable. In 1997, for centrally-owned state enterprises, the total revenue was 151 billion yuan, total cost was 130.8 billion yuan, taxes were 6.3 billion yuan, and the after-tax profits were 14.8 billion yuan. For locally-owned state-enterprises, total revenue was 18.3 billion yuan, total cost was 19.8 billion yuan, taxes were 0.9 billion yuan, and total losses were 2.1 billion yuan.[40] The profits from monopolist enterprises could be used for public infrastructures. Unfortunately, these tax revenue are

---

[39] State and local governments are profitable in some infrastructure services while experiencing losses in others. In 1991, in the U.S., for water supply, the net income ("profits") was $1.8 million for states, $98.4 million for counties, and $1996.7 million for cities; for transit, the net income was $-1376.9 million for states, $-423.2 million for counties, and $-2551.0 million for cities; for electricity supply, the net income was $132.6 million for states, $10.5 million for counties, and $2253.5 million for cities; for natural gas, the net income was $0.1 million for counties, and $303.1 million for cities.
[40] See China's National Bureau of Statistics, *Statistical Yearbook of China*, 1998, p. 573; Planning Commission of the People's Republic of China and China's Transportation Association, *Yearbook of China's Transportation and Communications*, 1998, p. 637.

usually used for other government expenditures.[41] Faced with more and more competition from private enterprises, the profitability of state enterprises may further decline. Thus, the role of state enterprises in infrastructure development may diminish.

5.6 Labor Services

Requiring citizens to provide labor services for infrastructure construction is a common way for infrastructure finance. In North America, from the beginning of the first permanent settlement, landholders were "taxed" three days a year to maintain the roads, i.e., keeping the roads in front of one's property safe for the movement of man and beast [see Cain (1997)]. Some European countries also used this method to build their infrastructures. Politicians in the U.S. are still advocating that people on welfare provide community services for the welfare benefits they receive. In some Latin American countries, rural people are required to provide a certain amount of community service to be entitled for medical insurance provisions.

In China, historically, bridges, roads, and canals were all built by extensive use of such labor. However, forcing people to provide excessive labor service often caused resentment and rebellions. Of course, with appropriate amounts of labor services, economic development can be speeded up. This approach of infrastructure construction was widely used by the Chinese government before the economic reform. About 70% of the population live in rural China, where the income level is low and where it is difficult for the government to collect taxes. However, this also means that labor is abundant in the rural places. Local

---

[41] China's tax system is severely distorted. Since it is difficult to collect taxes from private enterprises and individuals directly, the government has to collect taxes indirectly from the public through state enterprises. The government first grants state enterprises low-interest loans and allows them to charge monopoly prices, and then taxes their profits. In 1995, non-state (collective, individual, foreign, and other) enterprises produced 66% of industrial output, but only paid 29% of total taxes. They paid various fees to local government, which cannot be disposed of by the central government. In 1997, individual income taxes only accounted for 2.5% of total tax revenues — almost negligible!

governments may require rural residents to provide labor services for construction of local infrastructures (such as roads, streets, etc.) instead of paying fees and taxes.

6. Concluding Remarks

Chinese infrastructure construction and maintenance has lagged behind its economic growth in the last two decades. Slow development of infrastructures has negatively affected people's welfare, as well as economic growth. It is fair to say that China's infrastructure build-up before the economic reform has contributed to the fast economic growth in the country over the last two decades. However, infrastructures need maintenance and expansion. Long-term neglect of infrastructures will slow down economic growth. And since China is experiencing slow economic growth now, speeding up infrastructure development thus seems imperative for the country at this point. This paper concludes with the following policy recommendations.

First, China should pay more attention to inner city infrastructures. As mentioned earlier, local infrastructures (roads, water supply, sewage system, transit, garbage cleaning, etc.) are in poor condition. Local infrastructures are heavily used. Construction and maintenance of local infrastructure will directly increase employment and, therefore, increase output. Improvement of local infrastructure will raise people's living standard and increase people's demand for other goods and services. Improvement of local infrastructures will also increase local business activities and attract investment from other areas.

Second, the Chinese government should speed up development of rural infrastructures. Before the rural economic reform, people's communes organized farmers to construct and maintain rural infrastructures (roads, irrigation, streets, etc.). Since the establishment of the household responsibility system, small individual farmers only care for their own production and properties and not public goods such as streets and roads. Various fees paid by farmers are largely used for the salaries of village and town officials. With good roads, farmers may go to towns to buy more industrial or even domestic products. Currently, farmers complain about the burden of fees and taxes. However, if the fee revenue is used for rural infrastructures, farmers will then have no cause for complain. Rural fee reforms should thus focus on the allocation of fee revenue.

Third, China should decentralize its fiscal system and give local governments the right to issue bonds. Local governments do not have the right to issue bonds now. In many cases, infrastructures provide public goods of a localized nature. Decentralized responsibility, in which government authority is moved to sub-national levels of government, offers an opportunity to improve the provision of such goods. Local governments are better able to determine and respond to local preferences, and decentralization can increase user satisfaction and decrease the production cost of public goods. A study has shown that projects undertaken by local governments are executed at one-half to two-thirds the cost incurred by centralized agencies.[42] As mentioned, local governments in China still do not have the right to issue bonds. Although legislators at the provincial level have the right to establish tax laws, this right is seldom used. More fiscal freedom should be given to local governments for infrastructure finance.

Fourth, the authorities should heighten the enforcement of laws and reduction of corruption. Corruption is a major problem associated with the construction of public infrastructures in all countries, and China is no exception. For example, since the construction of the Three Gorges dam, about 500 million yuan has been misused or stolen.[43] Greater efforts should be made to improve the legal system, reinforce laws, and reduce corruption.

REFERENCES

Ashauer, David, "Is Public Expenditure Productive?", *Journal of Monetary Economics* 23, 1989, 177–200.

Barro, Robert, "Are Government Debt Real Wealth?", *Journal of Political Economy* 82, 1974, 1095–1118.

---

[42] See The World Bank, *World Development Report*, 1994.
[43] See *Lianhe Zaobao*, March 12, 2000.

_____, *Macroeconomics*, Fourth edition, John Wiley and Sons, 1999.
Cain, Louis P., 1997, "Historical Perspective on Infrastructure and US Economic Development," *Regional Science and Urban Economics* 27, 117–138.
Canning, David, "A Database of World Stocks of Infrastructure, 1950–95," *The World Bank Economic Review* 12 (3), 1998, 529–47.
Canning, David, Marianne Fay, Roberto Perotti, "Infrastructure and Growth," in Mario Baldassarri, Luigi Paganetto, and Edmund Phelps, eds., *International Differences in Growth Rates*, New York: Macmillan Press, 1994, 113–47.
Csernok, A., E. Ehrlich, and Gy. Szilagyi, 1973, "Numerical Results of an International Comparison of Infrastructure Development over the Last 100 Years," *European Economic Review* 4, 1973, 63–65.
China's Ministry of Finance, *The Finance Yearbook of China*, Publishing House of Financial Journals, Beijing, China, 1998.
China's National Bureau of Statistics, *Statistical Yearbook of China*, Beijing: China Statistical Publishing House, 1998, 1999.
_____, *A Statistical Survey of China*, Beijing: China Statistical Publishing House, 2000.
Diamond, Peter, "National Debt in a Neoclassical Growth Model," *American Economic Review* 55, 1125–50.
Editorial Group, *Modern Chinese Economic History*, Department of Economics, The Chinese People's University, People's Publishing House, Beijing, 1979.
Easterly, William, and Sergio Rebelo, "Fiscal Policy and Economic Growth: An Empirical Investigation," *Journal of Monetary Economics* 32 (3), 417–58.
Eisner, Robert, "Infrastructure and Regional Economic Performance: Comment," *New England Economic Review*, September/October, 1991.
Fisher, Ronald C., *State and Local Public Finance*, Chicago: Irwin, 1996.
International Monetary Fund, *International Financial Statistics*, 1998.
_____, *Government Finance Statistics Yearbook*, 1998.
Kuninori, Morio, "Financing Japan's Infrastructure: A Blend of Gradualism and Diversity in Financial Instruments," *Infrastructure Strategies in East Asia*, edited by Ashoka Mody, The World Bank, Washington, D. C., 1997.
Munnell, Alicia H., with the assistance of Leah M. Cook, "How Does Public Infrastructure Affect Regional Economic Performance?", *New England Economic Review*, September/October, 1990.
Lin, Shuanglin, (2000a), "The Decline of China's Budgetary Revenue: Reasons and Consequences," *Contemporary Economic Policy*, 18, 2000, 477–490.
_____, (2000b), "Resource Allocation and Economic Growth in China," *Economic Inquiry*, 38, 2000, 515–526.

———, "Foreign Debt and Economic Development: Lessons for China," in Doowon Lee and Jason Yin, eds., *Comparison of Korean and Chinese Economic Development*, Seoul, Korea: Yonsei University, 1999, 149–175.

Liu, Zhiyou, Liu Yinfeng, and Wang Jiahua, "Lun guozhai zhengce yu caizheng, huobi zhengce de xietiao peihe," *Caijing Yanjiu*, No. 1, 1997, 3–8.

Planning Commission of the People's Republic of China and China's Transportation Association, *Yearbook of China's Transportation and Communications*, Beijing: China's Transportation and Communications Publishing House, 1998.

Reinfeld, William, "Tying Infrastructure to Economic Development: The Republic of Korea and Taiwan (China)," *Infrastructure Strategies in East Asia*, edited by Ashoka Mody, The World Bank, Washington, D. C., 1997.

Wallis, John J., "American Government Finance in the Long Run: 1790 to 1990," *Journal of Economic Perspectives* 14, No. 1, 2000, 61–82.

Wang Junhao, "The Reform of Government Regulation in China's Running Water Industry," *International Symposium on the Reform of China's Infrastructures*, November, 1999.

The World Bank, *World Development Report 1994, Infrastructure for Development*, Oxford University Press.

Wu, Shi-an, *China's Fee Collection Research, Zhongguo Caizheng Jingji Chubanshe*, China Finance and Economics Publishing House, 1997.

Xia, Xinghua, "Reform and Development of China's Civil Aviation," *International Symposium on the Reform of China's Infrastructures*, November 1999.

Xiang, Huaicheng, "Guanyu 1999 nian zhongyang he difang yusuan zhixing qingkang ji 2000 nian zhongyang he difang yusuan caoan de baogao," *Gazette of the Standing Committee of the National People's Congress of the People's Republic of China*, No. 2, March 2000, 95–107.

Yu, Jianguo, "The Timing of the Reforming of China's Infrastructures," *International Symposium on the Reform of China's Infrastructures*, November 1999.

Zeng, Peiyan, "Guanyu 1999 guomingjingji he jihuan zhixing qingkang ji 2000 guomingjingji he jihuan caoan de baogao," *Gazette of the Standing Committee of the National People's Congress of the People's Republic of China*, No. 2, March 2000.

———, "Objectives of Economic and Social Development, Report on the Ninth National Congress and Third Session," *People's Daily*, March 7, 2000.

Zhang, Yunqiang, "Dui bashi niandai yilai woguo guo zhai zongliang kuozhang ji qushi de fenxi," *Sichuan Jinrong*, No. 12, 1997, 29–32.

Zhu, Rongji, "Report at the Third Session of the Ninth National Congress," *People's Daily*, March 6, 2000.

13
Building Up China's Telecommunications Infrastructure

LU DING*

On the eve of China's entry into the World Trade Organisation (WTO), the Chinese telecommunications sector has been undergoing a series of drastic institutional changes. To understand the significance of these changes, we will first review the features of China's telecommunications sector and discuss the political-economic factors that led to the emergence of domestic competition since 1993. With this background, we will examine how China is beefing up its telecommunications sector for foreign competition on the eve of WTO entry.

1. FEATURES OF THE SECTOR

1.1 15 Years of Hyper Growth (1985–1999)

When China was a centrally planned autarky (1950s–1970s), the

---

*Dr. LU Ding is Associate Professor at the Economics Department, National University of Singapore, and Research Associate at the East Asian Institute, NUS. The author thanks Messrs Gao Yangzhi and Shen Guanghui of the Shanghai Institute of Post & Telecommunications Economics for their valuable support and Wong Chee Kong, a postgraduate student at NUS, for his research assistance.

telecommunications infrastructure received low priority in the heavy-industry oriented development plans. The telecommunications sector was seen purely as a tool for meeting administrative needs. The state-owned telecommunications system was semi-military and had a rigid administrative structure and non-profit nature. In the early 1980s, when China launched into its two decades of rapid economic growth, the telecommunications sector was one of the worst bottlenecks in the economy. In 1984, the State Council acknowledged that the sector was "seriously backward" and there existed a "remarkable gap between supply and demand".[1] The government then introduced stimuli to the industry, speeding up development of telecommunications infrastructure in the mid-1980s to meet the booming market demand.

Since then, the telecommunications sector has possessed a strategic spot in China's industrial policy regime. The average growth rate of main telephone lines from 1988 to 1991 doubled the rate of GDP growth and accelerated above 30% after 1992. Through the 1990s the growth rate of telephone lines consistently exceeded that of GDP, on average three to four times higher (Figure 1).

Table 1 shows that China's telecommunications sector has developed much faster than its central planners envisaged. Again and again the explosive growth of the industry has made a mockery of government forecasts. Take the switchboard capacity for example. For the Sixth Five-year Plan, the capacity built was 25% higher than what was planned. During the Seventh Five-year Plan period, actual capacity built overshot planned target by 30%. In 1995 the capacity hit 200% higher than what was specified in the Eighth Plan! Only in the first half of the 1990s, China installed more than 73 million phone lines, more than all the rest of the developing world combined. Switchboard capacity leaped from 4 million lines prior to 1985 to 160 million by the end of 1999 (Table 2). The number of fixed-line phone subscribers increased from two million in 1979 to 110 million by the end of 1999 (Table 3). During the next ten years (till 2010), mainland China (excluding Hong Kong, Macau and Taiwan) will see fixed-line users increase to 200 million to 300 million.

---

[1] *Yearbook of China Transportation and Communications 1986*, Beijing, p. 243.

—□— Real GDP —♦— Telephone Lines

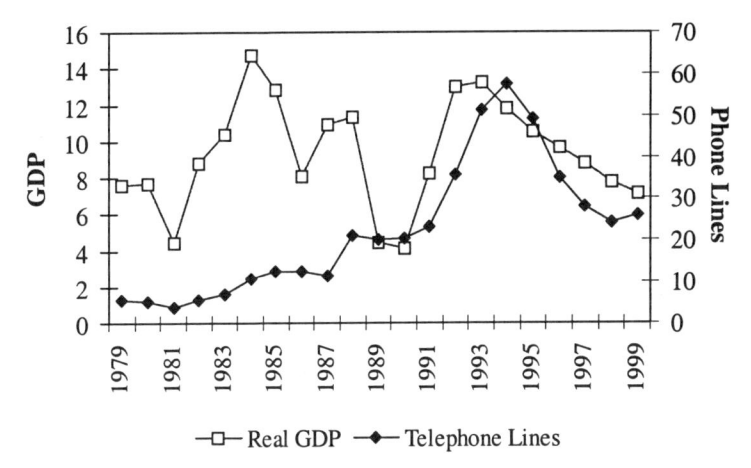

Sources: China Statistical Yearbook and Yearbook of China Transportation and Communications, various issues, Beijing. Ministry of Information Industry web site, http://www.mii.gov.cn/.

Fig. 1. Annual Percentage Growth Rates of Real GDP and Number of Fixed-line Phone Subscribers, 1979–1999

Since the mid-1990s, China's telecom growth has also been driven by an expansion of its mobile network. The number of mobile phone subscribers has now surpassed 43 million (Table 4). The Ministry of Information Industry (MII) anticipates the total number of mobile phone subscribers to increase to 70 million by the end of 2000.[2] A further 100 million mobile-phone customers are also expected to be added by 2003 and another 200 million by 2010.[3] Symbolic of the huge changes in this sector is the country's mobile phone code growing to 11 digits by July 1999. Such an increase amplifies the code capacity from 50 million to about 500 million, which should meet the country's demand by 2010.[4]

After a fifteen-year period of hyper growth, China will soon boast the world's largest telephone and mobile telephone networks, overtaking the United States in both categories. In 1985, China's telephone network

[2] *Mingbao* (Hong Kong), 14 January 2000.
[3] *South China Morning Post* (Hong Kong), 20 December 1999.
[4] *China Daily* (Hong Kong), 22 July 1999.

Table 1. Build-up of Telecommunications Infrastructure: Planned and Actual, 1981–2000

Items	The Sixth Five-year Plan (1981–85) Planned for 1985	The Sixth Five-year Plan (1981–85) Achieved by 1985	The Seventh Five-year Plan (1986–90) Planned for 1990	The Seventh Five-year Plan (1986–90) Achieved by 1990	The Eighth Five-year Plan (1991–95) Planned for 1995	The Eighth Five-year Plan (1991–95) Achieved by 1995	The Ninth Five-year Plan (1996–2000) Planned for 2000	The Ninth Five-year Plan (1996–2000) Achieved by end of 2000
Urban switchboard capacity (lines)	2.7 million	3.37 million	6.35 million	8.26 million	18 million	54.56 million	150 million	179 million
Long distance phone lines	28,011	37,551	109,615	112,437	350,000	735,545	2,800,000	5,490,000
Telephone terminals per 100 residents (up from 0.43 in 1980)	N/A	0.6	N/A	1.11	Above 2.0	4.66	National: 10 Urban: 30–40	National: 20 Urban: 39
Main telephone lines of which: mobile phone lines	N/A	N/A	N/A	N/A	N/A	N/A	123 million 18 million	215 million 85 million
Average annual growth rate of postal and telecommunications turnover	5.0%	9.8%	11.05%	22.5%	20%	35.1%	20%	30% (1996–99)

Sources: *China Statistical Yearbook* and *Yearbook of China Transportation and Communications*, various issues, Beijing; Ministry of Information Industry web site, http://www.mii.gov.cn/.

Table 2. Local Switchboard Capacity in China, 1985–1999

Year	Local switchboard capacity Million lines	% Change
1985	6.13	
1986	6.72	9.62
1987	7.74	15.10
1988	8.87	14.64
1989	10.35	16.63
1990	12.32	19.05
1991	14.92	21.14
1992	19.15	28.34
1993	30.41	58.78
1994	49.26	62.00
1995	72.04	46.23
1996	92.91	28.98
1997	112.69	21.29
1998	138.24	22.67
1999	158.53	14.68
2000	179.00	22.60

Sources: *China Statistical Yearbook* and *Yearbook of China Transportation and Communications*, various issues, Beijing. Ministry of Information Industry web site, http://www.mii.gov.cn/.

was ranked 17th in the world. Only twelve years later in 1997, it became the second largest, next only to the United States.[5] By 1999, the United States still had the world's largest telephone network, with about 180 million end-user connections compared to 132 million total connections in China in mid-1999. China, however, is adding between 20 and 30 million connections a year, while the US is adding only about 10 million a year. With these trends, China is set to surpass the United States in 2002.[6]

---

[5] *Far Eastern Economic Review* (Hong Kong), 30 September 1999.
[6] News report on a speech by Xie Linzhen, vice director of the Department of Electronic Information, MII. *The China Interactive Times Newsletter* (www.shanghai-abc.com), Vol. 2, No. 24, 21 August 2000.

Table 3. Number of Fixed-line Phone Subscribers in China, 1978–2000

Year	No. of subscribers (million)	% Change
1980	2.14	5.31
1981	2.22	3.74
1982	2.34	5.49
1983	2.51	7.04
1984	2.78	10.65
1985	3.12	12.43
1986	3.50	12.31
1987	3.91	11.50
1988	4.73	20.99
1989	5.68	20.16
1990	6.85	20.60
1991	8.45	23.37
1992	11.47	35.71
1993	17.33	51.12
1994	27.30	57.48
1995	40.71	49.13
1996	54.95	34.99
1997	70.31	27.96
1998	87.42	24.34
1999	108.81	24.46
2000	144.00	32.80

Sources: China Statistical Yearbook and Yearbook of China Transportation and Communications, various issues, Beijing. Ministry of Information Industry web site, http://www.mii.gov.cn/.

In the mobile communications market, China is currently adding close to four million mobile-phone users a month. It recently passed Japan as the world's second largest mobile-phone market with about 52 million users and is expected to pass the US for the number one spot by mid-2001. Meanwhile, for the user caller ID service, which usually piggybacks on the expansion in mobile phone service, China has already surpassed the US as the world's largest.[7]

---

[7] *The China Interactive Times Newsletter* (www.shanghai-abc.com), Vol. 2, No. 25, 25 August 2000.

Table 4. Number of Mobile Phone Subscribers in China, 1988–2000

Year	No. of subscribers (million)	% Change
1988	0.0032	
1989	0.0098	206.25
1990	0.0183	86.73
1991	0.0475	159.56
1992	0.177	272.63
1993	0.639	261.01
1994	1.568	145.38
1995	3.629	131.44
1996	6.853	88.84
1997	13.233	93.10
1998	23.863	80.33
1999	43.238	81.20
2000	85.260	97.00

Sources: *China Statistical Yearbook* and *Yearbook of China Transportation and Communications*, various issues, Beijing; Ministry of Information Industry web site, http://www.mii.gov.cn/.

As a result of the market expansion, the telephone penetration rate (measured by the number of telephone terminals per 100 persons) rose sharply from 0.6% in 1985 to 1.1% in 1990, and to 13% in 1999. In urban areas, the rate reached 17% by 1995 and over 28% by 1999. Many coastal cities, in particular, had raised their telephone penetration level from 2–3% to above 30% by 1995 in less than a decade's time. Teledensity (measured by main telephone lines per 100 residents) in 1999 reached 8.64% (Table 5). By international comparison, China has been remarkably successful in catching up with the rest of the world in raising its teledensity. As shown in Table 6, the middle-income country's average teledensity was 13 times higher than China's in 1987 but the gap closed up quickly in the following decade: by 1998 the former was only 42% higher than the latter.

Table 5. Penetration Rate and Teledensity in China, 1985-2000

Year	Penetration rate	Teledensity
1985	0.60	
1986	0.67	
1987	0.75	
1988	0.86	
1989	0.98	
1990	1.11	
1991	1.29	
1992	1.61	
1993	2.20	
1994	3.20	
1995	4.66	3.36
1996	6.33	4.49
1997	8.11	5.68
1998	10.53	6.96
1999	13.00	8.64
2000	20.10	17.80

Sources: *China Statistical Yearbook* and *Yearbook of China Transportation and Communications*, various issues, Beijing. Ministry of Information Industry web site, http://www.mii.gov.cn/.

Table 6. Catching Up in Teledensity

Year	1987 Teledensity	1987 Compared to China	1998 Teledensity	1998 Compared to China
China	0.37		6.96	
Low-income country average	0.29	22% lower	1.64	76% lower
Middle-income country average	5.27	1,324% higher	9.85	42% higher

Note: According to the World Bank classification, countries with per capita GNP below US$ 500 in 1987 or with per capita GNP below US$ 760 in 1998 are low-income countries. The per capita GNP range for middle-income countries is US$ 500 to 6,000 for the year 1987 while the range is US$ 761 to 9,360 for the year 1998.

Sources: *Yearbook of China Transportation and Communications 1991* and *ITU Statistical Yearbook 1995, 1999*, Beijing.

1.2 Reforms and Policies Driving the Growth

China's telecommunications sector developed in leaps and bounds since the mid-1980s largely thanks to the former Ministry of Posts and Telecommunications' (MPT) status as a privileged monopoly that enjoyed strong market demand and favourable state policies. Compared to other sectors in the economy, telecommunications has been one of the most centrally-planned and state-controlled industries in terms of market entry, pricing, and business organisation. In 1979, the State Council made the MPT the dominant central planner of the nation-wide postal and telecommunications development. Local postal and telecommunications enterprises were to be put under the "dual leadership" of provincial governments and the MPT, with the latter the main decision maker (Lu, 2000). With the reforms to put the local postal and telecommunications enterprises (PTEs) in a system of contractual responsibility, a vertically organised hierarchy emerged as the administrative structure of China's telecommunications. The national ministry at the top was responsible of overall planning and management of the industry. It controlled international and inter-provincial communications. It also set and enforced technical standards and formulates key policies and plans. At the provincial level, the Postal and Telecommunications Administrations (PTAs) performed a similar role within the province. Below them were hundreds of municipal and prefecture bureaux of postal and telecommunications (PTBs). Next, more than 2,000 county-level postal and telecommunications enterprises (PTEs) operated local service networks in the county capitals and extended lines into the surrounding rural areas. Below them were tens of thousands of branch offices operating exchanges at the village level. There were also many non-public branch exchanges (PBXs) owned and operated by work units and rural villages (Mueller and Tan, 1997).

The MPT system underwent a deeper revamp in 1988 amidst a major state-owned enterprise reform initiative taking place nationwide. The MPT granted its national manufacturing, construction, and purchasing departments status of separate legal entities or greater independence in financial accounting and human resource management. Meanwhile the MPT set up the Directorate General of

Telecommunications (DGT) and the Directorate General of Posts (DGP) to incorporate business enterprise functions. The DGT was later known as China Telecom, which comprised 29 provincial postal and telecommunications authorities (PTAs), all of which offered local and long-distance services through the 1990s. The PTAs in Beijing, Shanghai, and Guangdong also offered international services. The MPT itself handled regulatory matters through its Department of Policy and Regulation. The MPT's China Telecom eventually registered with the government as a corporate group in 1995.[8]

Over the years, the MPT received various financial stimuli from the state. In October 1984, the State Council stipulated a "six-point instruction" to give priority to postal and telecommunications development (Gao 1991). A policy of "three ninety-percent" was adopted:

- 90% of profit was to be retained by the MPT (in other words, the tax rate is 10%, well below the 55% tax rate for other industries);
- 90% of foreign exchange (hard currency) earnings were to be retained by the MPT; and
- 90% of central government investment was not considered as repayable loans.

In addition, PTEs and PTBs also enjoyed favourable interest rates when they borrowed from state banks. The preferential "three ninety-percent" policy provided favourable conditions for the sector's expansion until 1994 when a major fiscal- monetary reform unified corporate tax rates, simplified the tax levy structure, and made Chinese currency convertible for current account transactions.

In October 1988, Beijing announced the so-called "sixteen-character policy" for telecommunications infrastructure development (Jin, 1992). The policy was summarised by sixteen Chinese characters,[9] which outline four principles:

- Overall planning of industrial development should be unified under the MPT.

---

[8] *Yearbook of China Transportation and Communications 1996*, p. 234.
[9] In Chinese: *"tong chou guihua, tiao kuai jiehe, fen ceng fu ze, lianhe jianshe"*.

- Ministerial administration should be co-ordinated with regional authorities.
- Responsibilities should be defined and shared among different administrative levels.
- Construction of infrastructure should mobilise resources from all concerned.

Based on these principles, financing postal and telecommunications investment was largely decentralised in the late 1980s. The Seventh Five-year Plan (1986–90) stipulated that the intra-province telecommunications projects should rely mainly on local financing. Institutions or individuals should be encouraged to contribute to infrastructure investment. Those who had invested in telecommunications projects could benefit from receiving priority of being connected to the network and lower charges for telecommunications services. In the rural area, whoever invested in the infrastructure facilities could manage and operate the local exchanges (You, 1987).

An important state policy to facilitate telecommunications investment was to allow a faster pace of capital depreciation in the postal and telecommunications sector. The State Council's "six-point" instruction of 1984 promised to gradually raise the accounting capital depreciation of the postal and telecommunications sector to 7%.[10] From 1980 to 1990, the government adjusted capital depreciation rate upward three times.[11] A reform of the PTE accounting system in July 1993 again raised the capital depreciation rate.[12] In 1995, the gross fixed capital depreciation rate was as high as 16%. The capital depreciation amounted to RMB 40 billion, accounting for more than 40% of the total fixed capital investment.[13] Capital depreciation is the main source of technical

---

[10] State Council, "Instruction to the Postal and Telecommunications Management (12 October 1984)", *Yearbook of China Transportation and Communications 1986*, p. 243.
[11] *Yearbook of China Transportation and Communications 1990*, p. 271.
[12] The detailed depreciation scale is: 5–7 years for telecommunications equipment, 6–8 years for power equipment, 10–15 years for communications cables, 30–40 years for buildings (*Yearbook of China Transportation and Communications 1994*, p. 235).
[13] Wu Jichuan's interview, *Yazhou Zhoukan* (The International Chinese News Weekly), 19 May 1996, p. 58.

upgrading and transformation (TUT) investment. The higher depreciation rate in the postal and telecommunications sector led to a higher-than-average weight of TUT investment in total fixed capital investment. Thanks to the policy, the weight of TUT investment in the postal and telecommunications fixed capital investment increased from the mid-1980s to the end of the 1990s (Figure 2).

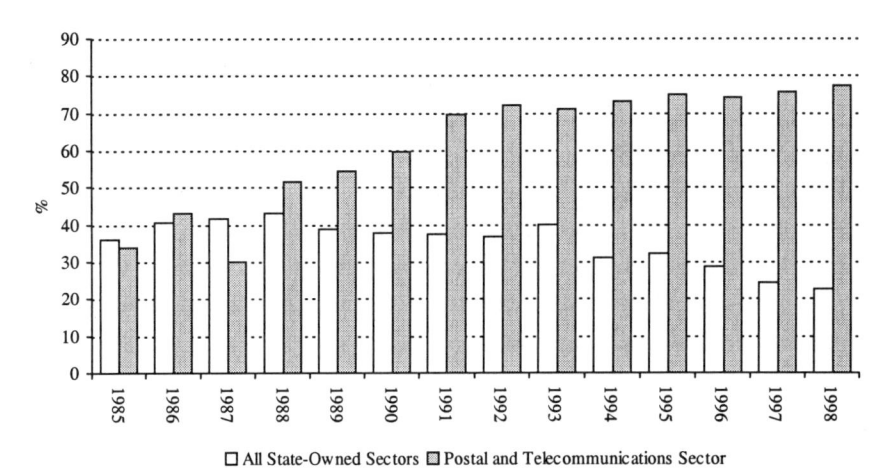

☐ All State-Owned Sectors ☐ Postal and Telecommunications Sector

Source: Yearbook of China Transportation and Communications 1991, 1996 and China Statistical Yearbook, various issues, Beijing.

Fig. 2. Weight of Technical Upgrading and Transformation Investment in Total Fixed Capital Investment, 1985–1998

To encourage telecommunications investment, import of telecommunications equipment has received preferential tariff treatments. In 1985, for instance, import tariff rate on automatic exchanges and telefax equipment was cut from 12.5% to 9%.[14] For projects involving foreign investment, import tariffs are usually exempted. In comparison, China's average tariff rate was 39.9% before 1994 and this was reduced to 23% by 1996. On top of that, domestic producers of electronic and

---

[14] Almanac of China's Foreign Economic Relations 1986, Beijing: Foreign Trade and Economic Cooperation Press, p. 129.

telecommunications equipment also enjoyed the lowest effect rates for sales-related taxes in the 1990s (Table 7). As for the "co-ordinating tax for directions of fixed capital investment" (introduced in 1991–1998 to levy on indigenous enterprises), the postal and telecommunications sector was levied a zero tax rate, which was meant for projects "urgently needed by the state".[15]

Low trade barrier has given rise to a highly competitive telecommunications equipment market, which in turn fosters the rapid growth of the telecommunications sector. The introduction of terminal equipment licensing under the MPT in 1989 largely deregulated the terminal equipment used by customers of the network.[16] As a result, telecommunications service providers can choose among competing domestic and foreign equipment suppliers to minimise their investment costs.

As China's economy expanded rapidly after implementing the open-door policy in 1979, the increased international interaction has created great demand for the transmission of information within the country. Telephone service is no longer only an administrative tool of the state, but a private good for business operation and household consumption. The customer base for phone service was quickly privatised in the late 1980s and early 1990s. In 1991, residential phones accounted for more than one third of the total phones in more than ten provinces and municipals (Hong and Qian, 1992). In 1995, more than 80% of the increased telephone exchange capacity was for residential uses.[17]

The strong demand generated fat profits for the telecom monopoly. In 1984 the MPT system received state permission to adjust its service tariff rates. During the period 1986 to 1990, the MPT made adjustments to a wide range of telecommunications service rates. Consequently, the rate of capital return in the industry increased from 9% in 1986 to 17%

---

[15] State Council, "The Provisional Regulation on the PRC's Direction-Adjustment Tax on Fixed Capital Investment" (16 April 1991).
[16] *Yearbook of China Transportation and Communications 1996*, p. 232.
[17] Wu Jichuan's interview, *Yazhou Zhoukan* (*The International Chinese News Weekly*), 19 May 1996, pp. 57–58.

Table 7. Burden of Sales-Related Taxes of Industrial Enterprises by Sector

Sector	1990 Pre-tax Profit (RMB bn)	1990 Post-tax Profit (RMB bn)	1990 Sales-Related Tax (RMB bn)	1990 Effective Rate (%)	1995 Pre-tax Profit (RMB bn)	1995 Post-tax Profit (RMB bn)	1995 Sales-Related Tax (RMB bn)	1995 Effective Rate (%)	1998 Pre-tax Profit (RMB bn)	1998 Post-tax Profit (RMB bn)	1998 Sales-Related Tax (RMB bn)	1998 Effective Rate (%)
Heavy industry	102.89	34.68	68.21	7.59	313.26	112.98	200.29	6.48	476.99	88.34	388.65	10.36
Manufacturing	38.25	17.52	20.73	5.13	110.94	42.60	68.34	4.79	233.78	40.96	192.82	10.77
Special purpose equipment	3.20	1.56	1.64	5.44	10.16	2.69	7.47	4.55	23.82	2.00	21.82	12.73
Electronic & telecommunications	4.26	2.29	1.96	3.77	18.50	11.68	6.82	2.81	50.82	21.69	29.13	6.47
Instruments, meters, cultural and official machinery	1.17	0.59	0.57	5.69	2.62	0.69	1.93	4.62	7.25	0.90	6.35	9.57
National total	194.59	55.98	138.61	8.25	505.03	163.49	341.54	6.45	749.33	145.81	603.52	9.41

Sources: *China Statistical Yearbook*, 1991, 1996, 1999, Beijing.

in 1990, much higher than the average rate of capital return for all industries. According to the World Bank, the rate of return of China's telecommunications industry in 1989, adjusted for accounting differentials, was equivalent to 12% by Western business standards (Ma, 1992). The price structure also had a clear cross-subsidising feature, with the rate of return much lower for local (intra-city) city services and higher for long distance and international services.[18] At the end of 1990, the intra-city telephone rates were widely adjusted. The ministry set a price cap according to local telephone companies' average costs with a mark-up for profit. Local telecommunications companies were authorised to set their own intra-city rates not exceeding the cap, subject to the approval of local government's price control authorities (Sun, 1992).

Under such a pricing framework, the PTEs faced an incentive structure that strongly encouraged business expansion. All revenues from local (intra-city) telephone services were kept by the PTEs. Their shares of revenues from inter-regional services were determined by unified national accounting rates and a regional cost coefficient. On top of that, they retained 20% of the increased inter-regional operation revenue over the previous year's basis. For the PTE employees and managers, the effective way to increase their wage fund was to increase the output/revenue of the enterprise and the MPT's national network by generating more telecommunications traffic. As service prices and tariffs for long distance telecommunications were set by the MPT and local rates and installation charges were capped, revenue maximisation was equivalent to output maximisation. Therefore the PTEs had strong incentives to increase revenue through expanding quantity of sales (Lu, 2000).

Before the mid-1990s, given the low teledensity, strong and growing demand, and infrastructure bottleneck, China's telecommunications market had been a supply-constrained one. The PTEs had no alternative but to make all-out efforts to increase their supply capacity by improving

---

[18] An MPT source disclosed that in 1993 the profit margin on local service was only 2 to 3%, while the margin on long distance calls was 25% and on international calls, 75% (Mueller and Tan, 1997, p. 41).

local telecommunications infrastructure. To meet the fast-growing demand and overcome fund shortage in telecommunications infrastructure investment, the central government authorised PTAs to collect installation fees within ranges set by the MPT in 1980. For commercial phone lines, the installation fee ranged between RMB 1,000 to RMB 2,000 per terminal. For residential users, the charge was between RMB 300 to RMB 500.[19] In 1990 the MPT adjusted its guidelines for telephone installation fees. The installation fee charges was then based on line connection costs. The decision making regarding installation charges was decentralised to the local level. In the early 1990s, the installation charges varied from around RMB 2,000 to more than RMB 5,000 per line (Liu, 1992). In comparison, in 1990, the average annual wage and per capita gross domestic product (GDP) were only RMB 2,140 and RMB 1,622 respectively. These figures indicate that, if an average worker wanted to subscribe a telephone line, he had to work 1 to 2.5 years just to pay the installation charge. Relative to per capita income, such an installation charge was the highest in the world.

In Table 8 we can observe that investment in the postal and telecommunications sector increased by leaps and bounds in the decade after 1984.[20] The growth was more spectacular in the first half of the 1990s. Fixed capital investment in the sector during the Eighth Five-year Plan period (1991–1995) was 11 times more than in the Seventh Five-year Plan period (1986–1990) (Wu, 1996). According to the MPT, during the first half of the 1990s, the investment in telecommunications infrastructure was mainly financed through three sources. One was the installation fee collected from the users, which accounted for 40% of the capital. The second came from domestic and foreign government loans, accounting for about 30% of the total capital. The remaining 30% came from PTE's profits and capital depreciation.[21]

---

[19] Directive issued by Ministry of Finance, the MPT, and State Bureau of Price On Urban Telephone Installation Fees (June 1980), in *Yearbook of China Transportation and Communications 1986*, pp. 344–345.

[20] The investment in telecommunications accounts for about 80% of the total fixed capital investment in the postal and telecommunications sector.

[21] *Lianhe Zaobao* (United Mornings, Singapore), 8 April 1994, p. 23.

Table 8. Fixed Capital Investment in Telecommunications Sector

Year	Fixed Capital Investment Billion RMB	% Change
1985	1.34	
1986	1.71	27.27
1987	2.14	25.29
1988	2.66	24.39
1989	4.01	50.60
1990	4.92	22.62
1991	6.89	40.09
1992	13.71	99.03
1993	35.30	157.52
1994	69.41	96.63
1995	85.60	23.33
1996	91.08	6.40
1997	105.60	15.93
1998	150.07	42.12
1999	151.81	1.15
2000	205.40	28.00

Sources: *China Statistical Yearbook* and *Yearbook of China Transportation and Communications*, various issues, Beijing. Ministry of Information Industry web site, http://www.mii.gov.cn/.

2. INTRODUCTION OF COMPETITION SINCE 1993

Despite the MPT's spectacular success promoting growth of the telecom industry, China nevertheless moved on to dismantle its monopoly and to introduce competition in the telecommunications market. In 1993 the State Council formally deregulated the paging service market and the VSAT communications by authorising the MPT to license these service suppliers.[22] By the end of 1995, the MPT had licensed 2,136

[22] State Council, "Approval of the MPT's Proposal to Enforce Regulation of Telecommunications Service Market (3 August 1993)", in *Yearbook of China Transportation and Communications 1994*, pp. 468–469.

paging service suppliers and 68 inter-province telecommunications service providers.[23] A landmark event occurred in December 1993 when the State Council decided to award a basic telecommunications licence to China United Telecommunications Corporation (or Unicom).[24] China Unicom was set up by the Ministry of Electronic Industries, the Ministry of Railways, the Ministry of Electric Power, and 13 major state-owned companies. The carrier intended to compete with the MPT in the long-distance and international services market. Meanwhile, another player, Jitong Communications Co. Ltd. (Beijing), entered the scene. It was a VAN (value-added network) operator set up by the State Economic and Trade Commission, aiming to build a nation-wide backbone linking the networks belonging to government ministries, universities, and research and state-owned organisations. It also was supposed to offer VAN services to government departments and the private sector. Both new players are shareholder-based but largely state-owned and state-controlled. Since then, China Telecom, the former MPT-controlled monopoly, has gradually lost its grip over the nation's huge telecommunications market and eventually succumbed to its fate of divestiture. A number of political-economic factors are behind these developments, as detailed below.

2.1 Driving Forces

The year 1992 was a turning point in China's economic development and market-oriented reform. In spring that year, Deng Xiaoping, China's late paramount leader, made a tour to several cities in South China during which he called on the new generation of leaders to speed up economic reform and make the economy more open to the world. Answering Deng's call, the Chinese Communist Party's 14th National Assembly (held in October 1992) formally adopted "a socialist market economy with Chinese characteristics" as the goal model of reform. This marked the beginning of a series of centrally initiated reforms to usher

---

[23] *Yearbook of China Transportation and Communications 1996*, pp. 231–232.
[24] The MPT, "Approval of China United Telecom's Scope of Business (14 April 1994)", in *Yearbook of China Transportation and Communications 1995*, p. 512.

in a modern market economy for China. The reform package implemented in 1994–95 covered the fiscal-taxation system, money and banking, and foreign exchange management. The central and the local governments made concerted efforts to attract foreign direct investment by offering low-priced land, quality infrastructure, tax concessions, and improved public services. Since 1993, China has been the world's second largest host country for foreign capital inflow, next only to the US. During the 1990s, China sucked in about half of all foreign direct investment that went to the developing economies. Thanks to these reforms, China's GDP grew at an annual rate of 11.9% and its investment at 14.1% during 1990–97, much higher than the rates for low and middle income economies in the same period (2.8% and 7.2% respectively).[25]

In this backdrop of market-oriented reform, the centrally planned hierarchy of the MPT monopoly was inevitably challenged. By then, the MPT was a traditional state-owned and state-controlled monopoly, which combined three functions under its umbrella: policy/regulation, service provision, and equipment manufacturing. All these major functions were challenged by other players in the sector. After China embarked on market-oriented reforms, many non-public networks (vis-à-vis the MPT-managed public network) were established by different government ministries, such as Ministry of Railways and Ministry of Electrical Power. The capacity of these networks was no inferior to that of the MPT-managed public network (He, 1994), posing a real threat to the latter's monopoly. As pointed out by Tan (1994):

> Big private operators and manufacturing ministries often confront the MPT in the arenas of policy and regulation. ... (T)hey have the same, or even stronger, levels of representation in the State Council, ... Large users and local governments also tend to favour a more liberal policy towards public service and they are dissatisfied with the MPT's monopoly. At the equipment end, Ministry of Electronic Industry (MEI) and some user ministries are the traditional competitors (to the MPT) ... (Tan, 1994, p. 175)

[25] World Bank, *World Development Report 1998/99*, Table 11, pp. 210–211.

Through the 1980s to the 1990s, rapid technological progress in telecommunications technology was moving the industry in many countries towards a more competitive and de-regulated regime. Telecommunications used to be a classical case of an industry with "natural monopoly" features. Economic efficiency brought about by economies of scale created formidable entry barriers for any firms intending to compete against the incumbent monopoly. Cross-subsidisation between profitable and unprofitable segments of the market was viewed as a necessary "sin" with the provision of "universal service" to the public. New communications technology has made such an industrial structure unsustainable and obsolete. Since the early 1980s, in developed countries like the United States, Britain and Australia, competition introduced by the regulatory revamp in the telecommunications market has greatly boosted the sector's growth and improved customer service.[26]

In China, this global trend lent strong support to challengers of the MPT monopoly. To the top Chinese leaders, the application of information technology (IT) is indispensable to modernising the economy and reviving science, technology and education. Aware of the rationale behind the global trend of market opening in the telecommunications industry, the Chinese leaders could not afford to allow China's IT industry to be constrained by inefficiency, poor service and high prices, which were associated with the MPT monopoly.

However, the central planning mindset has nurtured what Mueller and Tan (1997, pp. 56–58) called a "technocratic approach" to IT development. This approach takes technology as a paramount factor in economic development, as opposed to the "market-oriented approach", which sees market forces as the means to economic development. The Chinese leaders with technocratic views see the application of information technology as crucial to their attempts to bring the economy under some kind of systematic central control. They also view information networks as the equivalent of price signals, profit incentives, and legal structures that promote co-ordination in a market economy. These views

---

[26] *China Daily* (Hong Kong), 10 June 1999.

have prompted them to maintain central control over telecommunications network building while introducing competition in a prudent and gradualist manner.

In 1994, the State Council announced the "eight policies of telecommunications development",[27] which outlined China's strategies of developing the sector:

1. Giving priority and policy support to the telecommunications sector.
2. Central planning of network and service development.
3. Focusing on the construction of a unified nation-wide public network.
4. Licensing value-added and mobile telecommunications services; deregulating the equipment manufacturing market; conducting open tender for network projects.
5. Independent accounting and hierarchical administration for the PTEs; linking employee rewards to enterprise performance.
6. Supporting the PTEs to raise capital from various ways and collect installation fees.
7. Promoting network modernisation and human resource development.
8. Importing foreign equipment and technology and utilising foreign fund sources.

These policies reflect a gradualist and rather conservative approach to market opening. Within the MPT, a representative view towards competition and monopoly in the industry is based on the thesis of a "post-telephony era". According to this thesis, telecommunications development must go through two stages. The first was the telephony era, during which infrastructure building raised teledensity to meet the need of universal service for basic telephony. The second is the post-telephony era, featured by pluralised and more advanced communications services, which add values to the public network built in the first stage. In the first era, the industry had the features of a natural monopoly with strong economies of scale and therefore would be best managed in a centrally planned monopoly system. A competitive market would be efficiency-enhancing and conducive to technological progress only in

---

[27] *Yearbook of China Transportation and Communications 1995*, p. 225.

the post-telephony era. Therefore, in the case of China, the rapid build-up of telecommunications infrastructure could only be carried out under a state-planned, monopolist policy, especially during the industry's take-off period. With the basic public network in place, China quickly entered a transitional period between the two eras in the mid-1990s. In this period, state monopoly and central planning were still better able to raise teledensity and provide basic telephony to the population; as for the markets for plural and advanced services, it was better that they be made open to competition gradually (Jing, 1999).

2.2 Mergers and Divestiture

The birth of China Unicom in 1993 was a result of high-level "lobbying" by a political coalition formed by the Ministry of Electronics Industry, the Ministry of Electric Power, and the Ministry of Railways (He, 1994 and Tan, 1994). The State Council adopted the proposal to issue the licence to China Unicom while reaffirming the leading role of the MPT in the sector and its functions of network supervision and regulation. The emergence of China Unicom and other new players in the industry was "a product more of political power than of market economy. The competition arising from it was conducted in the absence of a developed legal framework" (Jing 1999, p. 7). As noted by Mueller and Tan (1997), the MPT's primary role in the telecommunications sector was severely circumvented since the new players like China Unicom had a power base outside the MPT that placed them "almost at the same level in deliberations regarding the sector's future structure". To resolve the inevitable disagreements among the ministerial stakeholders, in 1994 the State Council created a National Joint Conference on State Economic Informatization (JCSEI), chaired by Zou Jiahua, the then vice premier.

This institutional structure, however, failed to create effective competition in the sector. An original purpose to license China Unicom was to let the new company unite the domestic private networks and use their capacity to compete with China Telecom. China Unicom, however, was not able to fulfil the expectation largely due to its lack of expertise in telecommunications management and political clout to "unite" different stakeholders. In the first four years after the launch of Unicom, the company mainly focused itself on the mobile communications market, capturing only 3.5% of the market share, compared to China Telecom's 96.5% share (Jing, 1999). Meanwhile the temporary "task force" nature of JCSEI prevented it from performing the role of an effective regulatory authority.

After a few years of tussle for power, at the 9th National People's Congress (NPC) convened in March 1998, the Ministry of Information Industry (MII) was formed through the merger of the former MPT, the former MEI, and the Network Department of the former Ministry of Radio, Film and Television. This was a marriage between odd partners since the MPT and MEI had been rivals all these years. In addition, the new ministry took over information and network administration, handled previously by the former JCSEI and the former State Council's Commission on Radio Frequencies, the former MRFT, China Corporation of Aerospace Industry, and China Corporation of Aviation Industry. Wu Jichuan, the former Minister of Post and Telecommunications, took over the helm of the new ministry. A major objective of this reform was to fulfil the separation of the regulatory and commercial functions in the telecommunication sector so that competition can be developed under the supervision of a single regulatory authority, the MII.[28]

Since its inception, the MII has successfully revamped the former MPT's postal and telecommunications businesses. By early 1999, almost all assets and employees of the former PTEs under the MPT had been reallocated to the two separate business entities, China Post and China Telecom. After separation from the postal business, China Telecom had about RMB 600 billion worth of assets.[29] The next task for MII was to divest the former monopoly into smaller entities so that effective competition can prevail. At first, some scholars in Beijing proposed a "horizontal divestiture" of China Telecom into seven regional "baby CTs" following the US model of the AT&T divestiture in 1983. With

---

[28] "The Plan to Define the Functions, Internal Organizations, and Personnel Quotas of the MII", *Youdian Jingji (P&T Economy)*, 1998 no. 3, Volume 44, pp. 2–4.
[29] Interview with officials and scholars of Shanghai Institute of P&T Economy, 20 June 1999.

fierce opposition from the MII, the proposal was shot down after an official delegation that visited the US to investigate the background of AT&T divestiture reported that mergers, rather than divestiture, had become the trend in the industry. It also reported that even officials of the US Federal Commission of Communications (FCC) did not consider the AT&T divestiture model appropriate for China. After that, the MII won the State Council approval for its "vertical divestiture" plan. Based on this plan, the MII started in December 1999 to divest China Telecom into four separate companies serving different functions, namely, fixed-line, mobile, paging and satellite operations. In fact, before its formal divestiture, China Telecom had already been operating under the framework of four business lines in 1999 (Wu, 2000). These were the China Telecom Group Corp. (with an asset value of about RMB 400 billion), the China Mobile Telecom Group Corp. (with an asset value of RMB 180 billion), the China Paging Telecom Group Corp. (with an asset value of RMB 13 billion) and the China Satellite Telecom Group Corp (with an asset value less than RMB 1 billion). [30]

Meanwhile, the MII also tried to position China Unicom as an effective competitor to China Telecom and China Mobile. First, the MII made itself the largest stakeholder of China Unicom by transferring the assets of China Telecom's CDMA Great Wall Network and Guoxin Paging Company paging branch to Unicom in spring 1999.[31] Second, it revamped the management of China Unicom by replacing its executives with experienced ones from China Telecom. The staff exchange and asset transfer are said to have contributed to an improved business relationship between the two rival carriers.[32] Third, the MII allowed China Unicomto expand into mobile and Internet telephony. In particular, China Mobile is to retain only the GSM (global system for mobile communications) business and the analogue TACS (Total Access Communications System) network while leaving the whole CDMA (code

---

[30] Interview with officials and scholars of Shanghai Institute of P&T Economy, 20 June 1999.
[31] *China Online News*, 4 May 1999.
[32] Interview with officials and scholars of Shanghai Institute of P&T Economy, 20 June 1999, 8 July 2000.

division multiple access) market to Unicom (Li, 2000, p. 17). Last but not least, China Unicom got the MII's blessing to launch an IPO (initial public offering) to raise equity funds. It went "public" by launching IPO in the Hong Kong and New York stock exchanges in June 2000 with a plan to raise at least US$1 billion, but ended up with a listed market value close to US$ 5 billion.[33] Backed by the MII, in March 2000 China Unicom succeeded in procuring loans of RMB 10 billion and RMB 1.6 billion from the China Development Bank and the Bank of China respectively to finance its construction of mobile and digital communication networks.[34]

After signing an interconnection agreement with China Telecom in January 2000, China Unicom subsequently unveiled detailed plans to capture more than 30% of the mainland's fast-growing mobile-phone and Internet-related services markets in the next five years. It plans to boost the capacity of its CDMA mobile-phone network to 60 million lines by 2005, aiming to attract 45 million subscribers, with the network covering most of the country. It believes that the capacity of its GSM network will by then reach 15 million lines and attract 13 million subscribers, with the network covering the prosperous eastern and middle parts of the country.[35] China Unicom also received a boost in its efforts to compete against China Telecom when it obtained the government's approval to enter the international call market (IDD) in March 2000, thus effectively breaking the China Telecom monopoly in this lucrative market.[36]

Along with the divestiture of China Telecom and the beefing up of China Unicom, the telecom sector in 1999 and 2000 witnessed a series of reforms that featured opening, tariff readjustment and the formulation and completion of telecom legislation. The expensive installation fees have been cut. High rates for long distance and international calls have

[33] *South China Morning Post* (Hong Kong), 15 April 2000; Lin (2000); and *ChinaOnline News* 21 June 2000.
[34] *China Daily* (Hong Kong), 23 March 2000; *South China Morning Post* (Hong Kong), 1 April 2000.
[35] *South China Morning Post* (Hong Kong), 15 December 1999.
[36] *South China Morning Post* (Hong Kong), 11 March 2000.

been slashed. At the provincial level, however, the restructuring of the old PTA-PTB hierarchy had not been fulfilled by the early 2000 (Wu, 2000). Since its inception, the MII has also been the agency authorised to review, approve and grant operation licences to Internet Service Providers (ISPs). In 1999, the MII and its provincial PTAs approved more than 300 ISPs, among which 53 were approved for nationwide services.[37] With the blessing of the MII, China Telecom launched a nationwide Internet Protocol (IP) telephony trial in May 1999 in partnership with state-owned carriers Jitong Communications and China Unicom. After nearly a year of trial, in April 2000, the MII formally issued 4 IP telephony licences to China Telecom, China Unicom, Jitong Communications and China Netcom.[38]

Since early 1999, the MII has openly promoted the development strategy of "breaking up the monopoly and introducing competition" (*pochu longduan, yinru jingzheng*). The strategy seeks to rely on the market to improve telecommunications services and accelerate technological progress to prepare the sector for global competition.[39] More specifically, the basic idea behind the recent MII-initiated reforms consists of the following points (Jing, 2000, p. 6)[40]:

- Emphasising unified planning and co-ordination in developing the basic network to avoid repeated building up of expensive networks;
- Opening the service business to fair competition;
- Allowing access to the backbone network, which is to be kept under unified investment and management;
- Imposing strict regulation on basic services while having looser regulation on value-added services;
- Strengthening the role of dominant state carriers when opening the market to more competition; and

---

[37] Xinhua News Agency, 16 February 2000, http://www.xinhua.org/chanjing.
[38] MII's announcement on the opening of IP telephony market, 24 March 2000 (MII web site news, 30 March 2000, http://www.mii.gov.cn.)
[39] *Hong Kong Economic Journal* (Hong Kong), 10 December 1999.
[40] Also from Interview with officials and scholars of Shanghai Institute of P&T Economy, 8 July 2000.

- Continuing policies to favour telecommunications network development in rural and underdeveloped areas.

2.3 Issues and Challenges

There are several issues in the MII's market opening agenda. First, the MII appears to be ensuring that the service provided by other carriers simply complements that of China Telecom and is not in direct competition. The fear is that the vertical divestiture of China Telecom has only split the telecommunications market into four highly monopolistic segments and created only limited competition. The China Telecom-China Mobile business alliance continues to dominate the market for basic long-distance and mobile services. China Telecom still has about 99% share of the fixed line market. Its main competitor, China Unicom, has basic service network in only three cities, Tianjin, Chongqing and Chengdu. The presence of these new carriers may not signify genuine deregulation and competition, since it is the MII, not market demand, that directs their moves (Hsu, 1999). The historical links between the MII and the major state-owned carriers cast doubts on the MII's capacity as an impartial regulator. Notwithstanding these reservations, it seems that real competition has emerged in the mobile telephony and long distance services. In 1999, China Unicom had only 5% of the mobile phone market but it has been able to increase its share to 12% after it received asset and personnel transfer from China Telecom in early 2000.[41] The launch of IP telephony and Unicom's entry into the IDD call service in early 2000 marked the beginning of a more competitive market structure in the long-distance market. China's telecommunications sector has entered an era of competition (Table 9).

Other factors may threaten the MII's authority to control the pace of market opening. The ministry's endeavour to avoid repeated construction of basic networks has encountered political resistance. A plan to build a unified broadband network for Shanghai's Pudong area was challenged by the entry of a new operator, China Netcom

---

[41] *China Daily* (Hong Kong), 10 June 1999; 23 March 2000.

Table 9. Market Shares in the First Half of 2000

	China Telecom	China Mobile	Unicom	Jitong	Netcom
Total telephone user base	68.1	25.8	6		
Long-distance optical cable	86.6		13.4		
Mobile phone subscription		81.2	18.8		
IP telephony	54.4		31.2	12.3	2.1

Sources: Zhongguo Jingji Shibao (China Economic Times), 20 October 2000.

Corporation (CNC), in April 1999. China Netcom, which has Jiang Mianhong, son of Chinese President Jiang Zemin on its board, is a joint venture among the Chinese Academy of Sciences (with Junior Jiang as its vice dean), the Shanghai Municipal Government, State Administration of Radio, Film and Television (SARFT) and Ministry of Railways. It was created to provide high-speed voice and data service in 15 cities, and to connect with 70 countries.[42] To do so, it planned to build its own broadband network. Following Netcom's footsteps, Jitong Corp. also announced its plan to develop its own broadband network. The State Administration of Radio, Film and Television (SARFT) vowed to move into the telecom business by setting up "China Cable Television Networks Corp" and taking advantage of its national cable business networks. Netcom's ambitious project, interestingly enough, was not endorsed by the MII, but by the State Development Planning Commission under the State Council.[43] The political clout of these new players threatens to circumvent the MII's authority over basic network development.

The absence of a Telecommunications Law leaves the MII regulators vulnerable to political manoeuvres. Since its inception, the MII has experienced a difficult time in pushing through a Telecommunications

---

[42] *South China Morning Post* (Hong Kong), 15 December 1999.
[43] *China Telecom Weekly News* (Boston), May 17–21, 1999.

Act or Telecommunications Law in China's National People's Congress as a legal framework for regulating the industry, although talks about such an Act or Law have been around for years. The delay has been due to conflicting interests and rapid changes in the central government's policy. A preliminary regulatory framework was not in place until the State Council promulgated the Telecommunications Regulations of the People's Republic of China in September 2000. In coping with these manoeuvres, a strategy taken by the MII appears to be seeking reconciliation between different interests with the resources at its dispose. Following its successful revamp of China Unicom, the MII played a paramount role in arranging for China Telecom and China Netcom to sign a "Strategic Co-operation Agreement" in August 2000.[44] Whether this agreement will boost the MII's authority over unified planning for network investment still remains to be seen.

A related issue is the nature of the major state-owned telecom carriers. It is still not clear whether these carriers will be allowed to operate fully on a profit-maximising basis. According to Wu Jichuan, Minister of Information Industry, much work remain to be done to provide more Chinese with access to basic telecommunications services. By 1999, nearly a quarter of administrative villages still had no access to plain-old telephone lines.[45] Huge disparity in telecommunications development exists among different regions (Tables 10 and 11). Even areas with the highest telephone penetration rate (such as Shanghai with 29%) still need to work hard to catch up with the developed countries. In such a situation, will the dominant carriers be responsible to ensure universal service to residents in rural and underdeveloped regions? If so, some extent of cross-subsidisation in their tariff structure would be inevitable. This structure, however, is vulnerable to new entrants who are likely to "cream-skim" the lucrative part of the market. The impact of limited competition since 1994 and, in particular, China Telecom's divestiture process that went through the year 1999, had reportedly severely affected the planned programme of telecom infrastructure construction. Telecom

---

[44] The MII web site news, 10 August 2000, http://www.mii.gov.cn.
[45] *China Daily* (Hong Kong), 17 October 1999.

Table 10. China's Fixed Line Penetration Rate by Region, 1998

Area	Population (million)	Fixed-line subscribers (million)	Fixed-line Penetration (%)
National	1,248.1	87.40	7.00
Municipalities			
Shanghai	14.64	4.31	29.45
Beijing	12.46	3.13	25.14
Tianjin	9.57	1.66	17.35
Provinces			
Guangdong	71.43	9.58	13.42
Liaoning	41.57	4.77	11.47
Zhejiang	44.56	5.02	11.27
Fujian	32.99	3.47	10.53
Jiangsu	71.82	7.50	10.44
Jilin	26.44	2.42	9.14
Heilongjiang	37.73	3.41	9.04
Ningxia	5.38	0.37	6.96
Hubei	59.07	4.05	6.86
Xinjiang	17.47	1.19	6.83
Hebei	65.69	4.03	6.14
Shandong	88.38	5.26	5.95
Hainan	7.53	0.43	5.76
Inner Mongolia	23.45	1.25	5.35
Shaanxi	35.96	1.82	5.06
Chongqing	30.60	1.54	5.04
Shanxi	31.72	1.55	4.89
Hunan	65.02	3.16	4.85
Henan	93.15	4.43	4.75
Jiangxi	41.91	1.93	4.59
Yunnan	41.44	1.88	4.54
Anhui	61.84	2.74	4.44
Qinghai	5.03	0.22	4.43
Gansu	25.19	0.95	3.75
Guangxi	46.75	1.67	3.57
Sichuan	84.93	2.80	3.29
Tibet	2.52	0.06	2.35
Guizhou	36.58	0.80	2.18

Source: China Statistical Yearbook 1999, Beijing.

Table 11. China's Mobile Penetration Rate by Region, 1998

Area	Population (million)	Mobile phone subscribers (million)	Mobile Penetration (%)
National	**1,248.1**	**23.84**	**1.91**
Municipalities			
Shanghai	14.64	1.26	8.60
Beijing	12.46	0.99	7.98
Tianjin	9.57	0.48	4.97
Provinces			
Guangdong	71.43	3.63	5.08
Fujian	32.99	1.46	4.44
Zhejiang	44.56	1.51	3.38
Liaoning	41.57	1.29	3.10
Heilongjiang	37.73	1.02	2.79
Hainan	7.53	0.19	2.59
Jilin	26.44	0.60	2.27
Jiangsu	71.82	1.41	1.95
Shandong	88.38	1.49	1.69
Hubei	59.07	0.83	1.41
Hebei	65.69	0.92	1.39
Shanxi	31.72	0.42	1.33
Henan	93.15	1.19	1.27
Chongqing	30.60	0.37	1.22
Hunan	65.02	0.75	1.16
Inner Mongolia	23.45	0.26	1.10
Guangxi	46.75	0.51	1.09
Yunnan	41.44	0.44	1.05
Jiangxi	41.91	0.43	1.03
Shaanxi	35.96	0.37	1.03
Sichuan	84.93	0.85	1.00
Anhui	61.84	0.58	0.94
Ningxia	5.38	0.05	0.93
Xinjiang	17.47	0.16	0.90
Qinghai	5.03	0.04	0.70
Gansu	25.19	0.14	0.56
Guizhou	36.58	0.19	0.51
Tibet	2.52	0.01	0.46

Source: China Statistical Yearbook 1999, Beijing.

service reforms were also reported to have slowed some foreign telecom-equipment suppliers' business in the mainland market that year.[46] Without solving this issue, it would be hard to reverse the downward trend of fixed capital investment growth in the telecommunications sector since the late 1990s (Figure 3).

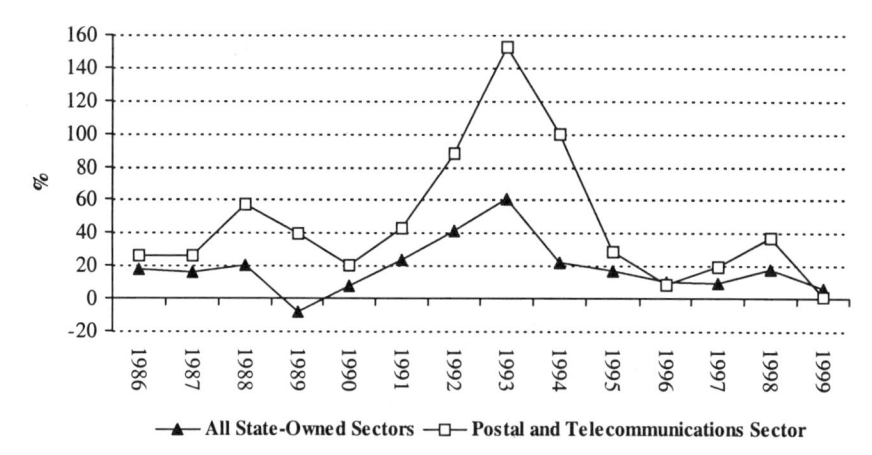

―▲― All State-Owned Sectors ―□― Postal and Telecommunications Sector

Sources: *China Statistical Yearbook* (various years) and *Yearbook* (various years); the 1999 figure is from Ministry of Information Industry web site, http://www.mii.gov.cn/.

Fig. 3. Growth Rate of Fixed Capital Investment, 1986–1999

To tackle the issue of raising equity funds, the MII has recently accelerated the pace of arranging for the major Chinese carriers to tap the Hong Kong and other overseas capital markets. In May 2000, the MII arranged for China Mobile Communications (Group) Corp. to become the 100% owner of China Telecom (Hong Kong) Co. by acquiring at no cost the 43% stake in CT (HK) from China Telecom Group Corp. After changing its name to China Mobile (HK) Co., the giant listed company in Hong Kong's stock market started preparations to purchase seven of the mainland's biggest provincial and municipal mobile-phone networks from its state-owned parent, China Mobile

[46] *South China Morning Post* (Hong Kong), 4 October 1999.

Communications Corp. The regions covered are Beijing, Tianjin, Shanghai, Liaoning, Hebei, Shandong and Guangxi.[47] This acquisition was backed by Vodafone, who agreed in October 2000 to invest US$2.5 billion to help fund the US$34 billion deal. With this investment, Vodafone would gain a 2.6% stake in China Mobile's current US$96 billion market value.[48] The MII's support of China Unicom's launching of a record US$5 billion IPO in Hong Kong and New York in June 2000 was another success of utilising overseas capital for China's telecommunications development. Following China Unicom, Netcom and Jitong also revealed plans to go public in Hong Kong and other overseas markets. Meanwhile the MII has plans to restructure the local branches of China Telecom in nine coastal cities into independent "public corporations" for IPO launches in Hong Kong and other overseas stock markets. It also proposed to apply the Build-Operate-Transfer (BOT) model to encourage investment in telecommunications infrastructure in China's inland regions.[49]

Public listing of the state-owned carriers has opened the possibility of privatisation of these firms in the long run. In the more immediate future, the issue is whether private companies will be allowed to enter the telecommunications service market. Currently, the value-added businesses, including the Internet Service Provider business, have already been opened to non-state firms. Paging service, which used to be in the category of basic service, is now put in the category of value-added service. New and private players are expected to enter this market soon (Wu, 2000).

Finally, there is the challenge of China's imminent entry into the World Trade Organisation (WTO). With the completion of the WTO entry deal, foreign competitors are now virtually at the doorstep. Currently telephone penetration remains far lower in China than in the United States, which has a population of about 280 million compared to China's

---

[47] *China Online News*, "China Telecom (HK) Changes Name to China Mobile", 22 May 2000, http://www.chinaonline.com.

[48] "Vodafone buys into China Mobile", *Straits Times* (Singapore), 5 October 2000.

[49] Interview with officials and scholars of Shanghai Institute of P&T Economy, 8 July 2000.

1.4 billion. By 1997, both the business volume and revenue of China's telecom sector exceeded RMB150 billion, ranking 12th in the world.[50] China Telecom, the country's dominant carrier, ranked 10th among the 50 leading world telecoms operators in 1998, with a total sales of US $24.16 billion.[51] The figures suggest that China's telephone market has far more potential than the US market. With its still low teledensity, a rapidly growing economy and a huge population, China is expected to become the No. 1 battleground for the world's major telecom players after its accession to the WTO.

3. Entering the WTO Era

After a decade-long negotiation, the US and China finally signed the Sino-US WTO accord in November 1999. To reach the final deal, China made significant concessions to a series of market opening terms. Those related to the telecommunications sector will pave the way for foreign investors to take controlling stakes in China's telecommunications service provision and also open the door for investments in the Internet sector (Table 12).

3.1 Implications of Openness

Policy changes in the telecom industry will focus on allowing foreign investment in the telecommunications service sector, as well as the popular mobile communications and Internet access businesses. In April 1999, in his failed bid to wrap up a deal with the US, Chinese premier Zhu Rongji offered up to 49% foreign ownership of all services and 51% foreign ownership for value-added and paging services within four years. The November deal is a small step backward, nonetheless, foreign firms are allowed to hold 49% stake in Sino-foreign ventures upon Beijing's accession into WTO and increase this to 50% after two years. As for the

---

[50] *Beijing Review* (Beijing), 21 June 1999.
[51] *China Daily* (Hong Kong), 14 October 1999.

Table 12. China's WTO Agreement Terms with the US

Sector	Maximum % of Foreign Ownership Allowed	Geographical Limitations
Value-added and Paging Services		
Upon accession	30%	Beijing, Shanghai and Guangzhou
1 year after accession	49%	Beijing, Shanghai, Guangzhou and 14 other cities –Chengdu, Chongqing, Dalian, Fuzhou, Hangzhou, Nanjing, Ningbo, Qingdao, Shenyang, Shenzhen, Xiamen, Xian, Taiyuan and Wuhan
2 years after accession	50%	Nationwide
Mobile Services		
1 year after accession	25%	Beijing, Shanghai and Guangzhou
3 years after accession	35%	Beijing, Shanghai, Guangzhou and the 14 cities
5 years after accession	49%	Nationwide
Fixed Line Services		
3 years after accession	25%	Beijing, Shanghai and Guangzhou
5 years after accession	35%	Beijing, Shanghai, Guangzhou and the 14 cities
6 years after accession	49%	Nationwide
Internet Content Providers (ICP)		
Upon accession	30%	Beijing, Shanghai and Guangzhou
1 year after accession	49%	Beijing, Shanghai, Guangzhou and the 14 cities
2 years after accession	50%	Nationwide
Internet Service Providers (ISP)		
3 years after accession	25%	Beijing, Shanghai and Guangzhou
5 years after accession	35%	Beijing, Shanghai, Guangzhou and the 14 cities
6 years after accession	49%	Nationwide

Sources: The Economist Intelligence Unit, *Telecoms & Wireless Asia*, 14 January 2000.

telecommunications equipment market, China's entry to the WTO is not expected to cause a drastic impact, because the country is already one of the most competitive markets in the world for telecommunications equipment, open to foreign players as well as domestic manufacturers.[52]

Until recently, China had upheld a policy prohibiting foreign equity investment in the telecommunications service sector. On May 25, 1993, the MPT announced that "no organisation, enterprise or individual outside China may engage in the management of China's broadcasting networks, special wire or wireless services, or become a shareholder in a telecommunications business."[53] Until China's accession to the WTO, most foreign participants would continue to be prohibited from holding a direct equity position in Chinese telecom service companies. They have also been barred from having any operational control without the approval of the State Council, which has been resolute in refusing to do so. As a result, foreign involvement has been limited to arm's length agreements, wherein foreign companies discreetly provide investment in exchange for a share of operating revenue (Hsu, 1999).

Investors had a short-lived optimism in 1998 when China Unicom, in need of capital, roped in 45 foreign companies to take US$1.4 billion worth of indirect equity stakes in its operations through the so-called "China-China-Foreign" (CCF) joint ventures. Under the "CCF" model, a "China-Foreign" joint venture is formed between a local company and a foreign firm, routing the funds through the joint venture into the network operator (e.g. Unicom). The deal opened a loophole in regulations barring foreign companies from operating a domestic telephone network and allowed them to earn money officially on installation and "consulting" fees. De facto foreign equity could reach as high as 90%. By the end of that year, however, the MII officials branded the joint ventures "irregular" and accused them of reaping profits at the expense of government programmes designed to subsidise telephone service in poor and remote regions.[54] Consequently in 1999 the MII

---

[52] *South China Morning Post* (Hong Kong), 20 December 1999.
[53] *Beijing Review* (Beijing), 14–20 June 1993.
[54] Reuters news, *Business Times* (Singapore), 2 December 1998.

forced China Unicom to wind up its initial commercial agreements with foreign investors in these projects. The foreign companies, which included Deutsche Telekom, France Telecom, Spring, NTT International and Bell Canada, had to re-negotiate to retrieve their investments.[55] A glaring point during this period was AT&T's winning of a joint venture project to build and operate an IP network in Pudong, Shanghai, in May 1999: the first time a foreign operator had been allowed to offer telecom services in its own right.

The Sino-US WTO accord of November 1999 is China's first official commitment to the opening of its telecommunications sector, both to the scope of services and to direct investment in the telecom business. Signing the WTO deal binds China to the principles outlined in the WTO Basic Telecom Agreement of 1997, which stipulates that a member country must implement regulations that deter anti-competitive practices. This includes separating the roles of the telecom regulator from the dominant operator, establishing an interconnection right and instituting a telecom law.[56] Through these commitments, China will become a member of the Basic Telecommunications Agreement. Specific commitments include: [57]

1. **Regulatory Principles** — China has to implement the pro-competitive regulatory principles embodied in the Basic Telecommunications Agreement (including cost-based pricing, interconnection rights and independent regulatory authority) and to follow technology-neutral scheduling, which means foreign suppliers can use any technology they choose to provide telecom services. As a result, new technology could be introduced in China "at the same

---

[55] *Far Eastern Economic Review* (Hong Kong), 30 September 1999.
[56] The Economist Intelligence Unit (London), *Telecoms & Wireless Asia*, 14 January 2000.
[57] *China Daily Business Weekly* (Hong Kong), 21–27 November 1999. For a summary of the Basic Telecommunications Agreement, see Organisation for Economic Co-operation and Development (OECD), July 1999. *Implications of the WTO Agreement on Basic Telecommunications*, Paris: OECD.

time or even before" other parts of the world, according to Ron Spithill, president of Alcatel for the Asia-Pacific region.[58]
2. **Scope of services** — China has to phase out all geographic restrictions for paging and value-added services in 2 years, mobile cellular in 3-5 years and fixed line services in 6 years. China's key telecom services corridor in Beijing, Shanghai and Guangzhou, which represents approximately 75% of all domestic traffic, will be opened immediately to all telecom services on accession.
3. **Investment** — Under the terms, China will not restrict the type of technology in which foreign firms can invest, nor are there any limitations on owned or leased facilities. Foreigners will also be allowed to own gateways as long as they adhere to the cited geographical and ownership limitations. The Sino-European Union accord on China's WTO entry (signed in May 2000) will further accelerate the opening in mobile telephony in two years' time. Foreign ownership of up to 25% will be allowed upon accession, 35% after one year, and 49% after three years. Leasing and resale of telecommunications circuits will be allowed for foreign firms in three years.[59]

What appeals to investors most are China's low telecom penetration rates, an imminent explosive growth of e-commerce and the expansion of international calling expected to parallel the country's trade growth. The snag is that there are still geographical and ownership limitations placed on foreign investment in telecom services (Table 12). Different interpretations of the deals will certainly arise as the paternalistic MII continues to oversee the interests of the descendants of the former China Telecom. On top of that, foreign investors are still likely to encounter hurdles due to the lack of transparency in rules and regulations. The problems of red tape, vague rules and unpredictable inventions that had in the past pervaded throughout the telecom sector will continue to plague the investors.[60]

---

[58] *Hong Kong Standard* (Hong Kong), 26 November 1999.
[59] AFP's report on the EU-China deal, *Straits Times* (Singapore), 20 May 2000.
[60] The EIU (London), *Telecoms & Wireless Asia*, 14 January 2000.

For the Chinese policy makers, the pace of opening hinges on considerations of national security, sovereignty, and protection of strategic industries and indigenous carriers, as well as political stability and ideological control. The Ministry of National Security has always been concerned about the potential threat to communications security and sovereignty once foreign companies are allowed to operate China's telecommunications network. Given China's century-long history of being intimidated and invaded by foreign powers, such a concern is understandable. As part of the efforts to protect national security, China's State Secrets Bureau issued the "State Secrecy Protection Regulations for Computer Information Systems on the Internet" on 25 January 2000. It stipulated in article 15 that "National backbone networks, Internet access providers and users shall accept the supervision and inspection conducted by departments in charge of protecting secrets and shall cooperate with them. They shall assist secret-protection departments in investigating illegal actions that divulge state secrets on the Internet."[61]

3.2 Implications for Domestic Reforms

China's accords with the US and the EU provide an incentive for the government to remove deep-rooted policy barriers in the telecommunications industry. The national treatment of foreign companies will inevitably have implications on the right of entry of indigenous non-state players. However, the extent to which the WTO entry will affect the pace of telecommunications reforms remains to be seen.

According to Minister of Information Industry, Wu Jichuan, entry into the WTO is unlikely to cause any big shock to China's telecom sector, given its considerable capacity and ample human resources. China's telecom sector, which ranks among the world's top 10 in terms of annual revenue, is strong enough to withstand the shock. Nevertheless, it will have to undergo a painful period after the WTO entry, as local enterprises

---

[61] China Online News, 26 January 2000, http://www.chinaonline.com.
[62] *China Economic News* (Beijing), 13 December 1999.

would be pressed to improve their management and quality of service that have become inefficient due to long-term monopoly.[62] Acknowledging that China's WTO entry has given an impetus to the country's ongoing reform, Mr. Wu pointed out that "without entry into the WTO, the reforms would still be cruising along its set course. The Sino-US agreement has made the issue more urgent."[63]

To withstand the anticipated shock brought about by the forces of competition, the Chinese government has adopted two strategies. The first was to negotiate for caps and geographic restrictions on foreign ownership and for a longer time period for removing the caps during the WTO deal making. The second strategy is to implement structural reforms in the telecommunications sector to pre-empt cream-skimming opportunities for foreign entrants after the WTO entry.

For China's telecommunications policy makers, the issue of providing universal service in a competitive market environment becomes more acute after the WTO entry. Given China's cross-subsidising tariff structure, foreign firms are likely to invest in cities with large populations but not in poor and border regions. This would be inconsistent with the MII's mission to continue infrastructure expansion to accomplish nationwide universal service. An urgent task for the MII is therefore to revamp the cross-subsidising tariff structure. From 1995 to 1999, the installation fee for a fixed phone line was cut from RMB 300–5000 to below RMB 800. In most rural areas, the fee is below RMB 500. Mobile telephone's access charge was reduced by 75%. IDD rates dropped by 60–70%. Internet access fee decreased by 70–80% (Qian and Zhang, 2000). In June 2000, China Telecommunications (Group) announced a plan to slash its international call charges by as much as 50% in order to strengthen its hold on the telecom market. It also vowed to cancel telephone installation fees and restructure charges for city calls from three-minute blocks to single minutes.[64] Such adjustments of rates are part of the MII strategy to pre-empt the cream-skimming opportunities open to the foreign carriers after China's WTO accession.

[63] *Beijing Review* (Beijing), 21 February 2000.
[64] *Zhongguo Xinxi Bao* [China Information News (Beijing)], 2 June 2000.

Entry into the WTO requires that China adequately cultivate local companies for global competition. According to Yang Peifang, chief economist of the Economic Research Centre with the MII, "the most important thing for the administration, at present, is to adjust its current industrial policies to make them suitable for WTO access."[65] There is a major concern that the government's preferential policy to support telecommunications sector could be taken advantage of by the foreigners. "For foreign companies investing in telecommunications operations, profits have been to a great extent attributable to preferential policies offered by the state," lamented an MII official in 1998.[66] A realistic way out for the Chinese policy makers would be to formulate China's development strategy without delay, so as to be positively prepared for the challenge of competition. Such is the rationale behind the divestiture of China Telecom and the administrative support favouring the competitor China Unicom. Other efforts to beef up Chinese carriers included the MII-sanctioned IPO launches by the Chinese carriers in offshore markets and the restruct of China Telecom (HK) to China Mobile (HK) with its consequent acquisition of the mainland's biggest provincial and municipal mobile-phone networks (as discussed in Section 2.3).

A subtle objective of these offshore fund raising efforts is to make it easier for these Chinese state-owned carriers to fulfil China's commitment to allow 49% foreign shareholding upon its entry into the WTO. In China's telecommunications circle, word has it that several more China Telecom subsidiaries at provincial levels are preparing themselves for overseas listing following the China Mobile (HK) model.[67] If every Chinese carrier had a significant portion of its assets owned by the overseas subsidiary of its state-owned parent, little will be left for the real foreign companies to snap up what is left in the 49% stake allowable for foreign ownership when China enters the WTO. Such a strategy will

---

[65] *China Daily* (Hong Kong), 21 November 1999.
[66] Reuters news, *Business Times* (Singapore), 2 December 1998.
[67] Interview with officials and scholars of Shanghai Institute of P&T Economy, 8 July 2000, 22 October 2000.

effectively sustain the state's control over the telecommunications business.

A real testing ground of China's commitment to telecommunications market reform and opening will be the legal regulatory framework. While a Telecommunications Law is still absent, the State Council approved and issued the MII-proposed Telecommunications Regulations of the People's Republic of China in September 2000, which standardises the regulatory framework for the telecom sector and unifies the existing regulations on tariffs, the issue of new licences, interconnections, network development and private/foreign participation.[68] The document spells out major principles of telecom regulation:

- Separating the administrator/regulator from the business operator;
- Breaking up monopoly, encouraging competition;
- Promoting development; and
- Maintaining openness, fairness, and justice in exercising supervision and administration over the industry.

A remarkable feature of this regulatory framework is opening of the telecom sector to non-state and foreign players. The new rules divide telecom companies into two types: one is the basic telecom business operator who provides public network infrastructure, data and voice transmission service. The other is the value-adding telecom business operator who uses the public network to provide telecommunications and information services. All basic telecom business operators and value-adding telecom business operators whose service scope covers two or more provincial territories must be licensed by the MII ["*guowuyuan xinxi chanye zhuguan bumen* (the State Council's administration overseeing the information industry)", as worded in the document]. Other value-adding telecom business operators should be licensed by provincial telecom regulatory bodies. A crucial requirement for a basic telecom business operator to be licensed is being a legally established corporation

---

[68] *The PRC Provisions on Regulation of the Telecommunications Sector* (issued by State Council on 25 September), the Ministry of Information Industry web site, www.mii.cn/news2000/1013_1.htm.

in which the state share or stake is no less than 51% (the controlling stake). As for the value-adding telecom business operators, there is no specific requirement for state control, thus clearing the way for foreign investors.

To ensure fair access to the public network by the new entrants, the Provisions specify that interconnection between different networks should follow the principles of feasibility, economic rationale, justice and fairness, and mutual co-operation. According to the Provisions, the dominant telecom operator is obliged to allow interconnection with other telecom operators and specialised (non-public) network units.

The promulgation of the new regulation was also a crucial step to establish the MII as a state regulatory authority. Under the new rules, telecom tariffs consist of market-adjusted prices (set by service providers), government-guided prices (i.e. floating ranges allowed for operators to set their prices/rates), and government-set prices (for important tariff rates). Pricing is mainly cost-based. The MII is authorised to play a pivotal role in government involvement in telecom tariff setting. The new regulatory framework also reconfirms that the state, through the MII, should centrally plan, manage, and allocate telecom resources such as radio frequencies, satellite positions, telecommunications network codes/numbers. The operators' possession and usage of such resources will be levied by the state at rates suggested by the MII and the fiscal departments of the State Council. Administrative assignment and auction are referred to as the two measures to allocate the telecom resources. Meanwhile, telecom operators are obliged to fulfil the responsibility of providing universal services, which are enforced through the MII's regulatory specifications or tender clauses. Finally, the Provisions reaffirm the MII's central planning authority over the development of public network, specialised (non-public) network and radio/television transmission network. Projects involving nationwide networks must be approved by the MII before they could go through the state approval procedure for capital construction projects. Telecom network's design, development and operation by any player must meet the requirements and standards of national security and network security. With these rules, the government is set to keep its control over the investment and development of the country's telecommunications infrastructure.

4. Concluding Remarks

To fulfil its commitments upon WTO accession, China would have to revamp its rules in line with international norms, perfect its laws and regulatory framework, increase the transparency of its legal systems and government administrations and ensure market order. With lower entry barriers, competition in the domestic market is expected to become increasingly fierce. The increased pressure to prosper or perish will in turn force Chinese firms to improve their management efficiency and hone their competitive edges. The telecommunications sector is no exception.

Recent developments in China's telecommunications sector clearly mark the dawning of a more competitive era featuring an oligopoly market. When China moves to fulfil all its WTO commitments with regards to opening its telecommunications market in the next few years, we can expect the following changes.

First, with the rise of new carriers like Unicom, Jitong Communications, and Netcom, the dominance of China Mobile and China Telecom will continue to decline. Competition among the major domestic carriers will intensify, thus dismantling the previous cross-subsidising tariff structure. This will effectively squeeze the profit margins of these oligopoly carriers and pre-empt the scream-skimming opportunities of foreign entrants.

Second, China's relatively low teledensity and the sector's dynamic growth suggest the potential of its telecommunications market. However, it is not realistic to expect infrastructure construction to keep pace with its explosive growth that started in the second half of the 1980s. In particular, given the withering of China Telecom-China Mobile's dominance and their responsibility to provide universal service, new infrastructure investment will tend to be focused on the more "creamy" part of the market. Basic network construction for the less lucrative underdeveloped regions will be slowed down unless the government intervenes actively or technology progress provides alternatives. No doubt more capital will flow into China's telecom sector, but not as quickly as before, especially in raising teledensity and penetration rate of basic services. The high end of the market (such as international calls and data transmissions, sophisticated mobile communications, etc. in more developed coastal cities) will be better serviced at the cost of affordability and availability of low-end market services (such as plain old telephony) for the local and rural areas.

Last but not least, because of the above, the MII is likely to remain highly interventionist, given its constant concerns over national security and sovereignty, universal service to the remote and underdeveloped areas, and indigenous carriers' chance of survival in an open market. Its endeavours to oversee infrastructure planning and construction will not fade, despite being challenged by various interest groups. China's industrial policy makers want to promote the information technology (IT) industry as the "foundation, guide and pillar" of the Chinese economy in the 21st Century. The official target is to maintain a 20% annual growth rate for the industry over the next five years (2000–2005), about three times the expected rate of GDP growth. That would double the size of the IT industry to about 5% of GDP.[69] "Speeding up the informatisation of the national economy" is high on the agenda of China's Tenth Five-year Plan (2001–2005). To the Chinese leadership, the possibility of using IT to accelerate China's industrialisation is an opportunity in the new century for China to catch up with the West (Zhu, 2000). As the engine and backbone of the IT industry, the telecommunications sector will surely continue to play a strategic role in the government's industrial policy.

Uncertainties still remain, like the extent the MII would separate itself from the business operations of the divested former China Telecom. Would it restrain itself to be a truly fair umpire rather than a quasi-player in the telecommunications business? By seeking to list Chinese carriers in overseas/Hong Kong stock markets, the government can technically retain its control over the telecom business as before without blatantly violating its commitment to allow 49% foreign ownership upon

---

[69] News report on a speech by Lu Xinkui, vice minister at the Ministry of Information Industry, *The China Interactive Times Newsletter* (www.shanghai-abc.com), Vol. 2, No. 25, 25 August 2000.

WTO entry. Since the MII still holds major stakes in the carriers descended from the former China Telecom (and even in China Unicom since April 2000), it is hard, if not impossible, to expect it to adopt a hands-off approach as a passive dominant shareholder if these carriers were to bleed or sink in the post-WTO-entry days. Until the state-owned giant carriers assume their place as pure commercial players and the MII limits itself to being an impartial regulator, a level-playing field is unlikely to emerge as foreign investors have hoped for. Thus the more successfully the MII beefs up these state-owned carriers to prepare for WTO entry, the less likely or necessary it would be for it to intervene to protect them when the market is fully open for foreign competition.

References

China Statistical Yearbook, various years. State Statistics Bureau. Beijing China Statistics Press.

Gao Yangzhi (1991) (in Chinese), "*Shanghai dianhua wang de fazhan xianzhuang he fazhan zhanlue* (Shanghai's telephone network: status quo and development strategy)", *Youdian Jingji* [*P&T Economy* (Shanghai)] 16, 22–28.

He, Fei Chang (1994), "Lian Tong: A quantum leap in the reform of China's telecommunications", *Telecommunications Policy* 18 (3), 206–210.

Hong Xiuyi and Qian Yongwei (1992) (in Chinese), "*Woguo chengshi zhuzhai dianhua fazhan qushi yu sikao* (The trend of residential telephone development in China)", *Youdian Jingji* [*P&T Economy* (Shanghai)] 21 (4), 19–23.

Hsu, Connie (1999), *Telecoms & Wireless Asia*. London: The Economist Intelligence Unit.

Jin, Jiyuan (1992) (in Chinese), "*Shenhua gaige, zhuanhuan qiye jingying jizhi jige wenti de tantao* (Issues of deepening reform of enterprise operational rules)", *Youdian Jingji* [*P&T Economy* (Shanghai)] 20, 1992(4): 4–6.

Jing Xing (1999) (in Chinese), "*Jianchi shishi qiushi, yiqie cong shij chufa — wei jinian gaige kaifa 20 zhounian zuo* (Insist on the principle of pragmatism — on the 20th anniversary of the commencement of reform and opening)", *Youdian Jingji* [P&T *Economy* (Shanghai)] 46, 1999(1): 2–8.

Li, Jiaju (2000) (in Chinese), "*Waixiang ershiyi shiji de zhongguo liudong dianhua shichang* (China's mobile telephone market towards the 21st century)", *Youdian Jingji* [*P&T Economy* (Shanghai)] 50, 2000(1): 14–19.

Lin, Sun (2000), "Exploring new avenues: Unicom's focus on growth", *Asian Communications*. August **14** (8): 12.

Liu, Zhaoquan (1992) (in Chinese), "*Youdian fazhan yu chanquan guanli tizhi gaige* (The development of P & T and reform of asset management)", *Youdian Jingji* [P&T Economy (Shanghai)] **18** (1), 2–4.

Lu, Ding (2000), "China's Telecommunications Infrastructure Buildup: On Its Own Way", in Ito, Takatoshi and Krueger, Anne O. (eds.), *Deregulation and Interdependence in the Asia-Pacific Region*. Chicago: University of Chicago Press, pp. 371–414.

Ma, Qiang (1992) (in Chinese), "*Dianxin zifei de pingjia fangfa ji guoji bijiao* (Ways to estimate telecommunications rates and an international comparison of rates)", *Youdian Jingji* [P&T Economy (Shanghai)] **18** (1), 27–30.

Mueller, Milton (1994), "China: still the enigmatic giant", *Telecommunications Policy* **18** (3), 171–173.

Mueller M. and Tan Z. (1997), *China in the Information Age: Telecommunications and the Dilemma of Reform*. Westport, Connecticut: Praeger Publishers.

Qian, Jinqun and Zhang, Yi (2000), "*Jin nian lai woguo dianxin zifei tiaozheng qingkuang* (Adjustment of telecommunications rates in the recent years)", *Dianxin Ruan Kexue Yuanjiu (Telecom Soft Science Research)* Vol. 3: 28–37.

Sun, Yaming (1992) (in Chinese), "*Youdian xin yewu zifei zhengce youguan wenti de tantao* (Issues related to pricing policies regarding P & T new services)", *Youdian Jingji* [P&T Economy (Shanghai)] **18** (1), 36–37.

Tan, Zixiang (1994), "Challenges to the MPT's monopoly", *Telecommunications Policy* **18** (3), 174–181.

Wu, Jichuan (2000) (in Chinese), "Interview on reform and opening of the telecommunications sector", *Youdian Jingji* [P&T Economy (Shanghai)] **50**, 2000 (1), 2–4.

Wu, Jichuan (1996), "Carefully study the experience of fulfilling the Eighth Five-year Plan, work hard to fulfil the Ninth five-Year Plan, and strive for making China a country with the most advanced postal and telecommunications sector by the year 2010". In *Yearbook of China Transportation and Communications 1996*. Beijing: China Transportation and Communications Society, 16–17.

Yang, Peifang (1991) (in Chinese), "*Lun dianxin hangye de mubiao he xietiao fazhan* (On the goals and ways of a harmonic development of telecommunication)", *Youdian Jingji* [P&T Economy (Shanghai)] **16**, 1991 (3), 2–4.

You, Zhengyan (1987), "Status of postal and telecommunications sector and industrial policies". In *Yearbook of China Transportation and Communications 1987*. Beijing: China Transportation and Communications Society, 766–768.

Yearbook of China Transportation and Communication, various years. Beijing: China Transportation and Communications Society.

Zhu, Rongji (2000), "On the drawing of the Tenth Five-year Plan", *People's Daily*, 20 October 2000.

APPENDIX

Basic Statistics of China's Telecommunications Industry, 1998

Items	China	Asia	World
Financial data (U.S.$)			
Income per main telephone line	235.00	652.00	871.00
Investment per main telephone line	207.00	316.00	215.00
Tariff structure for residential users (U.S.$)			
Installation charges	226.00	132.00	109.00
Monthly subscription	1.90	5.4	6.9
Local call rate (three minutes)	0.01	0.04	0.09
Residential subscription tariff as percentage of per capita GNP	3.1	6.9	7.5
Basic quantity data			
Main lines per 100 residents	6.96	7.34	14.26
Cellular mobile subscriber per 100 residents	1.90	3.05	5.38
Long-distance calls per main line	231.86#	4.61# (India)	412.88# (Brazil)
Outgoing international traffic (minutes per subscriber)	19.60	55.30	100.70
Waiting time for subscription (years)	0.1	0.5	0.7
Satisfied demand	99.1	95.4	95.9

Note: # 1996 figures.
Sources: ITU (1998), *Yearbook of Statistics: telecommunications services 1988–1997*; ITU (1999), *World Telecommunications Development Report 1999*.

14

Education and Development: Experiences from East Asia

JOHN WONG & LIU ZHIQIANG*

EDUCATION AND DEVELOPMENT: A COMPLEX ISSUE

Most development economists have long argued that economic development critically depends on investment in both physical and human capital. In many cases, it is the accumulation of human resources, more than capital or material resources, that ultimately determines the character and pace of economic development. Since a country's principal institutional mechanism for developing human resources (i.e., skills and knowledge) is its formal educational system, education therefore holds the key to economic development in the poor country. It thus follows that the more education a country has developed, the more rapid its economic development.

---

*Professor John Wong is Research Director and Dr. Liu Zhiqiang is Senior Research Fellow at the East Asian Institute, National University of Singapore. The paper was presented at the international symposium on "Guizhou Education Reform and Development, 2000," 16–18 May 2000, Guiyang, Guizhou, PRC. The authors thank Mr. Aw Beng Teck and Dr. Lin Shuanglin for their very helpful comments and suggestions.

Yet, while some developing countries have devoted a lot of resources to formal education, this has not resulted in significant economic development. In fact, in many developing countries, there is a serious problem of the "educated unemployed". On the other hand, education is known to have contributed a great deal to the economic success of East Asia. In view of this, this paper sets out to identify some lessons from East Asian countries with regard to how education has contributed to their success and how these lessons can be applied to China.

EDUCATION AND EAST ASIA'S DYNAMIC GROWTH

The East Asian region is commonly defined to comprise Japan, China, the four newly industrialized economies (NIEs) of South Korea, Taiwan, Hong Kong and Singapore, and the four Association of Southeast Asian Nations (ASEAN) of Indonesia, Malaysia, the Philippines, and Thailand. All have displayed a strong capacity for dynamic growth, with many having experienced high growth for two to three decades until the recent Asian financial crisis of 1997–98 (see Table 1). In fact, some of these economies have broken the past world growth records, so much so that the World Bank in its highly-publicized study referred to the high growth performance of East Asia as the "East Asian Miracle".[1]

Why has the East Asian region been able to sustain dynamic growth for such a long period? Development economists can easily explain this within the neoclassical framework. The high growth of these economies typically stemmed from their high levels of domestic investment, which were generally matched by their equally high levels of domestic savings. As can be seen from Table 1, except for Taiwan and the Philippines, most of these economies have devoted 30% or more of their GDP to domestic investment. High investment and high savings in these economies have created what may be called a "virtuous circle of sustained economic growth": High investment, high export growth, high GDP growth, high savings, and then high investment again. In fact, the ability of an economy to put aside a larger share of its rising income as savings

---

[1] The World Bank, *The East Asian Miracle* (New York: Oxford University Press, 1994).

Table 1. Performance Indicators of East Asian Economies

	Population (Millions) 1998	GNP per-capita, (US$) 1998	PPP Estimates of GNP per-Capita, (US$) 1998	Growth of GDP(%) 1960-70	1970-80	1980-90	1990-98	1998[a]	1999[a]	Consumer Price Inflation (%) 1999[a]	Annual Export Growth (%) 1990-98	Mfg exports as % of total exports 1997	Export-GDP Ratio (%) 1998	Gross Domestic Savings as % of GDP 1990-98	1998	Gross Domestic Investment as % of GDP 1990-98	1998
China	1,239	750	3,220	5.2	5.8	10.2	11.1	7.8	7.1	-0.6	14.9	85	22	43	43	39	39
Japan	126	32,380	23,180	10.9	5.0	4.0	1.3	-3.6	0.9	-0.7	3.9	95	9[b]	34	32[b]	30	29
NIEs																	
South Korea	46	7,970	12,270	8.6	9.5	9.4	6.2	-6.8	12.3	1.2	15.7	87	38	36	34	37	35
Taiwan	22	12,040[a]	17,495[a]	9.2	9.7	7.1	6.5	4.7	5.1	-0.9	8.1	98	23	26	25	23	21
Hong Kong	7	23,670	22,000	10.0	9.3	6.9	4.4	-7.0	4.5	-4.2	9.5	93	125	32	30	31	30
Singapore	3	30,060	28,620	8.8	8.5	6.4	8.0	-0.7	6.7	1.5	13.3	84	187[b]	48	51	36	37
ASEAN-4																	
Indonesia	204	680	2,790	3.9	7.6	6.1	5.8	-17.4	0.5	1.6	8.6	42	28	33	31	33	31
Malaysia	22	3,600	6,990	6.5	7.8	5.2	7.7	-8.6	8.1	2.1	13.2	76	118	39	47	38	32
Philippines	75	1,050	3,540	5.1	6.3	1.0	3.3	-0.1	3.1	3.9	11.0	85	56	17	15	22	25
Thailand	61	2,200	5,840	8.4	7.2	7.6	7.4	-6.0	3.5	-0.5	11.1	71	47	34	36	39	35

Notes: (a) Asiaweek Dec. 31, 1999–Jan. 7, 2000. (b) The data refers to 1997.
Sources: World Development Report 1999/2000; Taiwan Statistical Data Book 1999; Asian Development Outlook 1999.

for the purpose of investment is probably the most convincing explanation of the arithmetic of economic growth in the East Asian region.

Education has also played an important part in the growth process. Even critics of East Asian growth models, such as Alwyn Young and Paul Krugman, have conceded that a significant part of the growth is attributable to the sharp increase in human capital in these countries [Young (1994)]. But, according to the critics, what is lacking in the East Asia's growth process is improvement in productivity, and as a result, this high economic growth is not sustainable (because of diminishing returns to production factors).

In a way, this criticism is misplaced. The spectacular growth performance of East Asian economies was partly due to the catch-up phenomenon, by which the rapid growth in per capita income could be attributed to the high rates of technological change made possible by the diffusion of technology from the more advanced countries. However, such technology diffusion could not occur until these economies had reached a certain level in the development of their human resources which can enable them to master the technology and put it into use. On this count, human capital is pivotal to economic growth in East Asian economies.

This is not to argue that productivity is not an important growth engine in East Asian countries. Rather, the way that human capital contributes to economic growth may change as these countries enter the next phase of economic development. Before they caught up with the world's advanced economies, the human capital facilitated mainly the adoption of incoming new technology. After they have managed to catch up with the world's advanced economies, the human capital will then be chiefly devoted to inventive and innovative activities, hence resulting in more substantial productivity growth.

QUANTITY AND QUALITY OF EDUCATION IN EAST ASIAN COUNTRIES

Most East Asian countries have compulsory education up to the primary level, while some, such as Hong Kong, Japan, and Malaysia, make it compulsory up to the secondary level. Table 2 contains selected education

Table 2. Education Indicators

	Adult Literacy Rate (%)				Gross Enrolment Ratio: Primary School (%)				Gross Enrolment Ratio: Secondary School (%)				% of Age Group Enrolled in Tertiary School
	1980		1995		1980		1996		1980		1996		1995
	Female	Male	Female	Male	Female	Male	Female	Male	Female	Male	Female	Male	
China	52.7	78.6	72.7	89.9	103.7	121.0	119.9	120.9	37.4	53.9	66.9	74.2	5
Japan	-	-	-	-	101	101	102	101	94	92	100[b]	98[b]	40
NIEs													
South Korea	90.1	97.5	96.7	99.3	110.5	109.3	94.5	93.7	73.8	82.1	102.0	101.6	52
Taiwan	71.7	91.5	91.1	98.1	101[d]	99[d]	101.8	99.5	79.8	80.9	98.9	95.6	46
Hong Kong	77.3	94.2	88.2	96.0	105.7	107.4	98.1	96.2	65.4	62.9	77.3	72.8	22[a]
Singapore	74.0	91.6	86.3	95.9	106.2	109.1	92.9	95.3	60.3	59.5	73.5	71.6	34
ASEAN-4													
Indonesia	57.7	77.5	78.0	89.6	99.7	114.6	112.3	116.9	23.3	34.7	47.6	55.8	11
Malaysia	59.7	79.6	78.1	89.1	92.0	93.3	91.8	90.2	45.7	49.7	66.1	57.5	11
Philippines	88.7	90.6	94.3	95.0	109.9	113.8	118.7	116.4	68.8	59.7	80.2	78.1	27
Thailand	84.0	92.3	91.6	96.0	97.4	100.3	87.9	88.2	27.9	29.6	56.5	57.5	20

Notes: [a] – 1993 figures   [c] – 1995 figures
       [b] – 1994 figures   [d] – estimated based on Statistical Yearbook of the Republic of China 1998
Sources: World Bank, World Development Report 1999/2000 and UNESCO Statistical Yearbook 1998.

indicators by gender for selected years. Without a single exception, all countries have made significant progress in human resource development. This is evidenced by the across-the-board improvement in the adult literacy rate. The literacy rates among female adults rose substantially between 1980 and 1995, although these were still lower than the rates for males. In 1996, the gross enrolment ratio (GER) to primary school was close to or higher than 100% for most of the countries, except in Malaysia and Thailand where the GER stood at around 90%, which is below the world average (99%) but higher than the level in Less Developed Countries (65%).

The most significant improvement occurred in GER at the secondary school level. In 1980, Japan had the highest enrolment ratio of more than 90% for both sexes; it managed to raise the ratio to 100% for females and 98% for males by 1994. Among the four NIEs, only South Korea and Taiwan were able to catch up with Japan. Between 1980 and 1996, they were able to increase GERs at the secondary school level from about 80% to nearly 100%. In comparison, Hong Kong and Singapore saw their secondary school GERs rose modestly to just over 70% by 1996. Among the ASEAN-4, only the Philippines was on par with Hong Kong and Singapore. The rest of the group, although they experienced marked improvement, still lagged behind Japan and the NIEs.

The GERs at tertiary-level education vary greatly among East Asian countries. The ranking is in general similar to the ranking by GERs at secondary school level, with Japan, South Korea, and Taiwan leading the pack, followed by Singapore, the Philippines, Hong Kong and Thailand. Indonesia and Malaysia were at the bottom, both with 11% of the age group attending tertiary schools. It is worth noting that the GER (27%) at the tertiary level in the Philippines was higher than the GERs in Hong Kong, Malaysia and Thailand, even though the country's per capita GDP was less than one-twentieth of that in Hong Kong, one-third of that in Malaysia, and one-half of that in Thailand.

The quality of schooling is more difficult to measure. However, available information from 1980 and 1990 indicate that there were substantial variations in the quality of schooling among East Asian countries. Table 3 presents several rough but commonly used indicators.

Table 3. Indicators for the Quality of Schooling

	As a % of GNP 1980	As a % of GNP 1990	% of Private Enrolment Pri. 1980	% of Private Enrolment Pri. 1990	% of Private Enrolment Sec. 1980	% of Private Enrolment Sec. 1990	Student-teacher Ratio Pri. 1980	Student-teacher Ratio Pri. 1990	Student-teacher Ratio Sec. 1980	Student-teacher Ratio Sec. 1990
China	2.5	2.3	–	–	–	–	27	22	18	15
Japan	5.8	4.7	1	1	13	15	25	21	17	17
<u>NIEs</u>										
S. Korea	3.7	3.6	1	1	46	41	48	34	39	25
Taiwan	–	–	–	–	–	–	–	–	–	–
Hong Kong	2.5	3.0	94	–	96	–	30	27	29	23
Singapore	2.8	3.4	26	24	28	27	31	26	19	22
<u>ASEAN-4</u>										
Philippines	1.7	2.9	5	7	48	36	31	33	34	33
Malaysia	6.0	6.9	–	–	–	4	27	20	23	19
Indonesia	1.7	–	21	17	49	50	32	23	15	13
Thailand	3.4	3.8	8	10	13	10	23	18	18	18

Source: UNESCO, *World Education Report* (1993).
Notes: Pri.=primary school; Sec.=secondary school.

As a share of GNP, public expenditure on education varies from a low of 1.7% in the Philippines and Indonesia to a high of 6% in Malaysia in 1980. But all countries, except for Japan and South Korea, raised their education spending in 1990 compared with 1980. Under the column "% of private enrolment", there appears to be a negative relationship between the share of public spending on education and private school enrolment, i.e., countries that spent less public money on education tended to have more private schools. Furthermore, countries that had more private schools also tended to have lower student-teacher ratios.

IMPLICATIONS FOR CHINA

China's economic growth in the past two decades ever since the beginning of its economic reform and open door policy shows considerable similarity with other high-performance East Asian economies. On the surface, China's overall education achievements have lagged far behind other East Asian economies, implying that education might not have contributed as much to its economic growth as its other East Asian counterparts. But one has to remember that China's growth and development since 1978 has been concentrated in the big cities and the costal region, where most of China's capital and human resources congregated. This suggests that education and human capital have played an equally important part in China's economic growth. Indeed, according to a World Bank study, of the 9.4% annual GDP growth in China during 1978–1995, some 9% is attributable to the rise in human capital, 45% to capital and labor increases, and 46% to total factor productivity growth.[2] Although the contribution of human capital to the growth appears to be small, part of the increases in the total factor productivity may also be accounted for by the increase in human capital, as it facilitates the adoption of advanced technology.

Table 4. Ratios of Total Costs by Educational Level Per Student Year

	Relative Cost	
	Secondary vs. Primary	Higher vs. Primary
China (1990)	2.28	29.43
Malaysia, Ghana, South Korea, Kenya, Uganda, Nigeria, India (1960s)	11.9	87.9
U.S, U.K, New Zealand (1960s)	6.6	17.6

Source: Statistics on China from State Education Commission of the People's Republic of China, "Comprehensive Statistical Yearbook of Chinese Education", Higher Education Press, 1995. Other statistics from George Psacharopoulos, "The Returns to Education: An International Comparison", Amsterdam: Elsevier, 1972.

[2] World Bank, *China 2020: Development Challenges in the New Century*, The World Bank, Washington D.C., 1997.

As Table 2 shows, China has made significant progress in human resource development. Primary school enrolment has been maintained at over 100%, exceeding that of Malaysia and Thailand. China also experienced a steady increase in secondary school enrolment. Between 1980 and 1996, GERs rose from 37.4% to 66.9% for females and from 53.9% to 74.2% for males. These rates are higher than those attained by Indonesia, Malaysia, and Thailand, and are similar to the levels attained by Hong Kong and Singapore. But China clearly lags behind East Asian countries in tertiary school enrolment. In 1995, students in tertiary schools accounted for a mere 5% of their cohorts, compared with the enrolment rates that range from 52% in South Korea to 11% in Indonesia and Malaysia.

However, these statistics do not necessarily imply that China should allocate more resources to expand the capacity of its tertiary education system. Table 4 compares the ratio of total costs per-student year by educational level for China and a group of developed and less developed countries. The data reveal that the ratio of total per-student cost of secondary to primary education and that of higher education to primary are higher among less developed countries than among developed countries. The cost ratio of higher to primary education in China is 29.43, implying that for the equivalent cost of educating one university student for a year, 29 primary or 14 secondary school children could have received a year of schooling. This in turn suggests that, as in many less developed countries, China is spending a large proportion of its educational budget on a very small proportion of its students enrolled in universities.

Table 5 contains the relative average earnings of individuals by educational level. If we compare these data with those on cost (Table 4), it is clear that relative earnings differentials by educational level are much less than unit cost differentials in developing compared with developed countries. Whereas a university student costs 29 times as much as a primary pupil to educate for one year, the university student on the average earns only 1.35 times as much as the typical primary pupil. To the extent that average relative earnings reflect average relative productivity, the wide disparity between relative earnings and relative

Table 5. Ratios of Average Annual Earnings of Worker by Educational Level

	Relative Earnings	
	Secondary vs. Primary	Higher vs. Primary
China (1988)	1.12	1.35
Malaysia, Ghana, South Korea, Kenya, Uganda, Nigeria, India (1960s)	2.4	6.4
U.S, U.K, Canada (1960s)	1.4	2.4

Source: Statistics on China are derived from the authors' calculation according to the earnings function reported in Liu Zhiqiang, "Earnings, Education, and Economic Reforms in Urban China", *Economic Development and Cultural Change* 46, July 1998. Other statistics from George Psacharopoulos, "The Returns to Education: An International Comparison", Amsterdam: Elsevier, 1972.

costs of higher versus primary education may suggest that China might have unwisely invested too much in higher education. These funds might have been more productively used in primary and secondary school expansion. Thus, the cost-benefit analysis suggests that China should spend a larger portion of its education budget on primary and secondary schools, at least in the present stage of economic development.[3]

This does not necessarily imply that future relative cost-benefit ratios will continue to favor the expansion of schools at lower levels. In a market economy, market forces work to bring costs in line with benefits associated with education. Such is the case in most of the East Asian countries, in which human resource allocation is done through the market.

[3] These cost-benefit calculations are far from perfect. Earnings used here are private benefits, and social benefits are likely to be much larger than what the earnings indicate because education or human capital is known to generate positive external effects on the economy at large. The costs used here are government expenditures on education at various levels and exclude tuitions and fees paid by students' families. Therefore, the costs of education have also been underestimated. Thus, more detailed information are needed to provide an accurate picture. Nevertheless, our back of the envelope calculations are indicative of possible misallocation of resources between different levels of education.

Although, in recent years, China has made some progress in labour reform, the government still plays an important role in allocating jobs and in determining wages. Some recent studies on income distribution in China have shown that economic reforms have raised the rate of return to education; for example, the rate of return to education is higher in Guangdong than in other areas, and the rate of return to education is significantly higher in 1994 than in 1988. There is also some evidence that economic reforms have raised the earnings gaps between university and non-university graduates [see Li & Gustafsson]. This means that economic reforms tend to alter the cost-benefit calculation in favor of higher education.

Although in general the East Asian experience seems to suggest a positive relationship between economic growth and human resource development, this is not always true. Among the ASEAN-4, the Philippines had achieved the highest level of student enrolment rates in all three levels of education during the period 1980–96. But its growth record has been the worst of the ASEAN-4 since 1970s. This implies that investment in education alone is not sufficient to boost the rate of economic growth. The demand for educated labor must also increase if investments in schooling are to have an impact. As can be seen, this conclusion is in line with the argument in favor of higher education in the previous paragraph.

According to the World Bank study (1993), one major contributing factor in East Asia's successful education programs had been the overall budgetary commitment to education and the distribution of the education budget. In most East Asian economies, public investments in education were not only sizable but also efficient. By placing an emphasis on universal and high-quality primary education, these countries were able to achieve economic efficiency while at the same time attaining a fair degree of equity. The rising demand for secondary and university education was met by a combination of an expansion in the public secondary school system with meritocratic entrance requirements and a growing private school system.

In 1996, China spent 2.3% of its GNP on education. Although this figure is higher than that in Indonesia and the Philippines, public expenditure on education as a share of GNP has been on the decline in China since 1989, the earliest year for which data is available. Given rising enrolments at all levels of education, the lack of funding would undoubtedly jeopardize the quality of schooling. This gives cause for concern, because there is some evidence that it is the quality of education and not its quantity alone that best explains differential earnings and productivity at the individual level and economic growth at the macro-level [Behrman & Birdsall (1995)].

A major contributing factor to the decrease in the education budget share is that the tax revenue share of the government has been falling in the wake of fiscal reform. While fiscal decentralization is in general conducive to economic growth, it appears to have had an adverse effect on education in China.[4] What are the options for China in light of the East Asian experience? One possible strategy is to address the problem through education system reform that explores new financial sources for the education system. First, consumers of education services can be required to shoulder a bigger slice of the total costs. Parents in general do not object to a reasonable increase in tuition fees provided it is accompanied by a commensurate quality improvement. Second, the government should use the limited public funds to upgrade existing schools (i.e., focusing on quality improvement), while leaving quantitative expansions of schools in the hands of the private sector. In fact, the experience of some East Asian economies (such as Singapore) has demonstrated that the presence of private and semi-private schools has not only provided the consumers of educational services with more choices but also put competitive pressure upon public schools to improve their quality.

Concluding Remarks

It is clear that China's human capital formation in per-capita terms is

---

[4] For relationship between fiscal decentralization and economic growth, see Justin Lin and Liu Zhiqiang, "Fiscal Decentralization and Economic Growth in China", *Economic Development and Cultural Change*, forthcoming in October 2000.

still at a very low level. The next phase of China's development strategy should place higher priority on education. More resources should be devoted to improving the quality of existing schools rather than to quantity expansion. While the government should continue to take the lead in the development of the education system, market forces should be allowed to play a bigger role in mobilizing financial and human resources of the society towards improving the service quality of the education sector.

Education is a highly complex issue, given that the complex human psyche is involved and the fact that the shape and texture, and hence the quality, of an education system is invariably influenced by diverse local conditions, mindsets and governmental agendas. This paper has teased out in broad strokes some commonalities among the education systems of East Asian countries that had contributed to their development. What perhaps is more exciting and unexplored territory is the latest fuss in the region over the new economy. The demands of this new knowledge-based economy will no doubt heighten the role of education, and even re-education for those schooled in the ways of the old economy, as each country pushes to re-invent itself in the market place where old rules no longer apply.

References

Jere Behrman and Nacy Birdsall. "The Quality of Schooling: Quantity Alone is Misleading", *American Economic Review* 73, December 1983. See also Eric A. Hanushek. "Interpreting Recent Research on Schooling in Developing Countries", *World Bank Research Observer* 10, August 1995.

Li, Shi and Bjorn Gustafsson, "The Anatomy of Rising Earnings Inequality in Urban China", forthcoming *Journal of Comparative Economics*.

Young, Alwyn, "A Tale of Two Cities: Factor Accumulation and Technical Change in Hong Kong and Singapore", *NBER Macroeconomics Annual* 1992, MIT Press; Paul Krugman. "The Myth of Asia's Miracle", *Foreign Affairs*, Nov/Dec 1994.

15

China's Drive to Attract the Return of Its Expatriate Talents

YU WING YIN*

1. INTRODUCTION

In a recent interview with *Science*,[1] President Jiang Zemin said that since 1978, nearly 320,000 Chinese students have gone abroad to study, and of these, 110,000 have returned to China. This is approximately a one-third return rate, which has been the trend all the time.

The recent attention placed on attracting the return of personnel trained abroad reflects a change in circumstances in China's development. Economic progress has reached a stage where China can now make use of much more trained manpower.

The regulations enacted by the Beijing municipality[2] to encourage the return of its expatriate talents have been exemplary. They fall into

---

*Dr Yu Wing Yin was Visiting Senior Research Fellow at the East Asian Institute in 2000. The author gratefully acknowledges the guidance and support of Professor John Wong.
[1] "China's Leader Commits to Basic Research, Global Science", *Science*, 16 June 2000, p. 1950.
[2] Beijing Government Notice No. 19 (2000).

four categories: (1) to confer on returnees the same benefits as nationals residing in Beijing; (2) to confer on returnees the same benefits accorded to foreigners; (3) to ensure that returning compatriots are not disadvantaged by their absence from the country as compared with nationals who have not gone abroad; and (4) to grant additional incentives over and above the preceding three categories.

A statement by the central government[3] in August 2000 set the target of absorbing 10,000 returning students per year over the next five years. This 10,000 target is within the one-third rate, as the number of students going abroad every year is now in the region of 30,000. It is a modest target, as it has been reported that 13,000 students are expected to return this year, and the numbers are rising by 13% a year [Pomfret (2000)].

The liberal nature of the policy actions is significant. The returning expatriate is given the best of both worlds: he enjoys all the benefits of a national, at the same time he has also all the rights and privileges accorded to foreigners. Wherever possible without disadvantaging the local people, returnees are given benefits and incentives over and above these entitlements. Restrictive measures are never undertaken. President Jiang Zemin reiterated the liberal policy in the interview with *Science*: "Despite all the different views, we still believe that they should have the freedom to come and go."[1]

2. An Overview of Chinese on Overseas Study

In the 1950s, the major destinations of overseas study were the Soviet Union and the Eastern European countries. This was because of the economic embargo from Western countries following the Korean war. After the ideological split with the Soviet Union in 1961, the Chinese students were called back. It was estimated that China sent some 40,000 persons to the Soviet Union for study and training in the twelve-year period 1951–62 [Liu (1995)]. Meanwhile, China had also been sending

---

[3] *Singtao Daily News* (Malaysia), 7 August 2000.

small numbers of students to Italy, Belgium, Switzerland and the Nordic countries after 1957.[4]

In 1972, China entered the United Nations and became a member of UNESCO, whereupon it increased student exchanges with France and Britain. Vice Premier Fang Yi visited West Germany in 1978 and signed a Technological Cooperation Agreement initiating a flow of students to Germany. In the same year, US President Jimmy Carter dispatched National Security Adviser Z. Brezinski and Science Adviser Frank Press to visit China to discuss cultural and scientific exchanges. In 1979, Minister of Education Jiang Nanxiang visited the US and concluded an Agreement on Education Exchange Programs. The number of students going to the US have been on the increase ever since; it has been estimated that by 1984 the US was the destination of 50% of Chinese overseas students, and 75% in 1990 [Liu (1992)].

With Deng Xiaoping's return to power in 1978 came the great encouragement to send students overseas. In 1981, students were allowed to study abroad at their own expense [Du (1992)], though restrictions were placed on self-financed students in 1982 in that students in Chinese universities had to continue with their studies till graduation and work for two years before they could go abroad. But the restrictions were lifted towards the end of 1984, and the floodgates were opened.[5]

Following the Tiananmen incident in 1989, there was a hiatus in students going abroad. Upon Deng Xiaoping's Southern visit in 1992, the Chinese government reaffirmed the policy of "supporting students to go abroad, encouraging them to return, and allowing them to come and go freely".[5] Restrictions pertaining to age and years of service were removed; policies regarding overseas studies became very liberal. The

---

[4] The first impetus to send students abroad came in 1954, when a large amount of skilled manpower was needed to push forward the first Five-Year Plan. However, by 1957 the anti-rightist movement had already caused the number of students going abroad to dwindle to a trickle of a few hundred a year. In 1966 there was a large-scale recall of overseas students, to return to take part in the Cultural Revolution.

[5] As an indication, the number of students taking the TOEFL examination in Beijing increased from 285 in 1981 to 26,000 in 1987. See Kong et al. (1994).

number of students going overseas increased three-fold between 1991 and 1993 (Table 1). The large increase was partly due to the liberal policy and partly because students planning to depart after 1989 had been held back. Since 1993, the annual out-flow has exceeded 10,000.

Chinese policy regarding overseas study has gone through cycles of tightening and relaxation. At times the adjustments were necessitated by circumstances such as the Tiananmen incident. At other times, they reflected internal disagreement. Minister of Education Liu Xiyao was opposed to the liberal approach; it was after his replacement by Jiang Nanxiang in 1978 that the liberal policy went into full swing.

On the home front, there have been steady efforts to augment the education sector, where the participation rate in higher education had increased from 1.7% in 1980 to 5.7% in 1996,[6] and enrolment at universities quadrupled between 1978 and 1998 (Table 1). However, the demand for higher education has always outstripped supply, which in turn translates into pressure to go overseas. On average, for every five graduate students enrolling at universities in China, one student has gone abroad.

In the early fifties, one motivation to send students abroad was to acquire foreign language skills. Emphasis quickly shifted to science and engineering, which have been the dominant fields of study since then. In the beginning, overseas study was within the purview of the Ministry of Foreign Affairs and the Ministry of Education. Since the time of the first Five-Year Plan (1953–57), the State Science and Technology Commission has also been involved in discussions regarding overseas study. There had been very few students pursuing humanities and social sciences by mid 1980s. In response to American demand for a more balanced distribution of study fields, Li Peng in 1986 promised to increase the cohort of students pursuing social sciences.[7]

The Committee of Scholarly Communication with the People's Republic of China reported that the vast majority of students from China were in the technical fields, with humanities and social sciences

---

[6] *UNESCO Statistical Yearbook 1998.*
[7] *Renmin Ribao*, 27 October 1986.

Table 1. China's University Student Statistics

Year	Total Undergraduate Student Enrolment	Total Postgraduate Student Enrolment	Number of Students Going Abroad to Study	Number of Returning Students	Estimated Rate of Return*
1978	856 322	10 934	860	248	0.29
1979	1 019 950	18 831	1 777	231	0.13
1980	1 143 712	21 604	2 124	162	0.08
1981	1 279 472	18 848	2 922	1 143	0.39
1982	1 153 956	25 847	2 326	2 116	0.91
1983	1 206 823	37 166	2 633	2 303	0.88
1984	1 395 656	57 566	3 073	2 920	0.95
1985	1 703 115	87 331	4 888	1 424	0.29
1986	1 879 994	110 371	4 676	1 388	0.30
1987	1 958 725	120 191	4 703	1 605	0.34
1988	2 065 923	112 776	3 786	3 000	0.79
1989	2 082 111	101 339	3 329	1 753	0.53
1990	2 062 695	93 018	2 950	1 593	0.54
1991	2 043 662	88 128	2 900	2 069	0.71
1992	2 184 376	94 164	6 540	3 611	0.55
1993	2 535 517	106 771	10 742	5 128	0.48
1994	2 798 639	127 935	19 071	4 230	0.22
1995	2 906 429	145 443	20 381	5 750	0.28
1996	3 021 079	163 322	20 905	6 570	0.31
1997	3 174 362	176 353	22 410	7 130	0.32
1998	3 408 764	198 885	17 622	7 379	0.42
1999	4 085 874	233 513	23 749	7 748	0.33

*Rate of return is estimated by dividing the number of students returning by the number of students going abroad in the same year. However, students usually return in later years.
Sources: China Statistical Yearbook, 1993, 1995, 1997, 1998, 1999 and 2000.

amounting to only approximately 4%. The number of students sent abroad by the Academy of Sciences (CAS) were about 10 times those sent by the Academy of Social Sciences (CASS) [Liu (1995)]. As the CASS was the main dispatcher of students in the social science field while the CAS was only one among others sending science and engineering students, the proportion of social science students was far less than one-tenth, in fact almost one-twentieth. The distribution of study fields among self-financed students was less skewed towards the natural sciences. In the 1990s, many self-financed students opted to study business management with a view to entering the business sector.

In the 1950s and 1960s, those dispatched abroad were mainly scholars and scientists who were experienced and already possessed a career base. As university reform took place [Wang (2000)], there was a need for qualified staff, and overseas study began to emphasize study for masters and doctoral degrees [Hayhoe (1989)]. By the 1990s, there were already a huge number of self-financed students going abroad to pursue degrees, and consequently, the emphasis of public funding shifted back to scholars and senior professionals.

The statistics of personnel going abroad to study between 1978 and 1989[8] (Table 2) show a return rate of 52% for personnel sponsored by the state and public units against the return rate of 4% of self-funded students, giving an overall return rate of 41%. The 52% return rate of publicly-funded students is a clear indication of the liberal policy towards students studying abroad.

From the 1978–1989 statistics, it is interesting to note that among the publicly-funded personnel, doctoral students had the lowest return rate of 8.6%, while masters students had 23%. Visiting scholars had the highest return rate of 65%.

3. LIBERAL POLICY

When the policy regarding overseas study was promulgated, the percentage of students returning was left entirely open. There was no

[8] Guangzhou Government Network for Returning Scholars www.gzscse.gov.cn.

Table 2. Personnel Going Abroad for Study and Returning Between 1978 and 1989

		Outgoing Personnel			Returning Personnel		
		State sponsored	Enterprise sponsored	TOTAL	State sponsored	Enterprise sponsored	TOTAL
Publicly funded personnel	Visiting scholars	21 963	32563	54 526	15 624	19 928	35 552
	Doctoral students	5 003	7 562	12 565	653	427	1 080
	Masters students	1 947	2 819	4 766	366	722	1 088
	Undergraduate students	1 081	486	1 567	236	267	503
	TOTAL	29 994	43 430	73 424	16 879	21 344	38 223
Self-financed students *				22 677			960
TOTAL				96 101			39 183

Source: Guangzhou Government Network for Returning Scholars www.gzscse.gov.cn.

planned projection regarding students returning, and no targeted percentage of returning students. There is evidence to suggest that the return rates have been accepted with no expression of dissatisfaction, until perhaps very recently. Table 1 shows that the one-third return rate has been the consistent trend over more than 10 years. There has been no public outcry, not even against the one-half return rate of publicly-funded students.

Against the thinking that citizens should return to the state the benefits they derived, which was a concern of then Minister of Education Liu Xiyao, was the realization that at the stage of economic development at the time, China could not offer sufficient opportunities for personal development for its educated persons, and it might do the nation little harm but the individual a lot of good for them to be allowed to stay abroad, a point of view put forward by Qian Xuesen,[9] the mastermind of China's nuclear programme.

---

[9] *Shijie Jingji Daobao*, 26 September 1988.

While Chinese leaders might have expected a significant proportion of students to stay on abroad, it was not a point that could be conveniently stated explicitly. Most countries have a policy of expecting their foreign students to return to their own countries at the end of their study. While many developing countries are net "exporters" of people and talents, no country has an announced policy encouraging their nationals to stay abroad.

Deng Xiaoping's policy towards overseas study was predicated on the premise that training acquired by nationals abroad will eventually accrue to the benefit of the country in the long term. Deng said in 1978: "Even if half of those sent abroad do not return, there remains one half to help with the four modernisations. It is still better than not sending or sending less." [Kong et al. (1994)] Deng endorsed the policy to increase greatly the number of personnel going abroad.

Deng Xiaoping's policy was remarkable in three aspects. Firstly, it marked a significant reversal of hitherto strict control. Secondly, the policy action was taken intuitively against an absence of manpower planning since at that time there were no detailed calculations or estimations of numbers of talents staying abroad, nor would such forecasts be possible. Thirdly, the policy has been remarkably successful, as is borne out in hindsight.

The policy regarding overseas studies has been considered successful in the following aspects. It has enabled a much larger number of students to go abroad than would have been possible otherwise. Between 1978 and 1989, self-financed students accounted for 24% of the total going abroad (Table 2); in the 1990s this percentage increased to over 50%. The policy has ensured that returning students are suitably motivated; they were not forced to come back as there was no legal bond to return. Market forces ensure that returning students are appropriately placed in positions for which they are suitably qualified. China has not suffered from the brain drain, in the sense of a development setback or any undesirable economic effects arising from a lack of manpower. Also, there has been no sign of a general deficiency in manpower.

4. Early Measures to Attract the Return of Students

The Chinese government has taken steps to encourage the return of Chinese students overseas. The following are some measures [Liu (1995)] introduced in 1990:

- Sending visiting missions consisting of university presidents and professors to visit 48 universities in the US, and holding seminars and making house visits. In 1991 three recruiting missions consisting of government, provincial and city officials visited seven European countries and held 72 seminars.
- Establishing an overseas students page in *People's Daily* Overseas Edition, to carry information of interest to overseas students, for them to express their views, and to provide solutions to their queries.
- Inviting students to go on home tours to visit priority laboratories in Peking and Qinghua universities and other technologically advanced districts.
- Organising exhibitions of technological breakthroughs made by returnees to demonstrate that knowledge acquired overseas can be applied to good use at home.
- Providing funding for research.

The actions undertaken were remarkably imaginative and included all the modalities that had been tried by other countries. However, economic conditions in China were still backward, technology was not advanced and working conditions far from ideal. Despite doing all the right things, success was limited in the early 1990s.

The actions in 1990 were undertaken in part to appease students who were disturbed by the Tiananmen incident in 1989. Many had said they had changed their minds about returning to China [Qin (1999)]. At the same time, these activities were a continuation of the ongoing effort initiated in 1988. The State Council announced in 1992 an amnesty for overseas students who had taken part in pro-democracy activities in the aftermath of the 1989 Tiananmen incident.

5. Recent Manpower Needs

In the late 1990s, there was a large influx of skilled personnel in the field of information technology [Wong and Nah (2000)]. Compared to other areas of industry and technology, the IT sector requires much less investment in equipment as a prerequisite. Thus China is not hampered by its lack of capital to invest in costly equipment. As information technology allows participants and newcomers to reach the frontiers relatively quickly with little prior experience built up in the field, there is a much shorter cycle before efforts become revenue generating. Consequently a large number of entrepreneurs who may have little capital are encouraged to jump onto the bandwagon.

The demand for technical personnel in the information technology field is a worldwide trend.[10] Faced with a projected shortage of IT manpower in the next five to ten years, the United States as well as European countries have taken policy actions designed to procure and increase their IT manpower. In this regard, China is no exception.

China wants to attract the return of nationals in the following categories: (1) persons intending to invest or manage business, especially setting up new business, which may be technology related (technopreneurs, who combine business acumen, management expertise and technical knowledge); (2) professionals with know-how in product development and commercialisation; and (3) experts in the frontiers of research in their fields. The first category of persons are in short supply everywhere. Most countries have paid attention to conditions which would attract them and encourage them to stay. The second category of professionals are in severe shortages in China. The third category of persons in the frontiers of their fields are welcome in most countries. It is not particularly remarkable that China would like to attract such persons. It should be pointed out that China is not keen to take on lesser researchers. Research institutes in China are mostly fully staffed and often have to turn down the applications of many nationals wishing to return, a syndrome not uncommon in many advanced countries.

---

[10] "The Tug of War for Asia's Best Brains", *Far Eastern Economic Review*, 9 November 2000, p. 38.

Apart from specific needs, there appears to be no general shortage of technical manpower in China. It is significant to note that President Jiang Zemin mentioned the student statistics in a matter-of-fact way. He was neutral with regard to whether the one-third return rate was satisfactory or unsatisfactory. In the same interview he said, "Of course, for various reasons, quite a number of them have decided not to — at least for the moment — come back, which is understandable."[1] It was commentators and journalists who inserted the value judgment that the one-third rate was too low, in their attempt to provide a motivation behind recent policy actions.

6. Recent Ad hoc Measures

Against the background given in the above paragraphs, it can be appreciated that policy actions taken so far in respect of attracting the return of nationals trained overseas are not the result of overall manpower planning, but are undertaken on an *ad hoc* basis to address specific needs. They are demand driven rather than supply led, in the sense of catering to specific demands in manpower needs rather than planning for a manpower supply.

The most important examples of policy actions undertaken in recent months have been the ones by the Beijing municipality,[2] which are systematic and comprehensive and which are expected to be the model for actions at the city and provincial levels elsewhere. Some parts may even be implemented at the national level.

Highlights of the Beijing regulations are as follows. They can be classified into four categories (stated in brackets.) : (1) conferring the same benefits as resident nationals, (2) conferring the same benefits as foreigners, (3) ensuring no loss of seniority for time spent abroad, (4) benefits over and above the foregoing categories.

- Returnees who are engaged in technology ventures or advanced research are granted *hukou* or "permanent residence permits" of Beijing, irrespective of their original residence state before they went abroad (1).

- Returnees are eligible for government financial assistance for their research projects, which was hitherto limited only to local Chinese nationals (1).
- Returnees who have already acquired foreign citizenship or permanent residency overseas are entitled to enjoy the same privileges accorded to foreigners in China (2).
- Returnees can remit their salaries and profits abroad and are not subject to foreign exchange restrictions (2).
- Returnee's seniority is to be reckoned continuously uninterrupted by periods spent abroad (3).
- Children of returnees are eligible to enter schools for residents. Other things being equal, they are given priority in admission. Children of returnees are given special consideration for enrolling in good schools regardless of their Chinese language proficiency (4).
- Returnees can purchase a small domestic car for personal use on a tax-free basis (4). This has been a customs regulation in force nationally since 1992.[5]
- The salaries of returnees employed by enterprises owned by the municipality are negotiated on an individual basis; returnees can receive a subsidy of up to 10 times the salary allocated to the post (4).

While most of the incentives enacted by the Beijing municipality lend themselves to emulation by other cities and provinces in China, the Beijing *hukuo* is a unique attraction. Beijing's uniqueness is in no small part related to *Zhongguancun*, a district specialising in technology and knowledge-intensive activities, dubbed China's Silicon Valley, which poses a special attraction for overseas Chinese talents. Recent plans by the municipality to develop and expand the district has further motivated and hastened the promulgation of the incentives to attract the return of overseas talents. *Zhongguancun* has set up a representative office in Silicon Valley in the US to promote business and to facilitate the return of talented Chinese nationals currently working there.[11]

[11] "Overseas students target of tech park", *South China Morning Post*, 1 February 2000.

Elsewhere in China, similar trends are observed. In November 1999, Guangzhou introduced regulations encouraging overseas scholars to work in Guangzhou.[12] Returnees and their family members are eligible for the Guangzhou *hukou*, with a waiver of the usual application fees. Persons who have acquired foreign nationalities are allowed to remit their income out of the country. The period spent overseas, including time spent for masters and doctoral degrees, will be counted towards the calculation of seniority. Children of returnees will be given favourable consideration for admission to schools. One particularly favourable stipulation is that, where the returnee and spouse live apart, the employer should be responsible for the expenses of a round-trip visit once every year. When the need arises, returnees may be granted multiple exit and re-entry permits to travel to Hong Kong or out of the country. Technology transfer projects of returnees are eligible for priority accommodation in technology incubator parks at favourable rentals and for financial assistance from the Innovation Fund for Overseas Scholars, which can amount to more than 100,000 yuan. Approved commercial projects will also receive priority in venture capital support.

In a bid to improve the employment market for returning students, Guangzhou and Shenzhen have recently held highly publicized "talent fairs". The high profile events were charged with specific recruitment targets, and they have been hailed as eminently successful [Ye (2000)].

In Kunming, the High-tech Development Zone gives returning Chinese students the same incentives as overseas investors. In addition, the Yunnan government offers a bonus of up to 3 million yuan for outstanding contributions made by nationals or returnees toward the upgrading of the local economy.

In Hangzhou, returnees can register their new businesses as foreign-funded enterprises, and enjoy the same tax benefits as those provided for foreign enterprises. A start-up fund of 80 million yuan is put aside to assist returnees in setting up their businesses. Another fund of 20 million yuan has been set up to reward significant contributions to the local economy.

---

[12] Guangzhou Government Order No. 10 (12.10.2000).

Targeted at knowledge-based enterprises sponsored by returning and not-yet-returned overseas Chinese scholars, the Suzhou Pioneering Park for Overseas Chinese Scholars was set up in 1998 as an incubation site of the Suzhou New and Hi-Tech Innovation Service Centre. The Park features short-stay accommodation for overseas Chinese scholars. It offers a rental incentive of "first-year exemption and second-year reduction by half" to tenants engaged in developing or prototyping state-of-art products.

State funding to universities and research institutes has recently been increased in order to attract returning scholars. The Chinese Academy of Sciences was allocated an additional 600 million yuan to lure the return of senior Chinese scientists working overseas; the Ministry of Education has given 1.8 billion yuan to a group of elite universities, including Peking and Qinghua, for them to top up the pay of outstanding faculty members. In addition, a number of private sponsorship programmes, such as the Cheung Kong Fund financed by Hongkong tycoon Li Ka-shing, are in place to attract young, overseas mainland talents to take up professorships in key universities in China.

7. NATIONAL POLICY TO ENCOURAGE RETURN OF HIGH LEVEL TALENTS

Subsequent to the enactment of the Beijing regulations in May 2000, the central government in August 2000 promulgated a statement encouraging the return of high level expatriate talents.[3] The statement indicated that high level expatriate national talents can be appointed to leadership positions in the insurance and finance fields. They can take up professional leadership positions or senior executive management positions in state enterprises and tertiary institutions. They are also eligible for appointment to directorate positions not involving central government responsibilities. Permanent residency obtained abroad (e.g., green card) may be retained. Those willing to relinquish their permanent residency abroad are eligible to be appointed legal representatives of their units. The statement further expresses that compensation to returnees should be calculated according to their ability and contribution.

Apparently catering to the needs of those used to a western lifestyle, the statement stipulates that assistance should be given to find employment for family members of returnees. Assistance will also be provided to place children of returnees in better bilingual schools and in universities.

The statement of the central government is significant in that it provides important indication with respect to the eligibility of returning nationals to responsible positions. While singling some sectors for mention, such as insurance, and paying attention to details regarding employment of family members, the statement appears to be less than completely systematic and comprehensive. It is likely to be intended as an early indication of support for encouraging the return of talents, to be followed by a more comprehensive national policy at a later date.

The policy measures are pragmatic, directed towards providing specific economic incentives. No appeal is made to patriotism. Students opting to return to China do so because they know it is to their comparative advantage to live and work in the motherland. Ideological preparation used to be a prerequisite to studying abroad in the 1950s and 1960s.[5] Since the 1990s, it has no longer been mentioned.

REFERENCES

Du, Ruiqing, *Chinese Higher Education: A Decade of Reform and Development (1978–1988)*, Macmillan: 1992.
Hayhoe, R., *China's Universities and the Open Door*, M.E. Sharpe: 1989.
Kong, Fanjun et al., *Zou Chu Zhong Guo* (Leaving China), 1994.
Liu, Sun-Chi, *A Study of Mainland Chinese Overseas Students*, 1992.
Liu, Sun-Chi, *Education and Research on Human Studies and Social Sciences in Mainland China in the Past 20 Years (1975–1995): A Policy Approach*, 1995.
Pomfret, John, "Brain Drain Over, Chinese Return with Seeds of Culture Clash", *International Herald Tribune*, 17 October 2000.
Qin, Wenjie, *China's brain drain: a study of the factors affecting Chinese students' and scholars' decisionto remain in the United States and not to return to China*, Boston University doctoral thesis, 1999.
Wang, Jueichi, "Development of Higher Education in the Chinese Mainland in the 1990s", *Mainland China Studies*, Vol. 43, No.4, April 2000, pp. 59–79.

Wong, John & Nah Seok Ling, "Internet in China", *EAI Background Brief* No. 63, and "E-Commerce in China", *EAI Background Brief* No. 65, 2000.

Ye, Lou, "Overseas Students Coming Back at a Golden Time", *Beijing Review*, 7 February 2000, p. 20.

Part V

Regional Impact

16

Implications of China's Reform and Development on the Asia Pacific

JOHN WONG*

CHINA'S DYNAMIC GROWTH IN A REGIONAL PERSPECTIVE

The Chinese economy has experienced spectacular growth since it started economic reform and open-door policy some 20 years ago. Real growth during 1979–99 was at an annual rate of 9.7%. China's current per-capita GDP, just near US$900, is about the level of Taiwan in 1974. In 1978, China's total nominal GNP was only US$44 billion or just 60% higher than that of Taiwan. By mid-2000, China's total nominal GNP reached US$1 trillion, which was three times of Taiwan's and ranked the world's seventh largest.[1] In terms of purchasing power parity (PPP), the Chinese economy in 1999 became the world's second largest after the USA — one needs, of course, to qualify the possibility of the PPP measure to overstate China's real GNP.

---

* Professor John Wong is Research Director of East Asian Institute, National University of Singapore, Singapore. He would like to thank Research Officer Miss Nah Seok Ling for her valuable assistance in updating the statistical tables.

[1] World Bank, *World Development Report 1999/2000*. Also, *Mingpao* (Hong Kong), September 20, 2000.

According to the World Bank, it took Britain about 58 years to double its per-capita income from 1780–1838; 34 years for Japan (1885–1919); and 11 years for South Korea (1966–77); but only 9 years for China (1978–87) and another 9 years for it to double again (1987–96).[2] If the World Bank could also report on Taiwan's economic miracle, it would find that Taiwan's growth performance had been equally impressive: it also took Taiwan only a few years to double its per-capita income in the 1980s. This suggests that late-comers, once having successfully taken off, can achieve faster economic growth and take a shorter time span to double their per-capita income, because they can take advantage of the backlog of technological progress and surplus capital created by the forerunners.

China's economic performance in the past two decades has indeed been breath-taking. But viewed in the overall East Asian context, China's hyper-growth is not really exceptional. Nor is it unprecedented. However, on account of its vast size and diversity, China's dynamic growth has far-reaching implications for the East Asian region.

The East Asian (EA) region is commonly defined to comprise Japan, China, the four Newly Industrialized Economies (NIEs) of South Korea, Taiwan, Hong Kong and Singapore, and the four Association of Southeast Asian Nations (ASEAN) of Indonesia, Malaysia, the Philippines, and Thailand — the original ASEAN members. Situated on the western rim of the Pacific, all these East Asian economies (EAEs) have displayed a strong capacity for dynamic growth, with many having experienced high growth for a sustained period until 1997 when they were hit, in varying degrees, by the regional financial crisis. In fact, several of the EAEs had one after another broken the past world growth records, so much so that the World Bank in its well-know study referred to the high growth phenomenon of East Asia as the "East Asian Miracle".[3] (Table 1).

Japan was the first non-Western country to become industrialized. Its high growth started back in the 1950s after it had achieved its post-

---

[2] World Bank, *China 2020: Development Challenges in the New Century*, (1997).
[3] *The East Asian Miracle* (New York, Oxford University Press, 1994).

Table 1. Performance Indicators of East Asian Economies

	Population (Millions) 1998	GNP per-capita (US$) 1998	PPP estimates of GNP per-capita (US$) 1998	Growth of GDP (%) 1960-70	1970-80	1980-90	1990-98	1998	1999[a]	Consumer Price Inflation (%) 1999[b]	Annual Export Growth (%) 1990-98	Mfg exports as % of total exports 1997	Exports as % of GDP 1998	Gross Domestic Savings as % of GDP 1990-97	1998	Gross Domestic Investment as % of GDP 1990-97	1998
Japan	126	32,380	23,180	10.9	5.0	4.0	1.3	-2.5	0.8	-0.7	3.9	95	9*	34	32*	30	29*
China	1239	750	3,220	5.2	5.8	10.2	11.1	7.8	7.1	-0.9	14.9	85	22	43	43	39	39
NIEs																	
South Korea	46	7,970	12,270	8.6	9.5	9.4	6.2	-5.8	10.0	1.2	15.7	87	38	36	34	37	35
Taiwan	22	13,121	n.a.	9.2	9.7	7.1	n.a.	4.6	5.6	0.1	2.4	96	48	26	25*	23	21*
Hong Kong	7	23,670	22,000	10.0	9.3	6.9	4.4	-5.1	2.1	-4.2	9.5	93	125	32	30	31	30
Singapore	3	30,060	28,620	8.8	8.5	6.4	8.0	0.3	5.6	1.2	13.3	84	133	48	51	36	37
ASEAN-4																	
Indonesia	204	680	2,790	3.9	7.6	6.1	5.8	-13.2	0.1	1.6	8.6	42	28	33	31	33	31
Malaysia	22	3,600	6,990	6.5	7.8	5.3	7.7	-7.5	5.4	1.6	13.2	76	118	38	47	39	32
Philippines	75	1,050	3,540	5.1	6.3	1.0	3.3	-0.5	3.2	4.3	11.0	85	56	17	15	22	25
Thailand	61	2,200	5,840	8.4	7.2	7.6	7.4	-10.4	5.0	0.7	11.1	71	47	34	36	39	35

Notes: (1) a denotes data obtained from Far Eastern Economic Review; (2) b denotes statistics Asiaweek's estimates; (3) *denotes 1997 figures; (4) n.a. denotes not available

Sources: World Bank, World Development Report 1999/2000, Washington D.C.: Oxford University Press; Statistics Department, Taiwan Ministry of Economic Affairs, http://www.moea.gov.tw; "Bottomline", Asiaweek, 28 January 2000; and "Prices & Trends", Far Eastern Economic Review, 13 April 2000.

war recovery, and carried the growth momentum over to the 1960s. Japan's economic growth engine was initially based on the export of labour-intensive manufactured products; but it was soon forced by rising wages and increasing costs to shed its comparative advantage for labour-intensive manufacturing in favour of the four NIEs, which started their industrial take-off in the 1960s. These four NIEs, once dubbed "Asia's Four Little Dragons", constituted the most dynamic component of the EA region, and their near double-digit rate growth has been sustained for three decades, from the 1960s to the 1980s. By the late 1970s and early 1980s, high costs and high wages had also caught up with these NIEs, which had to restructure their economies towards more capital-intensive and higher value-added activities, and to pass their comparative advantage for labour-intensive products to the late-comers of China and the four ASEAN economies. Japanese scholars like to depict this pattern of development as the "flying geese" model.[4]

Japan today is a world-class economic superpower, second only to the United States. In 1998, Japan's nominal per-capita income, at US$32,000, was about 40 times of China's and some 20 times that of ASEAN-four's. However, the income gaps between Japan and the four NIEs have been closing up, as the NIEs have graduated to become "NDEs" or "newly developed economies". South Korea, with the lowest per-capita income of the four NIEs, is already a member of the OECD. For political reasons, Singapore has chosen not to join the OECD, even though Singapore's per-capita income now ranks the world's fourth highest — slightly higher than that of the United States.

More significantly, the ASEAN-four (which were originally resource-based economies, depending heavily on the export of natural resources and primary commodities for growth) have all become industrialized in the sense that their overall economic growth is now primarily fuelled by the growth of their manufacturing sector, particularly manufactured

---

[4] The "flying geese" concept of development was originally coined by a Japanese economist, Kaname Akamatzu. ("A Historical Pattern of Economic Growth in Developing Countries", *Developing Economies*, Vol. No. 1, March/August, 1962).

exports.[5] The same is true for China. When it started the open-door policy 20 years ago, half of China's exports still made up of primary products, compared to only 16% today. Suffice it to say that as a result of their sustained economic growth, the EAEs have also been rapidly industrialized.

An important feature of these EAEs is their growing economic interdependence. The EAEs, despite their inherent political, social and economic divergences, can actually integrate economically quite well as a regional grouping. This is essentially the underlying meaning of the "flying geese" principle. Thus, Japan is obviously the natural economic leader of the group and has in fact been the prime source of capital and technology for other EAEs. The resource-based ASEAN-four complement well with the manufacturing-based NIEs while both are also complementary with the more developed Japanese economy. Then the huge potential of China, with its vast resource base and diverse needs, offers additional opportunities for all.

Not surprisingly, the EA region has already developed a significant degree of economic interdependence as manifested in its fairly high level of intra-regional trade. As shown in Table 2, the EA region in 1998, despite the Asian financial crisis, still absorbed 48% of China's total exports; 43% of the average of the NIEs', 45% of the average of the ASEAN-four's, though only 33% of Japan's — still unusually high for Japan as a global economic power.

Apart from intra-regional trade, intra-regional foreign direct investment (FDI) flows has increasingly operated as a strong integrating force for the EA region, especially since a great deal of regional FDI is trade-related in nature. The EAEs are essentially open and outward-looking in terms of being heavily dependent on foreign trade and foreign investment for their economic growth. In particular, China and ASEAN

---

[5] Oil and gas used to constitute 80% of Indonesia's exports; Malaysia's exports used to be dominated by rubber, tin and palm oil; Thailand was used to depend heavily on rice and sugar; and the Philippines used to depend heavily on coconut products. See John Wong, *ASEAN Economies in Perspective: A Comparative Study of Indonesia, Malaysia, the Philippines, Singapore and Thailand.* (London, Macmillan Press, 1979).

410 CHINA'S ECONOMY INTO THE NEW CENTURY

Table 2. Intra-Regional Trade of the East Asian Region, 1998

	Total Exports (US$million)	Industrial Countries (%) Total	U.S.A.	Japan	EEC	China %	NIEs %	ASEAN-4 %	East Asia %	East Asia less Japan %
China	183,744	55.3	20.7	16.2	15.8	-	28.7	3.0	47.9	31.7
Japan	387,955	54.3	30.9	-	19.4	5.2	20.2	7.8	33.2	33.2
NIEs										
S. Korea	132,256	48.1	17.4	9.3	18.0	9.0	14.0	7.3	39.6	30.3
Taiwan	110,580	n.a.	26.6	8.4	16.7[a]	n.a.	26.7	6.5	41.6	33.2
Hong Kong	173,693	48.4	23.4	5.3	16.7	34.5	5.8	2.9	48.5	43.2
Singapore	109,886	47.2	20.0	6.6	17.0	3.7	15.0	21.3*	42.8	36.2
ASEAN-4										
Indonesia	54,341	55.2	15.8	17.7	16.6	4.2	22.8	5.4	50.1	32.4
Malaysia	73,470	51.9	21.6	10.5	16.4	2.7	28.0	6.1	47.3	36.8
Philippines	29,496	70.7	34.4	14.4	20.5	1.2	18.4	6.4	40.4	26.0
Thailand	54,489	58.2	22.3	13.7	19.0	3.2	18.1	6.5	41.5	27.8
Total Imports										
China	140,385	51.6	12.1	20.2	15.5	-	30.4	5.8	56.4	36.2
Japan	281,243	47.5	24.0	-	15.5	13.2	10.2	11.4	34.8	34.8
NIEs										
S. Korea	93,282	61.3	21.9	18.1	13.7	7.0	4.2	7.4	36.7	18.6
Taiwan	104,670	n.a.	18.8	25.8	16.8[a]	n.a.	9.9	9.1	44.8	19.0
Hong Kong	184,602	33.6	7.5	12.6	11.7	40.6	16.4	5.5	75.1	62.5
Singapore	101,606	52.1	18.5	16.7	15.0	4.8	9.6	22.6*	53.7	37.0
ASEAN-4										
Indonesia	29,185	48.3	8.6	16.2	16.9	4.4	25.5	16.3	62.4	46.2
Malaysia	58,319	55.5	19.6	19.7	12.9	3.2	27.0	8.8	58.7	39.0
Philippines	31,393	55.5	21.9	20.3	9.7	4.2	22.2	7.9	54.6	34.3
Thailand	43,108	54.6	14.0	23.6	13.8	4.2	16.0	8.6	52.4	28.8

Notes: 1) Singapore is also a member of ASEAN. 2) "East Asia" is defined to comprise Japan, China, 4 NIEs and ASEAN-4. 3) * Figure for Indonesia is not available. 4) n.a. denotes not available. 5) a denotes data for EU instead of EEC

Sources: IMF, Direction of Trade Statistics Yearbook 1999; and Statistics Department, Taiwan Ministry of Economic Affairs, http://www.moea.gov.tw.

have devised various incentive schemes to vie for FDI, which is generally treated not just as an additional source of capital supply but, more importantly, as a means of technology transfer and export market development.

Initially, Western capital, particularly that from the United States, dominated the FDI scene of EA. Then came the Japanese capital as the second wave, especially after the late 1970s. Today, the cumulative stock of Japanese FDI has surpassed that of American investments. Since the late 1980s, the EA region has witnessed a new but no less significant development, which is associated with the steady growth of FDI flows from the NIEs to ASEAN and China. The NIEs, particularly Taiwan, Hong Kong and Singapore, having transformed themselves from capital-shortage to capital surplus economies, became a new source of FDI flow into ASEAN and China to form the third wave. Table 3, on the intra-regional FDI flows in East Asia, serves to show how the EAEs have invested a lot in one another.

This is particularly the case for China, which in recent years, has become the most favoured destination of all developing economies for FDI. As can be seen from Table 4, the EA region, especially Hong Kong, Taiwan, Japan, Singapore and South Korea, accounted for an overwhelming share of FDI inflow to China. In other words, Japan and the NIEs have been able to capture most of the benefits arising from China's open-door policy. However, such regional predominance has been declining in recent years, as China made efforts to attract more FDI from North America and the EU. In 1998, the East Asian share of FDI in China declined to 59%, from 88% in 1992.

Suffice it to say that China's economic growth fits in very well with East Asian growth. In fact, China's dynamic economic growth since 1978 has interacted with many high-growth EAEs positively to each other's advantage. On the one hand, China has been able to harness the region's trade and investment opportunities to facilitate its own economic growth. At the same time, China's growing economic integration with the region also provides new opportunities to enhance the region's overall growth potential.

Table 3. Foreign Direct Investment by Countries (US$ Millions)

JAPAN'S FDI OUTFLOW

	1987	1988	1989	1990	1991	1992	1993	1994	1995	1996	1997	1998
China	1226 (3.7%)	296	438	349	579	1070 (3.1%)	1691	2565	3834	2628 (5.2%)	2266	1267 (2.6%)
ASEAN-5												
Indonesia	545 (1.6%)	586	631	1105	1193	1676 (4.9%)	813	1759	1596	2414 (4.8%)	2514	1285 (2.7%)
Malaysia	163 (0.5%)	387	673	725	880	704 (2.1%)	800	742	573	572 (1.1%)	791	614 (1.3%)
Philippines	72 (0.2%)	134	202	258	203	160 (0.5%)	207	668	718	559 (1.1%)	524	427 (0.9%)
Singapore	494 (1.5%)	747	1902	840	613	670 (2.0%)	644	1054	1152	1115 (2.2%)	1824	760 (1.6%)
Thailand	250 (0.7%)	859	1276	1154	807	657 (1.9%)	578	719	1224	1403 (2.8%)	1867	1637 (3.4%)

KOREA'S FDI OUTFLOW

	1987	1988	1989	1990	1991	1992	1993	1994	1995	1996	1997	1998
China	n.a.	n.a.	6	16	42	141 (11.6%)	264	632	824	836 (19.7%)	633	630 (16.2%)
ASEAN-5												
Indonesia	126 (30.7%)	20	75	164	170	164 (13.5%)	59	68	200	154 (3.6%)	178	75 (1.9%)
Malaysia	1 (0.2%)	1	3	18	-	24 (2.0%)	24	20	114	44 (1.0%)	17	21 (0.5%)
Philippines	n.a.	1	3	32	48	20 (1.6%)	14	45	57	49 (1.2%)	31	65 (1.7%)
Singapore	n.a.	n.a.	n.a.	3	5	13 (1.1%)	4	4	22	55 (1.3%)	11	128 (3.3%)
Thailand	n.a.	10	9	13	32	26 (2.1%)	37	27	22	24 (0.6%)	186	93 (2.4%)

TAIWAN'S FDI OUTFLOW

	1987	1988	1989	1990	1991	1992	1993	1994	1995	1996	1997	1998
China	n.a.	n.a.	n.a.	n.a.	174	247 (n.a.)	3168	962	1093	1229 (n.a.)	4334	2035 (n.a.)
ASEAN-5												
Indonesia	1 (0.9%)	2	0.3	62	160	40 (4.5%)	26	21	32	83 (3.8%)	56	20 (0.6%)
Malaysia	6 (5.7%)	3	159	185	442	156 (17.6%)	65	101	67	94 (4.3%)	85	20 (0.6%)
Philippines	3 (2.6%)	36	66	124	1	1 (0.1%)	7	10	36	74 (3.4%)	127	39 (1.2%)
Singapore	1 (1.3%)	6	5	48	13	9 (1%)	69	101	32	165 (7.6%)	230	158 (4.8%)
Thailand	5 (5.2%)	12	52	149	86	83 (9.4%)	109	57	51	71 (3.3%)	57	131 (4.0%)

Notes: (1) n.a. denotes not available.
(2) Statistics for Japan's FDI outflow to ASEAN-5 from fiscal year 1995 onwards were released in yen and hence, have been converted to U.S. dollars at average inter-bank rates.
(2) 1998 figures for Japan's and Korea's FDI outflows are estimated data.
(3) FDI figures for Taiwan actually refers to approved outward investment.
(4) Figures in parentheses refer to FDI outflow as a proportion of total FDI outflow of source country.
Sources: OECD, *International Direct Investment Statistics Yearbook 1999*, Paris: OECD Publications; Japan External Trade Organisation (JETRO), *Japanese Outward FDI Declines While Inward FDI Increases*, http://www.jetro.go.jp/; and Investment Commission, Taiwan's Ministry of Economic Affairs, http://www.moea.gov.tw/.

COMMON GROWTH-INDUCING CHARACTERISTICS

Why have the EAEs been able to sustain dynamic growth for such a long period? Development economists can easily explain this within the neo-classical framework. On the supply side, rapid economic growth in the EAEs, especially in their early phases of industrialization, was the outcome of their rising labour force and increasing productivity. Growth of labour productivity is associated with the shift of labour from low-productivity agriculture to high-productivity manufacturing. This has happened to Japan, South Korea, Taiwan and China.

Viewed from the demand side, the high growth of the EAEs stemmed from their high levels of domestic investment, which were generally matched by the equally high levels of domestic savings. As shown in Table 1, the EAEs, particularly China and the NIEs, have earmarked a high proportion of their GDP for domestic investment, which is generally matched by their high levels of domestic savings. High savings and high investment in the EA region have created what may be called the "virtuous circle of growth": high savings, high investment, high export growth, high GDP growth and then high savings. This is the simplest explanation of the arithmetic of the region's high economic growth.

To create wealth, capital must be combined with labour in terms of both quantity and quality. But continuing high economic growth cannot be sustained by just dumping more and more capital to an increasing size of the labour force. What is more crucial to the process of sustained economic growth is the condition of technological progress resulting from the acquisition of knowledge. Such is the "endogenous growth theory", which emphasizes improvement in productivity and investment in human capital.

Paul Krugman has argued that East Asian growth has been based exclusively on the accumulation of capital per worker rather than increases in output per worker, i.e. productivity growth. Accordingly, East Asian growth could be a flawed strategy of growth without "total factor productivity" (TFP) — the amount of measured overall growth that cannot be explained by such factors as capital or labour — and would eventually bring about a collapse in growth as in the former Soviet Union [Krugman (1994)]. His observation has since stirred up a lively debate among economists and commentators. Several researchers have argued that Krugman has exaggerated the TFP problem of East Asia, and that many EAEs have in fact experienced TFP growth [Young (1995)].

Productivity or technological progress is admittedly a nebulous concept, which is also empirically difficult to measure or quantify. It is well known that in East Asia, particularly Japan and the NIEs, the accumulation of human capital has been highly successful, much like its accumulation of physical capital. The best proxy to indicate successful human resource development of the EAEs is to examine their achievements in education. It is well known that many EAEs have made remarkable progress in education and human resource development. This, coupled with EAEs' superb entrepreneurship, must have made a positive impact on their TFP.

In the case of China, for instance, its high growth during the last 20 years has indeed been accompanied by substantial productivity gains. In accounting for China's 9.4% growth of 1978–95, the World Bank has identified 8.8% (elasticity: 0.4) for physical capital growth, 2.7% (elasticity: 0.3) for human capital growth measured by years of education per worker, and 2.4% (elasticity: 0.3) for labour force increases, leaving the unexplained share of growth at 46%. This means that of China's 9.4% GDP growth, 4.3% is the unexplained residue, which is unusually large, compared to South Korea and Japan for the appropriate periods. A substantial part of the residual portion could be the TFP, which was generated from economic reform and the open-door policy.[6] In other words, China's high growth for the past two decades has indeed been sustained by a productivity boom.

High savings and high investment alone would not have generated such sustained high growth for China. Operating under socialist planning before 1978, China also had relatively high savings and high investment because of controlled consumption. But China's average annual growth during 1952–78 was only 5.7%, which was achieved with gross inefficiency coupled with a great deal of fluctuation. After 1978, with the introduction of economic reform and the open-door policy, China's economy started to take off by chalking up consistently near-double digit rates of growth. Economic reform, by introducing market forces to economic decision making, had brought about greater allocative efficiency. The open-door policy, by reintegrating China into the global economy, had also exposed China to greater external competitive pressures. Hence, higher TFP for China [Hu & Khan (1997)].

This brings to the fore the importance of export orientation in East Asian economic development. All EAEs share the salient common feature of operating an export-oriented development strategy, as reflected in their generally high export-GDP ratios and high export growth as shown in Table 1. Not just for Singapore and Hong Kong on account of their entrepot trade role in the region, but South Korea and the ASEAN-four also have high export-GDP ratios. As a result of following the export-oriented strategy, the EAEs were able to reap the gains from trade and specialization and to attract more FDI. It also enabled them to capture a rising share of the world market for their manufactured exports.

Specifically for China, as a result of the open door policy, China's exports grew at the hefty annual rate of 17% from US$13.7 billion in 1979 to US$195 billion in 1999. China is now the world's 9th largest exporting country. China's success in attracting FDI has been even more impressive. For the period of 1979–99, total FDI inflow to China amounted to US$307 billion, making China the second-largest recipient of international capital in the world after the United States. In all, more

---

[6] World Bank, *China 2020*, op cit.

than 200 of the world's largest global multinationals have invested in China.[7]

All the EAEs have, in varying degrees, exploited the export-oriented development strategy for their economic growth. But China has been particularly successful, even though it is a late convert to this strategy.

CHINA'S COMPETITIVE PRESSURES FOR ASEAN

Suffice it to say that China, in sharing many of the common growth-inducing characteristics of the EAEs, has fit in well with the dynamic EA region. However, China's "hyper economic growth" has also created competitive pressures for other EA economies, particularly the ASEAN economies, which are also vying for FDI with China as well as competing head-on with China's labour-intensive manufactured exports in the developed country markets. For further discussion of this topic, see [Loungani (2000)].

How far has China's dynamic export drive been achieved at the expense of the other EA exporters? Since all the EAEs have derived an important source of economic growth by pushing their manufactured exports relentlessly to the US market, an analysis of the EAEs' shares in the US market would reveal in a broad way China's competitive pressures for the other EAEs. Chart 1 shows the steady rise of China's market share in the US since 1989, particularly after the *Renminbi* devaluation in 1994, while the share for the NIEs' exports in the US market has sharply declined in the same period.

This implies that China's export drive to the US market has produced a general displacement effect for the NIEs. But it also means that the NIEs have been relinquishing their comparative advantage for the labour-intensive products to China. In fact, a substantial part (about 40%) of China's exports come from the foreign-invested enterprises, particularly those from Taiwan and Hong Kong; and parts of China's manufactured exports actually belong to the NIEs. In this sense, the economic rise of China has really not been a threat to the NIEs, which are complementary

[7] *China's Statistical Yearbook 2000.*

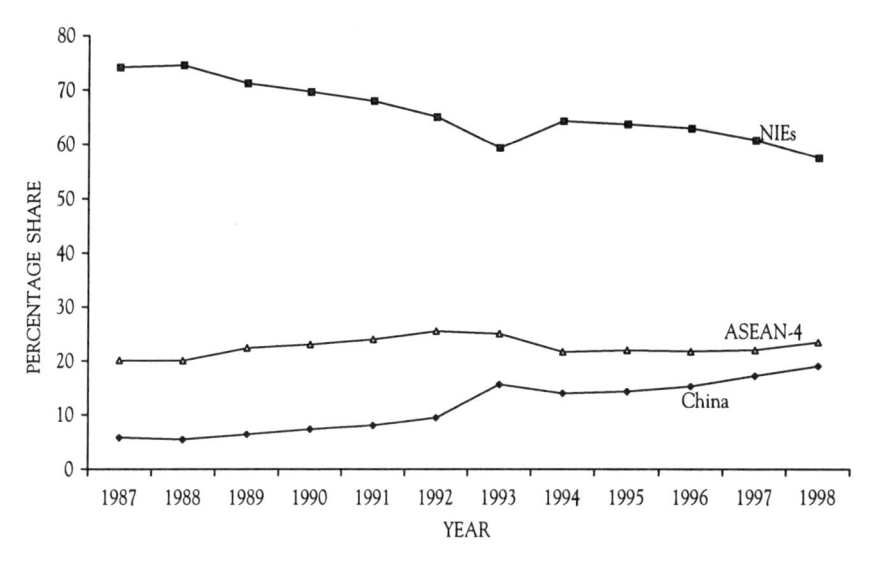

Source: IMF, Direction of Trade Statistics 1991 and 1999.

Chart 1. China and Asean-4 Increased their Market Share in US Market, 1987–1998

with the Chinese economy. China's economic growth, apart from providing trade and investment opportunities for the NIEs, has also facilitated their industrial restructuring.

At the macro level, the share of the ASEAN-4 in the US market has also increased over the years, suggesting that China's expansion has not been at the expense of the ASEAN economies. But a more detailed analysis in Chart 2 by focussing on China's dominant export items of apparel, footwear and household products brings out China's big jump in the US market vis-à-vis ASEAN's moderate gains, even after the latter's sharp currency devaluation in recent years. This indicates that China does pose serious competitive pressures for the ASEAN economies in respect of their labour-intensive manufactured exports.

The nature of China's economic relations with the ASEAN economies is actually much more complicated. In a broad sense, Sino-ASEAN economic relations are both competitive and complementary. But China and ASEAN at their present phase of development tend to be more competitive than complementary with each other. Both are

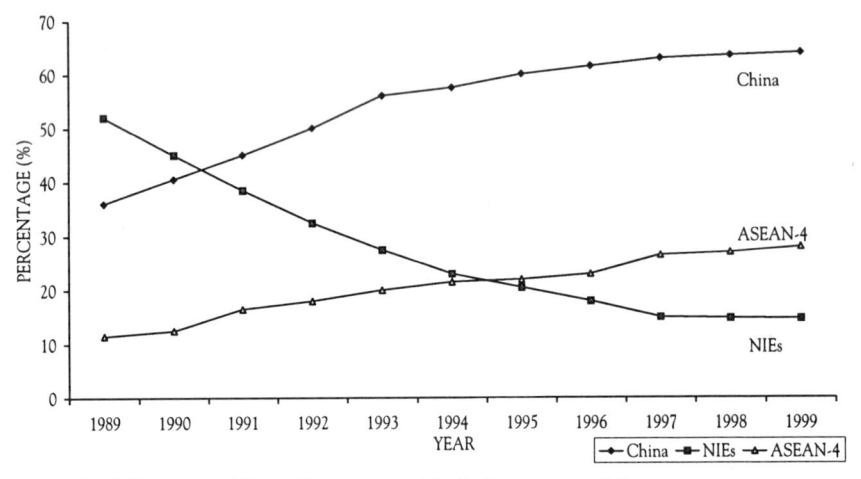

```
                                                                    China


                                                                    ASEAN-4


                                                                    NIEs

  1989  1990  1991  1992  1993  1994  1995  1996  1997  1998  1999
                              YEAR          ─◆─ China ─■─ NIEs ─▲─ ASEAN-4
```

Source: IMF, Direction of Trade Statitstics; and U.S. Department of Commerce

Chart 2. China's Gain in the U.S. Market have been Concentrated in Apparel, Footwear and Household Products, 1989–1999

economically oriented towards the industrial countries of the West and Japan. As shown in Table 2, in 1998, 55% of China's total exports and 59% of ASEAN's (average) were destined for the industrial countries. Furthermore, a great deal of the export items from China and ASEAN are quite similar, e.g., textiles and garment, shoes, toys and consumer electronics, as shown in Chart 2.

Accordingly, the level of Sino-ASEAN trade has been rather insignificant, particularly if Singapore (which is a member of ASEAN) is excluded from the group. As shown in Table 2, in 1998, China's exports to the ASEAN-4 were only 3% of its total exports while China as a market for the ASEAN-4 was also small, ranging from 4.2% for Indonesia to just 1.2% for the Philippines.

The structural weakness of the Sino-ASEAN trade is also caused by its high commodity concentration. In the 1970s and the first half of the 1980s, ASEAN's exports to China were made up of predominantly primary commodities, and usually a few items. For years, Malaysia's exports to China had consisted of virtually nothing but rubber. Sugar was an important item in the Philippines' and Thailand's exports to China and so on. At one time, China's exports to the Philippines and Thailand were dominated by petroleum products [Wong (1987)]. In recent years, though the commodity structure of Sino-ASEAN trade has become more diversified as a result of rapid industrialization progress on both sides, a few commodity items still figure prominently in ASEAN's exports to China. In 1996, for instance, crude petroleum and plywood accounted for 62% of Indonesia's exports to China while palm oil took up 28% of Malaysia's exports to China.[8]

It may be remembered that a substantial part of international trade nowadays is generated by foreign direct investment (FDI) or conducted by multinationals in the form of "intra-firm trade", especially for parts and components. If a country invests more in its trade partner, their trade will also grow faster. Thus, another reason for the present low level of Sino-ASEAN trade can be attributed to their small FDI inflow towards each other. As shown in Table 4, the bulk of FDI in China originated from East Asia comprising Hong Kong, Taiwan, Japan and South Korea, and hence, China's higher levels of trade with these East Asian economies. On the other hand, the FDI share of the five ASEAN countries in China had been rather small, rising from 2.4% in 1992 to 7.6% in 1996, and then 9.2% in 1998. Of the ASEAN share, Singapore is actually responsible for about three quarters of FDI inflow into China.

This also serves to dispel the often mistaken impression that the opening up of China has sucked away a lot of capital from the ethnic Chinese in ASEAN.[9] In the aftermath of the Asian financial crisis,

---

[8] For Indonesia, Biro Pusat Statistik, *Indonesia Foreign Trade Statistics 1996*; and for Malaysia, *Malaysia External Trade Statistics 1998*.

[9] For a detailed discussion of this topic, see John Wong, *Southeast Asian Ethnic Chinese Investing in China* (EAI Working Paper No. 15, Singapore, 23 October 1998). Many ethnic Chinese from Southeast Asia did invest in their hometowns in Guangdong and Fujian, but usually on a very small scale. The great unknown is about the exact proportion of Hong Kong and Macau FDI in China, which can be traced to the ASEAN origins. It is well known that many large investment projects in China by Southeast Asian ethnic Chinese are first incorporated in Hong Kong, which are then officially treated in China as "Hong Kong investment". However, not all the required capital for these kinds of projects had actually come from Southeast Asia and a great deal of it was in fact raised in Hong Kong or even in China.

Table 4. Foreign Direct Investment in China (US$ Million)

	1992 Actual Amount Invested	1992 %	1993 Actual Amount Invested	1993 %	1994 Actual Amount Invested	1994 %	1995 Actual Amount Invested	1995 %	1996 Actual Amount Invested	1996 %	1997 Actual Amount Invested	1997 %	1998 Actual Amount Invested	1998 %	1999 Actual Amount Invested	1999 %
Total	11292	100	27771	100	33946	100	37806	100	42135	100	45257	100	45463	100	40319	100
ASIA PACIFIC	9900	87.7	23333	84	28267	83.2	30235	80	32714	77.6	30389	67.1	26626	58.6	23210	57.4
Hong Kong	7706	68.2	17445	62.8	19823	58.4	20185	53.4	20852	49.5	20632	45.6	18508	40.7	16363	40.6
Taiwan	1053	9.3	3139	11.3	3391	10	3165	8.4	3482	8.3	3289	7.3	2915	6.4	2599	6.4
Japan	748	6.6	1361	4.9	2086	6	3213	8.5	3692	8.8	4326	9.6	3400	7.5	2973	7.3
South Korea	120	1.1	382	1.4	726	2	1047	2.8	1504	3.6	2142	4.7	1803	4.0	1275	3.1
ASEAN	271.6	2.4	1005.9	3.6	2240.6	6.6	2625	7	3184.3	7.6	3418	7.6	4197	9.2	3274	8.2
Indonesia	20.2	0.18	65.8	0.2	115.7	0.3	111.6	0.3	93.6	0.2	80	0.2	69	0.2	129	0.3

Sources: *Statistical Yearbook of China (1992–2000)*; and *China Monthly Statistics*.

ASEAN's FDI for China, with perhaps the exception of the capital-surplus Singapore, would be even less forthcoming. In any case, as China's FDI promotion is increasingly targeted at the more capital- and technology-intensive projects, FDI to China from the ASEAN will therefore remain insignificant.

In short, Sino-ASEAN economic relations in the foreseeable future will continue to stay at relatively low levels, even after China's accession to the WTO. Still dependent on capital, technology and markets of the West and Japan for its economic growth, China will continue to direct its major economic diplomacy efforts towards North America, Western Europe and Japan. The same is true for ASEAN. It is therefore difficult for ASEAN to develop a productive economic symbiosis with China in the way China's neighbouring economies in East Asia have done. Significant breakthrough in Sino-ASEAN economic relations will have to wait for the next phase of China's economic development when it has accomplished its economic reform and can operate effectively as an alternative engine of economic growth for the ASEAN economies.

A New Geo-political Role for China?

In the wake of the Asian financial crisis, most EAEs, with the exception of Indonesia, have rebounded. But the recovery has been uneven, as some EAEs have yet to tackle their structural reforms. But all will eventually recover and regain their high growth.

In the meanwhile, the patterns of geo-politics and geo-economics in the region are shifting, giving rise to a new configuration of economic and political relationships in the longer term. For one thing, ASEAN as a regional organization has already lost some of its political clout. How will China interact with the post-crisis region? What will happen to Sino-ASEAN economic relations? There will be new opportunities and new risks for both China and the region.

The recent economic crisis has amply shown that the Chinese economy is much less vulnerable to adverse external economic influences than the smaller ASEAN economies. Though China's externally-related sectors constitute the most dynamic part of its economy, external demand still accounts for less than 30% of its overall economic growth. China as a large economic entity has sufficient internal dynamics to maintain reasonable economic growth when the international economic environment becomes less conducive. Accordingly, China has emerged from the crisis much stronger vis-à-vis the ASEAN states. All this would position China to play a more assertive role in the post-crisis region. According to the 1998 Pentagon review of US strategic positions in Asia, "China has an important role in the evolving security architecture of the Asia-Pacific region".[10]

However, the ways in which China will play out its new geo-political role in the post-crisis region are admittedly more complex. Some Western commentators have exaggerated China's geo-political motives by assuming that China will take advantage of the weakness of other EAEs to push for a greater leadership role in the region in order to counter Western influences.[11] Perhaps in the long run, say in 10 to 20 years, but certainly not in the immediate future, as one finds little evidence that the present Chinese leadership is interested in seeking such a role in the ASEAN region.

China is, of course, fully aware of its legitimate political role in the region on account of geography and history. But having learnt a bitter lesson from its bad relations with Southeast Asia during the Cold War period, China is anxious to demonstrate a responsible and co-operative behaviour towards the ASEAN region. There is also cogent realpolitik rationale for China to continue with its low-posture towards the ASEAN region for many years to come. In any case, the ASEAN region will have to accept the gradual rise of China as geo-political reality and to adjust accordingly.

Apart from its many domestic preoccupation such as continuing with its unfinished economic and social reform programmes, China for the next five to ten years is likely to be fully absorbed in tackling its

---

[10] "Warning on role in Asian security", *South China Morning Post* (November 25, 1998).
[11] The Politics of East Asia's Economic Crisis", *Asia Wall Street Journal* (December 1, 1997).

thorny relations with Taiwan, which has recently taken a sharp turn for the worse following President Lee Teng-hui's demand for a "state-to-state" relationship with the Mainland. With the two Koreas having recently started the process of détente, the Taiwan strait remains a real hot-spot, which may flare up to upset regional stability. Singapore Senior Minister Lee Kuan Yew has warned against the "danger of miscalculation" by mainland China, Taiwan and the United States, the three parties directly involved. "Any misstep could upset growth and development in China and East Asia".[12]

References

Hu, Zuliu and Mohsin Khan, *Why Is China Growing So Fast?* (International Monetary Fund, Economic Issues No. 8, 1997).

Krugman, Paul, "The Myth of Asia's Miracle", *Foreign Affairs* (November/December, 1994).

Loungani, Prakash, "Comrades or Competitors? Trade Links between China and Other East Asian Economies", *Finance & Development* (June 2000).

Wong, John, "China's Emerging Economic Relationship with Southeast Asia", *Southeast Asian Studies* (Vol. 25, No. 3, December 1987).

Young, Alwyn, "The Tyranny of Numbers: Confronting the Statistical Realities of the East Asian Growth Experience", *Quarterly Journal of Economics* (Vol. 110, No. 3, 1995): Barry Bosworth, Susan Collins, and Yu-Chin Chen, *Accounting for Differences in Economic Growth* (Brookings Discussion Papers in International Economics, No. 115, 1995).

---

[12] *From Third World to First: The Singapore Story: 1965–2000. Memoirs of Lee Kuan Yew*, (Singapore, Times Edition, 2000), p. 731.

Table 5. Savings and Investment in East Asia

	Average Annual Growth of Investment (%) 1965-80	1980-90	1990-98	Gross Domestic Investment As % of GDP Average 1971-80	Average 1981-90	Average 1990-97	1990	1998	Gross Domestic Savings As % of GDP Average 1971-80	Average 1981-90	Average 1990-97	1990	1998
China	10.7	13.7	13.4	33.9	34.3	39.2	39	39	35.8	33.5	40.9	43	43
ASEAN-5													
Indonesia	16.1	7.1	4.4	21.6	32.0	33.4	36	31	19.3	30.4	33.1	37	31
Malaysia	10.4	2.9	10.8	29.1	33.0	38.6	34	32	24.9	30.8	37.8	33	47
Philippines	8.5	-2.5	4.4	26.5	22.3	22.4	22	25	27.8	21.9	17.3	16	15
Singapore	13.3	3.6	9.8	41.2	42.0	36.3	39	37	30.0	42.5	48.2	45	51
Thailand	8.0	8.7	6.5	22.2	24.4	39.4	37	35	25.3	26.7	33.8	34	36
South Korea	15.9	12.5	6.3	28.6	30.5	36.7	37	35	22.3	31.9	35.8	37	34
Taiwan	n.a.	n.a.	n.a.	30.5	22.6	23.2	23	25	32.1	32.9	26.4	28	26
Hong Kong	6.8	3.6	8.9	27.8	27.9	30.8	28	30	28.4	30.7	32.2	33	30
Japan	6.9	5.7	0.2	n.a.	n.a.	29.7	33	29*	n.a.	n.a.	32.0	34	30*

Notes: (1) * denotes 1997 figures. (2) n.a. denotes not available.
Sources: World Bank, *World Development Report* 1992, 1999/2000; and Asia Development Bank, *Asian Development Outlook*, 1992, 2000.

17

Has the Asian Financial Crisis Eroded China's Export Competitiveness?[†]

Friedrich Wu[*]

1. Introduction

Since the onset of the Asian financial crisis in mid-1997, there have been rising speculations that China could be losing export competitiveness vis-à-vis its regional rivals, especially the ASEAN-4 (Indonesia, Malaysia, Philippines and Thailand), whose export profiles are similar to China's. Evidence supporting this argument lies mainly in the sharp deceleration, and later contraction, in China's exports from mid-1998 to mid-1999 after years of double-digit expansion. This slowdown could be attributed to the forced depreciation of the ASEAN-4 currencies, which might have helped these countries to gain export competitiveness over China. With most of these crisis-hit regional economies now returning to a nascent stage of export-led recovery, it has been argued that China

---

[†]Reprinted with permission from *Asian Profile (Canada)*, Vol. 29, No. 1 (February 2001). ©Asian Research Serice.

[*]Dr. Friedrich Wu is Head of Economic Research at the Development Bank of Singapore. He is also Honorary Research Fellow of the East Asian Institute, National University of Singapore. Views expressed in this paper are those of the author and do not necessarily reflect those of the Development Bank of Singapore.

could also re-invigorate its sagging export sector, and hence its economic growth, by similarly devaluing the yuan.

This paper will examine whether China has really lost export competitiveness since the Asian financial crisis, and thus whether the calls for devaluation are valid. It will begin with some highlights of recent developments in China's export sector and its importance to the Chinese economy. Then it will assess whether the yuan is over-valued, particularly in light of the recent devaluations in Asia. Given that manufactured goods, particularly electronics and apparel & clothing, are the main drivers of both Chinese and ASEAN-4 exports, we will compare the competitive position of China's top two components of manufactured exports to the US vis-à-vis its Southeast Asian rivals before and during the Asian financial crisis by applying the shift-share methodology. A market-share analysis of the Japanese market will also be undertaken to determine if there has been any loss in China's export competitiveness against its ASEAN-4 rivals in Japan. Finally, the paper will conclude with an assessment of the implications of our shift-share analysis for the Chinese economy.

2. Recent Developments In China's External Economy

Weakening Exports and Balance of Payments Position

At the height of the Asian financial crisis when countries like Indonesia, Malaysia and Thailand were reeling from its effects, China managed to remain relatively unaffected due in part to its non-convertible currency and closed capital markets. However, its export sector began to deteriorate from the third quarter of 1998, resulting in flat export growth for the year (Figure 1). This lacklustre performance of China's export sector, coupled with the devaluation of other Asian currencies, seemed to indicate that its export competitiveness had deteriorated. With exports accounting for nearly 20% of GDP, their importance to the Chinese economy cannot be underestimated, especially when China's other engines of growth, such as private consumption and government spending, have either stagnated or performed sluggishly. Thus a protracted mediocre

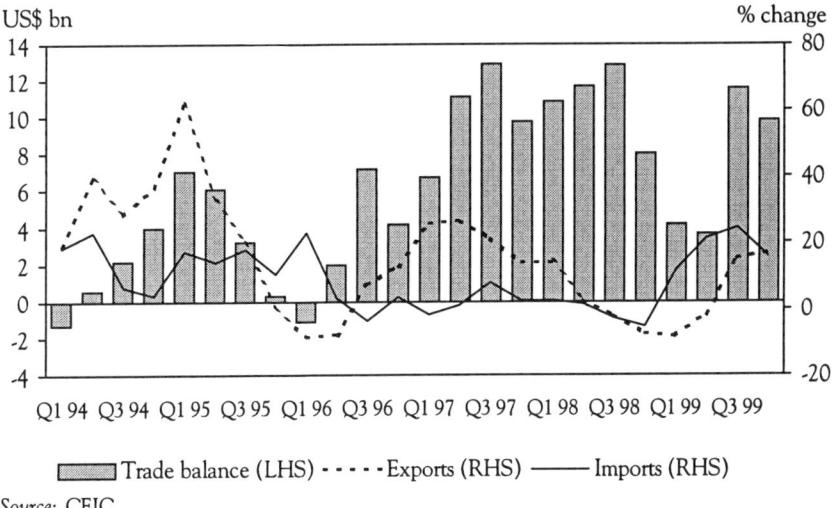

Fig. 1. China's Exports, Imports and Trade Balances

Trade balance (LHS) · · · · · Exports (RHS) ——— Imports (RHS)

Source: CEIC

performance of the export sector could hinder China's economic growth, and one possible solution to this problem would be to devalue the yuan.

The export sector is also important for the role that it plays in China's balance of payments. Despite the Asian financial crisis, China had managed to post a healthy trade surplus of US$43.6 billion in 1998, even though export growth was flat. This helped significantly to keep China's current account in surplus at US$29.3 billion in 1998 (Table 1). However, in 1999, the trade balance had plunged substantially to US$29.2 billion. Should this trend continue, the mainland's current account surplus could weaken even further from 1999's US$15.7 billion.

Is the Yuan Over-valued?

In addition to sluggish export growth and a deteriorating current account position, there have been concerns that the yuan is over-valued. One method of ascertaining the validity of this claim is to examine a country's real effective exchange rate (REER). The REER index measures the behaviour of a country's currency against currencies of its major trading

Table 2. China's Balance of Payments

US$ bn

	1994	1995	1996	1997	1998	1999
Current account	6.9	1.6	7.2	29.7	29.3	15.7
Financial account	32.6	38.7	40.0	23.0	-6.3	7.7
FDI	31.8	33.8	38.1	41.7	41.1	37.0
Portfolio investment	3.5	0.8	1.7	6.8	-3.7	-11.2
Other investment	-2.7	4.0	0.2	-25.5	-43.7	-18.1
Net errors & omissions	-9.1	-17.8	-15.5	-17.0	-16.6	-14.8
Overall balance	30.5	22.5	31.7	35.7	6.4	8.5
Foreign reserves	51.6	73.6	105.0	139.9	145.0	154.7

Source: CEIC

partners, and can be used in the analysis of its international competitiveness. A rise in the REER index denotes an erosion of competitiveness, while a fall indicates that a country becomes more competitive vis-à-vis its trading partners. In China's case, the general trend of its REER index indicates that it has been losing international competitiveness (Figure 2). In 1994, China's competitiveness slipped despite a devaluation of the yuan early that year, as its REER index rose to 103.4 in 1994 from 100.9 in 1993. Although it briefly recovered its competitiveness in 1995, the yuan's REER has since climbed steadily. Moreover, using the 100 level of the REER index as a benchmark for "fair" value shows that the yuan has been over-valued since 1996 (as the mainland's REER index has been above the 100 level). In contrast, the ASEAN-4's REER indices reveal that they have become more competitive since the Asian financial crisis. This is not surprising, given that the yuan has been held steady against the US dollar, while the currencies of some of its trading partners in Asia have depreciated substantially since the crisis.

To further gauge whether China has really lost its export competitiveness, a shift-share analysis will be conducted to determine the competitiveness of China's exports to the US (China's largest export market) (Figure 3) vis-à-vis its rivals in Southeast Asia. Since

Fig. 2. China's Reer vis-à-vis the Asean-4's

— Philippines(LHS)   ---- Thailand (LHS)   ······· Malaysia (LHS)
— China (LHS)   —■— Indonesia (RHS)

Source: DBS Bank estimates

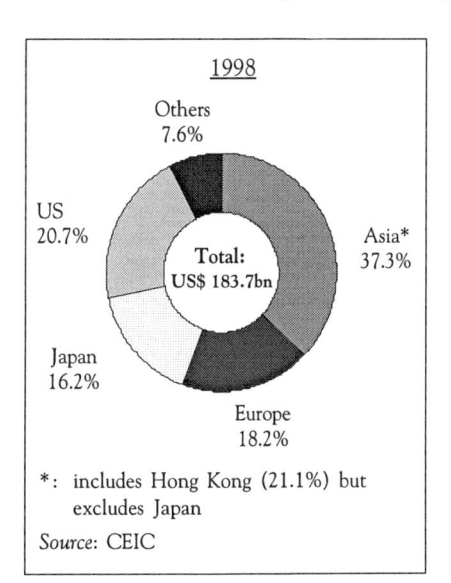

Fig. 3. China's Major Export Markets

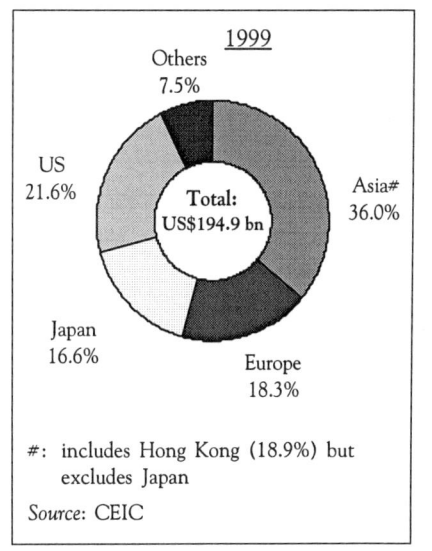

1998
Others 7.6%
US 20.7%
Japan 16.2%
Europe 18.2%
Asia* 37.3%
Total: US$ 183.7bn

*: includes Hong Kong (21.1%) but excludes Japan
Source: CEIC

1999
Others 7.5%
US 21.6%
Japan 16.6%
Europe 18.3%
Asia# 36.0%
Total: US$194.9 bn

#: includes Hong Kong (18.9%) but excludes Japan
Source: CEIC

manufactured goods make up the bulk of China's exports to the US, they provide a good proxy gauge of its overall export competitiveness in the US market as compared to the ASEAN-4. Manufactured goods are defined here as machinery and transport equipment (MTE) such as office machines and electronic products, plus miscellaneous manufactured articles (MMA) such as textiles and clothing, footwear and furniture. Together, these Chinese manufactured exports comprise nearly 85% of China's total exports to the US, while they constitute 63%, 91%, 90% and 72% of Indonesia's, Malaysia's, the Philippines' and Thailand's total exports to the US respectively (Table 2). As such, the US is an important destination for both Chinese and ASEAN-4's manufactured goods where they compete for market share for similar manufactured products. Trade data (at the Standard Industrial Trade Classification one-digit level) from the US International Trade Administration (ITA) and the Organisation for Economic Co-operation and Development (OECD) for 1994-98 are used in this study, since this period encompassed not only China's devaluation of the yuan at the beginning of 1994 but also the Asian financial crisis that began in July 1997. At the same time, an export-share analysis of the Japanese market (the second largest for China) will also be conducted to determine whether China's market share in that country has changed as compared to its ASEAN-4

Table 2. Relative Importance of US as a Market for China's and Asean-4's Manufactured Exports, 1999 (As Percentage of Total Exports to US)

(%)

	MTE	MMA	TOTAL
China	32.3	52.4	84.6
Indonesia	23.9	39.2	63.1
Malaysia	79.8	11.3	91.2
Philippines	66.5	23.4	89.9
Thailand	44.7	27.4	72.1

Note: MTE refers to machinery and transport equipment such as office machines and electronics products, while MMA refers to miscellaneous manufactured articles such as textiles and clothing, footwear and furniture
Source: CEIC

competitors. In this case, however, the shift-share analysis cannot be applied to the Japanese market due to the absence of product-level data.

3. THE SHIFT-SHARE METHODOLOGY

The shift-share methodology allows for a comparison of a country's exports to third-country markets with those of a "reference economy", which in this paper comprises China, Indonesia, Malaysia, the Philippines and Thailand. Rather than the usual static comparison, a dynamic approach is used here, that is, the yearly competitive position of a country is measured vis-à-vis the reference economy. In this way, any continuous changes in the industrial structure of an economy as well as changes in its export growth can be accounted for.

A country's export position in an overseas market is deemed to have improved (or deteriorated) if its exports grow faster (slower) than that of the reference economy, which is reflected by positive (negative) export differential. The *export differential* is measured in absolute US dollar terms. The export differential in third-country markets can be decomposed into three possible sources, namely *industry mix effect*, *competitive effect* and *interactive effect*, such as below:

(1) Export Differential = Industry Mix Effect + Competitive Effect + Interactive Effect

(2) Industry Mix Effect = $[E_{ij} - E_{oj}(E_{io}/E_{oo})]R_{io}$

(3) Competitive Effect = $E_{oj}(E_{io}/E_{oo})(R_{ij} - R_{io})$

(4) Interactive Effect = $[E_{ij} - E_{oj}(E_{io}/E_{oo})](R_{ij} - R_{io})$

where E_{ij} = exports of product i from country j to US
E_{io} = exports of product i from the reference economy to US
E_{oj} = total exports from country j
E_{oo} = total exports from the reference economy
R_{ij} = growth rate of country j's exports of product i
R_{io} = growth rate of the reference economy's exports of product i

Industry mix effect measures the portion of the export differential that is due to differences in the structure (or share) of a particular export industry of a country and that of the reference economy. A country has a structural advantage (that is, positive industry mix effect) if its share of exports in a particular industry grows faster and exceeds that of the reference economy.

Competitive effect measures the portion of the export differential that is due to the deviation between growth rates of a particular export product of a country and that of the reference economy. If a country's exports of a product grow faster than that of the reference economy, then it enjoys a competitive advantage over the reference economy in an export market.

Interactive effect measures the effect of export differential growth to a market that accrues from the interaction of the industry mix effect and the competitive effect. A positive (negative) effect results when a country's exports to a market are dominated by faster- (slower-) growing products or when its' exports are not concentrated in slower- (faster-) growing products.

Empirical Results

Empirical results from the dynamic shift-share analysis show that the overall position of China's exports of manufactured goods had been improving between 1994 and 1996 when compared to the reference economy. Its export differential deteriorated from –US$353 million in 1994 to –US$416 million in 1995, before improving markedly to US$1.5 billion in 1996 (Table 3). Even with the onset of the Asian financial crisis in July 1997, which resulted in the drastic depreciation of the ASEAN-4's respective currencies, China's manufactured exports to the US remained competitive, as reflected by large export differentials of US$2 billion and US$1.7 billion in 1997 and 1998 respectively.

When compared to the reference economy in the period before and during the Asian financial crisis, China emerged as the top export competitor among the five countries. The Philippines was the lone star-

Table 3. Results of Shift-share Analysis on China's and ASEAN-4's Manufactured Exports to the US, 1994–1998

US$ million

	1994	1995	1996	1997	1998
China					
Export Differential	-353	-416	1,519	2,031	1,705
Industry Mix Effect	319	284	126	230	121
Competitive Effect	-631	-668	1,347	1,746	1,551
Interactive Effect	-41	-32	45	56	34
Indonesia					
Export Differential	-452	-382	35	-348	-757
Industry Mix Effect	-270	-329	-194	-335	-213
Competitive Effect	-268	-80	336	-19	-739
Interactive Effect	85	27	-107	5	196
Malaysia					
Export Differential	1,273	1,143	-1,157	-2,427	-621
Industry Mix Effect	138	234	161	251	138
Competitive Effect	1047	818	-1,184	-2,432	-698
Interactive Effect	88	91	-133	-246	-61
Philippines					
Export Differential	-173	257	529	981	401
Industry Mix Effect	20	37	24	60	58
Competitive Effect	-188	211	485	876	323
Interactive Effect	-5	9	20	46	20
Thailand					
Export Differential	-293	-601	-926	-237	-728
Industry Mix Effect	-207	-225	-117	-206	-103
Competitive Effect	-104	-440	-926	-36	-689
Interactive Effect	16	64	116	5	64

Source: Estimates by Development Bank of Singapore

performer among the ASEAN-4, recording positive export differentials between 1995 and 1998 after experiencing negative export differential in 1994, while Indonesia recorded only one positive export differential of US$35 million (in 1996) during the five years. The worst performers in the US market were Malaysia and Thailand, whose overall export performances deteriorated before and during the crisis. Malaysia experienced the largest decline in export differential of US$2.4 billion in 1997, while Thailand recorded its largest contraction of US$926 million in 1996. Both countries' export differentials continued to contract in 1998. This implied that both China and the Philippines had gained export market shares at the expense of the other three ASEAN countries, which experienced negative export differentials between 1994 and 1998. Still, in the export of manufactured products to the US, no country in the ASEAN-4 grouping (even the Philippines) provided any serious challenge to China. This result was not unexpected, given that among the five countries in the reference economy, China remained the largest exporter of manufactured products (that is, machinery & transport equipment and miscellaneous manufactured products) to the US market in 1998 (Figure 4), even after sharp depreciation of the ASEAN-4 currencies.

An examination of the components of China's export differentials shows that its competitive effects in the export of manufactured products were sizeable, valued at over US$1.3 billion since 1996, when compared to its ASEAN-4 rivals. Before 1996, China's competitive effects were the worst among the reference economy, despite having depreciated the yuan in 1994. This could be largely attributed to high inflation of 18% per annum during 1994–95 which eroded any competitive gains from the yuan devaluation. By 1996, however, with high inflation tamed, China's abundant and cheap labour force gave it a cost advantage over the ASEAN-4 countries, and enabled it to experience faster growth in the export of manufactured goods to the US between 1996 and 1998. The only other economy in the reference economy that had a similar competitive advantage was the Philippines, though its competitive advantage was considerably smaller than China's. At the same time, China, together with Malaysia and the Philippines, enjoyed favourable industry mix effects during the period, though Malaysia enjoyed the largest structural advantage among them. This implied that though China's exports were dominated by the relatively fast-growing manufacturing industries, they still lagged behind that of Malaysia, as more of the latter's exports came from such industries. Finally, the combined positive industry-mix and competitive effects, which together

Fig. 4. US Imports of Manufactured Products from China and the Asean-4, 1998

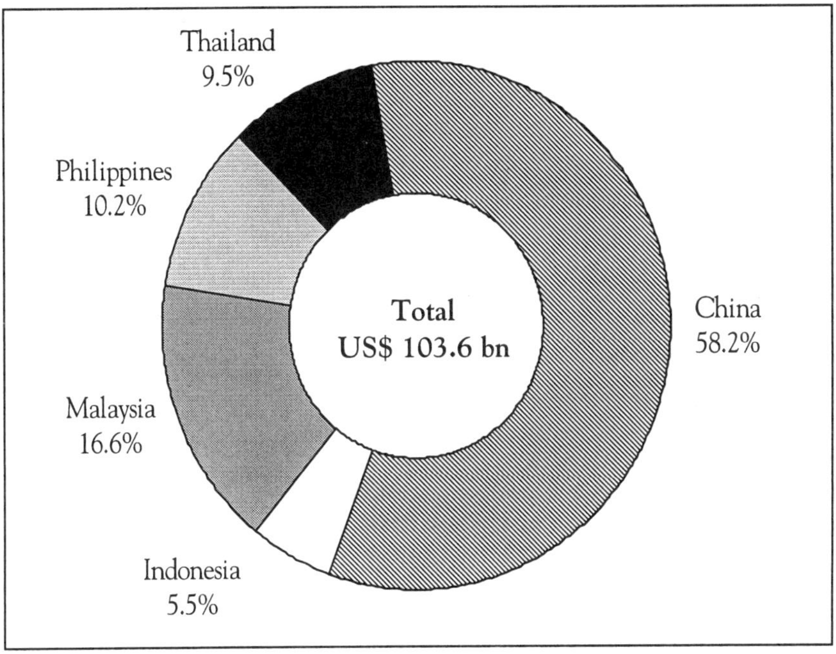

Thailand 9.5%
Philippines 10.2%
Malaysia 16.6%
Indonesia 5.5%
China 58.2%
Total US$ 103.6 bn

Source: CEIC

produced positive interactive effects over most of the period for China, suggested that the latter had chosen the correct path in its industrial policy, as compared to the reference economy, by emphasising on industries in which it had a competitive advantage.

In terms of export groupings, China's manufactured exports were boosted mainly by miscellaneous manufacturing articles (such as textiles and clothing, footwear and furniture) throughout the period, as reflected by sizeable positive export differentials, which were supported largely by the increasing share of the industrial grouping in the Chinese economy. Despite attempts to diversify its export sector towards more high-technology products, China's industrial output continued to be dominated by this manufacturing category, which tended to be more labour-intensive (Table 4). China's large export differentials were aided in part by its cheaper labour resources, which gave the country a competitive edge

Table 4. Results of Shift-Share Analysis on China's and Asean-4's Miscellaneous Manufactured Exports to the US, 1994–1998

US$ million

	1994	1995	1996	1997	1998
China					
Export Differential	674	648	1,397	2,166	1,238
Industry Mix Effect	423	678	714	1,275	643
Competitive Effect	185	−21	495	653	444
Interactive Effect	66	−8	188	238	150
Indonesia					
Export Differential	−170	46	31	−96	−411
Industry Mix Effect	−21	−40	−22	−37	−12
Competitive Effect	−166	99	57	−64	−417
Interactive Effect	17	−13	−4	4	18
Malaysia					
Export Differential	−156	−446	−454	−1,315	−426
Industry Mix Effect	−269	−441	−502	−810	−374
Competitive Effect	345	−15	159	−1,518	−164
Interactive Effect	−232	10	−111	1,013	112
Philippines					
Export Differential	−107	−10	−395	−424	−79
Industry Mix Effect	−20	−24	−35	−154	−128
Competitive Effect	−98	16	−409	−374	82
Interactive Effect	10	−1	49	104	−33
Thailand					
Export Differential	−241	−239	−579	−330	−321
Industry Mix Effect	−113	−173	−155	−274	−128
Competitive Effect	−197	−103	−633	−87	−290
Interactive Effect	69	37	209	31	97

Source: Estimates by Development Bank of Singapore

over its ASEAN-4 rivals, as reflected by its mostly positive competitive effects both before and during the regional financial turmoil. In this manufacturing grouping, China remained far ahead of its ASEAN-4 rivals, which all registered negative export differentials and they worsened with the onset of the financial crisis in mid-1997.

Between 1994 and 1998, China's export competitiveness in machinery and transport equipment (such as electronic products and office machines) was mixed, oscillating between positive and negative export differentials (Table 5). Besides Indonesia, China was the only other country among the reference economy during this period to exhibit negative industry mix effects, implying that its strengths did not lie in this particular manufacturing category, despite the Chinese government's attempts to promote it. However, China continued to enjoy competitive advantage

Table 5. Results of Shift-share Analysis on China's and Asean-4's Machinery & Transport Equipment Exports to the US, 1994–1998

US$ million

	1994	1995	1996	1997	1998
China					
Export Differential	-1,027	-1,065	122	-135	467
Industry Mix Effect	-1,464	-1,441	-619	-1,185	-1,111
Competitive Effect	720	586	1,114	1,547	2,285
Interactive Effect	-282	-210	-373	-497	-707
Indonesia					
Export Differential	-282	-428	4	-252	-346
Industry Mix Effect	-422	-399	-176	-313	-262
Competitive Effect	404	-70	430	132	-167
Interactive Effect	-265	41	-250	-70	83
Malaysia					
Export Differential	1,429	1,588	-703	-1,112	-194
Industry Mix Effect	1,597	1,585	691	1,174	925
Competitive Effect	-74	2	-705	-1,191	-591
Interactive Effect	-94	2	-689	-1,095	-529
Philippines					
Export Differential	-66	267	924	1,406	480
Industry Mix Effect	136	124	61	236	331
Competitive Effect	-164	118	711	834	96
Interactive Effect	-38	25	152	336	53
Thailand					
Export Differential	-54	-362	-347	93	-407
Industry Mix Effect	152	132	43	89	117
Competitive Effect	-180	-440	-357	4	-451
Interactive Effect	-27	-54	-33	0	-73

Source: Estimates by Development Bank of Singapore

in the export of machinery and transport equipment when compared to the reference economy, as reflected by the large competitive effects between 1994 and 1998. This meant that the growth of its machinery and transport equipment exports to the US had expanded faster than that of the reference economy during this period. The combination of negative industrial mix and positive competitive advantage during 1994–98 resulted in China's interactive effects for this manufacturing export grouping being negative, with its structural disadvantage offsetting the relatively competitive advantage of this export item. Still, on the whole, China's exports of machinery and transport equipment were relatively competitive when compared with that of the reference economy despite its mixed export differentials, with only the Philippines exhibiting a stronger performance during this period.

4. Export Competition In Japan

Japan is the second-most important market (after the US) for China, accounting for around 16% of its total exports. Similarly, Japan is also a relatively important market for the ASEAN-4, ranking as one of the top 3 export destinations for their exports (Table 6). As such, it would be interesting to see if China has lost export competitiveness in the Japanese market vis-à-vis its ASEAN-4 rivals. Unfortunately, a shift-share analysis cannot be conducted here as there is a lack of product-level data. A market-share analysis will be used instead. Thus, to determine any change in their respective market shares, aggregate exports of each individual country to Japan are calculated as a proportion of their combined total exports to Japan for the 1994–99 period (Table 7). An examination of China's and the ASEAN-4's export shares in the Japanese market shows that China's share of the Japan market had been relatively stable between 1994 and 1996, hovering around the 30% mark. Similarly, there were no drastic changes in the ASEAN-4 shares during the period. Even the devaluation of the yuan in 1994 did not increase China's market share in Japan at the expense of its ASEAN-4 rivals. Hence, from the time of the 1994 yuan devaluation to the period before the onset of the Asian financial crisis, there was no

Table 6. Asean-4's Major Export Markets, 1999

	Total Exports	US	Japan
Indonesia	US$48.7 bn	14.2% (2nd)	21.3% (1st)
Malaysia	US$84.5 bn	21.9% (1st)	11.6% (3rd)
Philippines	US$35.0 bn	29.8% (1st)	13.3% (2nd)
Thailand	US$56.8 bn	22.3% (1st)	14.5% (3rd)

Note: Figures in parentheses indicate rankings of the US and Japan as major export destinations for each ASEAN-4 country
Source: CEIC

Table 7. Export Shares of China and Asean-4 in the Japanese Market

(%)

	1994	1995	1996	1997	1998	1999
China	46.2	48.4	49.2	50.8	53.6	53.2
Indonesia	21.7	19.1	18.5	17.7	15.7	15.6
Malaysia	13.8	14.2	14.3	13.8	12.5	13.6
Philippines	4.5	4.7	5.5	6.1	6.4	6.6
Thailand	13.8	13.6	12.4	11.6	11.8	11.0
Total	100.0	100.0	100.0	100.0	100.0	100.0

Source: CEIC

discernible loss in China's export competitiveness vis-à-vis that of the ASEAN-4 economies that resulted in a significant reduction in China's market share in the Japanese market.

While no significant shift in export shares was apparent before 1996, the onset of the Asian financial crisis brought about some noticeable changes to their export competitiveness, especially China's. Between 1997 and 1999, China experienced an increase in its Japanese market share, expanding from 51% to 53%. Meanwhile, Malaysia and Thailand saw their shares fall marginally during this period, despite their depreciated currencies. In contrast, the Philippines saw its market share in Japan increase from 6.1% to 6.6%. Only Indonesia experienced a more significant drop in its market share, contracting from 18% in 1997 to 16% in 1999. Hence, it would seem that the onset of the Asian financial crisis dramatically raised the market share of China in Japan, mostly at the expense of Indonesia, while marginally affecting those of Malaysia, the Philippines and Thailand.

5. Implications For The Chinese Economy

No Devaluation on Export Competitiveness Grounds

According to our shift-share and market-share analyses, China had not lost export competitiveness either before or during the Asian financial crisis. In fact, China had a competitive advantage vis-à-vis the ASEAN-4 and had gained export market shares in the US and Japan at the latter's expense. This was despite the fact that the regional financial turmoil had forced the ASEAN-4 to depreciate their currencies, while the yuan continued to be fixed to the US dollar. However, a comparison of export growth shows that China's exports, like those of the ASEAN-4, began to slow with the onset of the Asian financial crisis (Table 8). While only Malaysia had experienced export contraction before the start of the regional financial meltdown, by the second quarter of 1998, exports of all the ASEAN-4 countries started to contract, except the Philippines, while China's exports began to contract by the third quarter of the same year. These events indicated that it was more likely that China's export growth stagnated in 1998 due to the drop in import demand from Asia than from a lack of competitiveness, since Asia as a whole absorbs over 50% of its exports (Figure 5). In fact, China's exports to Asian countries (including Japan) contracted by 9.9% for the whole of 1998, as compared to export growth of 18% and 16% to the EU and US respectively. Hence, there is little justification for the Chinese authorities to adjust the value of the yuan on the grounds of lost export competitiveness. Moreover, given China's export growth and strong FDI inflows during the Asian financial crisis years, there should be upward pressure on the yuan instead of the converse.

Table 8. Quarterly Export Growth: China vis-à-vis Asean-4

(%)

Country	Q1 97	Q2 97	Q3 97	Q4 97	Q1 98	Q2 98	Q3 98	Q4 98	Q1 99	Q2 99	Q3 99	Q4 99
China	25.8	26.6	20.9	14.0	13.9	2.5	-2.2	-7.6	-8.1	-1.8	15.0	16.7
Indonesia	10.4	7.1	10.0	2.4	0.9	-8.0	-9.4	-16.8	-18.8	-4.4	5.6	17.1
Malaysia	6.2	0.2	2.4	-5.7	-11.3	-10.1	-11.2	5.3	4.3	15.6	21.2	18.8
Philippines	17.5	26.5	24.7	22.2	23.8	14.4	19.2	11.5	15.2	12.1	22.9	23.8
Thailand	-0.9	2.2	7.1	6.7	-2.9	-5.3	-8.7	-9.9	-4.2	5.7	10.9	17.1

Source: CEIC

Fig. 5. China's Quarterly Export Growth to Selected Destinations

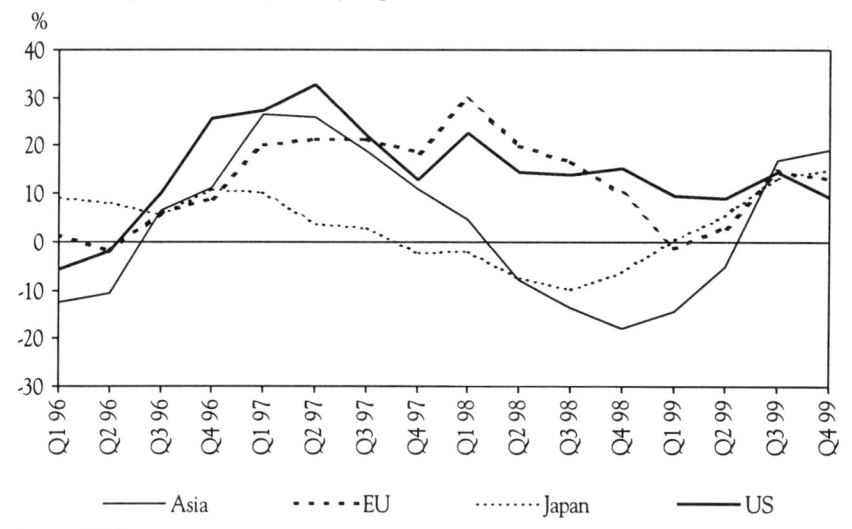

Source: CEIC

Devaluation May Not Enhance Trade Balances

On the other hand, while China apparently does not need to devalue its currency to restore export competitiveness, it might still do so in order to boost exports to improve its trade balances. Beijing's move to merge its two exchange rates at the beginning of 1994 had resulted in a surge in exports as well as an improvement in trade balances in 1994 and 1995. Since machinery & transport equipment and miscellaneous manufactured articles tend to be price sensitive, a downward adjustment in the value of the yuan could result in a surge in exports. However, on the flip side, a yuan devaluation could also lead to higher prices for imports and this could have an adverse effect on its export sector. This is because around 55% of Chinese exports use imported materials (components or intermediate goods) and this would mitigate any pricing advantage that a devaluation would gain. Our shift-share analysis has shown that the yuan devaluation in 1994 did not improve China's export competitiveness by much between 1994 and 1995 vis-à-vis the ASEAN-4. This could be due to high inflation that mitigated any competitive gains from the devaluation, as reflected by its large negative competitive effect vis-à-vis the ASEAN-4 during that period. China's overall export position improved only from 1996 onward when inflation started to moderate. Thus, a devaluation might not necessarily improve China's trade balances.

Devaluation May Jeopardise WTO Membership

China has just concluded WTO (World Trade Organisation) negotiations with its major trading partner, the US, for its entry into the world trade body. The agreement will lower tariffs on a wide range of products, allow foreign investment in telecommunication and the internet as well as provide foreign banks with greater access to the Chinese currency market. This agreement should reduce some of the tensions that have risen between the two economic powerhouses over the mainland's burgeoning trade surplus with the US. In 1998, China's trade balance with the US was US$21 billion and this figure surged to US$22.5 billion in 1999 (Figure 6). The wider access to the Chinese market should mitigate some of these concerns. However, should a yuan devaluation take place prior to China's formal accession to WTO, the bilateral trade balance between China and the US could deteriorate further due to increase US imports of cheaper Chinese products. As such, tensions between the two trading partners could heighten and would certainly adversely affect their bilateral relations. More importantly, this could anger the US Congress which could then delay its approval of the pact. Hence, a

Fig. 6. China's Trade Surplus with the US, 1994–99

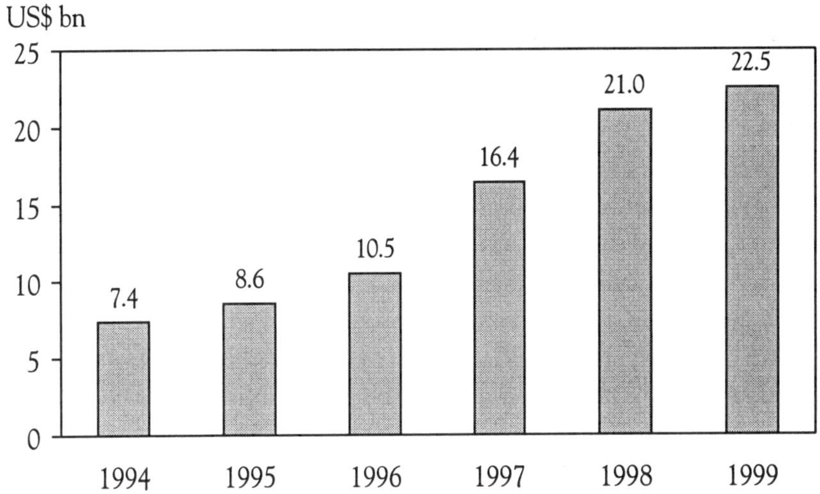

Year	US$ bn
1994	7.4
1995	8.6
1996	10.5
1997	16.4
1998	21.0
1999	22.5

Source: CEIC

premature yuan devaluation might not necessarily be beneficial to China in this case.

Should Devaluation Be Used to Reflate the Chinese Economy?

While devaluation would not solve China's external problems, it could go some way in helping reflate its moribund economy. China has been suffering from deflation for the last two years and the Chinese authorities have used all kinds of policy options to boost the economy but to no avail. A yuan devaluation could trigger a much-needed inflationary spiral, as it did with the 1994 devaluation when inflation sky-rocketed to 21.7%. Furthermore, with the expectation that inflation could rear its ugly head once again in the near future, this could spur private consumption and help revive an important engine of growth. At the same time, the resultant export expansion in the short-term would help to ease the over-supply and over-capacity situation in the mainland that has kept the lid on prices. However, whether the Chinese authorities would embark on such a drastic measure remains to be seen as they would have to balance the need to reflate the economy with the problems discussed above.

6. Conclusion

The findings of our shift-share analysis show that the competitiveness of China's manufactured exports have improved since 1994 vis-à-vis that of the ASEAN-4. Despite claims to the contrary, China has not lost its export competitiveness in manufactured products, even during and after the Asian financial crisis. Similarly, an examination of its export share to the Japanese market also supports this conclusion. As such, the argument for adjusting the value of the yuan cannot be made on this basis. In fact, devaluing the yuan could create more problems for China than it would solve. Therefore, the solution to China's domestic economic problems (such as deflation, excess capacity and high unemployment) does not lie with devaluation, but with the continuation and acceleration of domestic reforms since export expansion by itself would be insufficient to enable China to overcome these problems.

References

Herschede, F. (1991), "Asian competitions in third-country markets", *Asian Survey*, 21 (May): 434–41.

Herschede, F. (1991), "Competition among ASEAN, China, and the East Asian NICs", *ASEAN Economic Bulletin*, 7 (March): 290–306.

Hiley, M. (1999), "The dynamics of changing comparative advantage in the Asia-Pacific Region", *Journal of the Asia Pacific Economy*, 4: 446–467.

Lloyd, P.J. & Hisako Toguchi (1996), "East Asian export competitiveness: new measures and policy implications", *Asian-Pacific Economic Literature*, 10 (November): 1–15.

Wilson, P. & Goh, A. (1998), "The export competitiveness of dynamic Asian economies, 1986–93", *Journal of the Asia Pacific Economy*, 3: 237–50.

Wilson, P. & Wong Yin Mei (1999), "The export competitiveness of ASEAN economies, 1986–95", *ASEAN Economic Bulletin*, 16 (August): 208–229.

Index

Academy of Sciences (CAS) 392
Academy of Social Sciences (CASS) 392
administrative fee 176
agricultural residents 221
airports 310
ASEAN-four 408, 425
Asia's economic laggards 281
Asian financial crisis in mid-1997 425
Association of Southeast Asian Nations (ASEAN) 273, 374, 406
aviation routes 294, 296

budget deficits 115
budgetary expenditures 115
budgetary revenue 115, 149

capital accumulation 47
China Mobile Telecom Group Corp. 348
China Paging Telecom Group Corp. 348
China Satellite Telecom Group Corp. 348
China Telecom Group Corp. 348
China United Telecommunications Corporation (Unicom) 342, 346, 368
Chongqing 273, 283
competitive effect 432
county-level postal and telecommunications enterprise 333

Dalai Lama 248
de-nationalisation 229
Deng Xiaoping 239, 389, 394
Deng Xiaoping's Southern visit 389

development of science, technology and education 269
Directorate General of Posts (DGP) 334
Directorate General of Telecommunications (DGT) 333
domestic debt 314

East Asia 273, 406
East Asian economies (EAEs) 273
eastern (coastal), central and western regions 237
ecological problems 253
ecological protection 265
economic decentralisation 126
economic development 220, 373
economic interdependence 276, 409
economic isolation 281
economic restructuring 5
education 373
efficiency gains 49
Electric Power and Rural and Urban Electricity Supply Network 310
electricity 294, 296
endogenous growth theory 278
EU 363
export differential 431
export orientation 415
export-oriented development strategy 279
extra-budgetary revenue 132, 177, 202

FDI 415
federal relations 211
fees 313
fiscal recentralization 209
fiscal reforms 117, 148
fiscal system 151
foreign capital 317

gas and oil pipelines 309
GDP growth 11
government spending on infrastructures 305

highways 309
Hong Kong 279
hukou 397, 398
human capital 49

improved infrastructure 54
income equality 220
industrialisation 224
industrial restructuring 85
industry mix effect, competitive effect 431, 432
industry-structure adjustments 267
infant industry 81
infrastructure construction 260
infrastructures 291
interactive effect 431, 432
internet service 300
inter-provincial disparities 219
Inter-provincial Livelihood Disparities 229
irrigation system 310

Japan 274, 406, 438
Jiang Zemin 387
Jitong Communications Co. Ltd. (Beijing) 368, 342

Krugman, Paul 278, 414
Kuznets hypothesis 220, 223

labor services 320
Lee Kuan Yew 423
livelihood 219
livelihood indicators 220
local autonomy 152

MII 356
Ministry of Posts and Telecommunications (MPT) 333, 337
minority nationalities 247, 268
municipal and prefecture bureaus of postal and telecommunications 333
Muslim extremists 248

nationalisation policy 226
natural gas pipelines 294
Netcom 368
Newly Industrialized Economies (NIEs) 273, 374, 406
non-agricultural residents 221
nonperforming loans 17
non-public branch exchanges (PBXs) 333

OECD 274
operating fee 176
output 219, 220

paved roads 299
per capita consumption 221
per capita GDP 221
per capita national income 221
petroleum 294
petroleum and gas pipelines 296
pillar industries 88
Postal and Telecommunications Administrations (PTA) 333
preferential treatment 94
primary school enrolment 381
private enterprises 308
privatisation 37
productivity gains 46
profits from state-owned enterprises 318
provincial postal and telecommunications authorities 334

railroad construction 299
railways 294, 309
real effective exchange rate 427
regional economic disparities 219
reliability 65
resource allocation 50
returning expatriate 388
revenue-sharing 152
revenue-sharing contract 195

revenue-sharing system   196
roads   294, 296
rural fee reform   189
rural infrastructures   304
rural residents   221

san-xian ("third line") development plan   283
separatist movements   249
shortage economy   249
Singapore   274, 279, 408
Sino-ASEAN economic relations   421
Sino-ASEAN trade   418
socialist market economy   71
Song-Hu (Wusong-Shanghai) railroad   294
South Korea   274, 408
southern tour   239
Soviet Union and Eastern European countries   388
Special Economic Zones   241
state-owned enterprise   8, 306
statistical system   74, 77
surplus economy   249

tax reform   91
tax remittances   197
taxes   311
telecommunication   294, 296, 299
telephone   331
tertiary education   381
tertiary school enrolment   381
tertiary schools   381
Third Front   224
Three Gorges Dam project   287
Tiananmen incident   389
Tibetan Autonomous Region   248
total factor productivity   36, 44, 45, 278
tuigeng huancao   265
tuigeng huanlin   265

UNESCO 389
United States 363, 411, 430
urban public utilities 311
urban residents 221
user charges 313
U-shaped patterns 219

VSAT 341

Western Region 237, 257
World Trade Organisation (WTO) 325, 357, 442

Xinjiang Uygur Autonomous Region 248

yuan 426

Zhongguancun 398
Zhu Rongji 237, 259 284, 285